DEREK,
THANK YOU FOR
READING MY BOOK!

STANLEY
MAY 1, 2019

www.TheCleanerBook.com

The Cleaner

The Cleaner

The True Story of One of the World's Most Successful Money Launderers

Bruce Aitken

Although in essence this book is a work of non-fiction, the names of certain characters, places and incidents are products of both the author's imagination *and* historical facts. Any resemblance to actual persons, living or dead, business establishments, events or locales are NOT entirely coincidental. Where appropriate, names have been changed and noted.

Version BF-11

ISBN: 978-1-945190-19-3

First Edition 2017

Published by
:

www.IntellectPublishing.com

To The Reader

This book has been difficult to write on a number of levels.

First, it brings back memories of a very wonderful and exciting time, as well as a trying and challenging part of my life. In fact, although it is over now, just thinking about those years causes me to well-up with conflicting feelings of hopelessness and despair, as well as pure, adrenaline-pumping bliss. It feels as if it all happened yesterday.

Then there was the sheer volume of documents I had to go through to piece the story together as it actually happened— thousands of them! I had to make decisions as to what to include and what to exclude; a daunting task. Truth be told, after the first draft, this book was over 1,100 pages long.

In thinking about you, the reader, I decided to shorten the narrative, mention the facts and adventures, and leave you to read the extended versions of the documents on our web site.

Before I started writing, I decided I would tell the truth and nothing but the truth, *according to my best recollection.* Names have not been changed unless explicitly stated. The sequence of events is unchanged. Nothing has been added to the story for dramatic effect, allowing you to focus on events and put yourself in my shoes and try to feel what I felt at crucial moments.

I have tried to make sure that only the facts *as I remember them* are recorded. The deceptions, the double crosses, the lies, the broken promises, the illegal activities of each person involved, have all been exposed. And suffice it to say, more often than not, the U.S. government "alphabet" agencies were key players, as well as their investigators and prosecutors.

Invariably, I found it was those of us accused of wrongdoing who evinced the kind of integrity one would expect of those in law enforcement. It was the accused who looked out for one another and showed some serious cojones. These are the people I respect more than ever.

This is as much their story as it is mine, although both theirs and mine are certainly interwoven. Their lives, like most of our lives, have been impacted by government policy relating to the war on drugs, the question of legalization, the growth of the prison industry, the large number of fellow citizens experiencing incarceration, and the changes society is bringing about.

As for the writing style, I sought and received varied opinions from several prominent literary agents. In the end, I decided to keep my own writing style, which includes many flaws and a real lack of literary know-how. Regardless, I hope you will soldier through the book and find a few gems of meaning.

As I was writing, it also became apparent to me that, although I had not been religious in the past, a powerful spiritual element of faith permeated the events and decisions in the life of The Cleaner, hence the very detailed autobiographical slant.

At the heart of the story is a kid who was born in Hackensack, New Jersey, and grew up in Hasbrouck Heights, who through chance and circumstance grew up to become one of the world's most successful money launderers.

However...

There were unintended and devastating consequences.

Bruce Aitken
AKA Mr. Clean

www.TheCleanerBook.com

Foreword

Many of us have travelled through customs or airport security carrying something we should not. Possibilities include a scintilla of the finest squidgy Afghan hash, an extra bottle of duty-free booze, or a few thousand dollars that did not seem worth mentioning to the authorities. We know it can be a nerve-wrenching experience that precipitates sweaty palms, a pounding heart, and the persistent fear that the little old lady in the corner is actually an undercover drug squad officer, and we are aware it does not usually facilitate a relaxed journey. Imagine doing that day-in day-out for two decades. That is precisely what master money launderer Bruce Aitken did in the 1970s and 1980s. I can well understand why he turned to God in later life.

I never fully understood the terms "smuggling" or "money laundering" or why they became crimes. When I was "smuggling" or Bruce was "money laundering" all it meant was that we were moving beneficial herbs, in my case, or official banknotes in Bruce's, around the world. We happened to cross some artificial man-made boundaries called borders, but how could transporting something from A to B possibly be illegal? It never made sense to me and still does not.

The beauty of the book you hold in your hands is that it offers a unique and perfect insight into the money-laundering world of thirty-odd years ago. That was a time when, at one point, Bruce and his colleagues would be moving around huge amounts of currency by using golf bags with secret compartments within them. Indeed, Bruce estimates that his favorite golf bag, "Old Faithful," would alone have transported many millions-of-dollars-worth of notes between locations such as Guam, Japan, Vietnam, Hong Kong,

Switzerland, the Philippines and Australia. As with everything, it is often the simplest solutions that work best.

I first met Bruce in the early 1980s in Hong Kong, and we immediately formed a solid rapport. He was a master of his chosen trade and helped me clean up some cash that I had earned through smuggling. Reading about his two decades of laundering vividly brought back to me all the excitement, glamour and sheer fun that an international jet-setting life of crime invariably imparts.

In the first two years of his career, Bruce visited thirty countries and then escalated to going through two forty-eight-page passports a year. I travelled almost as extensively, but I tended to do so under several different identities backed by false passports. I could not build up a collection of air miles. Bruce, as far as I am aware, always travelled under his real name, and I cannot even hazard a guess at how many miles he managed to accumulate.

While Bruce fell into his vocation by accident, he took to it like a duck to water and was soon the go-to man for those who did not feel the need to tell the tax authorities about every penny they had earned, or were slightly cagey about exactly how they had earned the money. Bruce never asked many questions but, as with all these stories, governments began to ask too many questions, and snitches, that most vile sub-species of criminal, were eventually very happy to provide them with answers. I found Bruce's heartfelt tirades against *grasses* to be one of the funniest and most incisive parts of this fascinating account.

Bruce also captures brilliantly the paranoia and nerve-racking horror of his chosen lifestyle. There were so many near misses that it was only sheer luck and quick thinking that kept him out of trouble for so long. For example, who would have thought that one of the main ways to avoid a pull by airport customs was to join the queue directly behind someone of Indian descent? It turns out that our so-called color-blind airport officials will generally pick on our Indian brothers, who they assume are "always smuggling something," thus allowing the man with $600,000 wrapped around his number-five iron to pass through unimpeded.

The Cleaner introduces us to a host of incredible characters straight off the pages of a Len Deighton novel. These include Nicolas Deak—a Hungarian-born United States citizen, an ex-secret service soldier and former hero of the war in Asia. Deak established and was chairman of Deak Perera, a worldwide network of currency agents and smugglers, to service a multitude of clients, mainly the Central Intelligence Agency. Deak's murder, theoretically by a lone, demented female, is one of several mysteries that Bruce believes ends up at the feet of the biggest money-laundering, drug-dealing operation of them all: the CIA, Deak Perera's main client.

We also meet Father Jose, a Spanish Jesuit priest who lugged bags of money all over Tokyo making payments for Bruce's firm, Deak and Company, and sending all of his hard-earned commission of one-half percent back to a church he founded for prostitutes in Mexico City. The eventual arrest of this kind-hearted money launderer played a major role in the 1975 Lockheed disgrace that forced the then-Japanese-Prime-Minister, Kakuei Tanaka, to resign.

Bruce's activities were also interwoven with two of the most famous scandals ever to humiliate Australia's authorities: the 1988 drug-dealing Cessner-Milner affair and the earlier Nugan Hand affair, which involved the Vietnamese heroin trade (Golden Triangle), corrupt bankers, and, of course, the CIA.

When the net finally catches Bruce, we get firsthand insight into the nefarious activities of that most hypocritical of organizations, the United States government. The legal wrangling that could have resulted in at least two decades in prison for Bruce went on for many years, and Bruce's ability to survive the seemingly endless horrors that faced him is a true testament to the quality of his character and the strength that his powerful faith has imbued in him.

We are both proud of ourselves for explicitly refusing to co-operate with the institutionalized forces of injustice that wanted us to testify against any of our co-defendants. Although I got sentenced to twenty-five years, and you will read of Bruce's several hardships in the pages ahead, it was worth it.

Bruce now hosts a weekly Christian radio show in Hong Kong that has a phenomenal number of listeners.

Read this book and learn how good men can sometimes end up doing things that many regard as not so good. Learn as well how to ensure you do not get pulled by that nasty-looking customs official who seems to be staring directly at you.

Howard Marks
AKA Mr. Nice

Best-Selling Author of *Mr. Nice* and *Señor Nice: Straight Life From Wales to South America,* and *Mr. Smiley: My Last Pill and Testament.*

The Cleaner

Part One

Show me the money

The Cleaner

Prologue
The Pickup

1978

Standing in the twelfth-floor lobby of the MLC Centre in downtown Sydney, I suddenly felt very conspicuous. It was 11:30 am and the crowds in the offices would soon be heading out for lunch. I certainly did not want to meet or see anybody. All I could think was, *What the hell is keeping this lift!* I repeatedly jabbed my finger at the down button, feeling tired and irritable from the long flight; plus, the nylon travel bag was digging into my shoulder. Fifteen minutes earlier, it had been empty. Now, it was loaded with Australian dollars, $500,000 at the going rate, US $600,000. The thought of the money suddenly shifted my feelings from tired to a state of alert anticipation.

I had not wanted to take the lift, because I knew the wisdom of moving about unseen, but, as I approached the stairwell, I could hear people talking on the landing below. I was also repelled by the strong gagging smell of stale tobacco smoke. *Shit. People on a smoke break. Filthy habit.*

Suddenly, the bell on the lift rang. It seemed louder than normal and startled me. At that point, my senses were on hyper-alert. The door opened, and one of those automated lift recordings broke the silence: "Going Down." I instinctively turned and looked in. *Good, it's empty!* No one could see me, and the only recorded footage would be made by the CCTV cameras in the lobby.

I punched the button to the sixth floor, and was glad when the lift did not stop on any other floors. When the doors opened, I was relieved to find no one there. Hurrying down the corridor, I stopped at Room 606, took one last casual glance around, and rang the buzzer.

A shy, granny-like receptionist opened the door. "Come in, Mr. Bruce Walker. Harry has been waiting for you."

* * * * * * *

In the foreign exchange world of Deak & Company, arriving at Room 606 was just another "pickup," a term familiar to the free market, better known to the rest of the world as the "black market," a nebulous and murky world of unofficial foreign exchange. The term "pickup" refers to the seller's side of the transaction. Pickups and payments, and the bizarre ways of getting them done, were more typically known on the sub-continent of India and Pakistan and the Middle East as "hundi."

It is all illegal.

Governments frown on creative ways to hide money from their tax coffers. Deak & Company provided ways to get money in and out of a country without the government, or anyone else for that matter, knowing about it. It was Deak's specialty, and they had no equals. The stakes were high. If caught, I could be charged with money laundering, or heaven forbid, worse.

Much worse . . .

* * * * * * *

I had flown from Hong Kong to Sydney on the red-eye, and went straight to my hotel and checked in. No chance for sleep. It was just before 11:00 am when I left the Hilton, walked a couple of blocks down Pitt Street, then circled back around through some crowded arcades. Finally, I entered the office building's lobby.

That was my normal routine.

While Harry was expecting me on the sixth floor, my first order of business was on the twelfth.

Although I felt conspicuous, I did not feel there were actually any eyes on me. I pressed the twelfth-floor button on the lift and glanced at the coded message in my diary concerning the "tour," which I quickly translated to mean, "Pickup Australian $500,000 from Jeff." The code was changed for every transaction to ensure security was maintained; if I lost my book, the code would be meaningless to any other reader.

It was normal to pay "Jeff" a visit several times a year, and he was expecting me. He was one of the many prosperous diamond dealers in Sydney looking to get his money offshore to avoid the punishing Aussie income taxes.

When Jeff, in his mid-forties, appeared and motioned me into his library-like office, he was wearing a lightly starched white shirt with light-brown trousers and looking quite fashionable. He was always nervous, and beads of perspiration dotted his pale, wrinkled forehead. The sweat droplets on the bridge of his nose were reflected in his expensive horn-rimmed glasses. But in spite of his nervousness, there was a bond between us—a trust. His piercing brown eyes were clear and confident. It was not easy to hand over a half-million dollars to someone on a handshake, but he never hesitated. I quickly bundle-counted the money; each bundle of $100 bills, $50 notes, totaling $5,000. The Australian $500,000 fit nicely into my empty travel bag. Within ten minutes, the transaction was over.

"Please tell Brink to credit my account in Bank Leumi, Zurich, as soon as possible!"

Another handshake, and I was on my way.

"Brink" was Mr. Dirk M. Brink, Managing Director of Deak & Company Ltd., Hong Kong. He was also my mentor and direct boss. Not only was he one of the world's most eccentric characters, he also possessed a certain creative genius for moving money.

Having collected the "goods" from Jeff on the twelfth floor, I re-entered the lift and headed to the sixth floor. When the door opened, I exited, looked around, and made a quick turn past a few offices to Room 606. The sign on the door read "Harry & Allen Pty Ltd., Investment Bankers"—not a real name.

Always matter-of-fact, Harry was six feet tall with the posture and fitness level of a Marine; I guessed him to be in his early fifties. Brown-eyed and well-tanned, he looked like a banker in a dark-blue business suit and conservative gray tie. He quickly bundle-counted Jeff's cash, and with an aristocratic voice bid me farewell. Harry always had clients—the same clients belonging to most of the big-ten international accounting firms who stashed their gains offshore, usually without paying taxes. They periodically wanted to enjoy some of it back home, without the government getting wind of it.

"Need cash? Call Deak & Company. No questions asked." That was our motto.

Having taken the $500,000 from the "seller" on the twelfth floor and delivered it to the "buyer" on the sixth floor, the swap was complete. Neither party knew the entire deal had happened in the same building, just six floors apart. It had been a cakewalk, and took little more than half an hour for Deak & Company to earn a tidy five-percent commission on both transactions.

Sweet deal!

God willing, may we all never meet in the elevator.

* * * * * * *

This type of transaction constituted a typical day's work for me; one of many varied and fulfilling days in the world of cleaning money—"foreign exchange" we called it. It was a profession I neither chose nor sought out. Somehow, I not only became a money launderer, but I excelled at it. And I relished it. In fact, I loved every

Goddamn minute of it! Of course, when I first became a part of the money cleaning profession, I had no idea how it would affect my life.

I did expect to gain the perks of working for an internationally respected and trusted company. We provided a service that was in high demand by wealthy people, government agencies, world leaders, industry tycoons, ordinary people and plain old misfits; all sorts from all over the globe.

The profession commanded a certain amount of awe from clients mesmerized by the secrecy and mystery of how huge sums of cash could be made to disappear right before their eyes, then magically reappear in their offshore accounts. It involved a lot of glamour. I made life-long friendships, was treated very well, and with a lot of respect.

The *unexpected* effects of the job embroiled me in some of the biggest international money laundering scandals and drug busts in history. I would also find myself "kidnapped" by the United States government and facing life in prison.

God knows, it started out innocently enough.

The Cleaner.

CHAPTER 1
In the Beginning: Indochina on My Mind

Growing up is hard to do

"**H**ow in the hell did I ever get *here*?" I reminisced on the flight from Australia to Hong Kong.

My education into the money-moving world began in Saigon in 1969. The feeling that Asia would have a profound impact on my life made its first appearance when I was just a young boy. It must have been a premonition. Some say that when you cast your fate to the wind, there will be turning points or certain people that will have a major impact on your future. Some say it is a spiritual endeavor.

When I whispered my in-flight question to myself, two major turning points came vividly to mind, although there were many more.

The first event happened in Orlando, Florida, in the fall of 1969. If I hadn't been there, I never would have read the ad in the *Orlando Sentinel* that read "American Express International Banking Corporation, in Orlando, interviewing for positions overseas, degree in Business Administration, Economics, Political Science." I immediately thought, *That's for me!* and brimmed with enthusiasm as I read the rest of the ad.

The other important turning point involved a man who brought me to Florida in the first place: Ken Huebner, a friend I met playing high school and semi-pro baseball in New Jersey. He recommended me to his coach at Florida Southern College, and based solely on his recommendation and my pitching record, I was given a full scholarship. This was a big deal for a poor boy from New Jersey, and I felt blessed, indeed.

But then again, if it had not been for several major injuries while playing baseball for Florida Southern, I may have gone on to become what I had always dreamed of being—a professional baseball player. Of course, if it had not been for my torn cartilage, I would not have failed the Army draft physical and would have gone off to the killing fields of Vietnam. Is there such a thing as karma?

I think I was in the fifth grade when I became fascinated by a map of Asia with its exotic names and places: Hong Kong, Shanghai, Bangkok, Saigon. Back then, Southeast Asia was Indochina and Jakarta; the capitol of Indonesia was Batavia. Staring at that map, I felt something in my soul move with a feeling of excitement, and knew that one day I would see all of those amazing places.

Yes, if all the events and circumstances of my youth had not happened…but, then again, everyone's life has its own story. Is there something called fate?

Money for me always held some fascination, because as a youth it was a scarce commodity in our household. I grew up in a small town, Hasbrouck Heights, New Jersey, just eight miles from New York City. On a clear day you could see the George Washington Bridge. In the late 1940s and 1950s life was simple. We never locked our doors at night, and during the hot and humid summer both the front and back doors were left open so you could catch the breeze. Life was beautiful, although we were poor. I look back with nostalgia on lazy Sundays; "Blue Laws" required all commercial enterprises to be closed; Mom and Dad always had enough for an especially big, delicious noon meal.

The population of the town was about 12,000. We had a corner candy store, a Jewish butcher, a Polish ice man who delivered ice for the icebox, and an Italian man who sold strawberries. I played baseball from early morning until late at night with another young baseball fanatic, George Mayer (was there anything else?). It all started with Little League, where I developed good skills. Once, after pitching a great Little League game, the father of the pitcher on the opposing team got into an argument with my dad and told him, "Bruce is so damn lucky; if you dropped him into a sewer he would come up with a gold watch." *Wow! What a compliment.* I never forgot it. The luck of the Irish. I felt so blessed!

We were five children: a sister, Honey, seventeen years older; a brother Jim, ten years older; and twin sisters, Janice and Joanne, two years older. The twins and I were close and inseparable. We had been born and grew up in a slightly different era than the others. My elder sister and brother, unfortunately, had faced some abuse from our aunts and uncles.

My dad, "Irish" Jay Aitken (his mom was Irish and his dad was Scottish), was doing okay in a successful real estate business. At the time, he was married with one daughter. But one day he met "another woman" who became my mother. She was a beautiful girl named Alice Schonemann (her mom was Swedish and her dad was German). My stern German grandfather was head waiter at the Waldorf Astoria Hotel in New York. My other grandfather was Catholic, and a sailor on a ship that sailed frequently to New York. My parents must have created quite a scandal. My dad took off with young Alice, leaving his wife and daughter, and together the union produced five "illegitimate" children. I was the last and youngest of the union. (Strange words: *illegitimate children. Bastards? Not in God's eyes.*)

My dad was born in 1893 and my mom in 1903. I appeared as a menopause baby in 1945. My mom was surely an angel. Story goes that when the neighborhood doctor, Dr. Basralian, found out my mom was pregnant at her age, he was frantic and recommended she not have the baby. My mom replied without hesitation:

"Dr. Basralian, you can go to hell!"

My dad said it was the first and only time he ever heard my mom curse. Anyway, thanks to my mom, here I am!

Our family was ostracized. My father took to drinking a lot—like a true Irishman in both custom and appearance. His business failed, and not feeling welcome in the Catholic Church, he made up a story that the church did not give him some painting job so out of spite we never went to church. We lived downstairs in the family house, and our aunts and uncles lived upstairs. We had a small flat with two bedrooms with extra sleeping space in the living room. I was fourteen years old and in high school when my dad begrudgingly installed the first shower in the bathroom.

He could also play the piano by ear, so as soon as he heard a song, he could play it. Since we lived next door to Leo's Tavern, his musical gift was a recipe for disaster; many nights I had to pick him up off the bench outside the house and drag him home. I loved him dearly; after all, he was my dad. Besides, he's the one who taught me how to play baseball. Once, he even met Babe Ruth!

Both my mom (who looked angelic with a beautiful head of natural white hair) and my dad were ahead of their times. They lived together way before living together came into vogue, and my mom had to work to support the family. She was the bread-winner, and worked as a switchboard operator at the Physicians & Surgeons Exchange in Hackensack, New Jersey. She worked like a slave, putting in long hours for a pittance of forty cents an hour, until years later she reached the pinnacle—a dollar an hour. This was in the early 50s. She got paid every Friday.

As a consequence, my adorable, but not identical, twin sisters and I came to love Friday nights. By most Wednesdays, we had already run out of food and the cupboard was bare. So on Fridays, we would meet my mom as soon as she got off work, and head for the Safeway Supermarket, and then board the 102 bus and head home to feast.

I became an entrepreneur early, and took odd jobs whenever I could: I was a shoeshine boy, sold lemonade with my sisters, cut grass, shoveled snow, worked as a newspaper boy for the *Bergen Evening Record,* and later, set pins at the Pioneer Club bowling alley.

But my dad was a "ham"

There were times when my father demonstrated extraordinary chutzpah. I remember one hot summer Sunday, when Mom had been sick for a week. She couldn't go to work, and we were broke and famished.

Leo's Bar was an excellent restaurant, normally jam-packed with hungry diners every Sunday afternoon, and it was within stumbling distance. Suddenly, I heard the screen door open, shaking me out of a hot and hungry, sleepy summer trance. Dad came running in breathing hard, carrying a huge ham. The aroma was tantalizing.

My dad said, "Quick! Close the doors. Be quiet! No one is home!" My sisters and I ran for cover, but not before each of us grabbed a large chunk of ham my dad had sliced off. *Hallelujah, this was heaven!* I quietly rejoiced at the thought that we were going to feast on ham sandwiches for the next two weeks.

Suddenly, Leo, six foot tall, muscular, wearing a snarling face creased with a mean and ruddy complexion, came running out of the restaurant screaming and yelling, "Where is my ham!? Goddammit! Who took my ham?! Who stole my goddamn ham?!"

We froze.

Leo was followed closely by a herd of hungry diners who had been patiently waiting for Sunday lunch. Apparently, the big ham had just come out of the oven and had been placed on the window sill to cool off. Then someone started banging on the back door. My dad finally answered, and found a disbelieving, mean crowd of diners. Despite whiffs of delicious ham wafting throughout the house, when Dad opened the door, he mustered up a look of total astonishment and bellowed, "What ham!?"

I was damn proud of my dad. He was a real character.

Fruit of the Vine

My dad just could not hold down a job. He became a house painter and eked out a living sporadically. He taught my brother, Jim, and me how to paint houses, and my brother went on to make a good business out of it. My dad actually ended up working for Jim (provided Dad kept off the booze). When Dad got his own painting jobs from time to time, I would sometimes have to go finish them so he could get paid.

One day he came home and announced he had been hired to be a janitor at the nearby synagogue. We were so happy. He had the keys and all he had to do was keep the place straight. I laughed when he got the job because for reasons I never understood, his whole life had been spent blaming Jews for all the problems in the world. I can still hear my mom telling him, "Oh Jay, they are not all like that!" My mom loved everyone. Fortunately, I took after her. My best friends have been Christians, Muslims, Buddhists, and Jews—all sorts of people.

More importantly, the neighborhood's Jewish butcher actually saved my life when I was four years old. From his shop window, he saw me riding my tricycle into the path of an oncoming car; he dashed out, and snatched me off the cycle just in the nick of time.

Anyway, seems my dad started the janitorial job on a Friday, and immediately discovered the ceremonial wine cabinet. After all, he had the key.

The next morning being Saturday, the Sabbath, the Rabbi and some of his flock arrived early, only to find my dad and a couple of his red-faced Irish friends passed out on the floor, empty bottles of

14

wine strewn all around the ceremonial wine cabinet. Fired on the spot!

Man-Oh-Manischewitz...

Back at home, my dad continued to connive at every opportunity. We kids dreaded the unexpected, and jumped out of our skins whenever the doorbell rang. We were instructed *never* to answer the door—*never* to open the door, because it might be a bailiff serving a subpoena to appear in court for an unpaid debt. We normally had the TV on, blasting away, and when the doorbell rang we'd turn everything off and run out the back door, so technically nobody would be home.

The TV and radio were part of a deal we had that included an Amana freezer and food plan. A salesman appeared one day and we signed up. The deal was that you placed a quarter into the TV and it came on for two hours. We could watch the Brooklyn Dodgers with Happy Felton's Knot-Hole Gang, and the New York Giants baseball games. We hated the Yankees. When we ran out of money, we listened to the radio. Radio was great. You only had to use your imagination—imagination being that gift from God that can take a lifetime to appreciate. When the big Amana freezer arrived, it was stocked full of food. What a deal. We ate all the food and when it was gone, my father called the suppliers and told them to come and take the freezer back because we could not pay. We were all sad to see it go.

During my freshman year in high school, my aged and senile Aunt Mary, who lived upstairs, suddenly got a "wild hair." Since the family house was in her name, she went to court and had us kicked out on the street for not paying rent.

Rolling with the Punches

If anyone said anything against my family or anyone in it, there would be a big fight for sure. As we grew up, we learned not to take any crap from anyone. Not anyone. I don't know why, but some of the kids in my neighborhood were always fighting. I never *wanted* to fight anyone, but I fought from time to time. It was all about earning something called "respect."

I went on to play baseball throughout high school, and you might say that I was a star pitcher, managing a couple of no-hitters and a perfect game, then playing semi-pro with the Paterson Phillies. It was a time of deep confusion in my life, although being poor had made me tough.

When the electricity bill could not be paid, and the electricity was cut off, we studied by candle light. When we couldn't pay the heating bill, we froze.

I was a very confused teenager, confronting all the challenges that teenagers face. I was an honor student, but was losing interest in school. I lost interest in everything, in fact, except maybe girls, and they were a mystery. Sure, I knew I should go to college, but on what, thin air? Where was the money going to come from? I had decided, like my best friends, Vic Dragon, Richie Jaeger, Bob Soel, Phil Stroh, Eddie Geleski and Jeff Draesel, to go to Rutgers University and become a doctor.

When the mail came one day, Bobby found out he was going off to Lycoming on a football scholarship. Vic, Richie and Jeff got letters saying they had been accepted to Rutgers. So, I rushed home and found my letter from Rutgers. I was so happy! Of course, when I tore it open, it looked different than the others. In a few short words, I was told that the university was returning my application for admission, and that the check for the admissions fee in the amount of five dollars was being returned because of "insufficient funds."

I was so mad. I gave my dad the five dollars I had earned setting up pins at the local bowling alley every Friday and Saturday night— something I had continued to do even after I had suffered a broken right elbow. I could see that my dad felt hurt, so I gave him another five dollars and resubmitted the application. Two weeks later, another letter from Rutgers arrived. Yet again, the check had been returned for insufficient funds. "Do not re-apply," was the stern advice. All my friends were going away to college. I was alone and lost.

Fairleigh Dickinson University was nearby, and living at home and commuting was the only option that remained. Although it was a good university, I really needed to get away. I was not of a religious disposition as a young man, yet I always felt that God had a special plan for me. During the many times I had no guidance and had to learn from my own mistakes, I always felt everything would turn out okay. I prayed a lot. This, no doubt, was a result of my mother's influence. She was an angel, for sure. My mother always said, "If you don't have anything good to say about anyone, then don't say anything at all." I found out much later in my life that most of her words of wisdom came from the New Testament.

The Paterson Phillies and Florida Southern

I had just barely finished pitching my last game in high school when I got a call from a fellow named Bob Potts, manager of the Paterson, New Jersey, Phillies baseball team. Bespectacled, rotund, non-athletic in appearance, Bob was a baseball lover at heart and a quiet, nice fellow. He had been following my career in the newspaper, the *Bergen County Record*.

"How would you like to pitch for the Phillies this Sunday?" he asked.

I was in heaven. First big step into the pros! *"Come to the field in Hackensack at noon Sunday, and we'll have a uniform ready for you."* Turned out I pitched a good game, we won and I was on my way.

Semi-pro baseball was a great delight. I looked forward to every Sunday.

On one occasion I was about to leave for a game in Paterson when the phone rang. It was Mr. Dragon, the father of my best friend, Vic. Mr. Dragon was a pretty tough guy; an outstanding college football player in his time; he umpired semi-pro baseball games on Sundays, although his full-time job was working as a state parole officer.

"Bruce," he said, "are you pitching in Paterson today?" I told him I was.

"That's great, because my car won't start. Can I hitch a ride with you?"

As we approached the field in Paterson, Mr. Dragon suddenly yelled out, "Stop the car a couple of blocks from the field and let me out! I'll walk from there because it would be a scandal for the pitcher to drive up with the umpire!"

We were playing in New York City the following Sunday, then in Garfield, New Jersey, the Sunday after. One of the best players on the Garfield team was an outstanding baseball player named Ken Huebner. In both appearance and raw natural ability, Ken reminded me of a modern-day Babe Ruth. We knew each other from the newspapers. He was one year ahead of me. We became instant friends, and are friends to this day. He asked me about my college plans, and was very surprised when I told him my story.

"Listen," he said. "Let me see what I can do."

Ken had a full baseball scholarship at Florida Southern College in Lakeland, Florida, an excellent college with a great baseball program. It was mid-July, 1963. *What could he possibly do? It's too late.* A couple of days later, I went home after painting a house all day, and my mom informed me I had received a call from a man named Hal Smeltzly, the baseball coach at Florida Southern College.

All I could say was, *"What!?"*

I took a deep breath and dialed. "Hello, Mr. Smeltzly?"

For over an hour, we talked about my good academic and baseball records. He said I had been highly recommended to him by his star player, Ken Huebner. He said if Ken thought I was a great pitcher, that was good enough for him. An application for admission to Florida Southern would be coming in the mail. "Fill it out as soon as you receive it, and ask your high school to send me your transcripts. Don't worry about anything, but don't delay! You will be on a full scholarship for four years, half baseball and half academic."

I was speechless.

In late August, 1963, I met Ken Huebner at the airport in Newark, New Jersey. It was the first time I had flown on a plane. Always gracious, Ken let me sit by the window. First destination was Tampa, then Lakeland, Florida. To make a long story short, playing baseball for Florida Southern was a dream come true.

Over the four years I spent there, we won the Florida Conference Championships, and I made the All-American College Baseball Team in 1965, with the lowest ERA (Earned Run Average) in the nation. My record still stands at Florida Southern. The highlight of the year was playing against the Detroit Tigers during spring training.

My enthusiasm had me thinking: *Pro baseball, that's the next step for me—no doubt about it!*

FSC was a great school both academically and athletically. And to my surprise, at a Methodist school, I even enjoyed the mandatory Wednesday religious hour in the school chapel. I did not enjoy the mandatory military training—ROTC. Reserve Officer Training Candidates graduates could go to Vietnam as 2nd Lieutenants.

I still recall one of the lectures by a sergeant: "Gentlemen, this is the M-1 rifle. It weighs 9.5 pounds; with the bayonet attached it weighs 10.5 pounds. Therefore, the bayonet weighs 1 pound." There was a lot of laughter over that comment, but as for me, I just wanted to get back to baseball.

New York Times, Friday, June 4, 1965 / St. Petersburg Independent

College Baseball:

Draft Choices... Guerrant of Michigan, Fred Mazeruk of Pittsburg, Bill Monday of Arizona State **Bruce Aitken of Florida Southern**....*Terry Craven of San Francisco State, John Fause of Arizona....These are just some of the college baseball stars being watched eagerly by the scouts of the twenty major league clubs which will meet in New York next week to conduct their first free agent draft of college, high school, and sandlot players. Aitken, a right-hander, led all pitchers in earned run percentage with a 0.63 mark. He had an 8-2 won lost record for Florida Southern, permitting only 42 hits in 71 innings. He walked 16 and struck out 61.*

In addition, I had been invited to two back-to-back tryouts at the great Yankee Stadium, the "house that Ruth built." I recall pitching on the mound, mesmerized by the aura of the place; and, although frowned upon, I scooped up a handful of dirt as a keepsake.

After graduation

Before I knew it, I had graduated from Florida Southern. It was 1967, and I was poor as a church mouse. After college, I returned to New Jersey for the summer to play baseball, expecting to get drafted by a pro team. Ken went on to play for the Kansas City Royals. I was talking to scouts from several major league clubs. I was one of the upcoming top pro baseball draft picks, and was expected to sign contracts worth over $50,000, which was a fortune at that time.

Then, one hot New York City Sunday in June, while scouts were in the stands watching, it happened. I had been pitching a great game. All of a sudden, I felt a sharp pain in my right knee, then it locked. I could not straighten out my leg.

Soon, I was on the way to the hospital. The doctor at the ER applied enough force on my knee to straighten out my leg and put on a cast. A month later, the cast was off, and so were the baseball offers. I had thrown my last pitch in organized baseball.

My dreams were shattered.

Plan B

On a lark, I had applied for a job in Ft. Meade, Maryland, along with a good college buddy, George Kerekes. I passed the test and was offered a job at the National Security Agency as a cryptographer. The class was to start in September. It was the height of the Vietnam War, but the bloody job was not draft exempt. I received a notice from the draft board to report to Newark, New Jersey, for the Army induction physical. I was against the Vietnam War which I personally regarded as total madness. *I'll be damned if I am ever going to shoot anyone. America can go to hell first*! I was protesting in Greenwich Village and listening to Bob Dylan.

It was September 1967. There we were, my high school buddies and I, all together on the way to Newark to get physicals; and before long we'd surely be on our way to the killing fields of Vietnam. A couple of hours later, on the bus back to Hasbrouck Heights, we discussed our fate. One of them asked me what happened during my physical.

"I failed. The doctor moved my knee around, and said, 'Torn lateral meniscus, you fail.'" This was the first time in my life I felt a sense of joy at being a failure. The injury had turned into a blessing. But I wondered what the hell I was going to do

Just Lucky...

I had a 1954 Chevrolet I bought for $200. It took me three days to drive it back to Florida where I had friends. I was taking the Lakeland exit off I-4, when the car shuddered violently and stopped. *Shit! What happened?* I got out and looked under the car only to see that the drive shaft had imbedded itself in the blacktop. *Damn!* I only had a couple of miles to go. My friends, Ellis Shaw, a college basketball player from Coral Gables, and Norm Wolfinger, from Easton, Pennsylvania, were expecting me soon.

After pushing the car onto the grass and removing the license plates, I said good-bye, and started to walk down the ramp to hitchhike the rest of the way. Suddenly, a big semi-tractor trailer blew his horn and stopped to help me. The driver looked the car over, and pronounced, "I can fix it!"

Happily, I signed the Bill of Sale over to him and took him up on his kind offer of twenty-five dollars for the car and a ride into Lakeland.

Norm, who was later decorated after being wounded in Vietnam, was to become a top lawyer and well-respected prosecutor for the State of Florida. But the first summer out of college, in 1967, he drove a potato chip delivery truck. We shared some wild times during our college days.

He turned me on to Colt Malt Liquor beer and, taking after my Irish dad, I found myself getting drunk with my friends every weekend, chasing girls around in the boondock phosphate pits we called "High Tension." Our Friday night ritual was to wander down to Lakeland to "colored town" where we were treated like honored guests by all the "sisters" and Milton, a black fellow who ran a small bar.

One day Norm was so drunk he was arrested for peeing on the Golden Arches at McDonalds.

Years later, however, as a Florida prosecuting attorney, Norm went out of his way, as only a true best friend would, to write a letter on my behalf to a prosecuting attorney, supporting my bid for freedom.

Blind Faith

Ellis went on to Vietnam as a soldier and caught some mysterious illness while there. One of the saddest moments in my life was his death, which came within the short period of a year.

Florida Southern was a college with rich kids. Friends of athletes like me who did not have a pot to piss in. Ellis, Norm, and Ken Huebner, also poor, sympathized and hung out

That same summer of '67, I got a job working in Bartow, Florida, for the summer in the phosphate mines. The job title was "dam tender." It was forty miles away and I had no car. Work started at 7:00 am sharp and ended at 3:00 pm. I took the job. I really had no choice; I had to eat. Every day I woke up at 5:00 am. It was pitch dark.

I started to hitchhike. You could still hitchhike in America in those days. With luck, I would usually arrive in time, and reverse the process on the way home. I can honestly say I lived my life with some confident feeling of faith—or was it fate? I did not know. I felt ill-prepared for life and its mysteries, except for my mom's influence that told me to always trust in God.

"Dam tender." What a job. Long pipes gushed water and built up gravel underneath, and when the gravel came to the top of the pipe, you had to call for another pipe to be connected, otherwise it would back up into the system. That was the job—watching the end of a pipe all day.

I soon realized I needed a real job. So, before the end of the summer, I went to Orlando to see a girl I had dated in college. Terri Lulos was a beautiful girl of Greek descent who lived in Winter

Park. Her dad, Harry, was a very successful mutual funds salesman with Fidelity Funds. He opened my eyes to mutual funds as an investment, and to the lucrative commissions you could make selling them. But in my heart of hearts, I was not a salesman.

Good people, although perhaps a bit eccentric, they were always very kind, but they did not see much future in me for their daughter. I was staying in a cheap hotel near "colored-town," the black neighborhood that existed in every city in the South, signing up for daily jobs with Manpower for a fin—five dollars a day. On weekends, as the occasion permitted, I would walk to Winter Park to see Terri which was a good two-hour walk one way.

Interested in psychic matters, the Luloses decided to check me out by making an appointment for me to pay a visit to a mystic they trusted. His name was Robert Bos, and he lived in Cassadaga, Florida. Cassadaga, about an hour's drive from Orlando, is a lovely little town occupied by mystics, palm readers and other spiritual beings.

With nothing to lose and a certain amount of curiosity and hope, I decided to go. Mr. Bos asked me to sit in front of him across a small table in his living room. The place was plainly decorated, yet pleasant and comfortable. When Mr. Bos looked at me, I looked directly into his strange bright-gray eyes; he said nothing. After twenty minutes, he shook his head, which indicated the meeting was over.

Suddenly he said, "I am getting something."

What happened next was weird. He told me a few details about my early life that no one knew. He concluded by saying that to his amazement, I had thirteen guardian angels, and as such a person, I would have a life graced with amazing luck. Almost nothing could go wrong. However, there was something else he saw, and it was *not* good. That's when he frowned, and I saw fear and sadness in his mysterious eyes. I pleaded with him to tell me, but he flatly refused.

This was to bother me for years to come, until one day, over twenty years later, I finally found out what he saw.

But at that time in my life, I needed to get serious about my future, so I went to the office of a local headhunter and made a detailed resume´. After all, I had a college degree in Economics.

"On Wisconsin!" It's a song of victory...

After working with Manpower one day, I returned to the flea-bag hotel and found a message waiting. I had an interview the next day for a job as a claims adjustor. If I got it, I'd have a company car. This was to be another major turning point in my life.

The next day I put on my only white shirt and a tie, and hitchhiked across Orlando to a small office building: Employers Insurance of Wausau; I had heard of it.

"Hi, I'm Ron Langa," said the athletic-looking young fellow interviewing me. Ron wore a brilliant and broad welcoming smile, with a white short-sleeved shirt and tie, formal but at the same time carefree and casual. Ron was the only adjustor in Orlando, a one-man operation. A sharp, witty and fun-loving young bachelor, he hired me, and we became instant lifelong friends.

Later, we even attended law school together, and while I lasted only a year, he went on to become a top lawyer in Orlando.

Ken getting me into Florida Southern on a baseball scholarship, and Ron giving me the insurance job were probably the most important silent prayers God had answered in my life.

By the time I got back from a six-week training course in Wausau, Wisconsin, I had pretty much forgotten about getting a knee operation and playing baseball. I had a decent salary, a company car, and a big South Florida territory. Sometimes I would take off and return a couple of days later, spending Friday in the office doing the paperwork. I soon moved into a nice Florida house with Ron, and on weekends we partied.

At last, I had enough money to eat what I wanted whenever I wanted—three big meals a day on the road! Quickly my weight ballooned from the same 165 pounds I weighed when I graduated from high school, to a staggering 203 in less than two months. When I stepped on the scale, I was shocked, and started running. I also switched to cottage cheese and stopped eating like a pig, rapidly returning to 165.

My family was still in New Jersey, poor as hell. About three months after returning to Orlando, in the summer of '67, and getting my first pay checks, I sent for my mom and dad. I rented a trailer home for them to stay in temporarily, and asked my sister Joanne, one of the twins, to drive them from New Jersey to Orlando.

Element of surprise

A week later, expecting them to arrive at any moment, I stayed close to the phone. When it rang, it was Janice. "We are almost there. We just passed Daytona Beach." "We," to my amazement, turned out to be not only my mom and dad, but my twin sisters and their families, plus Honey and her current wild boyfriend, Lonny. Soon, a caravan arrived at our house. All my plans were upset. Ron was equally surprised. All I could think was, *it will take all my salary to support this family.*

Soon the situation degenerated into an Irish fighting match. The small trailer home was packed. Then, all of sudden, it was empty of my mom and dad. Honey had forced them to move into a room at a boarding house with her and Lonny, and they were sucking up the little cash I had given to my mom. I was livid. Arriving at their room, I threw a fit, took my old mom and dad and, much to their relief, returned them to the trailer.

Back home that night, there was a knock at the door. A police car with red lights flashing was parked outside. Ron answered. I waited, then came out.

"Are you Bruce Aitken?" the officer asked. "Come with me, you are under arrest."

This was the first time I had ever been arrested. Years later I would have a few more of these unpleasant experiences.

"Your sister has charged you with assault," the officer advised me.

Ron was livid and told the police the truth about what had happened, but the officer said, "Sorry, come with me and let the judge decide." I went to the police station and was formally charged, and ended up posting bail of a hundred dollars.

"Ok, you can go now," said the same policeman.

"Not so fast," I said.

"What is it?"

"I want to file a complaint. Can I do that?"

"Certainly!"

So, I filed a complaint against my sister, Honey, for assault. Within an hour, she was picked up and charged and brought to the same police station. I had gone home long before I got a call from my mom with the news. She asked, "Is Honey going to spend the night in the police station? She can't post the hundred dollars bail." The next morning I dropped the charges.

Honey had a penchant for having people arrested whenever they disagreed with her. It must have been the Irish blood. Years earlier in New Jersey, she got into a big fight with my brother, Jim, about who was to pay for the burial of my father when he passed away. My dad, still very much alive, had to go to the police station and bail them *both* out!

Get me out of here, before I go crazy

After a year I lost interest in claims adjusting. I was driving down the interstate one day, just listening to Glenn Campbell singing "Take Me Home, Country Roads" on the radio, and I pulled into a rest area and looked at the stack of files on the car seat. Confused and unhappy, I turned around, drove back to the office and gave my notice. I missed the excitement of playing baseball. Baseball was special. Once again, I found myself at a loss. Thankfully, Honey got a job and moved out, and I had rented a nice little house for my mom and dad, even though I was constantly broke.

I needed another miracle.

On a Sunday morning, just after I had joined the ranks of the unemployed and had about a month's savings in the bank, the next miracle happened.

I had one hell of a hangover from the night before, so I got up late. Ron was in Vero Beach for the weekend. Slowly relishing a second cup of coffee and feeling quite depressed, I turned to the "jobs" section of the *Orlando Sentinel,* and found my future in large black letters right there in front of me.

American Express International Banking Corporation. They were interviewing in Orlando for overseas assignments in something called military banking in Vietnam, of all places. College graduates with a BS degree in business or economics were "most welcome." My hangover suddenly disappeared and my spirits soared. I could see excitement returning to my life, and I forgot about the war. *Where would I go?* Vietnam to start, but then London? Paris? Amsterdam? Who knows? Thank God!

Suddenly, I was happy.

New York, New York

D.A. "Dale" Doll was Amex vice president at 65 Broadway. It was early Fall, 1969 and great to be in the Big Apple, in a training program, and employed by a big company. The interview had gone well in Orlando. In fact, what was required for Vietnam was just a warm body.

The training class was into its second week, when one of the executives walked into our class and dropped the bomb.

"Will the three staff assigned to Vietnam identify yourselves? Urgent openings are available right now, for a bonus."

Suddenly, three hands went up—the hands of the poor and hungry—me and two colleagues, Vince and Bill.

"Come with me right now," he said. "Go to Amex Travel and make the flight arrangements. You can finish the training on the way at Kadena Air Force Base in Okinawa."

Calling my family and friends in Florida with the news, they thought I was totally nuts. "Are you crazy? There is a war going on in Vietnam. You protested it! Don't go!" But the decision was a no-brainer. I felt driven by fate. I had to get away.

Forty-eight hours later I was staring out the window as the plane descended over the mountains on our final approach into Fairbanks, Alaska. Next stop, Japan. After arriving in Tokyo, I found a bar, chatted with the bar girl, was overcharged, and had my first taste of the exotic Far East.

Kadena Air Force Base was a sprawling structure. We stayed off-base and commuted back and forth with Amex staff for a couple of weeks. There was a steady flow of staff coming back through from Saigon on a military flight from time to time, full of war stories and telling us to change our minds while we still had the chance.

We were booked into a little hotel, the Koza Kanko, and we all suffered from culture shock. And yet, it was pleasant enough. It was simply exciting to be out of the USA and in a foreign country; and, quite frankly, I didn't give a damn which country it was. I just wanted excitement in my life again. I also discovered rice. Rice with sauces. We had never eaten the stuff. We ate potatoes, because rice was for "weaklings"—"the little people."

There was a street in Koza City called BC Street. It was seedy and run down with bars and girls catering to the U.S. military. I was shocked when I saw a row of small shacks linked up together, each about the size of an outhouse. There must have been a peephole for each occupant, because each time I approached one of the shacks, the door would swing open and a fifty-year-old female would jump out and ask me if I wanted a blow job. *What?* I was horrified. It was my first exposure to the ubiquitous skin trade in Asia, and the availability of women in the world's oldest profession, about which I had been totally naive. This was a new world, and I planned to take it all in.

Next stop, Vietnam, with its ongoing war and new levels of debauchery!

CHAPTER 2
Sunday in Saigon

I was feeling very happy to be leaving Okinawa and Kadena Air Force Base. Okinawa's daily rain and cold were getting to me—no sunshine that time of year. Moreover, I had not accustomed myself to all the sounds and smells of the place, so when the day finally came to head for Vietnam, I felt a mixture of anxiety and keen anticipation. I had time to worry about that later, however, because we had a stopover on the way to Saigon: Hong Kong.

Hong Kong had never held an attraction for me and I didn't really know what to expect. What could I do in a city that was a hundred percent Chinese? How could I get around or order a meal? I didn't even know if the Chinese spoke English.

Soon I was gazing out over an amazing sight, one of the most beautiful sights I have ever seen. I was on the Star Ferry crossing Victoria Harbor, from Kowloon to Hong Kong. It was a sunny day in late November, 1969, and at that moment I felt very excited to be alive.

The sunlight shimmered on the water like a million bright lights, while the sound of ships' horns wailed in the distance, all of them vying for space and the right of way. Organized chaos! There was a huge amount of traffic on the harbor. Large ships, small ships, dozens of Chinese junks with their big red sails, weaving their way between tiny boats called "wala-walas"—almost all of them seemed to be steered by smiling little old Chinese ladies dressed in black, wearing conical bamboo hats, their gold teeth sparkling in the sunlight.

Strange exotic smells assailed my nostrils and the salty water constantly slammed against the side of the ferry. Straight ahead of me was Hong Kong. Victoria Peak rose up from the central business district like a proud Phoenix. Although I had read all about it in *Taipan*, however, to actually be there held us in awe. Hong Kong was still very much a British Crown Colony, a fact I found reassuring. I loved it! Yes, all was well in my life again.

"Down with American Imperialists and their running dogs!" read the big banner draped across the wall in the China Products Store across from the Peninsula Hotel on Nathan Road, Kowloon. Quotations from Chairman Mao were posted everywhere, along with a counter piled high with Chairman Mao's *Little Red Book*. The very pretty and very tiny Chinese salesgirl noticed me frowning at the sign, asked me where I came from.

"Ah, New York...oh! An American?"

"Not quite the same," I answered, being "almost" a New Yorker.

"Are you a tourist?"

"No, I am on the way to work at my job in Vietnam."

"Vietnam? Oh yes," she said, glancing and smiling at the sign as I read her mind. *An American imperialist running dog!*

Because I had been totally against the Vietnam War from day one, I saw the irony, and realized I was about to discover the truth for myself.

We became so fascinated with Hong Kong, we decided to stay an extra day. This decision, as you will soon see, turned out to be a big mistake,

We went to the beach at Repulse Bay, up to Victoria Peak, to the Night Market, and to Causeway Bay Typhoon Shelter with those very same little boats playing music and selling seafood and San Miguel beer. The place was a beehive of activity: the trams, the ferries, it was magic. Here I was in the Far East, with a good dose of England thrown in. There was even a cricket pitch in front of the Hilton.

The next day, we tried to rebook our flights through AMEX and learned that all flights to Saigon were booked for the next three days. *Great news, three more days in Hong Kong!*

Expect the unexpected

Three days later, we left.

Staring out the window as the plane descended through light clouds, the voice of a pretty young Chinese stewardess brought me back to reality. It was the age of the mini-skirt and I could hardly keep my eyes off her lovely legs. *Asian girls are so very feminine.*

"Fasten your seat belts," she commanded in a perfect British accent.

Cathay Pacific Flight CX 106 from Hong Kong was on its final approach into Ton Son Nhut Airport. It was noon on a Sunday in early December, 1969, in Saigon, Vietnam. And there was a war going on. To our surprise, or more accurately, due to our ignorance, we did not realize the flight was via Phnom Penh, Cambodia. I got off the plane and walked around outside the terminal. The place looked just like Florida to me—flat with palm trees.

I saw a small group of people waiting to board and recognized one of them, a famous one at that, none other than the former Thai Prime Minister, Chavalit himself. I believe that was his name. He once acted in a famous movie, playing himself. I think it was called, "The Ugly American."

"Bruce...what the hell are we doing here?" Bill from Florida stood there, beads of perspiration, nervous sweat, congregating on his forehead, revealing his worst fears, while Vince, our other traveling companion, sat quietly in the aisle seat. Almost simultaneously, we all said, "The bread, man, the bread." Why else would anyone in his right mind be going to war-torn Vietnam unless he had to.

In fact, we were about to find out that we were already up shit creek without a paddle. Country bumpkins? We didn't think we were, but oh yes, we were. Like most Americans, we did not really know a hell of a lot about anywhere but America, the greatest country on the planet. Hong Kong had been an eye opener. We didn't know anything about Vietnam.

At last we were in Saigon, and it was a thrill to be in such a fascinating and completely different environment. After clearing customs and immigration, we piled into a taxi and headed to the American Express office. The streets were filled with people riding bicycles and motorcycles, and driving old French Citroen cars. The myriad smells were simultaneously strange, exotic and intoxicating. Tell you what, the French did leave some great things behind. The smell of freshly baked baguettes coupled with rich Vietnamese coffee mesmerized the senses.

We arrived at AMEX.

"Where the hell have you three morons been? What the hell are they doing in New York, sending me a bunch of morons?" Endless expletives followed. That was Reed Vauter, In-Country Manager, American Express International Banking Corporation, Vietnam, or AMEXVN. We had arrived three days late. Reed was six feet three inches tall and looked a bit anorexic. He wore faded blue jeans and a short-sleeved white shirt that looked like it needed a good washing. His thin face, bags under his eyes, and three-day stubble, reflected a torturous and extreme lack of sleep.

"Don't you morons know how to send a cable or make an international telephone call?"

In fact, we had no idea how to send a cable or make an international phone call, not to mention the thought had never crossed our minds.

"Check into the Astor Hotel on Tu Do Street, and get your stupid fat asses back here by 6:00 am tomorrow morning. Bruce Aitken, you moron, you're going up-country to Chu Lai!"

Bill was similarly dispatched to Pleiku in the Central Highlands, and Vince, I think, went to Phan Rang.

Picking up my bags, reality hit me. *Saigon. I'm in Saigon!* On our final approach into Ton Son Nhut Airport, I had seen the military aircraft on the tarmac, and dozens of helicopters parked under half-moon-shaped bomb shelters. Getting out of the plane, we had to wait for twenty minutes for a green military shuttle to take us to the terminal. Gasping, I could hardly breathe. The heat shimmering off the tarmac burned my face and eyes. I was sweating as if I were in a sauna. This place made Florida look cold.

The walk to the Astor Hotel on Tu Do Street, just a couple of blocks from the office, seemed to take forever, since I was sweating like a pig. The Vietnamese were not sweating at all. Every two steps someone approached, asking me to change money.

"Hey, you got green 'dolla!' No sweat! Me no cheap Charlie, I give you good rate, G.I.!"

Startling also, were the hordes of beggars, many missing limbs; the many ARVN soldiers, casualties of battle, pressed themselves close to us, begging for money while simultaneously trying to steal our watches.

Checking into the six-story Astor was a different matter. The front door was guarded by two Indian hotel doormen who chased away the street people. There was a curious mixture of furniture in the lobby: rosewood with inlaid mother of pearl, and a big tropical fish tank in the corner. I glanced at the ladies working at the reception, dressed in national dress, the *au dai*—sleek and sexy. *Score one on the plus side. These Vietnamese ladies are something to look at, all right.*

After checking into the room and taking a cold shower, I had the urge to get out onto the streets and look around. It was early evening, and the sun was starting to go down. Along with the night came a strong breeze and a remarkable drop in the heat.

As I walked, I thought about the black market. On the way over, we had been indoctrinated as to its perils, that it was illegal and to be avoided. I realized my throat was parched and decided to cross the street to a makeshift food stall selling cigarettes and canned drinks.

"I'll have a coke, please, with ice. Never mind, forget the ice, who the hell knows what's in it."

The little old Vietnamese man smiled broadly through his sharp-eyed wrinkled face, and betel-nut-red stained teeth, then gave me the coke and demanded, *"Hi Tram Dong, please,"* or *two hundred piaster, please.*

"What! Two hundred piaster? That's outrageous! That's almost two dollars. Are you nuts?"

"Dollar!" screamed the old man, his eyes lighting up and darting around to see if anyone was listening. "You have dollar! You give me one dollar, no sweat. I give you coke and give you back four hundred piaster, better known as 'P.' You have MPC. I give you coke, plus two hundred P."

He was mistaken about me having any "MPC," short for Military Payment Certificate. I knew I had just been introduced to the black market, or as businessmen called it, the "free market." This was bullshit, of course. I had just changed twenty dollars at the hotel at the official rate of P118 and this little drink stall was offering me almost P600? I knew something was not kosher, and that I needed to figure it out before I went broke.

Good Monday morning, Vietnam

"Hi, I'm Richard 'Dick' McKegny." A friendly voice awakened me from the radio's speaker well before 6:00 am the following morning; nice to hear since I did not sleep that well in the

Astor Hotel, due in part to having been ripped off by the hotel money changers. No wonder; there were three kinds of money circulating in Vietnam. The constant drone of helicopters dropping flares along the Saigon River had not helped me sleep, either.

"Looking for Viet Cong infiltrators," we were told. "Happens every night. Get used to it."

We were also told to, "Hurry. Pick up those sacks of computer readouts and beat feet." So we had to catch a C-130 to Chu Lai departing at 7:30 am.

I had been issued a MACV ID card (Military Assistance Command Vietnam) with equivalent rank of GS 13 (Government Service), so we could bump almost anyone off a flight, although we never did. No reservation necessary. We were, after all, "civilians" and considered the equivalent of a Colonel. Not a bad start. I didn't really like the trip, however.

The C-130 is a 4-engine prop transport aircraft. You have to sit along the sides in canvas seats, and there are no windows, so you don't know where the hell you are. I just listened to the engines for four hours and finally the thing touched down in Chu Lai, which was to be my home for the next nine months. Chu Lai by the sea! Home of the U.S. Army Americal Division (cavalry soldiers, hence Americal) and MAG 13, the Marine Air Group of Phantom jets and helicopters; over thirteen thousand souls in all.

It was hot and the place was a real dust bowl. Imagine an American Express bank in a place like that. Still, the U.S. military and personnel need all kinds of support. Life does not stop because you are on the other side of the world fighting a war. We bring America to you. The job was nothing special, and the Vietnamese staff did most of the work.

I worked with two Germans who had been borrowed from military banking in Germany. Civilians could go off the base at their own risk, and there was a little village called Tam Ky, a few klicks (kilometers) down the road; we visited as often as possible and got a few cold beers and a massage. The beer tasted better in the "vil," and most importantly, there were women there.

Nights spent on the base were either in the Officers' Club, perched on a hill where you could silently watch the Medivac helicopters landing the wounded at the field hospital, or at the NCO Club, drinking and listening to rock 'n roll belted out by some outstanding Filipino bands.

Then there were the Red Cross "Donut Dollies," an interesting mix of American girls who braved all to come to Vietnam to support the troops, and real troopers they were. Of course, some may have been lonely young ladies looking for love and companionship that they may not have found back home. In Vietnam they were in heaven, and in the minority, outnumbered by a thousand to one, surrounded by the U.S. Army, Air Force and the Marines. But to the last one, they were a bunch of good-hearted chicks, and as American as apple pie.

What amazed me were the unexpected things that were to be found in a war zone. The government spent a fortune bringing all kinds of civilians and services to the troops: banking, base exchange, life insurance salesmen, big construction companies like RMK-BRJ, and even car salesmen. That's right. A soldier could buy a Corvette, and have it waiting in his driveway on the day he got home—a short-timer's dream.

One day in early 1970, Chu Lai made the headlines in the USA by weathering the largest Viet Cong rocket attack of the war up until that time. I remember the morning well, running from the mess hall "hooch" with my breakfast in hand, to the underground bunker beside it. Over two hundred rockets were launched from the nearby mountain. By the time the base commander called the local Vietnamese village chief for approval to retaliate, the VC, having used time fuses, were long gone.

Funny how the Vietnam War was fought. There you were with incoming rockets blasting all around: *Step 1,* Call the village chief and ask for permission to bomb the piss out of the Viet Cong; *Step 2*, Permission granted several hours later; *Step 3,* Send up the Phantom jets and bomb the hell out of the mountain; *Step 4,* Kill the plants and the trees.

The field hospital was busy that day. It could have been much worse except, fortunately, most of the rockets overshot the base and landed in the South China Sea, a small fact overlooked or unknown as reported by the *Wall Street Journal.*

On the morning I arrived in Chu Lai, I met the AMEX staff member I was to replace. He was a fellow from South Carolina named Harold, and I was to move into his porta-camp, the little housing units provided by the company for the staff. The porta-camps were a leg above anything else on the base except maybe the general's quarters. You could call it a small trailer, but it was good enough; air conditioned with hot and cold running water. There was a loaded .45 caliber pistol under the bed at all times.

On the first night, I took the bullets out of the gun, walked up to a cliff overlooking the beach and tossed the damn things into the ocean. How the hell could I sleep with a loaded gun under my bed? I might end up shooting myself. Not all Americans are cowboys from Texas.

American Express International Banking Corporation, Military Banking Division, Chu Lai, Vietnam, APO 96302, was no slouch of an operation. I was surprised to find the place staffed with many expats: three Americans, two Germans, and one Japanese. The Americans were "assigned staff." Most were graduates of a school in Arizona called something like the American Institute of Foreign Trade, and were known as "tutors," or more precisely, "nerds." They were there for the money (we all were), but also to work their way up the AMEX ladder to a cushy spot in commercial banking. The Germans were there only for the money.

The Japanese fellow, Dick Hase, and I became best friends within the "group." Dick was a quiet fellow, and wise in many ways. He told me it was the sergeants who ran the military. They were the "wheelers and dealers," and this I found to be particularly true of an affable sergeant I was soon to meet, Sergeant Cruz. If you wanted anything, no problem, call Cruz. The guy was running a twenty-four-hour on-call operation Need a case of steaks? "How many?" "How many cases of beer you need, man?" It was party time!

The quid pro quo? We bankers were in a very enviable position; we were able to change money at ridiculous rates, and had access to "green" and to traveler's checks.

We also had access to the magical "black market."

One night, peering through cigarette smoke at the Officers' Club, I heard someone yell out my name.

"Bruce! Unbelievable. What the hell are you doing here?"

It was Bob Kimbrough, one of my frat buddies from college (Florida Southern), and he was right there on the same piece of sand. Bob was halfway through a tour as Warrant Officer, a 2nd Lieutenant, better described as a pilot flying Huey helicopters. *Damn,* I thought. *This was the result of staying in the college ROTC.* Later, I was happy to learn that Bob made it out of the place unscathed, but while there I was very pleased to provide for him, via Sgt. Cruz, an occasional case of steaks for the troops.

In the years I spent working in Vietnam, I met the troops, hundreds of G.I.s from officers to grunts, from all over the USA. They were all great young men serving their country in a senseless war that was not popular. I looked up to them, and prayed they would all make it back home safely.

"Bruce!" Dick Hase called out to me one Saturday morning. I never did like working on Saturday mornings. "Cruz came by and said to remind you to come to the party up on the hill behind the NCO Club in the afternoon. Don't go," Dick advised. "These G.I.s 'all no good,' all smoke that stuff, that 'mariana.'"

Mariana. Ha-ha! Japanese had a tough time saying "marijuana."

"Oh, really? Any ladies there?"

"Oh no, don't know, didn't say; don't go."

"Dick, you have anything better to do in this dust bowl?"

I was an athlete and did not smoke. I had smoked one joint with a friend as a teenager in New Jersey. I remembered it because after smoking it, we went for a beer at a topless bar in Garfield, and made fools out of ourselves ogling the girls.

"Where the hell is the truck?" shouted Sgt. Cruz, taking a long slow hit on a freshly rolled foot-long reefer before passing it around. "Shit. It is five o'clock, and they were supposed to be here an hour ago."

"What truck you talking about, man?" mumbled one of the soldiers as he exhaled smoke rings. He was a young black fellow from Georgia named Al, about nineteen years old and a "grunt" as we called them; he was just back from a mission. These were the young guys that went out in the bush looking for a fight for days at a time—the ones who did the actual fighting, many of whom did not make it back. For every one of these fellows, there were at least another ten military staff providing support and various other services.

A big scam! My mind went wild sometimes. *This war is only about business, about money—a huge mistake, and a shameful disgrace on the part of America. Send one of those bastards, Nixon, McNamara, Johnson or Kissinger out here and put a gun in their hands! Let them have a supply of those AMEX blood-soaked checkbooks that get handed in almost daily, with instructions to close the account and send the balance to the next of kin.*

"The ice cream truck, you idiot!" Just then, we heard the sound of a vehicle approaching. Everyone jumped up.

"That's the big f*cking surprise, Cruz? Ice cream?"

From the hilltop, we could see the big white ice cream truck with *Foremost Ice Cream* written in red on the front and sides, approaching at a very high rate of speed. It was about a mile down the road and was kicking up one hell of a trail of dust. Five minutes later, there it was, screeching to a halt right in front of us.

"What the hell took you so long?" screamed Cruz at the young driver, who was sweating profusely. Come to find out, the truck had been off base early in the morning, delivering a load of ice cream to the next base, a small Marine outpost or LZ (Landing Zone) about 20 klicks down the road. On the way back, it had picked up some very precious cargo.

The driver screamed, "Holy shit", I got behind a convoy of ammo that was coming down from Danang, and couldn't pass it. I got stuck just in front of the f*cking gate for an hour."

Murphy's Law.

"Quick. Open the goddamn ice cream truck door! The girls!" screamed Cruz. Suddenly a half dozen of us were standing behind the back of the truck refrigerator door when it sprang open.

Our jaws dropped! There they were, six lovely ladies. Three were barfing all over the place, and the other three were passed out, almost dead.

"Get them out!" The girls were crying, screaming in Vietnamese. It was pandemonium. "Holy shit!" We toted them out just in time. They all survived, thank God, but everyone was really pissed off. *No pussy today.* Cruz was worried, but worried only about one thing.

"The mama-san in Tam Ky is going to be so pissed off. No more pussy now or ever. It's a disaster!"

I went home drunk as a skunk. Cruz came in the following Monday, his usual smiling self.

"What happened to the girls?" I was genuinely concerned, amazed at the stupidity of what had happened, and terrified at the thought of what *might* have happened.

"Oh, no problem," Cruz casually replied. "Took them back off the base the next morning the same way they came in, in the ice cream truck. They first refused and put up one hell of a commotion. I had to put a gun to their heads, ha-ha."

Nine long months later and hallelujah! Due to the rapid rotation of AMEX employees who decided to quit and go home early, a chance opened for me to move closer to Saigon where I could get a real life, but not before I was sent to an air force base in Tuy Hoa; halfway back to Saigon in time and distance.

Tuy Hoa, South Vietnam – 1970/71

The difference between an army base and an air force base is like night and day. *Chu Lai was a shit-hole compared to Tuy Hoa, at least on the surface.* The roads in Tuy Hoa were paved, and the place was maintained. There was grass and trees. At Chu Lai, the only green I saw was that of army fatigues. It didn't matter much, because there was still a war going on.

American Express Bank, Tuy Hoa, was run by a happy-go-lucky character named Kerry Murphy, a really great guy with whom I became instant friends. He was Irish, a hard worker and a hard player. He was also a real fun-loving fellow. No wonder we hit it off instantly!

Soon we got into a good working routine, covering for each other. The "bank" opened at 9:00 am and closed every day at 4:00, and because Vietnam is hotter than hell, we got thirsty. By noon it was time for an ice-cold coke. We would pop one open, pour out the coke and fill the can with cold beer. By the time the staff had balanced out and gone home for the day, we were already drunk and heading for the NCO or the Officers' Club to continue our revelry.

Kerry had a cute Vietnamese girlfriend who worked for the bank, and he was hoping she would not get pregnant. More and more, we started leaving the security and boredom of the base and heading downtown to Tuy Hoa, where we each rented a room in his girlfriend's house. Transportation was in the form of Honda 90 motorcycles we had bought, and the distance from the base to the village was about twenty kilometers. The journey entailed riding down the highway, then turning onto a narrow two-lane road which passed straight through ten klicks of rice paddies, separated by two bridges over two rivers.

The bridges also held the railroad tracks for the trains, and the railings were separated by wooden planks, many of which were missing. You had to be damn careful and sharp-eyed, switching from plank to plank, when you saw one that was missing. Hit a pot-hole and you and the bike could be flipped over the side of the bridge and into the water, which due to fear, looked to be at least a hundred feet below. Nasty thought.

One night we had to make a quick decision. One of our staff, Miss Phung, was getting married, and we were invited to the party. But this also turned out to be the night when we had a shitload of problems at the bank. Saigon was calling about a shipment of American Express Travelers Checks that had not arrived. Where the hell was the courier? Were they sent to Air Force finance? We could not leave until they determined where the hell they were, and it was already dusk. The phone rang again and again, with either Saigon or the wedding party calling. Finally, around 8:00 pm we got word by telex. The courier had taken the US $100,000 T/C shipment and boarded the C-130 from Saigon to Pleiku by mistake. Hallelujah!

We were drunk by then, but managed to look at the clock. *Almost 9:00 pm, what to do now? We are the honored guests, right? But we never leave the base this late. What the hell, let's do it.* All the traffic, the trucks and a couple of jeeps were then traveling back to base, and there we were, trying to leave. The guard motioned us over to stop.

"Where the hell you two arseholes going? You f*cking crazy?"

"Yeah, we're crazy. Just lift the gate so we can get our fat asses off this shit-hole base. We're heading to a party. Besides," we said, "look up in the sky. What's that you see?"

"A bright full moon! You need more light than that. Good luck…you're totally nuts! Don't you know there are VC operating in the area?"

Kerry led the way and with not another vehicle in sight, we hauled ass toward Tuy Hoa. Once we passed through the mountainous area, the road sloped down a bit until it leveled out. Then it became an absolutely straight road for about five klicks through rice paddies. It was a beautiful sight in the full moon; beautiful, that is, until clouds passed in front of it and everything went pitch black. For the first time, I began to think the guard had been right. Kerry was about fifty meters ahead of me. In the silence of the night, the sound of the gunned motorcycles could be heard for miles, and we were only about halfway there.

All of a sudden, there was a flash of light, and the red brake lights on Kerry's Honda lit up like a Christmas tree as I heard his bike skidding on the asphalt, along with a very strange hissing sound. Adrenaline coursed through my body and I was instantly sober. A strange feeling flew through my mind and racing heart, and I thought about my family in America. I thought about my friends and everyone who told me I was nuts to be working in Vietnam in the first place. Were they about to be proven right? Most of all, I wished I was back on Tuy Hoa Air Force Base, safe and sound, totally bored, sucking on a cold beer.

"Kerry!" I finally realized the hissing sound was caused by rolls of razor-sharp concertina wire that had been rolled across the road in front of Kerry's bike, causing both tires to burst. The second coil rolled out behind him and in front of me, but I was able to skid off to the side and slam the bike into the gravel so it hit the side of my bike and missed me. I was no worse for wear except for scrapes on my hands; I saw the blood on my hands, but strangely felt nothing. I was totally numb. This is it. VC ambush! I prayed to God I would not be shot.

Suddenly, Kerry was surrounded. Ten, maybe twenty, soldiers jumped from the rice paddies from both sides of the road. I was a few meters behind. Brandishing M-16 rifles, they started screaming at us in Vietnamese. We started screaming back in English. Then one said, "Where you go, G.I.?" They were all wearing green. We had been ambushed, all right, but not by the Viet Cong. We were ambushed by "friendlies," by the ARVN, the Army of South Vietnam. The soldiers had been sitting in ambush, waiting for VC.

Instead of shooting us, an old man appeared with a set of wire cutters and we cut the wires out of Kerry's bike. It took about fifteen minutes to get the wire cut, and another two hours to get back to the air base, taking turns walking the bike with two flat tires, while riding mine next to it. The good news: a happy ending. We got back to the base just before the Officers' Club closed at midnight. Just in time for another cold beer!

Saigon, New Year's Eve, 1971

I had been "in country" for over a year, and continued to be amazed by many things. It's interesting to be in a country while a war is going on, especially a big, controversial war like Vietnam. Sometimes you stop and try to figure out just what the hell it is all about. The "anything can happen at any time" mentality sets in big-time; and that leads to an *"I don't give a damn about anything"* attitude; which leads ultimately to a complete breakdown of what is normally considered to be moral and ethical. At that, you move into the realm of *"live for the moment, because anything can happen."*

In reality, being a civilian in Vietnam was not particularly dangerous but the situation allowed me to use it as an excuse to succumb to temptation and decadence. In many ways, the experience changed me, and even as those changes were happening,

I knew I would never be the same, or at least not for a long time to come.

Hailing a small white taxi outside Tan Son Nhut Airport, I felt pretty good to be back in Saigon. Saying good-bye first to Chu Lai, then to Tuy Hoa was not a problem, something like going from a desert to a village and finally arriving in the big city. For the next couple of months, I was to be assigned to American Express at MACV Headquarters, Saigon. The compound was a sprawling set of buildings and facilities located between Tan Son Nhut and ARVN —Army of Vietnam General Command. The big guns, like General William Westmoreland, worked here. MACV came to be known as Pentagon East.

About twenty minutes later, the taxi pulled up in front of the villa rented by AMEX: 127 Ly Tran Quan, a nice place on a quiet shady street two blocks from the Saigon downtown cemetery. I remember the cemetery because it was the same one where the Viet Cong hid most of the ammo they used during the Tet Lunar New Year Offensive of 1968.

The villa had six bedrooms and a pool on the roof, ideal for rounding up a few girls from one of the local bars on Tu Do Street and throwing a party. The company also employed a little old lady named "Cupa" who was a great cook. She could only speak two English words: *"Eat now."* Each time she said it, she giggled heartily.

From the MACV office, I was able to get a new assignment in Di An and Phu Loi, about forty kilometers past the Ben Hoa Air Force Base. A sharp right turn on the highway led to the beach town of Vung Tau, about a two-hour drive south. One trip stands out— *New Year's Eve 1971.*

In the mornings, I often used a company jeep to collect some of our staff, drive them to the base and then back home at night. A couple of the office girls, a fellow I knew from RMK-BRJ Construction Company, and I decided to go to the beach for a party to bring in the New Year. We set out mid-afternoon and drove about a hundred kilometers south, arriving at Vung Tau before dusk.

I checked into our little hotel and took a shower before heading to the lobby bar where we were to meet for a few beers before dinner. I was almost dressed when someone started banging on my door. I mean *banging*. I opened it to find a colleague almost yelling at me, "Bruce, *they* are looking for you. I heard your name on the Armed Forces radio!"

"What…*my name*? What the hell are you talking about?"

"Your name, damn it. No joke, man. The message is to tell you to contact Saigon Red Cross immediately."

I felt sick; the air in my lungs turned hot and heavy. Whatever this was about, it could not be good. I called the Red Cross, and as I waited for the operator to come on the line, I became aware that it was almost New Year's Eve in America; all I could think was, *This has to be about my dad. My dad.*

The Red Cross told me my dad had suffered a heart attack and passed away. I was to return to Saigon immediately where the company would get me on the first flight to America. I just stood there, stunned, as a feeling of ineffable sadness and disbelief overcame me. My eyes reddened as the tears welled, and each heartbeat reverberated in my head.

After the initial shock hit me, I fumbled through getting my things together and my friend drove me to Saigon that night, even though it was after curfew.

Before we got to the highway, we were going breakneck speed through a small village when a dog ran out in front of us and *bam*, it glanced off the side of the jeep, making the most appalling, unbearable, loud wailing sounds I had ever heard. *The poor dog*! The neighborhood was waking up. Lights were coming on. What could we do? My friend punched the accelerator. We had probably killed that hapless dog, but we thought there was nothing we could do about it, so we kept going.

Memories of my dad flooded my consciousness over the days I traveled to Orlando; a forty-hour trip in those days. I felt especially sad that he died before my home leave, which was scheduled for the following month. It was a profoundly sad time.

Looking down from heaven, he would have seen the humor in my arrival in Orlando. My sister Honey, being a proud former U.S. Marine and real trooper of a sister, calculated when my flight would be arriving at the Orlando Air Force Base. Honey had called our sister, Janice, and told her, "Come, drive me there right now. *My brother is arriving from Vietnam!"*

As they arrived at the gate, Honey yelled, "Pull up!" and flashed her twenty-year-old Marine ID in the guard's face. The guard would normally yawn and wave anyone through, but in this case, he sat up and said, "Let me have a look at that! No, you should not have this. This is the property of the U.S. government." Then the ranting started and continued back and forth.

"Give it back!"

"Hell, no!"

Honey threw such a fit she had to be restrained by the MPs. Meanwhile, Janice was doubled over in a fit of uncontrollable laughter.

All of this was happening at the same time I was flying commercially on a Delta Airlines flight from San Francisco.

We got through Dad's memorial service as best we could. By the time I had been in America two weeks, I was itching to get out. My family and friends asked me to stay. Disney was opening, and the place was going to grow. There would be good opportunities. But my response was, "Once you have the itch you have to scratch it." I missed the Far East, and to my surprise, I missed Vietnam in particular. Orlando seemed dull in comparison.

Return to Saigon

I was sad to say good-bye to my mom, but I couldn't wait to get back to the excitement of travel and Vietnam. I had a lot to look forward to. I had talked with Amex Country Manager, Kurt Leutsch, before I left Vietnam, and he was going to find a spot for me in or near Saigon. Kurt, about five feet six inches and rotund with a Santa Claus-like red face, was one hell of a nice guy. All the Germans at AMEX were hard working and humble. It seemed their only pleasure in life was to drink a couple of six-packs of Budweiser after work. I always gave my ration card to Kurt, so he could buy another case every month. If Kurt was out of town, I gave my ration to his assistant, Hans Sowa. All the beer I had planned to drink, which was a ton, would end up in the presence of beautiful young ladies hanging out in the wall-to-wall bars on Tu Do Street or Nguyen Hue Boulevard.

Vietnam was a paradise full of ladies who spoiled a young, healthy bachelor rotten. Instinctively, I knew these experiences would change me. The vibe of the place included an ongoing war— you never knew when you might be in the wrong place at the wrong time and get your ass blown off. It was "live for today," because tomorrow you may not exist. Every day was lived on the edge. And sometimes shit happened, and it always seemed to happen before 11:00 pm, U.S. military curfew.

One hot evening, I was slurping a cold beer in My-My Bar on on Tu Do Street. It was nearing curfew. I had a young lady sitting on my lap when *bam*! The whole bar shook like an earthquake. Someone screamed, *"What the fuck was that?!"* We ran outside with our ears ringing, and looked across the street. The Bristol Bar had just been hit. A Viet Cong sympathizer had just driven by on a motorbike and flipped in a couple of grenades. There was not much left of half-a-dozen unlucky civilians and G.I.s who were sitting at the bar. The Bristol had been one of my favorite hangouts. The chaos that followed and the smell of explosives and flesh was nauseating. *"Fucking gooks!"* everybody screamed, shooting into the air.

Returning rapidly to "debauchery mode", because the civilian curfew was midnight, and the curfew for the military was 11:00 pm, I had it made. What a life! Just before 11:00 pm all the military fled, leaving all the ladies behind and at the mercy of the civilians. This was surely heaven!

Twenty-four hours after leaving Orlando, I was drifting in and out of sleep when I heard the Pan Am stewardess on the intercom:
"Fasten your seat belts. We are on our final approach to Kai Tak Airport in Hong Kong."
I was so happy to be back in Hong Kong, with a reservation at the Hong Kong Hilton for the night; I would be leaving for Saigon the following afternoon. I was looking forward to having dinner with a lovely Chinese girl named Jenny whom I had met at our usual spot, Jimmy's Kitchen. I loved the escargot. Breakfast would be on the balcony overlooking the cricket pitch, reading *Time* or *Newsweek*, listening to the BBC broadcast, tucking into a chicken-liver omelet and enjoying several cups of coffee while waiting for Jenny to arrive.

Pure decadence.

The market is "black"

By noon, I was out and about in Hong Kong, thinking about how I was going to double my money as soon as I got to Saigon. First stop, American Express. Next stop, the chemist. You never know about customs when you arrive in Saigon, so I cashed a check for two thousand dollars, asking for twenty crisp hundred-dollar bills. That was a hell of a lot of money in those days, and more

51

than I wanted to risk. Returning to my hotel, I wrapped the money in plastic and stuffed it into the back of a large tube of Colgate toothpaste I had sliced open with a razor blade.

The flight to Saigon the next afternoon arrived on time. After dropping my things off at the company villa, I jumped into a taxi and headed downtown to the Astor Hotel. The smell of Saigon was exhilarating. Inside, I closed the screeching gate of the old French-built lobby lift, and pressed six. On six, I had to get out and walk up a flight of stairs to the rooftop bar. Mr. Tai, my good Chinese friend, was one of the best black market money changers in Saigon. Next best were the Indians on the street, who hung around across from the Mosque.

"Mr. Tai, good to see you!"

"Mr. Bruce! You been up-country? Long time no see."

"Yes, up-country. What's the rate, Mr. Tai?"

"How much you got?"

"Two thousand green."

"Green! Great, man, great! I'll give you MPC 4,000 or local 1,600,000 in Vietnamese piaster, a big bonus!"

"Give me the MPC."

Being manager of a bank, I had access to all three currencies. I would put the MPC 2,000 away for now, and over time, exchange the remaining 2,000 MPC at 1:1 for another $2,000 green at my bank. Poof! I doubled my money like magic! I felt just like the Fed and the U.S. government—creating money out of thin air.

Had I been really greedy, or perhaps smarter, I could have made a small fortune, but I was happy stashing away a couple of thousand every few months. I foolishly, at the time, thought that was big money. I had discovered my mission in life. Little did I know how the black market would affect my future. It must have been fate that led me to Deak & Company several years later; Deak, with the black market at the core of its business.

Spending most of 1971 working out of Saigon for American Express International Banking Corporation, Vietnam. MACV Headquarters next to the airport provided a glimpse of where and how the top brass military lived—the colonels and generals who were running the war. What I remember most were the amenities: Olympic-sized swimming pools, golf courses, good restaurants, French Sports Clubs, and a BX (base exchange) that was well stocked with almost anything you could imagine. MPC was used to buy anything and everything on base—stereos, cameras, watches— most of which were also almost immediately sold at a tidy profit, and soon found on the street in markets all over Saigon and in Cholon, the large Chinatown at the far end of the city. That's where the black market for all manner of goods was located.

This is the Life! Tales to Tell!

This was the life in Saigon: working all day in the office, scamming to find ways to earn extra bread, partying every night until midnight. Living at the company villa was nice, but it restricted my ability to go out at night to change money at the top of the Astor, and to party. It was not long before I made a move.

Often, when I got caught out after curfew and had to get off the street fast, instead of returning to the villa, I took a room at the Astor, or the Cach San Vo Thanh, also managed by my good friend, Mr. Tai. He never charged me for the room. One night, what came to my immediate attention was a new pub that had opened just down the road, the 147 Vo Thanh. It was owned by a G.I. from South Carolina who had married a local girl and decided to stay.

The 147 Vo Thanh would become my virtual oasis.

The 147 featured southern-fried chicken and sizzling steaks served on a hot metal-and-wood platter. The whole place was decorated with that red-velvet wallpaper you can buy from a Sears catalogue. But the real attraction was the bevy of beautiful girls that served you. Since most guys were dining alone, these girls served the food, poured the beer, lit cigarettes and made conversation. The place was cozy, with less than a dozen tables and a small winding stairway leading up to a tiny bar in the loft. After dinner, you could invite one of the ladies for a Saigon Tea. I soon got to know all six beauties, and they soon learned that I lived in the building just across the street in an apartment on the top floor, and had a roof garden.

I thanked the Lord for midnight curfews, since it was not long before some of the girls were knocking on my door asking for a place to stay for the night. Neither the Vietnamese police, known as "little white mice" because of their white uniforms, nor the military, took kindly to girls roaming around after curfew, because Saigon was a very dangerous place.

I often found it difficult to wake up early in the morning and head off to work. I had an open jeep to drive to various work locations, like Cu Chi, Phu Loi and Di An. In Saigon, the day starts early in an attempt to beat the heat. Funny the things you remember, like the morning I stopped at a red light on a crowded street with the jeep full of young AMEX girls. Suddenly, an old Vietnamese bloke wearing filthy clothes made of black rags, stepped in front of my jeep, whipped his part out in front of us, and took a big long piss on the hood of my jeep—all to the delight of the girls. The light turned green, but I could not move until he finished.

Years later, it was revealed that Cu Chi Base was undermined by an amazing series of tunnels built right under the base—*right under us*—allowing the VC access whenever they wanted! The tunnels became a major tourist attraction after the war.

The attraction of Saigon at the time was that it was just a tantalizing place. Saigon bewitched and intoxicated like the exotic beauty that she was, her myriad and sensuous charms just waiting to be discovered. I never knew what to expect, but expected something every day. I never knew if the person smiling at me was friend or foe.

You might see a drunken G.I. shooting in the air after getting ripped off by a money changer on the street. Actually, that happened to me once. The guy offered me a rate to exchange $100 green for MPC at 300 and while I waited down an alley for the money to arrive, he bought me a couple of beers. I dropped my guard, and took the bundle without checking it; when I got back to my hotel and counted it, it turned out to be a bundle of piaster wrapped in a $20 MPC note. I took a loss of $75 on the transaction, and learned a couple of big lessons, one of which was not to be greedy.

Because I was changing green for piaster at up to P800/1, while the official rate was P118/1, I was able to live like a king on the local economy. French restaurants were cheap as hell. Everything was. It was U.S. government policy not to sell the greenback, because it would find its way to the enemy, the VC. I soon learned what a bunch of bullshit that was. Most of the "green" found its way into the Hong Kong bank accounts of wealthy Saigon Chinese and Vietnamese businessmen, or into Vietnamese gold taels; thin wafers of the precious metal known as *Kim Thanh*.

At the time I didn't know it, but after the fall of Saigon fifteen years later, I would find myself buying up huge numbers of gold taels from the Vietnamese at the request of the U.S. State Department.

Making light of things helped me overlook the serious side of what was really happening in Vietnam. The war was terrible, and it affected everyone. I don't know the term used by the other military banks there, Chase and BOA, but for AMEX, overdrawn accounts, which were a huge percentage, were called TIDS, or "Transactions in Difficulty." G.I.s who were rotated home were leaving behind a lot of checks that would bounce. We wrote them letters. The only reply I ever saw was a letter that came back with a picture. He had traced around his hand with a pencil—middle finger extended. The losses were all written off by the U.S. Treasury. AMEX really didn't give a shit. Under their contract with the Department of Defense, they would be reimbursed for all the losses.

On one occasion, we were about to ship a load of cancelled checks back to New York, when one of the girls spilled a whole bottle of *nuc mum* on top of them. *Nuc mum* was a liquid shrimp sauce the Vietnamese ate with everything, and it has a powerful foul stench that can knock your socks off.

What to do? Nothing. We packed it up and sent it through the Army Post Office to the New York office. About ten days later, we got a call from New York asking what the hell was in that box. I was told that when they opened it, half the staff in the New York office freaked out and started looking for a dead cat.

The TID's of some, often those souls of young guys barely out of high school who were killed in action, would be collected and shipped home with their personal belongings. Often, blood-stained checkbooks would be handed to us for account reconciliation. Each one affected my spirit. I could not see any reason on earth why we were there killing the Vietnamese, and they were killing us in return. What bullshit was this *"domino theory?"* Why not get those bastard politicians off their fat asses, and out here to do the killing themselves? This war was clearly about big business, big contracts, big money. In time, I decided not to be part of the machine.

After these realizations, I found myself sitting in a bar with a lady on my lap and one too many cold beers in my hand. Many impressions flooded my brain. I had decided to walk into the Saigon office on Plantation Road and quit; hand in my resignation. Nothing seemed to matter. I went to the USO to call home.

I'd miss the French restaurants, the good food at the Mosque, Cobra gunships close up, the Indian money changers, Huey helicopters showing off by skimming the streets, but I couldn't tolerate it anymore. I thought I had seen the best, but it turned out to be the worst. Song lyrics ran through my head: *"War! What is it good for? Absolutely nothing!"*

One of the Cobra pilots had made a tape of himself singing *"Here Comes Santa Claus"* over and over, but then you'd hear the rapid fire of the cannon as he blew away a dozen Viet Cong. Who could miss the fact that these were human beings just like us, who had mothers and fathers, sisters and brothers, grandmothers and grandfathers?

There was one AMEX staff who had been "in-country" for only one month when, quick learner that he was, he picked up on the black market in money and made a cool $100,000 before being caught by the military CID. What happened to him? We thought he would be tarred and feathered. Instead, he was sent out of the country within twenty-four hours, later to be hired by Chase in Germany, and given a good reference by AMEX who did not want to be embarrassed by the incident.

Totally nuts.

I resigned my position as I neared the end of my second tour in Vietnam. The US was pulling out, turning everything over to the Vietnamese, and AMEX was closing offices rapidly. The company offered me, and I turned down, a commercial post in Karachi, Pakistan, of all places.

Since Miss Tuy, the company secretary, agreed not to notify immigration until I gave her the okay, I decided to do a little more dollar salting before I left. So I went on one last spree, and made a little money by embarking on a month-long going away party that stopped only because Pan Am said they would no longer change my reservation.

During my spree, I saved every penny for the trip home and for school, and engaged in a few modest black market currency transactions. I needed to stay under the radar. My good buddy and colleague at American Express MACV Headquarters, John Langer, from Berlin, made that possible.

John had recently married a beautiful young Vietnamese girl who worked in his office. They rented a pleasant little house not too far from the center of Saigon. We are friends to this day and John is now living in HCMC. They had a big German Shepherd and a living room with a comfortable couch where I slept the days I remained in Saigon. Little could we have foreseen that many years after our beloved Saigon fell to the communists, John and I would still be doing "the deal."

John would become the chairman of a Frankfurt- and Hamburg-based international bank owned by the Turkish Chukurova Group. At that same time, in the nineties, I had great connections with the Vietnam ministries as a result of my company, Sports Asia Ltd., which would bring major sports events to the country. His tiny little Bank Kreiss AG, would receive one of Vietnams first banking representative licenses.

Little could I have imagined that Vietnam would be my saving grace at a time when the United States government was trying to lock me up and throw away the key!

Now, as I went about making money, I sensed the Army CID was watching me, because on my last day at AMEX, I was approached in the bank by a military intelligence operative named Albert, in civilian clothes, who asked me to meet him that night for a drink.

I knew I would be carrying a bundle of U.S. dollars and some traveler's checks, so I had a queasy feeling that it was either a setup or he wanted in on the action. I chose to meet him at the Roxy Bar on Tu Do Street at 10:00 pm. I knew the mama-san and many of the girls working there.

I had already been to see my money changer, Mr. Tai, who had kept me waiting at the Astor Hotel bar for almost two hours; this was unusual. By the time I arrived at the Roxy Bar, all the military personnel had already gone home.

"Bruce," said the mama-san, "someone was here waiting for you and just left. He had a few beers and asked a lot of questions. He very pissed off you no come on time! When he left, I watch him cross street and meet up with two army MPs and took off with them in their jeep."

A chill run down the back of my neck.

I needed time to think. My ticket to New York was written Saigon/Bangkok/Rangoon/Calcutta/Delhi/Karachi/Tehran/Tel Aviv/Athens/Rome/London/New York. I had a plan—law school, then run for some kind of office one day; do some good.

It was a good plan, but the best laid plans can change.

I had caught the travel and adventure bug, and when you have an itch……. Scratching it would lead me to become friends with one of the most charismatic intelligence operatives of the twentieth century, who was known as "The James Bond" of moving money.

Fate was about to deal me another hand.

END OF PART ONE

The Cleaner

The Cleaner

Part Two

The Laundry and Lockheed

The Cleaner

CHAPTER 3
Deak & Company

Winter, 1972 – Memphis, Tennessee

Some people are very calculating and plan their futures step by step, while others leave life to fate or blind trust. I suppose it depends a lot on the circumstances as well as your upbringing: your family, your education, your environment. I wondered if there really was such a thing as karma. In my life, I preferred to cast my fate to the wind, assured that the only direction to go was up. Of course, part of the magic and beauty of life is that things do not always turn out the way you expect them to.

I should mention that Jenny, the shy Chinese girl I dated in Hong Kong, turned out to be "The One." From the start, I saw something wonderful in her, and I knew it would last a lifetime.

I returned to America and decided to study law at Memphis State with my friend, Ron Langa, my buddy from Orlando. He'd given me my first real job with Employers Insurance of Wausau at a time when I was starving—long before I started my love affair with the Far East. Law school and family obligations in Florida turned out to be very expensive and I had either not saved enough money, or I had spent too much.

After a year at law school learning the basics, I determined I would be a lousy lawyer. When I analyzed the cases, I often came up with the wrong conclusion because I was basing my answers on common sense. And I yearned for the sense of adventure I had in the Far East. There, I felt alive every minute.

Before we were married, Jenny traveled to Toronto to study at a secretarial college. She would visit me in Memphis, and on one of the trips we decided, on a whim, to get married. Pooling our funds, we had a grand total of $1,800—one hell of a start. Ron was my best man, and he and his future wife, Lynda, were the only witnesses at our civil ceremony.

That night, Jenny and I shared a quiet dinner at a simple restaurant before we headed back to our tiny rented nest on top of a garage, just behind a big Southern mansion.

Jenny went to the Catholic Church nearby for Mass every Sunday, while I stayed home drinking coffee and reading the Sunday newspaper. Jenny had faith.

I was in the market for a job, and Jenny knew the name of a company in Hong Kong I could contact with hopes of finding a job. We both knew about a foreign exchange company called Deak & Company. Amazingly, when I contacted the Sara Beattie Agency, they referred me to Deak.

Deak had been known in Saigon as the biggest operator in the black market. In fact, that's where I often went to buy the U.S. notes I would smuggle back into Saigon; not too many, usually about a thousand dollars—an amount that I could comfortably stuff into the back of a large tube of Colgate toothpaste.

I had met the Managing Director of Deak & Company when he came running out of his office to the exchange counter one day, yelling "Goddammit. Doesn't anybody have a visa to go to Jakarta?" He calmed down, and then flashed me a smile that indicated this sort of thing happened all the time. We had a chat. I told him I would like to work in Hong Kong.

"Ah," he said. "You have an American passport. Good, very easy for you to get visas. Give me a call. Stay in touch."

I looked at the card he gave me: Dirk M. Brink, Managing Director, Deak & Company (Far East) Ltd., 406 Shell House, Hong Kong, Cable: Deaknik HX.

The call to Mr. Brink

Now, after opting out of law school, I searched around for that card from Dirk Brink. Jenny found it and I made the most important call of my life.

"Deak & Company (Far East) Ltd.," came the confident voice of the receptionist.

"Hi, my name is Bruce Aitken," I said, "and I am calling from the United States. May I speak to Mr. Dirk Brink?"

"Hold on," she replied. I did. I took a deep breath and prayed hard. I had no "Plan B." After several seconds, which seemed like an hour, Brink's deep voice answered with a tone of caution, uncertain as to as to who could possibly be calling from America.

Surprisingly, Mr. Brink remembered me almost instantly. He said that, as a matter of fact, he had an opening in Hong Kong right there and then, and he was looking for an assistant.

"I'll arrange for you to go to Deak & Company in New York as soon as possible to apply for the job and undergo training. In a couple of months, you'll come to Hong Kong. Bring your U.S. passport. Get the big fat one with forty-eight pages. The job involves a lot of traveling." My heart was racing. I hugged Jenny, and thanked God and her. *A miracle had just happened.*

On a winter morning in Memphis, I was thinking about the upcoming interview with Deak & Company. It was a very cold morning in January. My flight was scheduled to leave at 4:00 p.m., so I decided to go to work for a couple of hours to earn a few dollars. We were nearly broke at that time. The only job I could find in Memphis was as a laborer, working high up on the new bridge that was being built over the Mississippi River. It was dangerous work, but the pay was good, and I needed the overtime.

I rolled out of bed and said good-bye to Jenny. The old $200 Rambler started okay, but it was snowing, and the wipers didn't work. I had to stick my arm and hand out the window and move the windshield wiper manually just to see where the hell I was going. What a good start to the day. But, no problem, because in a couple of hours, I'd be in New York in a nice hotel at the expense of Deak & Company. That's great.

I got to the bridge and started to climb to the top level where the tools were kept; there was also a warm fire burning up there. "Good morning to all," I said. Then, as I bent down to pick up a wrench…CRACK, I heard a terrible sound and felt a cold steel wrench slam into one of my upper front teeth, breaking half of it, which fell into my hand. Shit. *"Arsehole!"* I spit out most ungratefully to the fellow in front of me.

"You *moron*! Look what you've done. *Fool!* I have a job interview tomorrow morning—my plane leaves in a couple of hours!"

Poor fellow. He thought he was doing me a favor by handing me a wrench. I cursed God, and said to myself, *"How, dear Lord, how could this have happened?"*

I regained my composure and ran down from the bridge as fast as I could. The foreman came rushing over, looked at my teeth and said, "Oh, shit." I let loose with a mouthful of expletives that I had to dig deep into my brain to dust off, jumped into the Rambler and drove home, my mind racing. I kept thinking, *What am I going to do*? Like many other times in my life when I was in deep shit, I prayed. I burst into the little apartment we rented over the garage.

"Jenny," I yelled, *"Look what happened!"* Much to my shock, she looked at me and laughed! She said I looked funny with a broken tooth.

"Oh, Lord, what am I going to do now? *Think,* Jenny!"

The solution? Call Dan Dooley. Yes! Memphis State University had a fine dental school, and our friend Dan was a graduate student. A couple of hours later, I was out of the dental chair, with a state-of-the-art, high-tech half-tooth called an "enamel etch." I asked Dan how long it would last. "Well," he said, "When you are in New York, chew all your food on the other side."

I did just that, beginning on my late evening flight. Instead of arriving early that night and chilling out for the interview, I arrived after midnight with a headache and one hell of a toothache.

The next morning I woke up very early, rushed into the bathroom and looked into the mirror. Thank you, God! The tooth was still there. Showered and dressed in my best suit, or more accurately, my only suit, I was beginning to feel a lot better as I took the subway to Wall Street and Deak & Company.

The winter sun was rising, but it was very cold. It was 8:00 am and the diner I stopped in for a coffee was already crowded. As I sat there enjoying a cup of real New York coffee, I could see a neon light in the foreign exchange shop at street level: "Deak-Perera Foreign Exchange." I felt a big knot in my stomach.

By nine in the morning, I was being introduced to the traders: Chief Trader, Raoul Del Cristo from Cuba, Lallo from Columbia, Michel from Egypt, and Manuel Van Gelderan who was visiting from Buenos Aires. All of them were laughing like hell over a joke in Spanish they said they would not dare translate. No doubt about it, I liked this place.

As the day was winding down, the secretary on the eighth floor motioned to me. "Mr. Roethenmund is ready to see you now."

This was it. Otto Roethenmund, the number two guy–Senior VP. I thought I'd surely be offered the job.

"Hello, Bruce," he said. "Welcome to Deak New York. What do you think of this place?"

Otto could not have been nicer or made me feel more comfortable. He was a Swiss banker and had the savoir faire of a gentleman. In the seventies, Swiss bankers were held in awe by Americans—envied because they could buy and own gold. After an extended and pleasant conversation, what came next was a bit of a shock.

"Well, Bruce, you are doing fine, and you are the kind of guy we feel is a good fit for the position in Hong Kong. Dirk Brink needs help. You have been in the Far East, you have a Chinese wife, and you speak a bit of the language."

It was about 6:00 pm and my headache was returning.

"One more thing before you meet Mr. Deak."

Meet Mr. Deak? Holy Jesus. I never expected to meet Mr. Deak!

"Here is the address of our colleague, Mr. Wilson. He can still see you tonight if you hurry; and if all goes well, then you can meet Mr. Deak tomorrow morning. Have you ever had a polygraph test?"

"Yes, as a matter of fact, I have. I had a polygraph when I applied for a job during my last year of college at Florida Southern. The job was with the National Security Agency in Fort Meade, Maryland." I had a sudden flashback to the blinking signs along the agency's corridors, "*Monitor Your Conversation.*"

I jumped into a crowded train and headed back uptown, almost subconsciously touching my tooth with my tongue to see if it was still there. I found Mr. Wilson, who administered the polygraph test.

Afterward, he said "nice to meet you" and told me to go back to Deak in the morning to get the results. That was it. I rushed out, feeling relieved that the long day was over. I must have passed because I told the truth, although at times I had felt my heart beating very fast.

Mr. Deak

"Good morning, Mr. Aitken. Mr. Deak will see you now."

This was it. I had awakened early, once again relieved that my tooth was still there. I really needed the job, and all I could think was, *What will happen to Jenny and me if I don't get this job? Please, God, please God. . .*

Mr. Deak stood up from his desk, motioned for me to come shake hands and sit down. The eight or ten steps to the desk seemed to take forever. I felt his awesome presence, no nonsense and stern, yet he had warmth in his eyes. The first thing he said was, "What did you think of the polygraph test?" The only thing I could think of saying was that I thought I had passed.

"Yes, you did," replied Mr. Deak, "but, actually, in real life it means nothing. We work with a lot of money in this company and with a lot of private clients who trust us to keep their identity and affairs confidential no matter what happens. People change."

We talked about many things. When the intercom rang to remind Mr. Deak of an appointment, I glanced at my watch and was surprised to find that most of an hour had passed.

"Well, Bruce," my heart sank, then rose when Mr. Deak finally said, "Welcome to Deak & Company."

"When can you return to New York for training?" he asked. "Next week? Fine! You will start downstairs with Deak-Perera, and the starting salary is one thousand dollars a month."

I was startled, and it must have shown instantly on my face. A grand a month in New York, even in 1974, was peanuts, chicken feed.

"What is your lovely Chinese wife doing?" Mr. Deak immediately asked. "Is she a secretary?"

"Yes."

"Okay, then she can work with us, too, if she wants to. She could start at six hundred a month while you are in New York. You can sort out your salary with Brink in Hong Kong when you get there."

I could not wait to get to a phone and call Jenny with the good news. Although she would not say so, I knew she must have been worried. I felt so proud to have gotten this job, as if I had regained my dignity as a person who could provide for my wife, and who had again rolled the dice in life and come out okay. The thought of returning to Hong Kong *employed* was exhilarating.

Sometimes, people just click. Thank God that was what happened with Mr. Deak and me. Over the years to come, we would become quite close, as he would often come to Hong Kong and invite Jenny and me to join him for dinner. Sometimes he would ask me to check out something for him confidentially and report back to him. And, like almost all people who met her, he really took a liking to Jenny; he no doubt felt I was a wise man to have married such a special girl.

Mr. Deak jogged every morning around the track he had built at his mansion in Scarsdale, New York, and he was very fit. He was disciplined in all ways and a strict vegetarian. Nothing, it seemed, was left to chance. He also married into the banking community, his wife being the daughter of an Austrian banker, Mr. Potter. I was blessed to meet him a couple of years later, when I made a courtesy call to Bankhaus Deak in Vienna.

One time I needed to take a quick lunch break, so I rushed across the street from our Broadway office to my favorite hot dog vendor at the corner of Battery Park. New York hot dogs are famous for being delicious, and I was stuffing a second one into my mouth, when I looked up and found Mr. Deak standing in front of me.

"Do you know what's in that hot dog you are eating?"

Sheepishly, I said I had no idea, but that it sure tasted good. On the walk back to the office, Mr. Deak said he would be coming to Hong Kong before the end of the year, and he would contact me via Brink in case of any special assignments.

Jenny and I enjoyed the time we spent working in New York City. We were squeezed into a tiny studio flat on 33rd Street. We worked long and hard during the week. Friday nights we went uptown to a pub called, "The Great British Disaster," and would meet an old friend from Vietnam. Charles "Ted" Stallone had been selling cars in Saigon during the war but was now studying history, and I knew he was destined to become a great university professor.

Saturdays were spent hanging around the city, and Sundays we read the *New York Times*, and walked around in Central Park. The *Sunday Times* took all week to read; it weighed about ten pounds back then.

For the first time in a long time, I was really happy. I had a future again.

In Confidence

Meeting and coming to know Mr. Deak made a lifelong impression on me. After all, as I would later find out, when he was in his early forties he had parachuted into the Burmese jungle and the Balkans on many covert missions as an agent of the Office of Strategic Services during World War II. As a major in the U.S. Army, he was the officer who took the Japanese flag of surrender in Burma. He was a brilliant and charismatic man.

In the business world, he established a worldwide network of currency agents and smugglers to service a multitude of private clients, as well as intelligence operatives. Some of the methods were quite sophisticated, while others were smoke and mirrors. Some methods were ridiculously plain and simple, like in South America, crossing borders over mountainous terrain with bags of money loaded on to the backs of donkeys. "Where there is a will, there is a way" rang true at Deak.

Winter turned into spring in New York, and just when Jenny and I were preparing to go to Hong Kong, Otto Roethenmund called me into his office.

"Bruce, would you mind going to Guam for a few months before going to Hong Kong? Tony Evans, our manager, needs an assistant, and needs to spend some time in the States soon. It is on your way."

Guam. I had heard about the place, but didn't know much about it.

"Sure, of course."

Two weeks later, Jenny and I were on the famous Pan AM 001 round-the-world flight from NYC through Los Angeles and Honolulu to Guam. I got off in Guam, and Jenny continued to Hong Kong. No sense in her staying in Guam; it would be better for her to be at home with her family.

Deak & Company (Guam) Limited

What a contrast between this island and the island of Hong Kong. I wondered why on earth Deak would bother to have an office in Guam. With a small indigenous population of local island people, almost all of whom worked for the government, known as "Gov-Guam," I could hardly imagine a reason. Knowing Mr. Deak to be no fool, I soon came to know there was a brisk business in Japanese yen, involving mainly young tourists on their honeymoons who were flocking there by the thousands.

The office also specialized in peso remittances to the Philippines collected from Deak offices worldwide. That was about it, except perhaps for business from the military. After all, the sprawling Anderson Air Force Base, located on the best part of the island, was the home of B-52 bombers flying from Guam to North Vietnam and back again. Total insanity! I could not seem to escape the damn Vietnam War.

What Guam did have going for it was nice local people, and a place to make friends. There were a lot of American libertarian thinkers hanging around Deak and buying gold. Some of those friendships have lasted until this day, such as those I forged with Mickey Howard, Chuck Nordquist, Ted Pope, and Dennis Mankini, four entrepreneurs selling insurance to the military; plus Roger Slater and Steve Deutsch. Chuck introduced me to Mickey, who together with Roger and Steve, would later offer to testify on my behalf.

Then there was Bill Thomasson, the local manager of a Guam finance company. Bill would later work for me when I started my own company—First Financial Services Ltd. Like a bull, Bill was ready to take off at a moment's notice—to smuggle money out of any country as required.

Thomas O'Donnell was a particularly fine young fellow who worked for Bank of America in Agana, Guam. He turned me on to a good Mandarin teacher. Tom later went on to become the representative for Philadelphia National Bank in Manila, and then joined me in Hong Kong as a partner in First Financial Services Ltd. Sadly, we would eventually split up.

Last but not least was Charles Provini. "Chuck" was a U.S. Marine captain, a decorated Vietnam vet, who really saw the action with special teams dropped into North Vietnam to clean up after the B-52 runs. Chuck Provini became my ticket off the island, and eventually replaced me at Deak Guam so I could return to Hong Kong.

Guam turned out to be a great place for someone looking for a sleepy tropical island to chill out; it was flooded with Korean and Taiwanese bars and clubs.

So what was Deak's main business? The Philippine peso remittances. Payment lists would come in day and night by telex from Deak offices around the world. Instead of going through the Central Bank of the Philippines at the official rate, Deak offered a better rate.

How?

Black markets exist because governments often restrict the flow of capital in order to hoard foreign exchange, while their citizens prefer the freedom to do what they want with their money. Black markets also exist because of greed and ill-gotten wealth.

Does clean money exist? Yes, it does—after Deak launders it.

There were so many people in Manila who were happy to give us cash pesos, paying up to seven percent over the Central Bank rate to get U.S. dollars into their account offshore with no record of the transaction. And there were tons of overseas Filipino workers ready to give you dollars in exchange for pesos in cash delivered to their families at three percent better than the bank rate.

Deak did the swap and pocketed the difference, making a cool three to four percent on every dollar.

Deak's partner company that made the deliveries could not have been a better company—DHL. They had heaps of workers on motorcycles who delivered documents all day, so why not deliver cash pesos, too?

DHL in Manila was the only DHL that was franchised and not a part of DHL International. It was owned by an American named Guy Coombs and his local partner, Rod Feliciano. The biggest sources of cash pesos were some of the banks themselves, or should I say, executives of the banks, as well as some prominent stockbrokers.

Oddly enough, the Central Bank of the Philippines daily quoted two rates simultaneously: their "official rate" and next to it, the "black market rate" of Deak & Company (Far East) Ltd., Hong Kong. *The Philippines is a lovely country.*

Little did I realize that my experience in Guam would last the better part of a year. However, it was to come in very handy a couple of years later.

Tony Evans, the Guam manager, ran an excellent office and was an extremely likeable fellow. He had been in the Navy, was hard-working and very intelligent, but also very overweight. A couple of years later, Mr. Deak would call to say that Tony had suffered a massive heart attack and passed away at a young 35 years of age. I was deeply saddened. His lovely wife, Trony, was from Cebu in the Philippines.

Being the only one with Guam experience, I soon found myself back on the island with no hope of leaving until Chuck Provini replaced me.

Kim Thanh Gold

Then it happened—the fall of Saigon: April 30, 1975.

For several days before the fall, I stayed on the telex in Guam frantically contacting American Express friends still in Saigon. I had just been there a few months earlier, in December 1974, on a holiday. I couldn't believe this was happening, much less so fast.

Three weeks before Saigon actually fell, planeload after planeload of Vietnamese started arriving at Anderson Air Force Base. A refugee camp sprang up near the Naval Air Station at Oroti Point. American Express staff I had worked with in Vietnam started arriving as well.

Fearing reprisals, anyone who had worked for the Americans was scared as hell to be taken prisoner by the Viet Cong or North Vietnamese troops who were approaching Saigon.

But something unexpected was also arriving. The Americans were providing transportation out of the country for the rich. Old ladies would arrive in black pajamas, setting off the metal detectors at the base. What was doing it? They were carrying taels of Vietnamese gold wafers called "Kim Thanh," Vietnamese-style gold, thin and pure; so thin you could easily smuggle or hide it by bending it around anything, including your body.

I received an urgent call from the State Department asking me if Deak & Company could help. My answer was a big yes.

Because I had been in Vietnam, I knew exactly what taels were, and I knew what they were worth. I offered the State Department a deal, and they accepted.

The deal was that Deak would buy the gold taels at the USD price *per ounce,* one tael for the price of one ounce. Simple. Since a tael was 1.2033 ounces, we had a good twenty-percent spread.

The gold would have to be bought for cash and transported to Hong Kong to be immediately melted into Chinese-style Hong Kong donut-shaped taels. Price was not hedged, so we took the risk of fluctuations. Gold was in a bull market trend.

First thing to do was telex Mr. Deak. Next was to have a meeting with trusted staff who were all Filipino residents of Guam: Hector Villanueva, Dos Devejos and Marietta. I told them, "Cancel everything and plan to put in some insane overtime."

Next, I called Dirk in Hong Kong. Dirk immediately set up a "gold train" daily courier service of Deak Hong Kong employees flying to Guam with cash and returning to Hong Kong with as much gold as they could fit into their hand-carry backpacks, or about twenty kilos each.

Planes were landing at the base daily, with passengers carrying thousands of taels hidden in their clothing. Most were being housed in a temporary tent city set up at Oroti Point. The military fenced it in, guarded it, and constructed a small shack on which we placed our sign, "Deak & Company Kim Thanh GOLD."

The State Department gave us strictly enforced operating hours from 9:00 am until 5:00 pm. And then the "Gold Train to Hong Kong" started in earnest.

The remittance arrived from Mr. Deak, US two million dollars to start. But hey, this was Guam, and Bank of America, Agana, was not used to having so much cash lying around.

I frantically transferred most of it to Deak & Company Far East Ltd. in Hong Kong with a request to send the cash back to me by courier on a flight the same day. The following morning, FX Chief Trader, Tony Pong, arrived with the "bread," landing at 2:00 am with a cool one million US dollars and by 9:00 am we were open for business.

For the best part of the next two months, we worked from 9:00 to 5:00, rushed back to the office to sort and weigh the gold, packed it into the backpacks of at least three or four couriers from Deak daily, and got them to the airport by midnight. More Hong Kong couriers carrying more cash for the next day arrived at 2:00 am.

Soon we were attracting one hell of a lot of attention in the Hong Kong physical gold market, and after about ten days, the *South China Morning Post* picked up on it, and my office was besieged by journalists. I could not spare them even one moment.

When they ran the story, the State Department was suddenly receiving applications from three or four other Hong Kong gold dealers, asking for space at tent city, and offering to buy at a much better price.

To make matters worse, the State Department started to come down on me hard, saying I was screwing the Vietnamese, and even worse, I was opening up after hours and staying open until midnight.

I was furious at the accusation, and stated I did not think twenty percent was too large a gross margin, given the expenses, and the price exchange risk, also, because we were the only company who could immediately provide the service.

I decided to lay a trap and find out if anyone was really using our shack to buy gold after hours. Much to my amazement, I pounced upon several expat friends of Dirk Brink who were sneaking into the camp at night and buying gold at my "shack."

"Calm down, don't worry, Bruce," they said. "There will be a big fat envelope waiting for you in Hong Kong when you get back!"

"Bullshit," I said. "Tell Brink to keep his fat f*cking envelope. Pack up, and get the hell out of here right now because the State Department is accusing me of violating the agreement and calling me a liar!"

They refused. I called my good friends—the Guam police.

Soon after, those guys were escorted to the airport and placed on the next plane to Hong Kong. Mightily pissed off at me, it was years before we ever spoke again.

The incident left a bad taste in the mouth of the State Department as well, and they actually mentioned it years later, when our paths crossed again during a major money laundering scandal. One of the qualifications required to work with the State Department is that you must be a nerd with the memory of an elephant.

Here's how the scene looked at the Oroti Point camp "gold market."

The small plywood and corrugated metal building had an entrance in front and an exit in the back. The Vietnamese selling gold would line up one by one at the first desk, which of course just happened to be Deak & Company (Guam) Ltd. Need I say more?

I observed with great admiration, Thomas Lee, the representative attending the second desk. Thomas was an employee of Lee Cheong Gold Dealers. Day after day, he watched us buy *all* the gold. So, one day I sent some customers to him, and when we met again in Hong Kong later, he told me it was something he would never forget. We have been friends ever since.

Within two months, it was all over.

Reflecting on this great adventure, I thought of it as pure luck, pure karma, to be in the right place at the right time. Happily, I returned to the Hong Kong office, and found a very nice bonus from Mr. Deak waiting for me and the Guam staff.

All the newspapers had reported:

Deak-Perera was one of the few financial institutions in the U.S. with a combined expertise in precious metals, foreign currencies and international banking. As a result of this knowledge, they were invited by the U.S. State Department in April 1975 to assist the South Vietnamese refugees that were pouring into Guam and the U.S. as Saigon fell.

Deak-Perera would soon be catapulted into the national limelight. Their role was to serve as the exclusive "money changer" for all five Vietnamese refugee camps.

The U.S. Military Payment Certificates (which carried the likenesses of movie stars) were worthless. Other items, even diamonds, jade and loose gems, were hard to exchange on the spot for a fair price. Only gold had a quick and ready resale value.

Of course, the Deak Guam gold-buying operation catapulted Deak into the national limelight. For a company that preferred to operate in the shadows, this, plus major scandals in Japan and the Philippines, would have serious unforeseen consequences. We did not realize at the time that it would attract the unwanted attention and criticism of higher-ups in the government intelligence community.

CHAPTER 4
Deak & Company - the Deal Maker!

A tale of two islands

Little did I expect the Guam connection to play an important role in my life as a money mover. As a U.S. Territory, Guam provided easy customs clearance into most destinations, especially Japan, the Philippines, Taiwan and Korea. From the Guam office, I was able to make some of my best contacts, many of which were to become good clients of Deak & Company in Hong Kong.

I was able to wear two or three hats at the same time, depending on where I was and who I was meeting, and I had four business cards: Deak & Company Guam, Horizon Travel Guam, Deak & Company Far East, and Compass Travel. Carrying the four business cards allowed me to be a chameleon, blending in anywhere, and in any discussion.

Home base

Shell House, 26 Queens Road, Central Hong Kong, was a very famous address. Looking straight up Pedder Street from Des Voeux Road Central, the building was "in your face" and commanded one's full attention. Across the length of the building, and four floors up, a bright-red neon sign read, "Deak & Company (Far East) Ltd."

This was the nerve center of Deak's Asian business and, outside of New York, the most important and profitable operation in the world. In Asia, it represented three Deak banks: Foreign Commerce Bank (FOCO) in Zurich and Geneva, Bankhaus Deak in Vienna, and Deak National Bank in Fleischmanns, New York.

Dirk ran the place like a well-oiled machine. A brilliant thinker and risk-taker, he was also cunning; definitely one of a kind.

He would usually arrive at the office before 8:00 am and was always the last to leave, which was normally just before midnight. He poured out more work in a day than most people do in a week, although sometimes much of it was nonsense.

Dirk could also pour on the charm and the charisma, and almost anyone who met him liked him. All day long there was a queue of people outside his office waiting to see him, plus dozens of phone messages from all over the world, a pile of telexes needing a reply, and journalists waiting to interview him. Everyone wanted Deak's point of view and predictions.

Dirk told me what he expected. "Bruce, you are now my assistant. What I cannot do, I will send to you to do. You handle it. If you don't know the answer, please do not bother me, just use your head; it's all common sense. Say anything you like; most people are idiots, and don't have a clue what the gold price will be tomorrow. Always tell them it is going to go sky high, you better buy now. It's always going up!"

Dirk spoke to the boys behind the counter in Bahasa Indonesian and Chinese, and struck a casual pose of knowledgeable, respectable authority.

Of average height, he appeared fit and healthy, and wore an almond-colored "safari" suit that matched his tan complexion. He had a full head of rust-brown hair, and his face was well-shaped; his piercing green eyes, sharp and bright.

Dirk Brink turned out to be one of the most interesting characters I would ever know. He had an amazingly clever mind for moving money, and a ruthless character.

The son of a high school principal, born of Dutch parents in Indonesia, he had led a colorful life. He was fluent in many languages: Indonesian, German, Dutch, French, Esperanto and

Afrikaans. He had an instant opinion about every subject in the world.

The *South China Morning Post* called Dirk almost every day, and Mr. Brink never hesitated to offer sometimes quite outlandish predictions about tomorrow's price of currencies, precious metals and the stock market. No problem.

Brink's office was a large space cluttered with heaps of newspapers, books and magazines. A huge desk sat in the center of the room, covered with telephones of all different colors, one for each language of the caller. Sometimes three callers were on hold as he switched back and forth effortlessly between them, quoting FX rates or whatever he felt like quoting.

Company dress for Brink and all other foreign staff was not the customary coat and tie; no sir, that was for bankers, lawyers and nerds. At Deak & Company, only safari suits were allowed. The company motto may well have been, *Have safari suit, will travel,* and, since the company also owned, and shared the floor with a major travel agency, Compass Travel Limited, travel, we did.

I soon got the hang of it. I was taking over from Brink's then-assistant, Ron Pulgar-Frame, a good-natured, chain smoking, tall and barrel-chested Englishman whose motto was "Have passport, will travel."

Three English ladies, Jill Lovatt, Julia Hayes, and Bernie Layfield, rounded out the foreign staff.

We were surrounded by about fifty Chinese who did one hell of a lot of work, led by Anthony S. C. "Tony" Pong, the hard-working expert head FX Trader, and Mr. K. M. Leung, the Treasurer and Chief Accountant who also happened to be Pong's father-in-law. Leung was known to all of us as "Dr. No."

Tony Pong ran a team of equally well-oiled, super-efficient "counter boys" who could handle multiple FX transactions in a flash.

At night, he turned into the "Emperor of Entertainment" for financially well-oiled Deak clients who wanted a night on the town. He had a little black book of ladies' telephone numbers, including those of bored and lonely, but attractive, housewives of local bankers—husbands who traveled a lot; their wives were looking for a little romance on the side.

Back to business, Brink would come rushing out of the office looking for huge sums to cover deals in progress, asking Pong at the FX counter, who always said "yes," and then got the deal *nixed* by asking "Dr. No." When Brink threatened to chop off his head, he invariably said yes.

Deak Far East was making millions, and sending millions back to New York, and sometimes Brink wanted some of it back. There was also a lot of under-the-table private business going on between Pong and Brink. Often the timing of such deals was given away by the tell-tale action of sending anyone who was overly inquisitive on a trip to nowhere.

Two-dollar bills

The corporate philosophy and culture of Deak & Company was very much couched in the feeling of *normalcy*. It was perfectly moral and just to avoid or evade taxes and insure your future well-being via the God-given right of privacy. After all, wasn't this the basis for having nominees, or Swiss bank accounts?

If Deak laundered it, you better open an account with one of Deak's banks and let it stay right there. Deak's banks issued ICD's (International Certificates of Deposit) at high interest rates, and paid one-percent commission to the selling agent or staff who completed the deal.

For example, I could do a "pickup," convince the client to place the money in an ICD, and get the commission. If he rolled the deposit over the following year, I received another one-percent commission. I loved Deak & Company!

Deak was totally up-front about their business. All you had to do was walk in and ask. Clients' legitimacy and trustworthiness were established instantly, under a "know your client" axiom that was part of the Deak "bible." Part of that bible was to grow the business based on a referral basis from already established genuine clients. To further ensure that potential customers were indeed bonafide clients, all Deak agents worked according to what we referred to as the Two-Dollar-Bill Rule.

The Two-Dollar-Bill Rule was simplicity itself, and it usually worked something like this: As we traveled around the Far East, or for that matter, wherever we had an "agent," upon request, we would from time to time leave the agent with a supply of US two-dollar banknotes. What made these notes unique was that we had cut them in half. The agent would give half a note to anyone he referred to our Hong Kong office to discuss confidential "free market" business or a transfer of money in cash.

For example, our Taiwan agent, "Mr. Hwang," would send a telex to Compass Travel, advising that his friend, Mr. Chan, would be coming to Hong Kong on such and such a date, and request that we assist him by arranging his "tour." When Mr. Chan arrived at the Shell House office, he would be accorded a warm welcome, and not long after the conversation began, would present half of the two-dollar bill he had been given by Mr. Hwang. His half would then be matched with the other half of the same two-dollar bill kept in the file in our office, and the discussion would immediately move on to the nitty-gritty of the money laundering business.

"Mr. Chan, you wish to sell us your New Taiwan dollars (NT$), the equivalent of US one hundred thousand dollars, and we are happy to buy them from you. You realize, of course, that Taiwan has very strict exchange controls and this is a very dangerous business.

"Our requirements are as follows: We need twenty-four hours notice and a good-faith non-refundable deposit of US three thousand dollars to cover the expense of sending someone from our office to Taipei for one day. The NT$ we buy from you must be in cash, in circulated currency, and never brand-new bills in consecutive numbers. We will quote you the exchange rate of the day and charge you a total fee of four percent. Agreed? Good!"

Four percent was very expensive. Of course, many locals were also doing the same business for less, but with Deak, the client was assured that the deal was backed by a solid company with liquidity, a company that would pay out the counter-value as agreed; it had a reputation it needed to protect.

But most importantly, no fellow local Taiwanese citizens would have knowledge of the transaction and could not, therefore, blackmail you later. Deak & Company was the Rolls Royce of money laundering.

Upon agreement of the terms, we would take a New Taiwan one–hundred-dollar note and cut it in half. Half would be retained by the client and taken with him. "Don't lose the damn thing," we would say, "or the deal is off." We never collected the money from a third party unless the other half of the note was presented first. Otherwise, who knows, we could have been set up for a sting.

Once the money was ready, someone from our office would fly to Taipei to meet the client, who would hand over the money in cash upon presentation of the other half of the one-hundred-dollar bank note.

Our agent, and others like him, were successful businessmen who were "dollar salting," or stashing away dollars overseas and not reporting this income to the government. They were happy to receive the local currency in cash at a rate over and above the official bank rate. It was a win-win situation for everyone.

It's a little blue book!

One of the trappings of the aura of legitimacy is called "substantiation." In their daily government FX quotation, I mentioned the Central Bank of the Philippines always quoted the black market rate quoted daily by Deak & Company. This bolstered my belief that laundering money was not to be taken seriously.

To beat it all, however, was a clever little piece of work created by Dirk Brink, which listed a simple and quick method of encoding that could easily be used to create almost any message by means of combining a series of two-letter combinations.

The code was simplicity itself.

The "Bible"

Most businesses operate with rules and regulations, by-laws and Articles of Incorporation. In fact, it seems that life revolves around rules of some sort. If not, there would be chaos.

A lot of entities such as governments and the military, the IRS and Congress, have enacted laws and rules so voluminous, and taken these laws and rules so far, that they can no longer be understood. Common sense is often relegated right out the window.

Why should the black market money laundering business be any different? If you are going to do it right, you need some rules; however, in this "profession" the rules are simple and written in code.

Remember Chairman Mao and his *Little Red Book?* Deak & Company (Far East) Ltd. had a *Little Blue Book* and it was the bible of free market foreign exchange. I am holding one in my hand right now, and it reads as follows:

INDEX: *(Applies to all countries and currencies)*

1. Do not write your assigned code number in this booklet.
2. Number consecutively all correspondence beginning with number 1.
3. To insure the safety and accuracy of coded instructions, no modifications or new definitions are to be made to the codes by clients. We have included blank code lines for future enhancements. If new definitions are developed, they will be forwarded to you.
4. Always, do business only by using banknotes cut in half.
5. We can accept customer defined codes from letters ZA through ZZ for names, addresses, and account numbers for individuals, firms, and banks for frequent transactions.

The index in the little blue bible covered the following topics: *Example, Payments/Receipts, Amounts, Currencies, Establishment Firms, Addresses, Dates/Times,* and *General.*

On call 24 hours

A requirement of the job was to have a good passport, and in those days, a U.S. passport was the best. I kept a small travel bag in the corner of my office, and was ready to fly off at a moment's notice.

When I left home in the morning, I never knew if I was going to be back home sleeping in my own bed, or not. But, hey, what the hell, this was a great life for a young fellow who loved to travel, and who had a reasonably understanding Chinese wife.

I soon found myself flying more than an airline pilot, and going through two forty-eight-page U.S. passports a year, with additional pages put in so that when I opened it, they fell out like an accordion. Kai Tak Airport was like a second home. Sometimes the trips were "same day" back and forth, and sometimes I was gone a week or more.

It occurred to me that because of the nature of the business, and the clients that would use Deak's magical money laundering services, I would be dealing with all types of unusual and sometimes very eccentric characters, from tax evaders to drug dealers, government agents to just plain old lunatics. To boot, there were many skeletons in the closets and never a dull moment.

The world was our oyster, with operations spanning the seven continents, including the communist Soviet Union and the capitalist USA. Brink had developed ingenious hundred million US dollar "Mother of all Laundry" methods he created especially for the good ole USA.

Oops!

What continually amazed me was the way Brink would make an instant decision, because when he did, there was no turning back. He was a natural charmer.

Bursting onto the scene at the money exchange counter early one Friday morning, he spied Helen Fennel, a delightful gray-haired elderly American lady, who always cashed her Social Security check at Deak's.

"Helen, have you ever been to Manila?" Brink uttered the magic words. *Oh no, here we go again.* Before she could even exhale, Brink motioned to the Compass Travel staff.

"Give Helen a round-trip ticket to Manila for the weekend. She is a good and loyal customer. Book her into the Manila Intercontinental Hotel in Makati at our expense."

"Oh, Mr. Brink," she finally exhaled, "Are you serious? You are so generous. Oh, my gracious, how can I ever thank you?"

"Oh, there is one thing," said Brink. "My friend will drop by with an envelope Sunday morning. They're documents. Put the envelope in the hotel safe, and check it in with your luggage when you fly back Monday morning."

Brink was either a devil or a wizard. No customs agent would bother to check a lovely white-haired granny like Helen.

The weekend came and went. Our Compass Travel driver "KK," using our authentic black London taxi, collected Helen from Kai Tak Airport on Monday morning, and brought her to the office. She could not thank Brink enough for the great weekend retreat. She had befriended a very nice Filipino couple on Sunday afternoon, and while they were waiting for a guest in the lobby, she was invited to the very exclusive Polo Club. She had a wonderful day and a few too many gin and tonics. Brink was so pleased.

Eyeing her check-in luggage, Brink asked her, "Oh, Helen, may I have the envelope with the documents?"

"What?" she said.

You could hear a pin drop as the room went eerily silent. Helen paused and thought for a moment as her face turned crimson red and then pale as a ghost.

"Oh, my God, I completely forgot about it! It is still in the hotel safe!" Barely able to control himself, now Brink turned red, then suddenly pale.

"Bruce..." *Damn it, Brink you fool!* I had just returned from Jakarta that morning.

"What time does the next flight leave to Manila?"

Two hours later, there we were, old Helen, who could have been my mother, and I, on the Cathay Pacific flight back to Manila.

Returning to Hong Kong late that night, I handed the envelope, which contained US two hundred thousand dollars in cashier's checks, to Brink, who took it all in his stride, laughing heartily, seeing only humor in the fiasco.

"Have you ever been to…? Moscow? Leningrad?"

Brink's favorite words when setting someone up in a sting were, "Have you ever been to. . .?" He was talking to me when he asked, "Have you ever been to Leningrad?"

"No, not recently," I replied sarcastically. Brink had already spoken to David Mok, the manager of Compass Travel. David was one hell of a nice bloke, very savvy and smart, and he carried money like the rest of us.

"Listen, Bruce, you know that we have been selling those damn worthless Aeroflot tickets for a couple of years now, and the Russkies never pay the travel agent commission. They owe us plenty! I want you and David to use two of the free tickets, go to Moscow and Leningrad, and stay at their *Intourist Hotels*. At least we get some benefit in return. Take some tours, meet their management, and ask for payment. Teach them how capitalism works. We are not running a charity!"

Looking at David, I wondered *what's the catch?*

"Oh yes, one more thing!" *Here comes the catch.* "When you get to Leningrad, check into the hotel. Take this little black envelope—it is from Bankhaus Deak, Vienna." *Or, maybe it is from Mr. Deak?*

Brink logic: "Take this small black envelope along with you, be sure to sew it into the lining of your coat. Take it out when you get to Leningrad from Moscow. Walk to the river front and stroll around on the night you arrive. This will be next Thursday night at precisely 9:00 pm. Don't be late. There is a famous boat docked on the side of the river, the *Aurora*. It is thought to have fired the first shot in one of the World Wars.

"On the second night, at 9:00 pm, hang out in the corner of the hotel bar and wait. If all goes well, a group of drunken Georgians will come in and start up a conversation with you. Slip the envelope to the one who introduces himself as 'Alexandre,' and who will be wearing a Harvard sweat shirt. That's it and it's so simple...you're done. So go and enjoy a couple of days at the Hermitage."

Of course, this was 1977 and Russia was *very* communist, and had parked KGB on every corner. Brink made it sound like child's play.

Flashback! Mr. Deak was no fool! I remembered my visit to Bankhaus Deak in Vienna just a few months earlier. What struck me was the very brief introduction to a visitor from Russia. I tried to recall his name; I thought it was Yuri. The head cashier had made a point of introducing him. He said he had been an exchange student at Harvard. I was wishing I had paid more attention. *No, it could not be; or could it be?* In simplicity, there is beauty. I recalled his parting words, "Hope to meet you again one day."

The next night, we found ourselves at Bangkok airport ready to board an aging Tupelov for the ten-hour flight to Moscow. No one was going to Russia in those days and the plane was carrying only a few foreigners, mostly Russian diplomats, and embassy staff. After a couple of hours in the air and a few vodkas, the chap across the aisle caught my eye.

"Hello, I am Constantine," he said. "Your accent is American. Why are you going to Russia?" The conversation continued, and when it turned into more of an inquisition, I said, "We are traveling to Moscow for meetings with Aeroflot and Intourist. We are travel agents who love to bring guests to Russia."

"Oh, I see. Be careful! Watch out for thieves and illegal money changers!" he warned.

Money changers? God forbid! I thanked him.

"Yes, do not change your dollars on the black market. You will be sent to prison for a long time." Given the gleam in his eye, I thought he was going to quote me a rate and offer to change the dollars for me instead.

Moscow customs was *totally* military style. My American passport was stamped with unusual fury. I had almost forgotten about the little black envelope I had simply placed in the back pocket of my jeans. There was no body search, just a lot of suspicious glances, until we walked out to be greeted by a friendly sign with our names on it from "*Intourist.*"

The next morning started a series of meetings involving vodka breakfasts, vodka lunches and vodka dinners, of which I have almost no recollection, except that we talked about the same things over and over again.

Two days and dozens of bottles of vodka later, still under the influence, we bear-hugged Russian style, said good-bye at the domestic airport, and headed for Leningrad. The Russian mission was accomplished. They had plied us with extravagant amounts of vodka and told us how all of their financial problems were caused by America. We totally forgot, or could not bring ourselves to ask Aeroflot when they would pay the money they owed Compass Travel; but that was not our purpose, anyway.

Couldn't believe our luck!

By the second night in Leningrad, I was sort of getting used to the place. What a *beautiful* city. At night, Moscow was totally dark with the exception of a few large red stars on the top of city landmarks. Leningrad was much more cosmopolitan.

I found the *Aurora*. It was docked right in front of my hotel; I could look down on it from my room on the sixth floor. Remembering Brink's instructions, I went down to the river and had a good look at it the first night, precisely at 9:00 pm, spending half an hour walking around the vicinity. So far, so good.

Suddenly, a young Russian woman approached me and started a conversation. She spoke a few words in Russian. When I replied in English, she froze for a moment, and a look of both shock and fear flashed across her face. She looked in all directions to see if anyone was watching from the shadows, then did a pirouette and took off like a bat out of hell.

There was a tennis exhibition in town, and when we got to the hotel bar on the important second night, we were greeted by the entourage of none other than Billie Jean King.

By 9:00 pm the small bar was already full of people and cigarette smoke. I approached Billie Jean's table and asked for her autograph, all the time sensing that a pair of eyes was watching me.

Just then, a friendly Russian chap approached me and asked if I could speak English. Sure enough, he was wearing a Harvard sweatshirt. I could feel sweat on the back of my neck. What were the odds that someone else would be wearing a Harvard sweatshirt? It seemed ridiculous.

I wondered about the message in the little envelope. It would certainly have been in code—perhaps account balance and payment details? This was the first, and only transaction, I would ever do absent the comfort of having a two-dollar or Russian ruble bill cut in half.

I could only assume that Mr. Deak, or someone from the U.S. Embassy, had written the message a couple of weeks earlier. Brink had told me it was supposed to be sent from the embassy in Vienna, by courier via U.S. State Department. But Mr. Deak thought otherwise and passed it along to Brink.

My brain was racing: *Could this be another one of Brink's tall tales? Maybe he just wanted David and me out of the office for a week. What if the guy freaks out after I hand it to him? Why didn't I think of these things before?*

I decided to switch my attention to the nice fat bonus Brink had promised would be waiting for me back in Hong Kong. I sure as hell could use the bread. I decided to make that my only thought.

It occurred to me, and I was informed later, that the Georgian I had just met had also been in Vienna, and had been on the same flight David and I took from Moscow to Leningrad. I believe he saw me looking at the *Aurora* and knew the deal was on.

Dealing in the currency black market in Russia was a very serious matter and not to be taken lightly. KGB eyes were everywhere. Brink assured me that Deak was operating a "pickup and payment" facility on a select basis for a U.S. intelligence agency out of Vienna.

Any and all communications would be made only by courier because the coded messages would instruct the local agent in Moscow to deliver rubles to a third party in exchange for U.S. dollars in an account with Foreign Commerce Bank in Switzerland or Bankhaus Deak in Vienna. The person I gave the envelope to could be passing it along until it reached Deak's agent who would always be unknown to us. Could it be James, as in Mr. Bond?

Billie Jean King and her minders seemed mildly annoyed with my request for an autograph, although she signed the piece of paper I offered to her.

I immediately took it over and handed it to the grateful fellow wearing the Harvard sweatshirt, along with the little envelope I was concealing in my palm. My heart was racing. It was cold in the bar, but suddenly I felt hot. I could see his pupils dilate as he became aware of the envelope in his hand. This was the split-second that would reveal the truth.

Seemingly a bit drunk, he shook my hand and patted me on the back, offering to buy me a vodka. At that moment, I felt many eyes on me and was stricken with a sort of paranoia. What really mattered, though, was the look of assurance in the eyes of the guy wearing the Harvard sweatshirt. Seeing I was a bit wobbly, David Mok came to my rescue, saying "How about me, can you get an autograph for my son, Anthony?"

"Sure!"

Mission accomplished!

A moment of euphoria came over me then, a little like "007" must have felt. We waited another hour while downing several more vodkas, until the Georgians left. I was looking forward to a visit to the Hermitage in the morning.

Go to Bombay!

I strolled into the Shell House office just before opening time the following sunny Friday morning. I had flown in from Moscow the night before, and I felt exhausted, unwell, and seriously jet lagged. In reality, it had been a tense and dangerous trip.

"Good morning," I said, anxious to tell Brink all about the events.

Brink and Ron Frame were arguing like hell. The door to Brink's office slammed and Frame, normally calm, cool, and collected, came out huffing, and was soon puffing on a cigarette.

"Brink!" he shouted, his face turning red. "I'm off to London on home leave for two weeks starting tonight," he turned and looked at me. "And the bastard wants me to go to Bombay for a pickup."

"Have a good trip," I laughed.

"What the hell are *you* laughing at? You are the only one in the office with a valid Indonesian visa so guess where you will be going tonight?" I was instantly sick. I knew I should have stayed at the airport. I remember struggling through the day, canceling a quiet, romantic dinner at home with my lovely wife.

By 8:00 pm my Compass Travel bag was filled with one million U.S. dollars in new hundred dollar bills, and I was waiting for the call from our driver to take me to the airport for the four-hour flight to Jakarta. I was chatting with Brink in his office when the green phone rang—the phone used by staff and agents when calling from a public phone overseas.

"Bruce, pick that up would you?"

I picked up and turned to Brink, "Mr. Brink, it is Ron Frame."

"What!?" Brink exclaimed. "Where the hell has he been all day, I thought he was going on holiday?"

"Mr. Brink," I whispered. "Remember this morning? He is in Bombay."

"Where?"

"Bombay."

"Oh, shit!" he said loudly, and then "Oh, shit" again softly. "I forgot all about it. The deal fell through. You can't trust those Goddamn Indians!"

"What about Ron?" I asked, handing Brink the phone.

"No, no, no, I can't take it. You tell him, Bruce."

"Tell him what?" I asked, finding it impossible not to laugh. Brink rolled his eyes and whispered it to me. I paused a moment and took a deep breath.

"Ron, you there?"

"You bet I am here. What the hell did Brink say?"

"He said, 'Tell him to come right back.'"

"What! That's it, that's all? 'Come right back?'" The cursing on the other end of the phone continued until it was drowned out by Brink's fit of uncontrollable laughter and a loud noise as Ron Frame slammed down the receiver.

Welcome to Jakarta

Damn, this was a crazy business! With the one million dollars in my carry-on bag, I was taking the late flight to Jakarta. I would be met at the airport by our agent, P. T. Iriawan, who was to deliver the cash to our customer, Bank of Tokyo. I was tired but resigned to my fate.

In Indonesia, oil companies' wages are paid in cash, and when the U.S. dollars dried up, we filled the demand; one or two million dollars could be delivered instantly, in exchange for a one-percent fee that amounted to a cool two million and twenty thousand by telegraphic transfer to Chartered Bank of London from Bank of Tokyo.

At least this transaction did not involve any deception—lying made me uncomfortable. I declared the money when I arrived in Jakarta, and was met at the airport by Iriawan staff, then taken to the closest hotel, an old one, the Kartika Plaza. They picked me up the next day and took me to the airport to catch a noon flight back to Hong Kong.

Josephine Iriawan ran a tight ship at her P.T. Jalan Iriawan Foreign Exchange Office. It was Indonesian style, and she ran the business out of her beautiful home; I liked this way of doing business very much.

Her office was located in a nice residential neighborhood. You entered an open gate and walked down the driveway to the office which was attached to the house which was a large villa. The large living and dining areas were in the back, and the whole place exuded wealth.

Even so, I detected a feeling of sadness surrounding her relationship with Deak & Company.

One day, suffice it to say, after many happy years of doing business with Deak & Company, there had been a big loss by Iriawan of over US one million dollars which had been stolen and never recovered. This amount would take Josephine forever to repay, even if she sacrificed all her commissions on future business.

Never at a loss for ingenuity, and realizing that Josephine had two sons, Brink decided to take out a life insurance policy on the eldest son, and wait for the day Deak & Company, the beneficiary, would be repaid.

Given that the son was probably only in his mid-thirties, I marveled at Deak's patience, while at the same time dismissing any possibility that they might have anything more sinister planned.

Josephine's other son, whom they did not choose to insure, was much younger—sort of a high-flying playboy who raced fast cars in all the circuits around Asia.

You may perhaps already be able to guess what happened. Soon after the money fiasco, the younger son was racing in the Malaysian Grand Prix Race in Kuala Lumpur when he lost control of his car and was killed instantly. This explained the deep sadness in Josephine's eyes.

Every time a Deak employee arrived to do business, she was reminded of the fact that Deak and Company, in a cold and calculating way, had managed to insure the wrong son.

CHAPTER 5
The More (Deals) the Merrier!

Clank! Clank!

Brink had so many deals going on at once that he could not find enough warm bodies to handle them. He sometimes became careless and used anyone who looked like he had a good passport and needed a bit of cash or adventure.

One day, a low-level CIA operative named "Doug Smith" came strolling through the lobby. He was highly recommended by Barry Clark, a close confidante of Brink. Doug later went on to work for the corrupt investment bank, Nugan Hand Bank.

He was a tough Vietnam vet who knew Mike Hand, a highly-decorated Vietnam vet who, along with Frank Nugan, formed the investment bank of Nugan Hand. They had offices in Hong Kong, Bangkok, and most suspiciously, in Chiang Mai, Thailand, an area made infamous by the drug trafficking in the Golden Triangle. Most people would assume that any bank that maintained an office in Chiang Mai would surely be involved in the drug trade and money laundering. More about Nugan Hand later.

To make a long story short, Doug had the misfortune to walk into the office while Brink was there. What do you think Brink said?

"Doug, so nice to meet you. Have you ever been to Nepal?"

The question was so familiar.

Doug was temporarily unemployed and looking to earn a few easy bucks.

"Here's the deal," said Brink, "there is nothing to it. Here is some money, go and buy yourself a good pair of Nike running shoes."

We were actually sending people to Kathmandu a couple of times a week wearing running shoes with the soles removed and stuffed with gold teals. There was a big margin in smuggling gold into Nepal that would quickly find its way into India; you could hide a kilo of gold in two shoes. Doug returned with his new shoes and was elated at the prospect of picking up an easy US five hundred dollars and an all-expense-paid trip to beautiful Nepal.

Late the following evening a frantic call came in from his friend, Barry Clark, also a tough former marine. A sharp-eared customs officer at Kathmandu Airport had been walking among the passengers who had just arrived when he seemed to detect a faint "clanking" sound coming from the shoes of one of the passengers.

"Brink! Doug has been busted in Kathmandu with a kilo of gold in his shoes!"

He may have had a few too many beers on the flight over, or perhaps he forgot to wrap the taels so that they wouldn't clank on the hard floor of the arrival hall.

The gold was forfeited, and in lieu of a fine, Doug spent a couple of months in the slammer. So much for a free holiday in the Himalayas. We never saw Doug in the Hong Kong office again.

Deak & Company Taipei

Taiwan was another location that produced milk and honey for the Deak black market machine. Taiwan's exchange controls were very strictly enforced and the place had a very serious aura about it.

We had about three dozen regular clients, many local, and some expatriates who had plenty of New Taiwan dough to sell. Many locals were in the black market money changing business as well, probably with good connections and paying off the right bankers to turn a blind eye. Deak operated primarily by doing swaps. Our most important agent needed NT cash. I won't mention his name, as I hope he is still alive. During the 1980s, he was indeed a very good friend.

My friend, let's call him "Sam," had a tremendous business. Every day his agents would buy tons of fish and pay for it in cash. The tuna was frozen and flown directly to Tokyo and Osaka on a daily basis and would eventually reappear as sushi in the markets and restaurants of those two great cities.

It was always wonderful to see Sam. Short and rotund, he was always smiling, and looked like a Buddha. He loved Deak & Company very much. We would collect NT dollars in huge suitcases from sellers and then deliver them to Sam for buying his fish. His Japanese buyers would send their payments back to his account with Deak in Hong Kong in U.S. dollars. A sweet deal indeed!

Sam was the ultimate host, so much so, I used almost any excuse *not* to avoid the Taiwan trips. For Sam and his trusted staff of eight, Deak & Company bi-monthly visits were a cause for celebration. On the first night, off we would go to the finest Chinese restaurants to be plied with endless good food and beer, after which we would be regaled with a bottle of XO. By 9:00 pm, I was usually passed out in my hotel room.

The night before returning to Hong Kong was even more special. Sam and I would drive up to the red light district, Pei To in Taipei, to a beautiful Japanese-style villa operated by his friend, Yoshi. The place had to be experienced to be believed.

In elegant surroundings, we were looked after by beautiful Japanese kimono-clad young ladies who would serve the food and pour the beer and sake. While smoking a Cuban cigar after dinner, you could hear the water running in the rooms next door in preparation for a bath and a massage or anything else that struck your fancy. A massage made me more than happy.

Sam loved Deak so much, one day he sent us a very big surprise. One of our customers casually mentioned the fact that he had officially bought some U.S. dollars at our Deak office in Taiwan.

"What?" we said, in disbelief. "We have no office in Taiwan!" Mr. Deak in New York was livid, and immediately asked Brink to check it out.

Sure enough, there it was. A small foreign exchange office on Nanjing East Road in the heart of Taipei, *Deak & Company Taiwan*, staffed and run by none other than Sam & Company, our cover blown by Sam himself.

Confronted by Brink, Sam was shocked by all the commotion. He said that he had simply opened the exchange as an official business in admiration and honor of his good friend Nicholas Deak!

He offered to change the name of his business.

The Philippines and the Manila envelope scandal

I became fond of the Philippines during my first trip to Manila around 1971. I was on R&R from Vietnam.

I was attracted to the people because they seemed to be good folks, always ready with a smile. It occurred to me that they must all be musicians, because in every Officers' and NCO Club you went to in Vietnam, you always found a Filipino band playing on Friday and Saturday nights.

At Deak's offices, all of the employees were Filipino and U.S. residents of Guam. Many were in Guam as contract workers in the construction business. They were our customers who sent peso remittances, or *padala*, back home to the Philippines. Over time, I got to know the geography of the Philippines pretty well, at least the names of the cities and provinces.

Deak & Company Guam survived on peso remittances. Filipinos from the world over would go to Deak in places like

Hawaii, San Francisco and Los Angeles, via Hong Kong and Europe, to send peso remittances back home.

Every morning when I went to the office, there would be a long ticker tape payment list at least ten feet long overflowing from the telex machine onto the floor. The tape would list the names of the sender, the beneficiary, and the peso amount to be paid, either by hand delivery in metro Manila or by bank transfer to the provinces. We would use the same tape to send details to our agents.

Here's how it worked...

Given the strict exchange controls that existed in the Philippines, there was always a lucrative and thriving black market for dollars, or for dollar salting.

Those who had pesos stashed away, but were not able to use them to buy dollars to credit to their offshore accounts (which they were not even supposed to have), or those who needed dollars to pay bills outside the country, found it much more convenient to use the services provided by Deak, rather than going through the hassle of getting Central Bank approval, leaving a tax record, and getting a lousy rate.

Stockbrokers and bankers provided Deak's agents with more pesos than they could handle—such was the demand for dollars. The remitters would give us the dollars outside, in exchange for the pesos inside, to make their remittance.

It really was that simple!

Another lucrative business involved U.S. cash dollars. You could buy cash dollars in Manila, provided you could get the dollars out and into your offshore account. Many ingenious methods were used to do this because the old saying is true: "Where there is a will, there is a way," and where there is demand, there will be supply—at a price.

One method was initiated by a leading Manila stockbroker. It was simple and straightforward. He simply sent twenty to thirty thousand dollars in "manila" envelopes by post to Deak Hawaii,

Deak San Francisco and Deak Guam. The package would arrive, and immediately a telex confirmation would be sent to him. This method worked well as long as such transactions were infrequent. The broker, whom we shall call "Arthur" since he is still alive, did it for quite a long time, until one day the package was lost or stolen, and did not arrive.

Furthermore, although it was a long time before the inevitable happened, the packages did eventually become suspicious, and caught the attention of Hawaii customs; this resulted in a major legal case, a currency violation, and the imposition of a fine against Deak & Company in San Francisco.

The same method was used by a travel agent in Chinatown, near downtown in old Manila. But this guy got very greedy. In fact, "George," we shall call him, went completely wild.

Starting with a single package of twenty thousand dollars a week, he soon increased it to the point where he was sending one package a day, and sometimes even two or three a day.

Needless to say, the Deak offices were being flooded with packages, catching the eye of all of the postal services. After all, how many packages marked "Travel Brochures" could be of interest in little bitty Guam? Either someone alerted the Manila post office, or the Manila post office caught on by itself.

Then, suddenly, the packages stopped arriving. George was frantically calling in disbelief from Manila every hour on the hour. After at least twenty packages mysteriously disappeared, he stopped to lick his wounds, and went to the post office to personally inquire, and was promptly arrested. Fortunately for him, in the Philippines, if you have money, and he did, you can get off with a slap on the wrist and a big fine.

Then one day, it all blew up in our faces.

Deak & Company San Francisco was indicted because they had never reported receiving currency shipments in excess of five thousand dollars, as required by law. The identities of Arthur and

George were exposed. It soon became a major problem for Deak, drawing the company and its operations squarely into the crosshairs as a target of the government. Over eleven million dollars had been received (just from Arthur, by the way) but not reported.

Arthur, however, was far more ingenious in a very simple way. Barry Clark, also a mutual friend and an avid golfer, observed that golf was a very popular sport in Manila, with over eighteen golf courses in metro Manila alone. Some time in 1973, the "light-bulb" in Arthur's head glowed brightly in an inspired "Eureka!" moment. Arthur and Barry came up with the brilliant idea to fill the golf bags with money.

Arthur then enlisted a group of reliable couriers, paying travel expenses and a fee, and presto, let the fun begin! Soon, every flight going to Hong Kong had at least one courier who had checked in one loaded golf bag. More about this later because it was to become a staple method, a way I would move money when I set up my own company.

The soul brothers of Seoul

Two dapper brothers of Indian descent, I'll use the names Madan and Ram, operated a thriving business out of their trading company in Seoul, another country where you just would not want to get caught doing black market currency business.

Korea had a very protected economy in the '70s and '80s, and the government wanted to know where all the money was and where it was going. Transactions were equally cumbersome, because the Korean "won" was only printed in small denominations. You needed huge boxes of the stuff to add up to any interesting amount.

Still, with big margins, we had an excellent partner for making profitable pickups and payments.

This business paled in comparison, however, to the transactions we were asked to make by the U.S. government for reasons unbeknownst to us. Sometimes, they would amount to several hundred thousand dollars, usually payable to Korean generals in the military, often having the same name, "General Chul." I often made the payments to then-retired General Chul, because it was easy for an American passport holder to get visas for Korea and to travel there often.

According to Brink, the order once came from the U.S. Embassy in Hong Kong—from an agent code-named Bernie Blair, or from Mr. Deak in New York, direct to Deak Far East.

I would contact our agent and ask him to buy dollars in the local market. From time to time they would lie very low, and were unwilling to risk the exposure, and in that case I had to smuggle the dollars in myself. One hundred thousand dollars was not a big package, so I spread it around my luggage in gift wrapping and simply checked it in. No sense hiding it in a golf bag in the middle of winter.

Upon arrival in Seoul, I looked for an Indian or an old lady to line up behind as I went through customs and held my breath. I always prayed and literally imagined I had cleared customs with ease—and I always did. They never asked me to open my luggage, which reminded me of Brink's adage, *"Smuggling is a white man's privilege."*

When I got to the hotel, I called the number given to me by Mr. Brink or Mr. Deak, and usually a very excited voice greeted me. Soon the "general" and I would be having a sumptuous dinner, coupled with an offer to provide me with anything I wanted, such as a beautiful girl, after which the "general" hurried off with the important package in hand. What could it have been for? I never gave it a second thought until sometime after news of the Lockheed scandal broke in Japan in 1975.

My mind was clicking:

Could those have been bribery payments in exchange for buying something from the good old U.S. Department of Defense?

New Zealand

"Bruce, have you ever been to New Zealand?"

Brink was at it again. Of course I had not been to New Zealand. It was a cool autumn morning when I checked into a little hotel Compass Travel had booked for me. New Zealand was a beautiful country. Our agent there operated out of an oriental antique shop in Auckland.

There was not much to do, just review some of the account transactions and pickup the balance which Brink said would be small. He also said, "Just check it in inside your suitcase."

The work finished, I was booked on the following morning's flight to Hong Kong. After feasting on a steak dinner, I was wide awake and looking for some excitement. New Zealanders are very friendly people. I met several at a pub, and before I knew it, it was 3:00 am and I was wasted. I asked the hotel for a 6:00 am wake-up call. I drifted off thinking, *I only have NZ fifty thousand to check with my luggage and I'll sleep on the plane.*

I vaguely remember getting a wake-up call, but when I rolled over and finally looked at my watch, it was 8:00 am; I was supposed to be on the nonstop to Hong Kong. I was in deep trouble. I had to be back in Hong Kong that night.

What the hell was I going to do?

A call to Air New Zealand revealed, thanks to God, there was another flight leaving at 10:00 am via Sydney. If I hurried, I could catch it. Nursing a mighty hangover and cursing myself for being a schlep, I made the flight just in time.

To my shock, however, customs was being very strict and carefully checking luggage. I must have looked ill, because, to my surprise, I was passed over and went straight through. Had I been sober, they may have checked more carefully and found the money.

My feeling better would only last a little while, because upon arrival in Sydney, I was whisked off the plane to the awaiting flight to Hong Kong. The door to the ANZ plane closed immediately behind me, and I found myself facing an eight-hour flight in a cabin full of economy class passengers, who seemed to be extremely irritated with me for causing the delay.

"Miss," I asked the stewardess, "what about my luggage?" I had told the airline it was urgent, that I had to get back to Hong Kong immediately, which was true. My luggage, however, wouldn't be coming until the next day. Oh, shit! I felt sick for the next twenty-four hours until I was back at Kai Tak Airport in Hong Kong, praying as I went to collect the luggage. It had arrived, and I had learned a very big lesson.

Where the hell am I?

It was 1977, and it had been a long time since I had been able to take a break and chill out in Orlando with the family. It was time for a holiday, and I was looking forward to what I would call "home leave." I relished the thought of two glorious weeks in one place where I could completely relax and recharge mentally and physically.

Arriving in Orlando, I spent a few blissful days being pampered by my mom, peace be with her.

Then it happened.

Just as I was beginning to feel good, chilling out with a cold beer in my hand and watching a New York Mets baseball game on TV, the phone rang. My mom answered it in her usual sweet voice, and I heard her say, "Hold on, Mr. Brink, he is right here."

"Bruce, how soon could you be leaving for Australia?"

"What the hell are you talking about," I shouted, "I just arrived in Orlando!"

"Please, we need someone to go to Sydney right away to do a series of pickups. It is a *huge* deal, and I'll pay you a big bonus. Leave as soon as you can. David Mok is already there waiting for you; please do the first pickup, put it in the bank and stay for a week, as we will be sending at least a half dozen more couriers." There was a short pause before Dirk added, "Did you bring a golf bag with you to Orlando?"

36 hours later

Soon I was really feeling like shit. The flight from Orlando to Los Angeles and Western Samoa, and then on to Sydney, was certainly not a stroll around the block.

David met me at the airport, and we went directly to a bank where Deak maintained a very special account, in which I surreptitiously made the first deceptive deposit of five hundred thousand dollars. (More about this amazing bank account later.)

I met the client the same afternoon and received the balance of the A (Australian) dollars that needed moving. It was over A$ two million. I bid David farewell, and as I slogged into the Hilton that night, I felt Brink could not pay me enough.

Tony Pong arrived the next morning, and Ron Frame the day after that. The bank account was getting far too hot in my opinion, and Brink was clearly out of control. After three days, he called me and asked if I could go into the bank again.

"No problem!" he said. "Just *pretend* you flew back to Hong Kong, then returned to Sydney. It's a piece of cake, Bruce."

My answer was, "Go to hell, Brink! Come do it yourself!"

Three or four Chinese counter boys were sent instead of me, and the balance was sent back with them in golf bags. By this time, I was looking forward to getting back to Hong Kong. It had been three weeks since I had seen my wife.

I hesitated to pick up the hotel phone when it rang, but pick it up I did. It was Mrs. Alice Silva, Brink's trusted and super-loyal and efficient secretary; she was a short, fat little lady of Portuguese descent, who had a charming round face, which always possessed a big and cunning smile. With my ear to the receiver, I could hear her trademark giggle, and "see" the twinkle in her eye, that always telegraphed that Brink was up to no good.

"Hold on Bruce. Hold for Mr. Brink."

Salt lick what?

"Bruce," Brink said, "I want you to meet me in a couple of days."

"No problem," was my reply. "I am heading back to Hong Kong in the morning."

"No, not in Hong Kong. I am leaving for Zurich tonight to meet Mr. Deak, and then I'll be flying back to my farm in White River, South Africa. Meet me there. Compass Travel has already sent you a new ticket by DHL; it will arrive in the morning."

"But listen," he went on, "The routing is Sydney, Perth, Mauritius, and Nairobi, as in Kenya. You're booked into the Nairobi Hilton. Our new agent, who only you have met in Hong Kong, Mr. Shah, has a pickup, just a couple of hundred thousand US dollars. Coded details of the client have been sent with the ticket. He is already waiting for you at the Hilton. It will take you an hour to collect and deliver to Mr. Shah. This is a big favor for Mr. Deak, and he asked me to personally thank you." This last comment was probably another one of Brink's lies.

"After the pickup, enjoy the weekend in the bush with the Masai natives at the Hilton's Salt Lick Lodge; you'll love it. After that, come and see me in White River on the farm."

Needless to say, the ticket arrived, the pickup took place and I spent the weekend out in the bush, watching elephants come drink at a salt pond. It was amazing.

Nairobi was simply out of this world in terms of exotic atmosphere. I had to pinch myself to believe I was there. Mr. Shah was a gracious host. We walked from the Hilton to a restaurant across the street, and then enjoyed a night on the town in one of the local nightclubs.

By the time I arrived in Johannesburg and flew on to Pretoria and White River, I did not really care what happened next. I spent two days at Brink's farm waiting for him, until the third night when I heard the telex pattering away in his office. It was a most unusual office indeed, perched about thirty feet up in a tree house near the guest house. The mountain view looking towards Kruger National Park was gorgeous.

I carefully walked up the wooden and rope spiral staircase that snaked its way around the tree a half dozen times. By the time I reached the top, I was dizzy. The message was short and to the point. "Trip home cancelled. See you back in Hong Kong. Mr. Deak says thanks." Of course, I knew that was bullshit.

I arrived in Hong Kong, having been away for well over a month, and within twenty-four hours, I was at Kai Tak Airport, boarding the red-eye Qantas flight for another deal waiting in Sydney.

I decided I may as well work this business on my own. One day I would opt out, and become an independent agent and refer business to Deak & Company for the commissions, and spare myself working for Brink, who by then, was totally out of his mind.

It is said that the genius has no common sense. This statement truly applied to Mr. Brink, and it occurred to me that some of the outrageous stories I had heard about him may actually have been true.

One story that really takes the cake concerns the small monkey Brink had sent from Jakarta all the way to South Africa in his German friend's hand-carry. His friend's name was Von Biernerstam. People will do anything for a free trip. The monkey was to mate with the one and only remaining rare, healthy Indonesian female monkey living on Brink's farm. Somehow, a very important detail had been lost in translation: they sent a female instead of a male.

On another occasion, Brink had a valuable parrot sedated and hand-carried back to Hong Kong on a flight from Jakarta. Upon reaching his home in residential Shousen Hill, Brink excitedly opened the box to admire the parrot. Sensing its chance, and by now wide awake, the parrot bolted and flew straight for the only window that Brink had forgotten to close.

Knowing Brink, I never asked if the stories were true. It really didn't matter. However, the fact that such an extraordinarily large number of beautiful parrots still inhabit Shousen Hill is really quite a coincidence.

CHAPTER 6
The Two "Mothers of All Laundries"

Australia

Australia was a very important income earner for Deak & Company Far East, and all the credit goes to Dirk Brink for his ingeniously simple methods that were used to move large sums of money from all the major countries to Hong Kong (and to anywhere in the world), without leaving the country of origin. It required some nerve to do that, especially the first time, and then each and every time thereafter; a lot of deception was involved.

Strange how one can rationalize something that goes directly against the conscience, such as deceiving people. I never felt comfortable with deception, and dreaded it. I had to lie, or at least not let others know the truth, while anticipating what they were thinking about me.

Flying to Australia for Deak & Company was always a pleasure and an experience, to say the least. I got to see much of the country, at least the cities, and to meet a lot of great folks.

I was going there so often during the late '70s and '80s, that I was beginning to develop an Aussie accent. "Good on ya, mate!" I thought "Waltzing Matilda" was the national anthem. I got to know Sydney and the surrounding suburbs so well that I ended up taking a small flat across the harbor, in Neutral Bay, and renting a car as soon as I arrived at the airport.

Here's How my Trip Typically Worked

It began the night before when I took the usual Boeing 707 CX overnight flight from Hong Kong to Sydney, then booked the Sydney/Melbourne leg under the name Bruce Smith, paying cash. No real record existed of me leaving Sydney.

From Melbourne airport, I took a taxi straight to Melton, a suburb of Melbourne, to the home of two characters named Abbie and Charlie. Both these characters were Russian-Jewish immigrants who were running a slick money laundering operation from their spartan, completely unassuming little house. Melton was a very basic working class neighborhood, nothing fancy.

Abbie and Charlie's code name was "movado." I don't know why.

I remember the first time we met; it was a very cold winter's day. It was a cloudy, unusually dark, and windy afternoon in July. Melbourne weather can't hold a stick to Sydney sunshine. I walked up to the front door and pressed the buzzer. A light went on in the foyer and another in the living room. I knew they were expecting me.

The door opened quickly, and standing right in front of me was big and massively overweight Abbie. I smiled; Abbie frowned. He spoke in a voice that made you think he was crying, constantly whining. His six-foot-tall frame carried what I guessed to be around two hundred and thirty pounds of mostly fat.

"Come in, quick, come in," he stuttered, obviously startled. "You must be Bruce."

Abbie was wearing a heavy wool coat, a white shirt that had turned yellow around the collar, crumpled baggy corduroy pants, and worn-out shoes. He looked like he didn't have a pot to piss in.

Right away he started yelling at Charlie in Hebrew or Yiddish, I don't know which. He squinted at me through beady, thick-lensed bespectacled eyes.

114

"Charlie, get Brink on the phone. This guy looks too young. How old are you anyway?"

"Thirty," I replied. The inquisition in the foyer lasted several minutes, until Abbie's whining was interrupted by Charlie.

"Abbie, it's cold in the foyer, let him in!"

Clarlie offered to make hot tea, and turned on the heat in the extra room in case I needed to lie down for a while. Having been on the plane all night, I could not wait for a hot shower, and I would have difficulty sleeping due to the adrenaline pumping during and after the grilling I got from Abbie. I had actually come close to telling Abbie to go to hell and find someone else to launder his f***ing money.

I marveled at Abbie's frugality. My dad would have made a comment like, "That's typically Jewish or Scottish or Dutch, or…"

They only had heat in the living room. The rest of the house was like the North Pole, which was weird because they had enough money stashed to last them literally hundreds of years.

Abbie was the nervous one, asking me over and over, "Are you, okay? Did anyone follow you? How is Dirk Brink? Please call him…you look far too young to carry half a million dollars in cash."

Over the course of the next several years, the tone never changed much.

Charlie, on the other hand, was the opposite; very generous, relaxed and dapper—a real ladies' man. Charlie was half the size of Abbie, and dressed with exquisite taste; dark-brown flannel pants, a dark-yellow long-sleeved shirt under a beautiful thick-knit dark-blue sweater, and a handsome dark-brown blazer. His leather shoes sparkled.

He frequently told Abbie to sit down before he had a heart attack, and said, "What is the big deal anyway?"

We went through this routine *every month* for years. Once Charlie had made up his mind about me, he never hesitated to hand over the big bundle of cash.

That first night, I was indeed very tired after the overnight flight, and was really not in the mood for Abbie's inquisition; but Abbie was our respected client, so I took it in stride and was thankful for Charlie who always said, "Abbie, leave him alone!"

After a shower and a bit of rest, Charlie always made me boiling hot vegetable soup and a roast beef sandwich before we got down to the hard work, which was only interrupted by phone calls to Charlie from a bevy of ladies.

"Hard work" meant quickly bundling while also counting the money. It usually came in Australia fifty-dollar notes, the largest A$ denomination at the time, normally between four hundred thousand and five hundred thousand in total; one hundred notes in a pack totaled five thousand dollars. I would have up to one hundred bundles to sort out on the overnight train.

Abbie and Charlie had no idea how the money was moved, and to their credit, and unlike many others, they never asked. I always grew suspicious of the Deak clients who became overly friendly, trying to get me to reveal our secret methods. I could be quite brusque if necessary.

One day in Sydney, for example, a client was proving to be most annoyingly inquisitive, so I simply said to him, "Now, Dr. Ted Krauss, my dear friend, if I told you how we did it, then you wouldn't be needing to see me again, now would you? And wouldn't that be a pity?"

I took the flat bundles from Charlie and stacked them into a pile of ten, totaling fifty thousand dollars, and placed the ten stacks of ten neatly into my travel bag. Abbie stared glassy-eyed at the Compass Travel bag full of money, with his face turning green at the thought of never seeing it again.

Finally, around 7:00 pm, when it was pitch-black outside, it was time to take a taxi to the Melbourne train station for the overnight express to Sydney. After sitting on the plane all night, I was not really looking forward to the train ride, because I knew I would be working all night. But I was sorely looking forward to being alone.

This was the life!

One night with no sleep on the plane, followed by one night with no sleep on the train, was part and parcel of my lifestyle in those days.

I had a couple of hours to wait, then I was able to settle in the train, the conductor collected my ticket, and I simply pressed the *Do not Disturb* button.

Armed with the day's *South China Morning Post*, I began to fold the money Hong Kong Chinese style, end over end, wrapped into squares, not elongated.

It was tedious and dirty work, made slightly easier by using one of those little rubber money-counting "condom-like" finger covers, like rubber thimbles placed over my thumb and index finger.

In between dozing off and packaging, I finally had all one-hundred bundles changed to look as if they had been wrapped in Hong Kong.

After taking a break, I wrapped the package in the newspaper, then wrapped the whole package in clear plastic, and lastly brown paper. I had brought along *the tools of the trade*. Even though I was a non-smoker, I was in a smoking compartment, armed with a pack of Marlboro menthols and a little red lighter. Next, I located the metal seal and small bar of red wax I had hidden in the lining of my luggage.

After melting the wax, I made a puddle on all four corners of the package, and pressed the metal stamp into the wax, Chinese style. Then I stood back to admire my handiwork. The imprinted seal, *Deak & Company (Far East) Ltd., Hong Kong,* completed the package perfectly; it looked exactly as if it had originated from Deak & Company, Hong Kong.

Glancing at my watch, it was almost 4:00 am, and time to put everything away. I let cold air in through the vent in order to eliminate the smell of the burning wax, and tried to get a little sleep.

The Fifty Million Dollar ANZ Deception

The train pulled into Sydney just after 8:30 am. I foolishly drank a cup of the unforgivably vile concoction that no self-respecting connoisseur would call "coffee," and I alighted from the train.

Approaching my favorite phone booth, I dialed the number for Cathay Pacific flight information, and got a recording: "Flight CX 101 nonstop from Hong Kong has arrived at 6:30 am." The flight was scheduled to arrive at 5:30 am, and the delay worried me somewhat.

I cursed Dirk Brink for not sending Tony Pong, our head foreign exchange trader, or one of the counter boys ahead of me to do the preparation work. It would have been best if someone met and handed me the package as soon as I got off the plane. Going solo involved a lot more risk.

I thought, *I must be crazy to keep doing this stuff. What kind of a job is this anyway? Let me think, let me think...shit, I'm tired! Decision time. Okay, I'll finish the "work" before checking into the hotel. I'll go straight to the bank.*

Downtown Sydney was a quick taxi ride from the train station, and I soon found myself a couple of blocks from the ANZ Bank at the corner of Pitt and Hunter. Unbeknownst to all, it was Deak's number-one money laundering factory par excellence.

Brink said it was the brain child of his good friend and Deak client Richard "Dick" Hughes. He was an Australian war correspondent and generally considered a British spy, or even a double agent? They often met at the Hilton's Eagles Nest, top floor lounge. Dick was the inspiration for the fictional character Dikko

Henderson in Ian Fleming's James Bond novel, *You Only Love Twice*, and for Old Craw in John le Carre's *The honourable Schoolboy*. Dick was a real life character! Ron Frame told me it was all his idea.

It was then a few minutes past 9:00 am, and the bank had just opened. Walking in, I caught the eye of a familiar face, Richard Jenkins, the head cashier. The receptionist noticed me immediately, and a feeling of intense suspense permeated the lobby right before I was whisked back toward the vault.

As we walked, I could hear whispering: *"Deak & Company has arrived. They have another deposit of repatriated Aussie dollars collected from Aussie tourists and travelers."* Yet another illusion created to avoid a world of draconian foreign exchange controls.

Right away there is small talk, suspicions at times, about the flight, what time I arrived, whether or not I had encountered any problems with the customs. All of this, of course, was a cunning ruse, a clever ploy, so I quickly changed the subject to rugby, and asked where everyone would like to go to lunch and have a few beers.

Obviously, although the bank management always asked, they understood we could never give advance notice of our trip for security reasons. But this time, I ran into a question. "Bruce, Adrian our Vice President asked to have a word with you the next time you make a deposit. He asked to see you last month, but you had already left."

"Sure, no problem," I said, as a bead or two of sweat began to appear on my forehead. I tried to shake off the tiredness.

This was the worst and most dangerous time. While the five hundred thousand dollars was being counted, I watched as my handiwork from the night before was destroyed, and the Chinese style money was converted back to Aussie style.

This is the time when questions were asked, which I always endeavored not to answer. A lack of sleep on the plane and focusing on the counting were my standard "excuses." Then, presto, everything would be finished.

Since the money had come from Hong Kong, Australia Reserve Bank gave approval for same-day value for US$ telegraphic transfer of the counter-value to the account of Deak & Company Limited at Chartered Bank of London in San Francisco. The money was magically "laundered" and yet another cool five percent went into the coffers of the company.

What did Deak do with the money? We simply credited Abbie's account with Bank Luemi or Bank Leu in Zurich for the counter-value of four hundred seventy-five thousand dollars while keeping twenty-five thousand for our efforts.

Taking the lift to the third floor, I was greeted by Adrian. Suddenly, I had a throbbing headache.

"Bruce, Brink never comes here himself anymore, and we just need to verify audit procedures— routine you know. We have been doing business together for many years, and we realize Deak & Company Hong Kong is the company's world collection point for overseas Aussie dollars you return here. I believe, very conservatively, it has been well over fifty million dollars over the years."

We went through the procedures, the questions about the flight and clearing customs.

Just then, I thought of my insurance policy.

Brink always complained like hell, but I always insisted if I were going to the bank solo I wanted a second dummy ticket from Compass Travel with the arrival date the same as the deposit date. Fortunately, I remembered to tear out the first ticket coupon. Then the bank manager popped the question.

Checking off an "audit" form, he asked, "May I see your ticket?"

"Sure," I calmly replied, shuffling through my briefcase. "I am returning on the flight tomorrow."

Checking that it was dated for arrival that morning, Adrian smiled, changed tacks completely, and proceeded to bend over backwards to say what an important account ours was and what a pleasure it was to do business with Deak. We passed again!

The deception always left me with a bad feeling and tainted my conscience. I was born with an honest-looking face, and over the years easily passed through customs at dozens of international airports while smuggling millions of dollars in my golf bag. I overcame my anxiety by using my imagination.

Before facing Adrian, I had said to myself, *I have just come from Hong Kong, bringing five hundred thousand Aussie dollars which I just deposited in the bank. How dare anyone question it!* I went over this again and again, using the silent soliloquy to quietly embolden myself; it gave me the necessary confidence. Later, of course, I would say to myself, *What an insane way to make a living!*

But truth be told, my chosen modus vivendi suited me to a tee. I loved the excitement and the glamour that went along with the turf of being a professional money launderer. How else could I travel the world all expenses paid, stay in five-star hotels and get paid for only one hour of "work?" I also had time to read, take flying lessons, and meet wonderful, interesting people. For a poor boy from New Jersey, the choice was easily rationalized.

Tired, I checked into the Sydney Hilton in yet another deception. As staff of Compass Travel, I would be instantly given the fifty-percent travel agent's discount. To my dismay, however, a message from Brink was already waiting for me; he wanted me to come back to our Hong Kong office immediately. I think, *Give me a break! I'll call him later and let him know the deposit has been made;* but in the shower, I hear the phone ringing.

"Hello, Brink, I said calmly, "What the hell is it?"

"Bruce, please get back here right away."

121

"What did you say?"

"You heard me. You are the only one with an Indonesian visa, and we have a big urgent order. We need you to go to Jakarta tomorrow night."

Over the years Deak maintained the ANZ deception, I would conservatively estimate we deposited well over fifty million Aussie dollars into the account, all sourced locally, and all disguised as coming from Hong Kong.

The USA one-hundred-million-dollar washing machine!

Dirk Brink never hesitated to physically move money by checking it into the belly of an aircraft. There were no terrorists to speak of in those days, and if luggage was X-rayed at all, money never set off any alarms. *Still,* you think, C*ome on, what about Murphy's Law?* One day the golf bag or the suitcase is not going to arrive. The client was paying us nice fees to move the money. They would be shocked to know that from time to time our system of "hundi swaps" was down, and we had to resort to the primitive methods they could have done themselves, if they had dared to take the risk.

After so many trips to so many countries, it actually became routine for me. Once the golf bag was checked in, I never gave it a second thought, until I was standing in front of the carousel on arrival, deep in prayer.

One day in 1977, Brink found a much better way—for the USA, that is.

Here's how it worked, as set up by Mr. Brink

To check out the lay of the land, we first sent two big red Hong Kong phone books to Deak & Company in San Francisco, to see if such packages were routinely inspected or not. The package was about the same size as the one that would contain one million dollars in US one-hundred-dollar bills.

Next, we ordered from Deak's USA offices a large supply of U.S. one-dollar banknotes, spreading the order around so as not to attract suspicion, even amongst our own offices. Our managers, Otto Beusch in San Francisco, Tom Kelly in Los Angeles, and Robert Maier in Honolulu, must have wondered what kind of a promotion or FX advertisement the eccentric Mr. Brink was up to.

We accumulated the one-dollar notes until we had exactly ten thousand pieces placed into one hundred stacks of one hundred pieces. If they had all been one-hundred-dollar bills instead of one-dollar bills, the package would be worth a cool one million instead of a measly ten thousand.

Next, we placed a one-hundred-dollar bill, top and bottom, one on each end of each stack. The total package at that point was worth thirty thousand dollars, but at a glance, the package looked like it was worth one million dollars.

As usual, the package would be vacuum-sealed in clear plastic, and possess the red wax seals. It would be hand-carried on the flight to San Francisco and declared a cool US one million dollars upon arrival at customs. The package was addressed from Deak & Company (Far East) Ltd., Hong Kong to Chartered Bank of London, San Francisco—"Repatriated U.S. currency for deposit."

When customs opened the brown paper wrapper on the package and saw the money, which certainly looked like one million dollars, their first response was to ask if we had security waiting. "Yes, of course!" was our reply. "Security" was a taxi ride downtown to the Downtown Holiday Inn to meet our staff waiting to switch the parcels, exchanging the package with the one-dollar bills for one that contained one-hundred-dollar bills, the real million dollars, wrapped and sealed exactly the same as if it had been brought from Hong Kong.

A quick taxi ride to Chartered Bank of London, San Francisco, and the deposit would be made. Just like that, another million would be laundered right there under everyone's noses. All in a day's work and for a tidy five percent. One or two staff suffered the small hassle of loading the one-dollar bills into a golf bag, then bringing it back to Hong Kong and standing by until it was time to do it all again.

It did not take long for Brink to turn the "Magic Money Movement" into a gigantic "Mother of All Laundries." It was sensible. Since we were already shipping huge amounts of foreign currency all around the world, millions of Japanese yen, millions of Philippine pesos, Swiss francs, deutsche marks and pounds sterling by *insured air freight,* why should sending dollars back to America be different?

Brink's brilliant "light bulb" had turned on again!

Hey Brink! Use Brink's...

It seemed only natural. Brink's armored car transport service had just opened in Hong Kong, and we would become a valued account. They would deal with customs and airport handling formalities, and door-to-door services with full liability coverage.

It was only a matter of time, Brink feared, until U.S. Customs would scrutinize the fake one-million-dollar shipment. The other weak link was the human factor—the courier. There was a great temptation to disappear with the package on a flight to another country.

Brink laughed when he envisioned such a scenario. The courier would have been shocked and disappointed when he discovered he had stolen a bunch of one-dollar bills! Ha-ha! They would be easy to trace.

It was not long before Pan Am cargo was carrying the "high value" cargo package of one-dollar bills thought to be a million, cosigned from Bankhaus Deak Representative Offices in Hong Kong, or Deak Far East, to several of the "cooperating" Deak offices or agents in the U.S. as "repatriated U.S. dollars." It worked like a charm.

Brink told me, perhaps honestly mistaken, that since the shipments were coming from the same organization, there might not be a need to make a currency declaration.

The last time I saw Dirk Brink, around 1984, he told me he had washed over US one hundred million dollars by this method. Could it have been true? Always prone to exaggeration, I knew in this case he was cutting it pretty close to the mark. We were sitting in his office quite late one night, and a file on his desk marked "Airway Bills—USA," was so thick it could have choked a horse.

We reminisced about the very first shipment several years earlier. Sitting in the same office, we had admired the handiwork of the fake, but very official looking, "million-dollar" package resting on his desk in front of us. "Ah yes," he had said, with unabashed admiration, "It looks good."

Indeed it did, and the system was, truly, the mother of all laundries.

As a matter of fact...

My many appearances at customs as an avid golfer (while actually being a "flying dollar caddie"), or holding a plain old money-filled suitcase, was the result of many meetings with some of the world's most unique characters. All of these experiences were to provide, simultaneously, tantalizing opportunities, horrific experiences and, of course, the inevitable consequences thereof.

CHAPTER 7
The Lockheed Scandal

Agana, Guam

It was not long after I had arrived back in Guam, on one of my several trips there over the years, while simultaneously enjoying all of the previously mentioned experiences at Deak and Company in Hong Kong that the telex in the Deak & Company office started tapping out messages in the middle of the night. Things were happening rapidly in Deak's world of Japanese yen pickups and payments. The special assignment discussed with Mr. Deak in New York was already being put into action, driven by the need for yen in Japan and a warm body to deliver it. Dirk Brink was on the case right away.

In the beginning, Guam was not my favorite place; I felt so isolated, although over time I began to relish that feeling, and grew to like the place.

When we worked, New York slept, and so it was with Hong Kong that we communicated daily.

It was a hot and steamy morning in 1973 when I walked into the office, about an hour late. The morning heat was getting to me. *I wish I were back in Hong Kong.*

Tony Evans, Guam's manager, startled me when I walked into the office. I said "Good morning!" I was taking over for Tony, who was soon off on a three month overdue home leave.

He said, "Bruce, where have you been? Brink has been calling every five minutes. Would you please get back to him and see what the hell he wants; and, by the way, ask him today's rate for pesos in

Manila, and what the hell to do with the Yen fifty million we bought over the weekend. Tell him I need a good rate, or we'll sell it to Bank of America!"

Suddenly, my spirits picked up. *Dirk Brink calling? Maybe I'll be heading to Hong Kong soon.*

I heard the familiar, quick double ring of the Hong Kong telephone system, and then the friendly voice of the receptionist, "Deak & Company (Far East) Ltd, who's calling?"

"This is Bruce from the Guam office."

"Oh… hold on, hold on," she said it twice. *Must be important.* I was not even put on hold, and I could hear her yelling, "Mr. Brink, Mr. Brink, Guam on the line."

A split-second later, I heard the calm voice of Brink.

"Bruce…," in his usual charming manner, "How would you like to come to Hong Kong for a couple of days?"

"Fine, how about today?"

"Yes, please come today; something important we need you to help us with.*"*

"On the way!"

Deak & Company Hong Kong was a beehive of activity. I arrived the same night after a four-hour flight from Guam, and checked into the Hong Kong Hilton, just a couple of blocks down the road on Queens Road Central.

Brink met me the next day at the twenty-four-hour coffee shop at street level. I always enjoyed a stay at the Hong Kong Hilton. I had fond memories of the days when I was working for AMEX in Saigon.

"Bruce, Tony Pong and the counter boys and all the staff at Compass Travel in Hong Kong have been to Japan far too many times, and we're attracting too much attention. New blood is badly needed. Mr. Deak and I want you to make some trips for us, coming from Guam." Brink cleverly included "Mr. Deak" knowing that he would not be questioned, making it nearly impossible to say no.

Like Hong Kong with Compass Travel, we had the perfect cover, using our subsidiary Horizon Travel in Guam. Guam, the paradise island, was known as "Honeymoon Island" in Japan, and 747 jumbo jets full of Japanese newlyweds descended on the island each and every day, seven days a week, bringing bundles of Y ten-thousand-dollar notes; so many you could fill up a truck! And, not surprisingly, being the avid golfers that Japanese men are, the husbands liked to bring along their golf paraphernalia. This inevitably included large, heavy *golf bags*. Unlike in Japan, there was ample opportunity to play golf on Guam.

"Do you play golf?" Brink asked.

"What did you say?" I asked.

We walked from the Hilton Hotel to Deak's office at Shell House where he had several nice sets of golf clubs in the closet.

"Not today," I replied.

"Good, because we don't want you to play golf. Just take the golf clubs from Guam to Tokyo from time to time."

"Okay, Dirk," I said. For the first time, I asked, "How much yen do you put in them?"

He proceeded to show me how to open the rivets on the bottom of the bag, and slide out a specially made compartment, lined with black carbon-paper-like cloth.

"Each golf bag can comfortably hold millions of Japanese yen in ten-thousand denominated banknotes," blurted Brink, bubbling with childlike excitement.

"OK, I get the picture. Have you done it before?"

"Yes, of course, all the time…but never in Japan."

This was the very first time I was made privy to his ingenious golf bag system, and the first of many times that I would have to pass through customs with a hollowed out golf bag filled with 'Ben Franklins'.

"So, Brink, you want me to be the first guinea pig. Why don't you just swap the yen already in Japan, as usual, with someone who wants the U.S. dollars outside? You know how strict Japanese exchange controls are and how dangerous it is doing unofficial business there."

"Sure, of course. If I could do that, I wouldn't be asking you to take the yen to Japan now, would I? Our agent there, code name 'Sanyo,' is scared as hell. He thinks his phone is tapped. He thinks he is being followed, that somehow they are on to him, and he needs to disappear. The Japanese police are ready to pounce. He cannot supply me with any yen.

"We have these urgent payments piling up, and I'm getting calls every hour from..." Brink suddenly hesitated, "you don't want to know who from, I can't say who, but he is attached to your bloody consulate here in Hong Kong."

"The United States Consulate?"

"No, the New York Yankees!" he said sarcastically.

So, we are making black market payments for the U.S. government. I pondered the thought almost with a trace of patriotism.

I remembered Mr. Deak's past with the OSS, and his contacts with the intelligence community; it was assumed, but not spoken of. Now it was out in the open, and it was not a surprise. Was it true or was this typical Brink hoopla?

Eventually, I would meet the embassy contact on numerous occasions. Standing about six and a half feet tall and weighing at least two hundred and fifty pounds, he was easy to remember. His code name was "Frank Price."

The same night, I was on the flight back to Guam, arriving just after 2:00 am. Guam flight schedules really suck since Guam is in the middle of the ocean. This is where America's day begins—in the middle of nowhere. The flights arrive in the middle too—in the middle of the night.

By the time I cleared customs and collected my golf bag, I realized I was already booked on the JAL afternoon flight to Tokyo; I suddenly felt a strong sense of unease. I could still hear Brink's parting words as I was leaving the office, "Don't worry, man...there is nothing to it. Remember, smuggling is a white man's privilege."

A lot of comfort, especially coming from a self-confessed racist Afrikaner.

I reminded myself that Dirk Brink was a very clever man, with a quick and razor-sharp mind. He had a gift for thinking of ingenious ways to move money, from the complex to the simple. This was one of the simple ones.

"When you get to Tokyo, check into the Okura Hotel, which is not far from the embassy, and wait for Father Jose to call."

Father Jose. I had heard about him and was looking forward to meeting him. Turns out he was Deak's other agent in Tokyo, and the most important one in Japan. "Sanyo" would pick up the yen from the Yakusa, or even from our high-placed mole at American Express Bank, or Manufacturers Hanover Trust, or anyone who was selling, and give it to Father Jose, who would make the payments.

It was essential that those responsible for the pickup were kept separate from the payment receivers, or else the agent could quickly put two and two together and, presto, match up the buyer and seller and perhaps do the business himself, cutting out the four-percent commission for Deak.

Why the "father" in Father Jose? Well, it was because he was a Spanish Jesuit priest. That's a fact. He lugged bags of money all over Tokyo making payments for Deak and sending one-hundred percent of his hard-earned commission of one-half percent back to a church he founded for prostitutes in Mexico City. Truly a wonderful man.

Suddenly, I felt much better about this business, knowing the deal came from the U.S. Embassy, and our agent was a Catholic priest. I believed it was good karma.

My thoughts were quickly interrupted by the Agana, Guam, airport announcement, "JAL Flight 306 bound for Tokyo, boarding at Gate 3; all aboard." It was now almost 4:00 pm. I had come to the office early, filled the golf bag with Y fifty million, and arrived back at the airport at 2:00 pm. I waited for a couple of jam-packed tourist buses to arrive, and chose a check-in line along with about a dozen other fellows with golf bags. As I stood there, I noticed the colors of everyone's golf bags.

I got a little nervous. *Shit, mine is kind of heavy, and it's white and red. And so are a couple of the other golf bags. Brink, you are either an idiot or a genius; this must be the most popular color. I hope no one picks up my golf bag when we get to Tokyo.* Suddenly, I did not feel so good, but what the hell could I do about it?

The attendant at the check-in counter stapled my luggage stub onto my ticket, and I watched the golf bag slide into the belly of the airport luggage system. Good-bye. *Don't lose the luggage check-in stub,* I told myself.

Tokyo immigration

It was close to 9:00 pm when I touched down at the old Tokyo Haneda Airport, ready to make my way to the hotel. I had drunk a couple of beers during the last hour of the flight and felt quite relaxed. Japanese are always polite, even immigration and customs. I lined up behind other non-Japanese at our designated counter.

"Ah, sooo. Why you come Japan? How long you stay and where?"

A few short questions and off I went to the luggage carousel. I was beginning to feel the sweat on my palms as I searched three carousels, looking at all the red and white golf bags. I watched as they were picked up by others, my eyes watering, straining to have a look at the numbers on the check-in tags. I felt the eyes of the custom agent nearby staring only at me.

Suddenly, I saw mine. Thank God! I watched it come around the corner until it passed in front of me. I flipped it onto a luggage cart, put my hand-carry on top and went to the nearest customs check, all the while looking for an Indian passenger to get behind. *"Customs will surely tear them apart because they are always trying to smuggle something, and they'll just wave you right on through!"*

Next best to standing behind an Indian is lining up behind a little old lady. With not an Indian in sight, I managed to find a little old couple to fall behind. They were from Guam and spoke no Japanese. It did not matter. They were waved through, and then the customs agent who had been staring at me asked me to go to his counter. He noted I had nothing to declare. So much for Brink's number-one theory—it didn't work here. I could feel a knot building in my stomach, and my palms beginning to sweat.

"You play golf here in Japan?" he asked, taking a long hard look at the red and white bag I had just placed in front of him. Apparently, it is very rare for a non-Japanese to bring a golf bag into Tokyo; and in the winter?

"Oh no," I replied truthfully, "I don't know anyone who will invite me and besides, the weather is too cold now. I plan to play a few rounds in Manila." As insurance, my ticket had been written Guam/Tokyo/Manila/Guam.

He asked to see my ticket. He hesitated for what seemed like an eternity. I stared him in the eyes, and my eyes told him I was beginning to become annoyed. Regaining my confidence, I asked quickly, "What is the problem?" He still paused. I lied, and told him I had to leave the golf bag in the stored luggage locker at the airport until my flight to Manila. (Of course, I had no intention of doing so.)

"Okay, go ahead," he finally said.

I let out a sigh of relief and cursed Brink for saying it was "as easy as pumpkin pie."

When I arrived at the Okura, there were already three messages waiting for me from a "Mr. Chan" calling from Hong Kong. *"Charlie Chan" Brink.*

Rooms in hotels are small in Japan, although the Okura is a five-star hotel. Once in my room, I transferred the yen to a Horizon Travel shoulder bag, and leaned the golf bag in the corner.

It was past midnight when the phone rang. It was Father Jose, calling to tell me he would contact me early the next morning. It was good he did not want to meet in the hotel. We agreed to meet at a Spanish restaurant, Los Platos, this first time and later at El Castellano. I just needed to confirm the time. "Come at noon," said Father Jose, "and make sure you come alone."

I checked the map, took the underground, then a taxi, and almost got lost walking the last ten blocks or so, looking over my shoulder all the while. Shit! Everyone looked the same to me. How do I know if I have "company"?

After a bottle of Father Jose's favorite wine—shipped from Spain—and a great lunch, I was feeling fine. A couple of hours later, I put Father Jose into a taxi, bag of yen in hand, and returned to my hotel. Father Jose had given me some accounts and coded payment records to send back to Brink. I decided to telex the info when I returned to Guam.

Father Jose was worried, and would become more worried each time I came to see him, which turned out to be more than a dozen times over the next two years. We decided to meet closer to the U.S. Embassy.

In Hong Kong, I saw the settlement accounts, and came to know our customer to be none other than Lockheed Aircraft Corporation. Point of contact: John W. Clutter, Lockheed Tokyo Office Chief and an assumed payment agent for the CIA, or even CIA Country Head himself.

Father Jose, Sanyo and I became good friends. Father Jose was concerned about security and asked me to watch his back. We never met in public or were seen together, except at the little Spanish restaurant, and Father Jose knew everyone there.

I would watch Sanyo meet with several Japanese gentlemen over the course of time, sometimes in the hotel car park; sometimes we met at the British Embassy car park, or at a residence, even a couple of times in a phone booth.

But what was it all about? Why was Lockheed Aircraft Corporation using the services of Deak? I was to find out the answer to that question two years later.

The nightmare –1975

Brink's secretary, Alice, really ran the place while Brink was away, which was quite often. Brink commuted every other month between Hong Kong and White River, South Africa, to his family residence on a beautiful small farm. As "Assistant Manager" I sat at his desk during the months he was away, and got to see firsthand what was really going on.

Much to my relief, Brink had just returned the night before, and we were waiting for the "master" to arrive when Mrs. Silva came running in, frantically waving her arms.

"Bruce, the *RED PHONE* has been ringing all morning!"

"What?" I didn't believe it.

I had worked in Hong Kong for almost two years, and the red phone had *never* rung. And it was *never* touched.

There was a battery of phones on Brink's desk, each with a special purpose. One was only for calls in German, another only in French, and there was even one for Esperanto. Brink was a brilliant eccentric.

But the *RED PHONE* was a very special phone with a special number that only special agents around the Far East knew, and they had to memorize it. It was only to be used in case of dire emergency.

"What are we to do, Mrs. Silva?" The words had barely left my mouth, when the red phone suddenly came to life: *RING! RING! RING! RING!* I had never heard it ring and when it did, the sound was totally unexpected...fast and shrill, with a sense of urgency about it.

"Don't touch it!" Mrs. Silva said.

Brink had told me to answer—if it ever rang and he was not there, then answer it! I hesitated as long as I could, hoping the damn thing would stop ringing.

It didn't. I picked up the receiver.

"Hello," I answered quietly and calmly, in a voice not at all like my own. To my shock, the voice on the other end recognized my voice anyway.

"Bluse," he said, in a heavy Japanese accent. It was Sanyo calling from Tokyo. He never could pronounce my name. "Is Mr. 'Blink' there?"

"Yes, on the way soon. What is it?"

"Big, big, very big problem! Oh, my God, oh, my God, it is on the TV, and in all Japanese newspapers! Father Jose has been arrested by Japanese internal police! Oh...it big news, you see! You watch TV. Good-bye! Sayonara! Tell Blink I go to hiding." A loud click followed.

I felt sick. Father Jose was my dear friend. Brink arrived a few minutes later and turned slightly pale at the news, but then the adrenaline kicked in. His first thought: what about the money, the accounts? Only Father Jose would have this information, not written down, only in his head. Many millions of yen paid out in recent days and weeks had to be accounted for.

"We must inform Mr. Deak!" Brink said,

"Yes, let's ask Mr. Deak what we should do."

For the first time, I was seriously asking myself, *What was all this money we paid out really for?*

The TriStar

We were about to find out what it was all about, because it became a story of immense interest and importance

In the late 1960s and early '70s the airline business was booming, and the market for wide-body planes was taking off. The 747 had changed the world. Competition between airplane manufacturers and airlines was fierce, and this was also true in Japan, with government-owned Japan Airlines (JAL) and All Nippon Airways (ANA). In an attempt to level the playing field, ANA bribed the Transport Minister, to buy time for Lockheed to compete against the "Big Two."

On the manufacturer's side, the big three U.S. corporations—McDonnell Douglas, Boeing, and Lockheed—all wanted to see their aircraft win, with Lockheed being, along with its trading-house partner, Marubeni, the long-shot by far. It became part of a sumo match involving the Prime Minister, no less. The matter came to be known in the media as Tanaka vs. Japan, and some thought it to be an even match.

Mr. Deak responds…

Around 9:00 pm the same evening, Hong Kong time, which was 9:00 am New York time, we were still in the office when the black phone began to ring. The black phone was a direct hot line and reserved *only* for calls from Mr. Deak, and *only* to be answered by Mr. Brink. I thought it might have been Mr. Deak's way of checking to see when Brink was in Hong Kong or South Africa, but in fact, when he was not in the office, it never rang even once.

When the black phone rang, everyone normally fled the office, leaving Brink to close the door and deal with the matter at hand. Strangely, this time Brink motioned for Ron Frame, the assistant manager, Tony Pong, Mrs. Silva and me to stay.

The conversation is etched in my mind. Much of it switched back and forth between English and German, which only Brink understood. But what I remember clearly was the solemn look on Brink's face. He just kept nodding his head, listening, nodding his head again, and then continued listening in silence. Obviously, this was extremely serious. After about twenty minutes, he slowly hung up.

Everyone started to speak at once. "What did Mr. Deak say? What can we do? What about Father Jose?"

There was a long pause before Brink said anything. "What about Father Jose?"

"Yes," we all said in unison. "What about Father Jose? Damn it! What in Jesus' name did Mr. Deak say about Father Jose?"

After a long pause Brink finally looked at us, and with a sly grin on his face again said, "About Father Jose?"

"Yes, God damn you, Brink!"

"Mr. Deak said, about Father Jose, about Father Jose?..he said to *pray for him.*"

"Shit! That's all he said? Pray for him?"

So praying was Plan A.

The reality was much more serious.

Plan B would be created three weeks later, after Father Jose had been thoroughly interrogated by the police and let out on bail. We kept a close ear to the ground until one day Sanyo called and said he had seen on TV that Father Jose had been released. The news said Father Jose knew nothing, and was only delivering documents for Deak & Company.

Sanyo said the police had been watching Father Jose for a long time, and knew it was Deak & Company that was delivering money, that they knew all the Deak and Compass Travel couriers were coming from Hong Kong. But they had no idea about the golf bags coming from Guam. To this very day, they *never* could figure out where most of the money was coming from or determine the source of the money.

"Bruce, can you go to Tokyo right away?" Brink asked. "You know where to meet Father Jose."

I had been the only one besides Brink and Pong who had ever been to Father Jose's little flat from which he provided his translation service, in Shibuya-ku, near the university in Tokyo. He would be expecting someone, and that could only be me. I felt that big knot return to my stomach.

"This may give me an ulcer," I said out loud to myself. I weighed the risks, and stupidly talked myself into believing there were none.

The next day, I was on the plane to Tokyo, having first flown from Hong Kong to Guam. I was not relishing the thought of showing up at Father Jose's flat at two in the morning, but that is what the situation called for. I took the train and walked the last ten blocks, then circled around from across the street. I had a good vantage point, and could see three hundred sixty degrees; I saw no one.

The entrance to the building was partly obscured by bushes, and if anyone approached me, I could keep on going around the building towards the university.

In the spirit of convincing myself I was helping my dear friend, and doing nothing wrong, I walked along the sidewalk, around the bushes and toward the entrance and lobby door. As soon as I appeared on the sidewalk, less than ten yards away from the entrance, the door sprang open. My heart stopped for what seemed an eternity. Much to my relief, a young man in his twenties walked out, took no notice of me at all, then walked across the road at a quick pace and disappeared into the metro.

I walked up to the entrance, glanced at the selection of doorbells, found 8C, and rang the buzzer. Almost instantly, I heard the deep voice of Father Jose.

"Father Jose," I said.

Silence, for a split second, and then a loud buzzing that broke the night silence. The front door opened. I walked in alone, and took the lift, pressing the button for the fifth floor, then took the stairs up to the eighth.

Father Jose and I drank my duty-free bottle of Johnny Walker Black Label, and talked nonstop for the next three hours. He gave me all the account balances, payments outstanding, deliveries pending—the works, to bring back to Brink. We shared a lot of whiskey and emotion due to the uncertainty of his future. He felt that the prosecutor would look kindly upon him, given he was only playing a small role in the Lockheed scandal and had no direct knowledge.

Interestingly, when I asked Father Jose if he liked being famous, to my amazement he said yes; that since he had been on TV he had received many calls from young Japanese stewardesses flying the TriStar with ANA, thanking him for supporting ANA TriStar. They were knocking on his door day and night. When I had knocked earlier that night, he thought I was another one!

I left Father Jose's flat before sunrise, made my way back to the train station, then to the airport for the flight to Guam and Hong Kong.

The police had been very thorough in monitoring airport arrivals, and had been watching employees of Deak & Company and Compass Travel, Hong Kong, over a full two years. They saw them come and they saw them go. Every time they entered Tokyo, an alarm went off. They had seen them every time they met with Father Jose. All the meetings were photographed and documented.

I was very fortunate not to have been connected to Deak Hong Kong or Compass Travel Ltd., and I thanked God for my good fortune in having made all my trips from Guam undetected.

When word broke that all the bribes were paid to Tanaka, the Prime Minister, reporters descended onto the office of Deak & Company Hong Kong, looking for the big boss, "Mr. *Blink.* That's right, *B-l-i-n-k.*" Dozens of Japanese reporters incessantly asked for Dirk. "Ah sooo, where Mr. Blink? Mr. Blink please! Must see Mr. Blink!"

On the morning I returned to Hong Kong, I went to the office about 9:00 am. It was a beautiful sunny day, and I was feeling pretty good and looking forward to a weekend at home. I pressed the lift button at 406 Shell House and suddenly five Japanese with cameras appeared behind me, all trying to squeeze into the same lift. I looked at them, and they looked at me. One of them pressed "four" and I thought to myself, *This time the shit has really hit the fan.*

When the lift stopped at four, they looked at me, hesitated, and when I went out first, they immediately yelled, "Ah sooo, you Mr. Blink?"

"What? Who?" I yelled back.

"Mr. Blink! Mr. Blink! Mr. Blink!"

"No! No! No!" I said, truthfully. "I don't know any Mr. B-l-i-n-k!"

I walked over to the Compass Travel counter, pretending to be a customer, and called Mrs. Silva, who had just come running out of his office.

"What's happening?"

"Oh!" she said, with a hearty laugh, "There are twenty Japanese journalists and photographers here, and all of them have been trying to squeeze into 'Mr. Blink's' office since early this morning."

All of a sudden the Japanese chatter stopped, instantly quiet. Brink was an avid non-smoker, you see; and that's why he had that big red and white NO SMOKING sign behind his desk. When he pressed a button on the floor with his shoe, the thing would light up and start flashing.

Brink was standing there, staring at the Japanese, all of whose shirt pockets were bulging with cigarette packs. They looked totally amazed when Brink pointed to the sign.

"You came to see 'Blink?' There, watch this 'No Smoking' sign blink! And by the way, I'm Dirk *Brink*. First, before we begin with your questions, please let me tell you a true story about my experience with the Japanese army."

The silence was broken only by the occasional sound of shuffling feet and muffled low voices.

"You see," he continued, "I was a soldier in the Indonesian Army, and when I was captured, I spent four years as one of your prisoners of war in the jungles of Thailand. I was slave labor, forced to build a railroad through the jungle on the River Kwai."

They looked at him in shock. The room went stark silent. They seemed to forget about Lockheed. One by one, each got up and walked out with a downcast face. Brink went on about how he was treated as a POW, and continued doing so until the last one left. Then you could have heard a pin drop.

Guilty

Prime Minister Kakuei Tanaka was eventually found guilty, along with a series of lesser figures who played into the scenario: ANA President, Marubeni; Lockheed President, Kotchian; and Chief John Clutter, who had testified before Congress.

Deak & Company had been exposed. Deak had made all the payments amounting to at least US thirty million dollars, and much of the money had either come from right there in downtown Tokyo or by delivery from Guam.

What was all the "hoopla" about anyway?

Well, as I mentioned, it seems there were three major U.S. airline manufacturers, each represented by its local giant trading "Hong" partners—all trying to sell their airplanes to ANA Airlines. Lockheed was by far the underdog, trying to sell its TriStar with the help of Marubeni. The other planes were McDonnell Douglas' DC 10 and Boeing's 747.

How Lockheed evened the playing field makes this story worth telling. Lockheed sought the help of an old friend, Yoshio Kodama, who had previously helped them with sales to the Japanese military. Lockheed was told it needed to be creative.

History of the "scandal"

As a consequence, Lockheed President, A.C. Kotchian, approved a payment of Yen five hundred million to Prime Minister Tanaka for influencing ANA. Tanaka agreed to do it. Tanaka then approached ANA President Wakasa, who agreed, and a couple of months later, presto, much to the surprise of Boeing and McDonnell Douglas, the contract was awarded to Lockheed for a fleet of TriStars at US thirty million dollars per aircraft.

In essence, Lockheed Corporation got the contract, while Marubeni got the commission; ANA got twenty-one Tri-Stars (over six billion dollars), the Japanese public got a good plane, and Tanaka and the "agents," Osano and Kodama, got a little pocket money.

The only problem was that it was all illegal, a minor detail that wasn't taken seriously until the 1976 U.S. Senate Sub-Committee Public Hearings under Senator Frank Church.

What followed was a complicated saga that would take years to unfold in the Japanese court system. After the story blew up,

142

Tanaka quickly and quietly tried to return the money through his secretary, Enomoto, but it was simply too late. Marubeni wanted nothing more to do with it.

With the final arguments concluded, judgment day was set for October 12, 1983. On that day, the last of one hundred and ninety hearings (which altogether had involved more than one hundred witnesses and lasted six years and eight months) finally took place.

It had been a spectacular show. Three of the sixteen defendants had fallen ill, and three witnesses and one judge had died. More than twenty books concerning the trial had been published; most of them became best sellers.

When the date arrived, the whole nation had reached fever pitch. The nation's televisions and radios were all turned on, seventeen helicopters were in the skies covering Tanaka's drive from Mejiro to the courthouse, four hundred and fifty members of a special police unit were deployed, fifteen hundred news personnel had descended upon the two key locations, and four thousand people were lined up for the fifty-two available court galley seats. Live coverage began at 7:00 am.

The Tanaka Chrysler motorcade left Mejiro and arrived at the courthouse shortly after 9:30 am. Even though this was only the first trial, Tanaka already had incurred legal fees estimated at four million dollars. The cost to the state was considerably more, and media expenses were incalculable.

Judge Okada delivered a fifty-five-thousand-character ruling, in which all of the defendants were found guilty. Okada admonished Tanaka for damaging the reputation of the nation and "forfeiting the people's trust in public offices." The judge threw the book at him; he was given a sentence of four years with a five-hundred-million-yen fine—almost four and a half million US dollars.

* * * * *

Deak & Company merrily continued on its way as if nothing had really happened, recruiting new couriers to service existing accounts.

Father Jose was defrocked, but happy. We continued to meet over the years whenever I was in Tokyo or whenever he visited Hong Kong on his way to Macau to visit his sister, who was a nun.

The ramifications of the "Lockheed Scandal" for Deak & Company in America and for Mr. Deak himself, however, were to be far-reaching and disastrous.

Shockingly, the TriStar selection over the MD, DC 10, and Boeing 727 could only be described as a miraculous, mind-boggling turn-around that reeked of impropriety.

Although just a pawn in the game, Deak was greatly affected because of the public's shocked reaction to how Lockheed President Kotchian, with the alleged tacit "nod" of the CIA, had resorted to bribery to win the contract. Was this the typical modus operandi of U.S. companies in foreign lands? The U.S. Senate Investigation Committee, led by Senator Church, would be shocked when it discovered the truth.

The Lockheed Bribery Scandal, with Deak and the CIA at its center, led to the passage of the Foreign Corrupt Practices Act, the first-ever law criminalizing bribery of foreign officials.

The Japanese populace was equally shocked. It was another scandal of "Watergate" proportions—dirty laundry, thrust into the open for all to see. Why the investigation? You might say that the center of political power and corruption in America had changed after Watergate. Nixon was out, and there were a lot of angry people thrown off the gravy train. Boeing and McDonnell Douglas would certainly not take things sitting down.

Lockheed became a great embarrassment to the U.S. government, which subsequently put a "gag order" on the scandal under the guise of protecting "national interests;" and so the truth about what we all know, namely that the CIA was a Lockheed collaborator, never came out. Several of the Japanese players who had been involved in the scandal, suddenly—and rather conveniently—"passed away," taking their knowledge to the grave.

According to my dear friend, Dirk Brink, who said to me one day in confidence, "Look to Clutter for the truth; he was our contact." Clutter had been the bridge between Deak and the CIA.

"Did Clutter work for the CIA?" I asked Brink, whose eyes darted around the room quickly in confirmation.

"Ask Mr. Deak," was his reply.

Truth or silence...

Even today, speculation is rife that the despicable murder of Nicholas Deak that happened in 1984 was the final straw. Could those responsible for his death consider murder to be the best way of ensuring that the truth, not only about the whole sordid Lockheed affair, but also a host of other "off balance sheet' transactions done for and on behalf of Uncle Sam over several decades, would quite literally be "buried?" No one on the planet believes the bizarre story that a deranged woman just happened to appear in his office and shot him.

Nothing that had happened in my life to that time was more shocking to me personally than the death of Mr. Deak, a man I considered to be truly extraordinary in intellect and charisma, and a personal friend, in such a "cloak and dagger" manner. I remember the day as if it just happened.

I was in my office early on the morning of November 20, 1984. Tony Pong called with the sad news. I was stunned. In a state of shock, vivid memories of Mr. Deak flashed through my mind, along with the words spoken many times by Dirk Brink.

"When you are dealing with clandestine government agents or agencies, you are dealing in a murky world. They are the real criminals and they will stop at nothing."

As for myself, when I found myself "kidnapped" by the U.S. government and incarcerated in 1989, facing two major money laundering indictments, I was asked by my investigator, Steve Swanson, whether I had anything on the government as a result of Deak & Company being the so-called "paymaster" for the CIA. I immediately thought of Lockheed and Clutter. More about Steve, a former DEA agent, later.

I proffered this information via Swanson to the prosecutor. Suddenly, the government was ready to deal, although in their own words:

"That Lockheed scandal is ancient history."

Oh, really?

In fact, as an interesting footnote to the scandal, at a chance meeting at the Hong Kong Foreign Correspondence Club in the fall of 2013, I met Japanese author and investigative journalist Eiichiro Tokumoto.

Familiar with, and intrigued by the scandal, he wrote about it in an article published in the influential publication, *Bungei Shunju*, the magazine that originally broke the story wide open in 1975.

His article in May 2014 revealed for the first time how most of the payments were made.

END OF PART TWO

The Cleaner

Part Three

Lessons in the Laundry

The Cleaner

CHAPTER 8
On My Own

Laundry blossomed like a flower

Some years later, in 2007, suitably revealed in the book *Reefer Men,* Tony Thompson described, in stark detail, the beginning of my company. In a flashback to 1980:

"Brian and the other members of the ring became increasingly successful, so they began to amass increasing amounts of cash and needed a way to launder it. The solution was provided by Tim Milner who, while investing his own earnings in a Hong Kong-based finance house, Deak & Company, became particularly friendly with an American banker named Bruce Aitken, friendly enough to admit that the money he was investing came from the drug business.

"Unfazed by the revelation, Aitken calmly offered to launder Milner's cash, first moving it around the world's money markets and then ultimately into offshore accounts and tax havens, for a modest commission. So efficient was Aitken that he was soon performing a similar service for them and for others. Within a year Aitken had quit his job at Deak and set up his own company, First Financial Services Ltd. His work consisted almost entirely of moving money for marijuana traffickers."

A critical decision

There was another salient issue that spurred me to take the plunge and go on my own. The whole Lockheed scandal brought an issue to the forefront that had been bothering me since the CIA fellow with the gold in his Nike tennis shoes had been nicked in Kathmandu. What about me?

What if it had been me instead of Father Jose who was arrested in Japan? I knew what we were doing was beyond slightly illegal, but in my mind, it was "different." Moving money was not the same as smuggling guns or drugs. It was simply an off-the-radar way to get money moved around the world. It was all about privacy. It seemed "happy-go-lucky" and was no big deal. Moreover, we were very good at it. Experts, in fact.

Yet, each time I flew somewhere, I was risking my freedom, because most countries held a decidedly different view of my chosen field. The Lockheed scandal brought everything to a head.

In the wake of the scandal, gradually over time, the mental burden finally came to a boil. I walked into the Hong Kong office one day in early September, 1977, and sat down in front of Brink. He didn't look up but simply asked, "What is it?" He must have sensed that something was wrong.

"This whole Lockheed thing has gotten me thinking. Remember we sort of left Father Jose swimming in deep shit without even so much as a paddle to help him out, didn't we? So, what about me, then? Where does that leave me, exactly? How would you feel, may I ask, if you were in my shoes, after what happened to him?

"Tony Pong just told me about a huge pickup in Taiwan tomorrow, and he is asking me to handle it. What would happen if I got caught in Taipei tomorrow? Please tell me. What is the position of Deak & Company?"

"What do you mean?" He lifted his head and looked directly at me, brows furrowed, almost angry. I was slightly taken aback.

"What do you mean, what do I mean? What I mean is this: What if I am arrested while on company business working for Deak? Will you guys back me up? Will the company back me up?"

Tony Pong, the head trader who worked the counters exchanging money, had joined us at my request and watched as I sat waiting for an answer.

"You know I'd have to speak with Mr. Deak about that, Bruce," Brink said. "But in the meantime, you're scheduled for that pickup in Taipei tomorrow."

"You're going to call Mr. Deak today?" I questioned Brink.

"Of course, Bruce. I'll call him as soon as possible."

I went home that evening not feeling at all well.

Recalling when I had gone to see Father Jose, I felt at times that "they," whoever they were, were watching me. It was not my imagination. I could feel eyes on me. I also knew that if I should get caught with any large amount of money or accounting records, they would not be as lenient with me as with a priest. They respected Father Jose because he was a man of God. Me? I would be nothing more than a dirty money launderer trying to steal taxes from their coffers.

I did not sleep well that night. For the very first time, I felt fear of the unknown and a stark realization of the risk I was taking. The Taiwan deal was big and involved a new client. The next morning, by the time I woke up, I had made up my mind. I didn't even bring an overnight suitcase with me to the office.

When I walked in before 9:00 am, there was the usual chaotic motley crew of people and deals just starting to whirl around Brink and Tony.

"Hey, Bruce, you ready to go?" Brink asked.

"Any word from Mr. Deak?" I asked.

"Nothing yet, Bruce. You're booked on the early afternoon flight."

I stood there staring at Brink intensely while I gathered my resolve. "Well, in that case, screw it. I'm not going!"

"What? What do you mean you're not going? Someone has to pick up that money! The guy is waiting in the Taipei Grand Hotel, for Christ's sake!"

Tony chimed in—I did not like his tone—"Yeah, Bruce. Please just go over there and get that money; deliver it to our agent and come right back. No problem!"

I ignored him.

No problem? I thought about that for a few seconds, remembering the look on Father Jose's face as we spoke about the Lockheed ordeal.

"Look, Brink. I'm not going unless I hear from Mr. Deak that I will be backed up by Deak & Company. I'm an employee. What if something goes wrong in the course of my employment? I have a wife to think about. Will the company continue to pay my salary if I'm in the slammer somewhere?"

"Nothing is going to go wrong," Brink said. "You've done it a dozen times, two dozen times, who knows?" Brink's eyes were piercing. His face was beginning to turn red. To my surprise, he was becoming very angry. I felt intimidated, but it served to strengthen my resolve.

Then Tony said, "Yeah, Bruce, if you don't go then I'll have to go."

I hesitated for a split second and decided.

"Well, then, get packing, Tony, because I'm not going!" He stormed back to his desk and slammed down some papers.

"Okay, okay, Bruce. Let me speak to Mr. Deak. I am sure it will be all right. You'll see." Brink tried to pacify me.

"Here's what I see. If I am not backed by the company, then I'm not going anywhere anymore, at any time, understand?" I took a deep breath and looked Brink straight in the eyes. "You see, I'd want much more than your prayers to help me if anything unexpectedly happened."

I left the office with a sense of peace and relief. I did not go to Taiwan. To his credit, Tony made the Taiwan pickup, and had no hard feelings afterwards. He was a pro, and in fact, he too was anxious to know the company's position.

We both already knew the answer.

Now I urgently needed a new game plan or a new job.

"Plan B"

Fortunately, it happened that Mr. Deak planned to visit Hong Kong in November 1977, and I had a chance to discuss my plans with him over dinner as we enjoyed a pleasant evening on a yacht moored beside Sai Kung. Pan Am was still flying into Kai Tak Airport in those days, and the owner of the yacht, as it happened, was a Pan Am captain by the name of Steve Meuris. Steve and his wife were a great couple.

I remember the conversation with Mr. Deak clearly, because he saw the advantage to both the company and to me, in my becoming a free agent, with the title "Business Development Manager."

"Mr. Deak," I said, "I have been traveling to different countries doing pickups and payments on almost a weekly basis. As soon as I arrive I do the deal, and when it's finished, I barely have time to catch my breath before I fly back to Hong Kong to start the next transaction.

"But what if I had the time to stay in Australia, for example, a while longer, and ask our happy clients to introduce me to new clients? Then I could also service their businesses."

Mr. Deak thought it was a great idea Deak & Company would quote me a preferential rate. I would give my client my quotation, and keep the difference. A wonderful arrangement for all concerned.

I'll always remember that night for another reason: Jenny was there. Mr. Deak was very fond of her, and remembered that when I started with the company he had given her a job in New York. Everyone was talking happily when I needed to get something from my briefcase. Steve's wife motioned that my briefcase was downstairs. On the boat, of course, our shoes were off; we were all in our socks.

I started to walk down the stairs.

In honor of Mr. Deak's visit, the whole boat had been thoroughly cleaned and waxed from top to bottom. Suffice it to say, as soon as I took my first step on the newly polished teak stairs, I found myself airborne, flying through the air like a *mis*-guided missile, completely out of my control; and I landed flat as a pancake on my back with such force that the whole boat shook as if a bomb had just exploded.

Funny how you remember things. My father was a house painter, and sometimes he fell off the ladder. He told me that if I started to fall, I should relax, and then I would be all right. I tried to relax during that twisted, airborne fall, and the next thing I felt was *WHAM!* The breath was knocked out of my lungs right before a shock wave ran across my entire body, emanating from the center of my back.

Everyone rushed to see if I were dead. A look of shock covered their faces. Being very embarrassed, and stubborn, I got up as fast as possible and brushed the whole thing off, saying that I was perfectly fine. Mr. Deak observed me closely, looking me straight in the eye over dinner, realizing that I was in some kind of pain, but he said nothing; neither did I.

By the time dinner ended, I had recovered and was feeling much better; not much worse for the wear, but sore as hell the following week while I nursed a bruised ego.

I'm free!

DEAK – PERERA GROUP
INTER-OFFICE INFORMATION BULLETIN

No. 253   New York, February 1, 1978

Deak & Company (Far East) Ltd., Hong Kong:

As of January 1, 1978, Mr. Bruce Aitken has opted to become a freelance agent for the Deak-Perera group with the title of Business Development Manager. He will continue to be closely in touch with the Far East office through which he can be contacted at any time. We wish him good luck.

Prior to the announcement from Deak & Company, I had done a lot of soul-searching. It made sense to become an agent for Deak & Company, giving up the big salary and benefits as an employee, in exchange for something better: commissions, my time and my life.

At least, that is what I thought.

I'm hooked

It did not take long.

Soon after I became a freelance agent in November 1977 my first deal materialized—a pickup from a client in Sydney. The amount was two hundred thousand dollars, and my fee three percent, or an easy six thousand for my efforts. This would be the acid test.

What were my efforts?

Having met the client, I packed forty bundles of fifty-dollar notes of five thousand each into "Old Faithful"—my favorite golf bag. Doing deals for myself was totally different from doing deals for Deak. I felt a thrill, something like an adrenaline junkie might

155

feel, as I prayed at the airport check-in, and then said another prayer— of thanksgiving—when I collected the money upon arrival in Hong Kong.

The next day happened to be a beautiful Sunday morning. I had slept well. Jenny and I had breakfast at the American Club at St. George's Building in Central, Hong Kong. I pondered the six thousand dollars I had just made. It was a lot of money at the time, and I savored an amazing feeling of being a good provider—the man of the house, a feeling men love. Smuggling money was so easy it felt like a drug addiction. Breakfast at the Club that morning never tasted so good. Suddenly, I felt alive.

I was hooked.

Christmas, 1977

Personally, I could not have been feeling better or more satisfied with life. Although my new arrangement was officially announced as of January 1, 1978, it was the last working day before Christmas and I was looking forward to chilling out over the holidays. The new arrangements with Deak were working well. A pragmatic Mr. Brink understood, saw the advantages and was actually happy with the new arrangement. He even gave me the full use of the office—no hard feelings.

Mrs. Silva referred a caller to me. An American chiropractor, Dr. Ted Krauss, who was based in Sydney, was calling from the five-star Peninsula Hotel in Hong Kong. He wanted to see me. When? I could not believe it. *Christmas Day.* "With humble appreciation, he thanked me profusely. Dr. Krauss came highly referred, and besides, he was due to leave Hong Kong the day after Christmas.

Christmas afternoon, I pressed the buzzer on the door of Room 806 at the Peninsula. I heard footsteps coming from behind the door. In front of me stood Dr. Krauss. About five feet nine inches tall, in addition to a warm and inviting smile, he wore sharply-creased designer jeans, matching dark-blue leather loafers, and a smart, white loosely flowing silk shirt. He was an affable fellow with a head of curly hair. Smoking a cigarette in a long holder, *dapper* would be a fitting word to describe the elegantly attired gentleman standing before me.

He offered me a cigarette. I declined. Five minutes later, he offered me a joint. *Now, this is one interesting fellow! Surely, he is up to something besides being a chiropractor.*

He wasn't.

Over the following years, Ted became a very good friend. He was a very sociable character, and a casual user of weed and wine. He wanted most of all to socialize with people he saw as interesting and living on the edge—like his friend Ray Cessna.

The phone tap

As fate would have it, Ted had a circle of friends I never knew, but which the authorities came to know quite well. A tap on his phone led them to some of our mutual friends.

I was to read the following sometime later, in a stinging report from a Royal Commission in Australia:

"Early in 1979, New South Wales police tapped the telephone of a suspected drug dealer at Cronulla. This led them to Moseman and then to Drummoyne, which led to a tap on the phone of Dr. Theodore Frederick Krauss, a chiropractor. Krauss had conversations with an American, Roy Bowers Cessna, but was cautious in his remarks, so a tap was placed on Cessna's phone. Soon after, on Wednesday, 14 March 1979, the tap enabled police to arrest Cessna and an Englishman, Timothy Lycett Milner, in possession of 110,000 Buddha sticks weighing some 137 kilograms. This amount suggested an intention to supply the drug, so the

offence would thus be indictable, and carried a maximum penalty of either ten or fifteen years in prison, depending on the strength of Indian hemp in the material."

Cito & Lynn

It is indeed a small world, and in it was a small circle of souls all mysteriously connected. Tim Milner, mentioned in the above report, and I went back a few years, and were comfortable, good friends. We would meet in Sydney from time to time, do some quick business, and, as birds of a feather, we would flock together.

Dr. Ted Krauss, as it turned out, was also a good friend of Lynn and Ray "Cito" Cessna—more birds of a feather.

After a few trips to Sydney around 1976-7, while I was still employed by Deak, I was invited by Tim to have dinner with Cito and Lynn. The first time may have been at a restaurant—they were strict vegetarians and knew some really excellent veggie restaurants around Sydney and Moseman on the North Shore.

Cito and Lynn had a nice home in Lane Cove, stuffed with beautiful Afghan, Persian, and Pakistani carpets, and it was always a joy to get an invitation to their home for an excellent dinner washed down with a couple of bottles of choice Aussie wine. I had no idea vegetarian food could be so delicious.

The house was well guarded, namely by two large Great Danes that growled at you as soon as you drove up to the front of the house, which was located about fifty meters from the road. I always hired a rental car, and by habit, parked it in front of another house a couple of blocks away, then walked the rest of the way.

In the beginning, Cito was very uncomfortable about the fact that I had been brought into the inner sanctum and into his home. He was not friendly towards me, and I did not feel welcome. Although I handled the money, I think he wondered if I could be trusted.

After several trips and cash pickups, Cito and Lynn and I became the best of friends; so much so, they insisted I go to their house every time I was in Sydney. I loved sitting on a large stack of carpets and hanging out with Cito. After all, he was an American who had found his way to Australia via rugged places like Iran, Pakistan and Afghanistan, and had many interesting experiences, friends and tales to tell.

Cito only had one bad habit—he chain-smoked unfiltered Camels, and he always had one in his hand. One day, we told him it would do him in. We were right, unfortunately. Thankfully, it took thirty years.

One thing about Cito, when he was your friend, he was a true friend, just like Tim and another great mutual friend named "Brian".

Cito also happened to be well-connected through his gracious and lovely Australian wife, Lynn, and through the folks he sold carpets to, like Dr. Ted and the likes of some very capable solicitors.

One of these was Morgan Ryan.

Morgan Ryan

Morgan Ryan and his mates were class acts. You had to admire both the way they lived their lives with genuine gusto, and the way in which they operated in and out of the system. If they weren't looking for loopholes in the law, they were looking for ways to win at the horse races at Randwick.

I remember the first night I was invited to go along and meet Morgan at his home in Neutral Bay. By that time, I had already moved a lot of money for my good friends, and, I suspected, for Brian, as well. Of course, I had not met Brian yet.

The only reason I was being introduced at all, was the magical service I had performed in making money disappear in Sydney, only to make it reappear somewhere else. Everyone, it seemed, had a need for this service. Likeable and shrewd from the onset, Morgan

Ryan was as sharp as a tack, a funny Irishman who had a great zest for life.

Morgan stood about five feet eight inches tall, and was always impeccably dressed. His face was round and warm. He wore beautiful tweed sport jackets that mirrored his enjoyment of the good life. We hit it off the moment we met. I expected the introduction would result in some pretty good business in the future, provided everyone could keep their heads down.

One day, however, fate proved otherwise.

March 1979

With dozens of successful deals already under my belt since 'going it alone', early March started uneventfully as I sat in my little office at Deak & Company in Hong Kong. Surveying my list of accounts, I noticed that in spite of every effort to develop relationships and accounts with straight-arrow types, I had an overwhelming imbalance of business that had to do with money laundering from the sale of marijuana.

It was March 9th. The phone rang. It was Brink.

"Bruce, pick up line one from Australia."

It turned out to be from a Mr. Piano—not his real name. He was calling from Perth.

Mr. Brink passed the account to me for consideration, because I had met Mr. Piano once in Hong Kong and again in Melbourne. He was a lawyer. Somehow, I was of two minds as to whether to take the call or not. I wondered why Brink passed him along to me.

When I first met Piano, I told him how we operated, gave him half a two-dollar bill in Melbourne, and didn't give it any more thought.

But, sure enough, he wanted to proceed. Could I immediately come to Australia for the first and only transaction? I quoted him my fee of five percent for the first and only deal, which he confirmed would be A$ three hundred thousand. The location was Perth.

Thinking out loud, I felt Deak & Company would earn their three-percent fee if I ran it through their account at ANZ Bank in Sydney. I checked with Brink, but he said he had no orders pending and did not want to use the account for Piano's business. This sounded a bit strange. It worried me. Brink, however, advised me that this was a "one-off" deal and that was the reason why he had passed it to me.

You know when you have that feeling deep down in your gut, a *premonition* telling you not to do something, but you do it anyway? That was how I felt. I buzzed Compass Travel.

"Please book me a ticket on the CX nonstop flight to Perth, and make me a reservation at the Perth Hilton." The Hilton was directly across the road from a big park where I could do some jogging in the mornings. I decided to bring "it" back with me in Old Faithful, and pocket the full five-percent fee.

A big problem with Perth was that there were only two direct flights a week. I would have to stay more than one night. I hoped Piano had his shit together and was ready. He said he was. Armed with Old Faithful, I arrived on the morning of March 12.

Tired, I got right on the deal, phoning Piano as soon as business opened at 9:00 am. By 10:00 am he was at my hotel. He was very nervous and sweating profusely; he was hesitating. It had been so much easier to agree to the deal in Hong Kong at the office than it was to actually do it.

So, there I was with a highly agitated individual standing in front of me, shitting himself, seemingly unable to make up his f*cking mind. I asked myself how hard it was going to be for him to hand over a cool three hundred thousand in cash and not get a receipt. At this point, he was starting to seriously piss me off.

Finally, I gave him an ultimatum.

"Look, my friend," I said as politely as possible. "Either bring me the cash within twenty-four hours, or no problem; as agreed, we simply walk away from the deal as if nothing happened. However, you will have to forfeit the expenses and the fee for breaking the deal. Please bring me either three hundred thousand dollars, or the fee of five thousand dollars for my time and expenses."

Frankly, either way I was happy. I honestly hoped he would just bail out and pay the penalty.

Upon arrival, unbeknownst to me, a golf tournament was taking place with registration beginning at the Hilton the same day. I could not believe my luck! There were golf bags all over the place. The hotel lobby looked like the eighteenth hole.

Later in the day, Piano rang my room. He said he had spoken to his advisor and was prepared to go ahead. I was shocked.

"Who is your advisor?"

"My banker, of course," was his curt and somewhat rude reply.

"You have violated a very important rule, and broken the confidentiality of the deal and *substantially* increased the risk." I wanted to add, "*You moron!*" but held my composure. I wasn't sure what to do. He then assured me his banker was a lifelong friend and trustworthy, and that he, Piano, would be delivering the goods to my hotel by 4:00 pm, just after the bank closed.

I told him to come alone.

He did.

It was then late afternoon on March 13. I called the airline and made a reservation on the early morning flight to Sydney for March 14. The flight connection to Cathay Pacific's daily return flight to Hong Kong was good, except for one crucial hitch. It was fully booked. I would have to return to Hong Kong on March 15.

I resigned myself to spending a day in Sydney babysitting the golf bag, because I never felt comfortable leaving it alone. I would be in Sydney for one night, but would not be able to call either Cito or Dr. Ted Krauss.

The doorbell rang at 4:30 pm and in came Mr. Piano, alone and sweating. I did my best to reassure him. He said he had been referred to Deak by a well-known Perth businessman by the name of Mr. Newton. He gave me the money. I gave him a pat on the back. I told him I needed to act immediately and transfer the money without hesitation or delay, so he would have to excuse me. He understood and quickly left the room

Immediately, I bolted and double-locked the door, took out the golf bag, which had been out of sight in the closet, unscrewed the bottom and quickly packed the cash into the specially made sleeves. This time, I was the one who was sweating. This was the time that I was most vulnerable.

The whole operation was completed in ten minutes. I breathed a sigh of relief. It was so good to have the cash out of sight, and I placed the golf bag back in the closet where I knew it was safe and sound.

About an hour later, the phone rang; it was Piano. "Was everything okay?" he inquired.

"Yes," I assured him. "As a matter of fact, not only was everything okay, but the goods are already on the way."

He expressed shock, verging on panic. "What?" he stuttered and mumbled something incoherent.

"Yes, sir," I continued, "no turning back now. It will be deposited within forty-eight hours to your account in Switzerland, as per your instructions."

He didn't say anything.

"Are you all right? Hello? Hello??"

An ominous silence then followed. We were disconnected. I called him back. He did not pick up.

I was worried.

I was feeling particularly concerned and very paranoid, and decided I needed some fresh air.

Opening the door to my hotel room at the end of the corridor, I glanced all the way to the end where the lifts were located, immediately making eye contact with two men in black suits, just standing there staring right back at me. *Oh shit! They look like police. What the hell am I to do?* I was already halfway out the door. *Keep going, Bruce.*

I walked slowly down the corridor and approached them. One had a big ring of keys in his hands, which gave him the appearance of a member of the hotel security staff. I nodded. They nodded back. I waited for the lift, which seemed to take forever to arrive.

I could see that the men in black were becoming uncomfortable, too. They walked slowly down the corridor toward my room. As they walked, I was stealing glances out of the corner of my eye to see where they were going. The lift bell rang too soon and the door opened. I let it pass. They would think I had taken it.

I looked for the door to the stairs, but first, stealing a last glance down the corridor, I saw them unlock the door to my room and enter. I felt a swath of heat on my forehead as my temperature rose, and my heart rate shot up as I walked down one flight of stairs and pushed the button for the lobby. I suddenly felt very sick. *What the hell should I do now?*

I waited for a short while in the lobby. No one appeared. I went out to the street for a walk to clear my head. A half hour passed, then an hour that seemed like an eternity. If I returned to the room, what would I find? Would they be waiting for me? Would they have checked the golf bag? Would it be gone? If anything, my curiosity became even more overwhelming than my fear of what might happen next.

With the only option being to return to the hotel, I proceeded to my floor. The lift opened. I looked down the corridor—there was no one there. I stopped in front of my door and listened. Silence. I took a deep breath. My heart was racing. I prayed. I approached the door lock. Turning the key, I slowly opened the door. The room was dark with just a reflection of light coming from outside the window. I turned on the light. No one was there.

Immediately looking towards the closet, I breathed a sigh of relief to see the golf bag was still there. Bolting the door, I carefully opened the bottom of the bag. *The money was still there.* I could not wait to get the hell out of there, and onto the morning flight to Sydney. The golf bag had passed the test. If someone was looking for the three hundred thousand, they had been very disappointed.

The next morning, I flew to Sydney. While checking in Old Faithful, I had a terrible feeling that many eyes were looking at me. Taking it all in calmly, I was happy to see the golf bag move along the conveyor belt on its way into the plane's belly and out of my hands. I froze for a split second, imagining that a customs agent or the police might still tap me on the shoulder.

Arriving in Sydney in the afternoon, I proceeded to the Hilton, golf bag in hand, happy just to stay in my room, order room service, enjoy a quiet dinner and a couple of beers. I was tempted, after the beers, to call Cito or Dr. Ted, but I felt I had already had enough excitement for one day and needed some peace and quiet. The golden rule of money laundering is never to mix the business of babysitting cash with pleasure.

Late that night, my peace was shattered by the phone ringing. It was Jenny.

"Hi, Jenny!" I said, "Do I have something very interesting to tell you when I get home." But she interrupted me. The news was more devastating than I could ever have imagined.

"Bruce," she said, "Bad news...are you sitting down?" My stomach turned over as I waited for her to speak. Silence.

"What is it, Jenny?" Someone unknown had called from Sydney and left a shocking message on our home phone. Cito and Tim had been arrested the day before in Lane Cove, through an undercover operation, with a huge stash of one hundred thousand Thai sticks.

As I would learn later, Tim, the expert yachtsman, would sail the weed from Thailand and bury it on one of the uninhabited islands off the coast of Western Australia. Cito would recover it and drive the loaded truck 3,934 km back to Sydney.

The message, which came from Morgan Ryan, was for me to be "ultra-careful." He had been so right! They had no idea who created the leak or who was being watched.

My first worry was about Cito and Tim. It had been over two months since my last trip to Sydney, and on that trip I had met Cito and Tim downtown. They must be in *very* deep shit. I hesitated, wanting to call Dr. Ted but decided not to do so.

It suddenly occurred to me just how exposed *I* was, and how serious my situation was at that moment. The flight to Hong Kong was leaving in a little over eight hours. Could I be taking a bigger than usual risk checking this golf bag full of money onto the plane? If I were stopped, I might be linked to the case against Tim and Cito. I wished I had never even heard of Mr. f*cking Piano in Perth, and that I had never become involved with his bloody transaction in the first place.

Decision time…

I checked out of the hotel early the next morning, and took a taxi to the airport. Everything looked normal. I checked in at the Cathay Pacific counter, and checked in "loaded" Old Faithful at the same time. It seemed a long time until we were finally called to start boarding. Up until then, I feared anything could happen.

As the plane taxied onto the runway, I said one last prayer. The pilot gave it full throttle. The aircraft reached rotation speed. I felt the lift on top of the wings as we quickly became airborne. At long last - lift off! I sank into my seat and pondered what in the world would happen next. I had a much more important deal coming up in Melbourne in April. I would have to be very careful.

The arrest of Ray (Cito) Cessna and Tim Milner was the result of the "tap" on the phone of Dr. Ted Krauss; it was yet another scandal of the highest order. At risk would be the lives and livelihoods of not only Cito and Tim, but those of top solicitors, magistrates, judges, and the police commissioner, himself—all Irishmen, I might add.

"A la Lockheed Japan," this new scandal would almost bring down the New South Wales government. Eight years later, it would take another major scandal—a kidnapping—to again expose this scandal, this time in minute detail, and reveal the payments made to certain beneficiaries. But first, it's important to put it in perspective.

Oh, no! Return to Sydney

The day after their arrest, I could not stop thinking about Cito and Tim being in the slammer and facing God knew what. I was grateful to have flown out of the country with Old Faithful safely checked in the belly of the plane.

When I got to Hong Kong, I knew there would be more news. Sure enough, when I went to work the next morning several messages were waiting for me from Cito's wife, Lynn, with instructions from Morgan. Lynn was calling collect from a pay phone. Later that day, Cito was bailed out. Things were not looking good, but Morgan was assuring Cito and Tim that he would get to work on it right away. Naturally, there would be expenses: Tim's bail and the grease to hopefully get a good result.

The task of bringing in the "bread" could only fall to me; however, I hesitated to return to Sydney immediately. I would wait one week until I could find a seller of Australian dollars in Sydney, rather than carry the cash from Hong Kong. The amount required for bail and solicitor fees would be between Australian fifty and seventy thousand dollars. We had agreed on a place and time I would make the delivery to Cito himself—a little vegetarian restaurant in Moseman.

When we met at the restaurant, no one seemed to have an appetite. I hugged Cito and Lynn, wished them well, and asked them to let Tim, who was in Long Bay prison, know that I would do as he instructed regarding any payments; plus, I would hope and pray for him.

CHAPTER 9
The Cessna-Milner Affair – As Reported

1979

The illegal phone taps on my Aussie friends, we would later learn, had yielded evidence that would result in a Federal Commission called the "Costigan Commission into Judiciary Corruption." A big-time scandal had reached a boiling point in the pot of intrigue and, moreover, it was boiling right under my very unsuspecting nose.

A voice deep inside said, *time to disappear until this blows over.* Little did I envision that what would become known as the "Cessna-Milner Affair" was about to explode and quickly take on the same proportions as the Lockheed scandal.

The trouble began with the illegal telephone wire tapes that were reported by *The Age* newspaper, and came to light as the result of the Stewart Royal Commission inquiry into the *Age* tapes.

Who could have imagined that the "truth" of this amazing "scandal" would finally come out eight years later? What, in fact, was the scandal all about? Morgan Ryan and his pals were clever as foxes, and ingenious in their creating environments that would lead to favorable outcomes for their clients. Little did I realize I would one day need their professional services.

Getting back to the scandal in question, when Tim was kidnapped for ransom eight years later in 1987 in Thailand, he was forced to spill the beans under duress about the Cessna-Milner Affair.

In essence, in Tim Milner's words, "I stayed on bail for two months until my case came up. I was told by Ray Cessna that if I paid money, things would be easier. He would say a figure, and then a different one, ranging from fifty to seventy thousand dollars. I went to court and was sentenced to eighteen months. Then, when I was inside, my lawyer visited me, and I signed a letter to Deak & Company (Far East) for an unlisted order for thirty thousand dollars. I knew it had to do with my case, but I did not know who was getting paid, or how it was done. They also took my twenty-thousand-dollar bail money."

Their attorney, Morgan "The Magician," with the aid of a bit of grease, was able to convince certain key decision makers in the case that the amount of THC in the hemp in the possession of Cito and Tim when arrested was of a very low quality and percentage so as to make this a very minor drug bust. The potential criminal liability exposure they would face if caught in possession was nothing like that of one hundred thousand Thai Buddha sticks.

Plus, to top it all off, on the day of sentencing, the case was magically transferred to a Magistrate's Court with a magistrate's decision instead of a jury trial, and with no recording equipment in the courtroom to boot. So, Tim and Cito surely got very good value for money.

To quote Andrew Keenan, reporting eight years later in the *Sydney Morning Herald*, "...Timothy Milner has admitted that he paid at least fifty thousand dollars so 'things could go easier' for him after he and Ray Cessna were charged with supplying Indian hemp in 1979. Although Milner said he does not know to whom the money was paid, he 'knew it was to do with my case.'"

The Herald article also reported that there was a *sixth* person involved: "Regarding the 'cast,' it was not five, as was always reported, but six."

The joint NSW-Federal police task force, headed by detective Chief Superintendent Ron Stephenson, had been set up during the previous year in the wake of the findings of the Stewart Royal Commission into the *Age* tapes.

As reported in the *Herald* at the time, Judge Stewart concluded that the three leading figures in the Cessna-Milner Affair—Solicitor Morgan Ryan, former Chief Stipendiary Magistrate Mr. Murray Farquhar, and police chief Mr. Wood—had been involved in a conspiracy to pervert the course of justice.

Much to my chagrin...

Among other things, Tim's statements indicated that the syndicate used a Hong Kong company (Deak & Company (Far East) Ltd.) to send all its drug profits from Australia to Southeast Asia.

Merv Wood, a former NSW Police Commissioner, was instrumental in insuring that the charges against Tim and Cito were dealt with by a magistrate rather than go to a trial.

"The other leading figures in the affair," the Herald article continued, "were Milner, former solicitor Morgan Ryan, then-Chief Stipendiary Magistrate Mr. Murray Farquhar, and the other defendant, Ray Cessna."

So all of the "cast" members were accounted for except one: me. The article concluded:

"Bruce Aitken would nicely fit the role of a 'sixth man' in the Cessna-Milner Affair. Aitken's involvement and background are less well-known than those of Messrs. Raymond Cessna, Timothy M., Morgan Ryan, Mervyn Wood and Murray Farquhar. Bruce Aitken was the "*mystery* money mover".

According to Milner's statements describing several cannabis imports in which he was involved, dating from 1975, 'the money was taken out by a Deak Company representative on all the trips.' He later identified 'Aitken' or 'B. Aitken,' a sometime Deak employee or contract agent, as being the man to whom he gave money from drug sales in Australia to be sent back to Southeast Asia. A final specific reference to Aitken concerned Milner's twenty-thousand-dollar bail money,which he says '*Cessna arranged for me via Aitken.*'"

More on Mr. Ryan and the "Affair"

Morgan was indeed an extraordinary and brilliant man, at times a lawyer and partner for noted crime figure, Abe Saffron. The Cessna-Milner matter was allegedly handled over dinner at Morgan's home in Neutral Bay on May 10, 1979. As reported later in the *Herald,* here is how it happened:

"The dinner was held on Thursday 10 May 1979 at Ryan's house in Neutral Bay. Present were Lionel Murphy, Ryan, Farquhar, Wood, and Magistrate Briese, by then NSW Chief Stipendiary Magistrate-elect, who was invited by Farquhar. According to Briese, a function of the dinner was to determine whether he would be a 'flexible' chief magistrate. What interest the various parties, including a justice of the High Court, would have in any such flexibility remains a matter for speculation.

"On the Monday following the dinner, Ryan and a legal associate, Bruce Miles, conferred with a former Drug Squad officer to see if the Cessna-Milner case could be heard on a summary basis. Maximum penalty would then be two years. This was referred to the chief of the prosecuting branch, Supcrintendent G. Fryer. He directed that the case was to be dealt with by indictment only.

"Around 9.30 am the next morning, Tuesday 15 May, the day the case was to be heard, Wood rang Fryer. According to Fryer, Wood said: 'Mr. Farquhar has indicated that he would be prepared to deal with the matter summarily if the prosecution consented. He is the chief magistrate and also the chairman of the drug authority and is an expert on these things, and if he is prepared to do that, then that's the way I want it handled'. Fryer said he accepted this direction. Wood claimed he gave no direction, but did confirm that he suggested to Fryer that Farquhar's guidance be sought.

Farquhar shifted the court to one in which there was no sound recording equipment, and gave Milner eighteen months, of which he served six. On 24 May, the day before Farquhar's retirement, he fined Cessna one thousand dollars and gave him an eighteen-month bond.

On 29 April 1980, Senator Gareth Evans was quoted: *"The standards we require of our judiciary are higher than might be reasonable to require of anyone else."*

I'm exposed...in the Herald

"According to the public records of the Stewart Royal Commission regarding the *Age* tapes, phone taps had been placed on various drug dealers, then moved to the phone of Dr. Theodore Krauss, the Sydney chiropractor. In early March, the taps were moved to the home phone of Raymond Cessna, one of the two Americans overheard speaking to Krauss. The other was Bruce Aitken.

"On March 21, 1979, two months before the Cessna-Milner case was finally disposed of, the NSW Police Crime Intelligence Unit sent a telex to Interpol in Hong Kong requesting certain 'discreet inquiries.' In particular, the CIU wanted to know the occupants of 406 Shell House, Queen's Road, Central, and whether 'Milner is in any way connected with the address, and also a man named Bruce Aitken.'"

Of course, the address was for Deak & Company, described as a "foreign currency specialist" and a fully-owned subsidiary of Deak & Company New York. In 1984, the U.S. President's Commission on Organized Crime made Deak a target of its inquiry into money laundering. It found Deak had been used to launder millions in the USA and Asia.

The Costigan Royal Commission noted that Deak had "acted as the agents for the infamous Nugan Hand in Hong Kong for the purpose of moving money." More about Nugan Hand later.

The inquiry revealed that Aitken had been transferred to Deak's Hong Kong office from Guam in November 1975 at the direction of Deak's New York office, and by 1978 had become a general agent or a commission agent.

In addition, the Costigan Royal Commission noted that he had traveled a great deal.

"During the three years up to 1981 Aitken was known to have visited Sydney more than fifteen times, Manila and Tokyo more than ten times, Taipei more than eight, and Bangkok more than seven. He had also visited Singapore, San Francisco, Honolulu, Macau, Brunei, Kuala Lumpur, Jakarta and Melbourne, and several countries in Europe and Africa. Although his name might not have emerged publicly during the Cessna-Milner matter, by late April 1980, NSW police had him listed as being an 'associate of Ray Cessna and Ted Krauss.'"

Under surveillance!

Thus, sometime after I arrived in Sydney on April 16, 1980, near ly a year after the resolution of the Cessna-Milner case, I came under surveillance by the Criminal Investigation Unit. Less than two weeks later, on April 29th, I was recorded in conversations on one of Morgan Ryan's tapped phones.

According to summaries of the calls recorded just before my arrest: "Morgan Ryan says, 'We all have to be ultra-careful,' and they arrange to meet at the Hilton at 5:45 p.m."

A note on the summaries has Morgan being overheard to say, presumably to someone in the room, that he would be late getting home that night: "He wants to see me. It's about this bloody money over in New Zealand."

The following day, the two spoke again. The summaries indicate that Ryan told Aitken to, "Put all the information in an envelope and put it in my letterbox.

"CIU surveillance running sheets noted that early that morning, April 30, Aitken drove from his apartment at McMahons Point to Ryan's Neutral Bay home. He was seen to walk down the steps to the front door, go to the letterbox, and then walk back to the front door before leaving."

They continue:

"That night Aitken drove to Double Bay…and later on in the evening was stopped by police in William Street. In the boot of his car was a canvas bag containing about sixty thousand dollars wrapped in two brown paper packages. He was subsequently charged with 'goods in custody.'"

Judging from the illegal police phone taps, May 1 was a busy day for Morgan Ryan. First, he learned of my arrest from Cito who, according to police summaries of the proceedings, told him that Aitken would not make a statement, and that I had said that I was simply on company business.

Morgan later called Cito back and was told that I "had been picked up carrying company funds." Morgan was concerned that "they should not get any of the *paperwork.*"

Morgan next called Mr. Abraham Saffron, asked him if he knew anyone high up in the Criminal Investigation Branch, and told him about my arrest. According to the summaries, "Abe said he will think about it."

The infamous paperwork? Morgan was known as the "magician" when it came to arranging Australia resident visas for Asians. He had some good Irish buddies high up in Immigration. The truth be told, the paperwork was for the expeditious handling of a resident visa for an old friend from the Philippines.

It was a traumatic experience to be arrested. Most of all, I dreaded telling Jenny. She would be very disappointed in me.

I had foolishly gone out to a party that night, invited by one of my very best mates, Peter King "The Duck," as in "Peking Duck." A lot of alcohol had been consumed, and there was a lot of hashish smoke floating in the air. The police put me in a holding cell. It was 3:00 am. I was miserable. I cursed myself profusely, and wondered what had happened to my character.

Once I bailed out, I called Jenny. Instead of adding to my torment, she comforted me. What a woman.

I had to appear in court and return to Sydney for the hearing the following month. I was sick with worry, but comforted because Morgan assured me of the outcome.

The truth about the $60,000

This particular bundle of cash actually belonged to a good friend of mine, a merchant banker named Warren Magi. I had been to Warren's house earlier the same morning to deliver the funds, unaware that the police had been following me. Warren's arrival in Sydney had been delayed, and his wife refused to take the money. The irony was that this particular sixty thousand dollars was not drug related.

The news of my arrest caused a bit of a panic in the Cessna-Milner camp, with concern over some paperwork that I was "supposed to have" from New Zealand mentioned by Solicitor Morgan Ryan.

The sixty thousand dollars I was found with was held as "goods in custody," since I had indicated that I had brought the funds with me from Hong Kong, and that I would prove that fact to the court. Morgan said the funds would have to be returned to me if I could prove that I had withdrawn it from my account in Hong Kong.

Although this was not the case, I returned to Hong Kong and obtained the back-dated official sixty-thousand-dollar withdrawal slip I would need to redeem the funds from my good friends at Deak & Company—and that is exactly what happened.

Police inquiries directed to Deak & Company in Hong Kong produced the reply that I had withdrawn sixty thousand dollars from my own agency account with Deak before coming to Sydney.

On May 10, 1980, a police inquiry to Interpol in Washington produced the reply: "Subject is known to drug enforcement agency as a drug trafficker under particulars supplied."

The "goods in custody" charge against me was dismissed on June 4, 1980. According to the confidential report of the Stewart Royal Commission concerning the magistrate who heard the matter, "The magistrate did not accept the allegations of the prosecution that the money had been in Aitken's possession as a result of drug transactions, in the light of documentary evidence from Hong Kong as to the origin of the cash."

Ironically, after I was arrested, Dr. Ted, via his lady, Jinny, promptly posted my bail of ten thousand dollars, and I was released from custody just minutes before I was to be transferred to the notorious Long Bay Prison.

I had dreaded having to return to Sydney for that pending court date, and agonized that I had taken such risks knowing that it had become very hot in the kitchen.

Although I knew the outcome of my case before I left Hong Kong, having reliable information from Morgan that two thousand dollars would cover the "expenses," I realized my days in Australia, a country full of my friends, a country I had come to love, had come to an end.

Our conversation

There are times in life when although you see the approaching "tsunami," you cannot seem to get out of its way before disaster strikes. For me, it was as if a foolish, loud noise rang in my ears, and drowned out the whisper of common sense that was screaming, *"Danger!"* Against my better judgment, I did not heed the voice of reason that was speaking to me from within; more worldly considerations prevailed over common sense.

I recalled Morgan phoning me just before my departure for Sydney to attend the court case. The conversation was short and sweet, something like this: "Don't worry, Bruce, it is all done. After the decision, you'll be able to claim your money. Don't forget to bring the paperwork, and what was agreed."

I had a feeling, which later proved to be correct, that the phone call was being taped, and I said, "Thanks, Morgan, the truth always wins in the end!" and I promptly hung up.

My only recollection of the court proceedings in Sydney was the comment from the very old and frail clerk in the police evidence department who gave me back the funds. While scratching his head, the old man said:

"In all my years as custodian of evidence, over forty years in fact, this is the very first and only time that I have ever given back the money!"

Hallelujah!

CHAPTER 10
Enter "First Financial Services Ltd."

The laundry

During my sojourn in Guam, I had the pleasure of befriending a young fellow American, Tom O'Donnell. Tom was fit, of average height and build, light brown hair and confident blue eyes, twenty-five years old with a happy and outgoing personality. I liked him instantly. He was working for Bank of America, and was a sharp, fun-loving bachelor. He introduced me to Irene Cheng, a Chinese lady from Taiwan, who gave us each Mandarin lessons.

Over time, Tom went on to work as the representative of Philadelphia National Bank, living in Manila in the exclusive neighborhood of Forbes Park.

Although he seemed to have it made, he was not really the type who would work for just one company forever, and eventually he cast his fate to the wind and joined me as a partner in First Financial Services Ltd., also called "FFS," in Hong Kong. The excitement of the free market exchange business, magically moving money, the travel, the characters, were all enticing. The deal was done.

Guam produced another character who was to join us later.

Bill Thomasson was head of Guam Savings and Loan Association, but resigned from that position about the same time Tom and I were establishing FFS. Fatefully, we had a conversation one day and I confided in Bill, telling him about the nature of FFS business, how money was smuggled in and out of countries by the millions on a daily basis in suitcases, *in golf bags,* by amazing sleight of hand, out-smarting customs officers and reporting requirements.

Being a straight-arrow type, I expected Bill to be shocked. But I was the one who was surprised.

"What a great business," he said. "Amazing! Like taking candy from babies! When can I start?"

Bill was six feet tall, sported horn-rimmed glasses and was prematurely gray – a distinguished looking gentlemen. He was sociable, and had an executive air that resembled, let's say, a banker or a professor. Customs officers would always wave him through with little more than a nod or a wink.

How it all began…

In the fall of 1980, *Mark Tier's World Money Analyst* organized a seminar. *Mark Tier's* was one of the first investment newsletters to be published touting precious metals and privacy.

I had just finished giving a talk when Tom and I were approached by an American attorney named Ed Seltzer. Ed told me he had listened with great interest to my speech entitled, "Hong Kong and Your Financial Privacy." This speech was, in fact, a remarkable prophecy regarding the loss of future personal financial privacy, the extent of which I could not foresee at the time.

"Bruce," he said, "Can you help my client? He wants to buy gold here in Hong Kong, but the problem is his funds are in cash, and in Australian dollars in Australia."

"What's the problem, Mr. Seltzer? This is Hong Kong." Ed always wore a business suit with a light-blue shirt and dark-blue tie. About five feet nine inches tall, he was a typical lawyer whose tired face and droopy eyes made him look as if he never slept.

"The big problem is that the funds are in Sydney, and impossible to deposit into the bank or remit out without the government looking at it." *So much for privacy.* "You know how damn tough those Reserve Bank exchange controls are."

"Well, Ed, you have come to the right place. This is not a problem that we cannot solve—that is, for a fee of five percent."

He smiled broadly, "That's a deal!"

Presto! First Financial Services was about to do its first deal and launch into the shadowy world of international money laundering. Blocked funds in Australia, to my mind, were a piece of cake. Yes, exactly like taking candy from a baby. Little did I know that almost eight years later, Ed Seltzer would play a very important role in a huge money laundering disaster.

From my early days in Vietnam, to the days I worked for Deak & Company, to the establishment of FFS, money laundering seemed to be my fate—my destiny, of sorts. Was my "career" always to be based on laundering money? I made a good living at it, and no one got hurt. If that were not enough, the people in this business had higher integrity and morality, ethics, than any businessman, banker, or lawyer I ever met. So, in spite of a slight cringe of conscience, my rationalizations were easily made.

Our first transaction with Ed was done just after the seminar. Initially, Tom met with Ed and was very excited about our first deal. Ed had arranged for A$ two hundred thousand to be in Hong Kong, and we bought it at a good rate, including our special two-percent handling fee. FFS was off to a flying start and thinking about the wonders of Hong Kong.

Over the years with Deak, I had come to know the heads of the major banks' cash departments, and no one ever raised an eyebrow when I walked in with large amounts of cash to deposit.

Hang Seng Bank was my favorite. Calling Rex Young, the head cashier, either in advance or just showing up, I was given the V.I.P. red-carpet treatment, and treated to a nice cup of coffee in the lounge while the money was counted in the presence of my accountant, "Y.C." Ah, the good life! How America has changed the world; today, Hang Seng Bank, or any bank for that matter, would instantly file a report to the police.

Thank you to the Fed

In addition to this, interest rates were sky high in the late '70s and early '80s and it was important to develop good banking relationships.

As beginner's luck would have it, out of the blue and by complete mistake, we received a credit from the USA to our newly opened FFS account at Hang Seng Bank. The Federal Reserve Bank of New York sent us one hundred thousand dollars, which I deposited at an interest rate of twenty percent.

I telexed the Fed immediately, and followed up again after thirty days, asking for instructions about how to apply. I didn't get a response for two years; then one day, they inquired. We gladly sent back the one hundred thousand and kept the interest. Off to a good start.

Good times were ahead dealing with carefree, good, non-violent people whose word was their bond, and whose handshake sealed a deal based on trust alone.

Love those Aussie dollars

It was not long before Ed referred one of his clients who had another nagging problem, having stashed away almost two million A dollars in safety deposit boxes in Singapore. He was scared as hell to try to exchange it there, and it was just sitting there collecting dust, instead of earning high interest.

Our modus operandi was the same as Deak & Company. If there was a deal, the golden rule of deals was to immediately say "Yes, no problem," and then figure out how the hell to do it. We offered the client two options.

One option was for him to bring the money to us, and we would buy it and charge the usual two percent for going to the bank, exposing ourselves instead of our client, depositing the money with no questions asked.

The second option was to give us the money in Singapore, then we would pay out the counter-value two days later, less our fee of five percent. Of course, this plan was based on our excellent contacts in Singapore who would launder the money without it ever leaving the country.

They chose option number two.

Tom, Bill and I said, "Okay, now that we have the deal, just how the hell are we going to do it?"

I did have good contacts in Singapore, especially with the Indian money changers, and one or two Chinese bankers, but I knew they would be expensive. We decided the simplest and only confidential way to proceed was to bring the money back to Hong Kong ourselves, in golf bags of course!

So, I traveled to Singapore with Jenny and our baby son, Matt, and stayed in the Shangri-La Hotel. Every day, for seven or eight days, I received A$ two hundred and fifty thousand from the client. Bill, "the Bull," loved to fly, so he would fly to Singapore, arrive late in the morning, then take the evening flight and the money back to Hong Kong.

The following morning, he would fly back to Singapore again, and we would repeat the process. Tom would meet him at night on arrival in Hong Kong, take the money and do the banking the next morning. By the time it was all over, Bill had flown to Singapore from Hong Kong, a four-hour flight each way back and forth, seven nights in a row.

Celebrating over dinner and champagne at the Mandarin Hotel back in Hong Kong, I felt life was so good. The best way to move money was the most obvious way.

We developed a simple new slogan: "Just move it."

Best friends, best clients

Even prior to my opening FFS, Tim introduced me to his good friend, "Brian," and over the years we three became best of friends, always living close to the edge and sometimes falling over it.

The Deak philosophy was, "Show me your money and no questions asked." As a result, it was inevitable that some of the money, sometimes all of it, was tainted. Although Rule #1 was "Know your client," if you could not satisfy this Rule, then you simply passed over it and followed your gut feeling before moving immediately to Rule #2 which was, "Don't ask, just do it."

Tim, from Cape Town, South Africa, stood six feet tall with a slim build, was always casually dressed, and wore a pleasant and carefree smile that matched his personality.

The master of hyperbole, Brink described Tim as a smuggler who had a large catamaran twin-hulled vessel that would slowly sail along, until, at the slightest sign of trouble, a switch would be flipped, revealing two jet engines; and, presto, the boat would become a hydrofoil to escape the authorities. Cool! Tim had a good chuckle some years later when I mentioned this to him.

"Brian," was to become a very special friend, indeed. I suppose you could describe him as the most generous, good-hearted person you could find on the planet. About six feet tall with light-brown hair and a pleasant gentle-but-firm disposition, he was an accomplished sailor and yachtsman, and was a class act. In addition, we had a lot in common, both being the same age and coming from New Jersey.

Brian grew up on Staten Island, about twenty miles from my home town. He had traveled across the world, married, and settled in Thailand, the "Land of Smiles." He spoke Thai like a native. If we had met earlier in New York instead of halfway round the world, it probably would have been at a peace rally in Greenwich Village during the Vietnam War.

Life was indeed good and only getting better. The only downside was quite a bit of decadence, good beer and liquor, and partying into the night.

Tim and Brian became First Financial Services' best clients.

The bread and butter business...

FFS had all the trappings of a normal and respectable business. We opened a nice little office in Central Hong Kong, on the fifteenth floor of the Connaught Centre. Jenny was my confidante and assistant, and her cousin, Patty, was our receptionist. Sisters Catherine and Maria were sent on trips on occasion to meet me or my brother, Jimmy. They would stay in the same hotel on the same floor, and babysit the cash until either Jim or I could fly it to Hong Kong.

The risk was always present, but I always prayed to God that the suitcase or golf bag would show up, and it always did. Over the many years, there was, in fact, only one incident where I thought the game was finally over.

In 1987, Maria met my brother, Jim, in San Francisco and was given a suitcase full of dollars to check in on the Cathay Pacific nonstop flight to Hong Kong. Maria arrived, but the suitcase, filled with a quarter of a million dollars, did not. We waited and waited for word from Cathay Pacific. In the meantime, the client was pressing me for his money, demanding it be sent by telegraphic transfer to his account.

I was so anxious and nervous that my arm muscles began twitching at random. I woke up during the night in a cold sweat. Then, three days later, Cathay Pacific called and informed Maria that the suitcase had been traveling around the world, but was finally in Hong Kong. We breathed a big sigh of relief and our confidence returned.

Maria went to the airport to collect the suitcase. She still had to pass it through customs, of course, and thank God, she was waved through without even a glance. There was nothing wrong with bringing any amount of money into Hong Kong, but it was best that no one ever knew about it.

The money was still in the bag.

The Philippines & FFS

As I mentioned, during my Guam sojourn the Philippines became one of my favorite countries. You always feel good arriving in Manila. The country's people blend a certain mixture of native big-hearted hospitality along with a big portion of Latin or Spanish fiesta, topped off with the legacy of years of American occupation—and almost everyone speaks English.

While working out of the Deak Guam office, I was introduced to our Manila agent, "Arthur". Arthur was well connected in banking and stock brokering circles; however, the backbone of his business was foreign exchange.

Clients and share buying customers were all the same—in need of dollars and needing them "offshore" in their Hong Kong accounts, rather than in the Philippines where they would be subject to high taxes. Nobody in the Philippines, it seemed, especially not the rich and well-to-do, wanted to pay taxes, and most of them did not.

More and more golf bags

One day in Manila, as I indicated earlier, but woth repeating, Arthur and Barry got an idea for a quick, new way to get the money to Hong Kong. This was the original initiation of the golf bag scheme.

There are eighteen or more golf courses in metro Manila alone. Basically, the golf bags would be filled with the money. Soon a system was up and running whereby a group of couriers, mostly American, Australian and Swiss, were flying to Hong Kong for the cost of the ticket and a couple of hundred dollars for expenses.

The golf bags were beautiful to behold—lined inside with black silk and a black plastic container. The story told, when he prepared the first bag for its trial run, he almost had a heart attack.

Arthur was standing right there next to the courier when he placed it on the conveyor belt, but just when the golf bag was passing through the X-ray, the technician was distracted by her colleague cracking a joke, and she wasn't even looking at the screen. Arthur had to go back and test it another time, and, of course, it passed.

Working with Arthur, within a month or two, we became so busy I had to rent a small flat near my office and stock it with rivets and tools to open the bags, take out the money, reseal the bags, and give them back to the couriers for the return trip to Manila. We were going to the airport every day, sometimes two or three times, to meet golf bags. We had found a steady line of work.

Upon ordering a nice supply of golf bags from Arthur, I soon found out that they worked equally well everywhere. Golf bags were going to England, to America, to Australia, everywhere, and they always worked like a charm. No one, and I mean no one, ever questioned the weight, which was probably up to ten kilos heavier than any normal golf bag, even after removing most of the clubs and shoes.

The Manila case and Arthur

We had a very good run, several years in fact; but all good things are said to come to an end.

We were operating during the Marcos era. Confidence in Manila was high. Some people loved Marcos because, however brutal and corrupt, he was a strong leader. The First Couple, Marcos and Imelda, were also glamorous, and the everyday people loved glamour. Of course, other people despised Marcos.

What was unique in the Philippines was that in spite of being poor, people seemed to be happy. The weather was good, and you could pick fruit right off the trees and eat it. Filipino families tend to be close and help each other, and the Filipino people were strong in their faith, thanks to the church. But corruption was also rampant, and spread like a disease. Salaries were so low that many government employees in positions of any authority, and most of the police, were corrupt.

It did not go unnoticed by the authorities that large volumes of cash were somehow being moved out of the country, but they didn't know how; no one could figure it out. They needed to take action, and they did. The military and Marcos' government intelligence, by paying informants, and even moving money themselves, were able to identify the six largest money movers and shakers in Manila. Five were Chinese syndicates from downtown Chinatown, and the sixth was my very good friend, Arthur.

Early one morning, the doorbell rang at Arthur's office. When he opened the door, he found himself suddenly confronted by three military policemen and a one-star general.

"Arthur, please, you must come with us. Our boss, General Fabian Ver, Marcos' head of the military, has some questions he wants to ask you; something to do with moving money. You wouldn't happen to know anything about that, would you?"

"Of course not!" Arthur replied, "Not me!"

To cut to the chase, what occurred thereafter was a shakedown of accusations and denials, all done in a somewhat congenial atmosphere. Arthur was told that it was time that the military took over the laundering of the money business, and all they wanted to know was how to do it. Until Arthur would tell them how he did it, he could stay under house arrest at Fort Bonifacio in Manila.

From that point on, our little business stopped. I was very concerned about Arthur, and after a couple of months was able to visit him and his wife, Baby.

"What happened?" I asked Arthur.

"No choice," he replied. "After a couple of weeks, General Ver sent for me again, and I told him the truth—how to move the money."

"Very good," the General said. "Thank you, Arthur. You will soon be released, and you can go home."

About three months later, Arthur was able to get a message to General Ver to ask him when he could go home. Seemingly shocked and surprised, General Ver said, "Arthur, my friend, are you still here?" He laughed heartily. "I will follow up on the paperwork. I thought you went home a long time ago!"

Who put the "H" in DHL?

Our local agent in Manila, Guy Coombs, was a kind and generous friend of mine for many years, and he was a colorful fellow in his own right. In appearance, he bore an uncanny resemblance to a large Buddha. Guy was in the military on Guam when he bumped into a character by the name of Larry Hillblom in a bar in Agana. The meeting was to change his life.

Attending law school at night, doing odd jobs and with no money, Larry was so poor he was forced to live rough, sleeping in his car. Whenever I feel sorry for myself, I think of what Larry was able to accomplish—rising out of the ashes.

Larry got a part-time job with a law firm in San Francisco that had a branch office in Honolulu. From time to time, important documents had to be urgently posted to Honolulu. One of the partners got the bright idea to fly Larry over and hand-deliver the documents to the office.

Well, after a couple of trips, it did not take Larry long to have an even brighter idea: send the documents on the plane as cargo, then send a multitude of documents with a courier, and charge a fee to them all. He convinced two friends to join him, and combining initials, they formed DHL. Larry was the "H" in DHL.

Soon he opened an office in San Francisco, then Hawaii, and then Guam, where he met Guy Coombs and asked him to open the DHL office in Manila. On the side, Guy became Deak's agent as well. With a stable of delivery boys on motorcycles already going around metro Manila, why not deliver pesos, too.

Larry was an eccentric fellow, if there ever was one. He was an introvert, and unusually shy until you got to know him. He came to be worth many millions, but he refused to wear a coat and tie, and hardly ever wore a proper shirt. With his six-foot height, ruddy complexion and skinny build, he seemed to have only one set of clothes: jeans and a faded white t-shirt. It was said that he was once not allowed to enter the boardroom at a DHL meeting in Seoul, because he was dressed like a slob. Larry cancelled the meeting and threatened to replace the board.

Larry also had a penchant for street food. DHL had a very nice executive dining room in the Manila office, and when Guy invited me there for lunch, I gladly accepted. Larry would go out and buy food in a plastic bag from the street, bring it back to the dining room and eat it.

The one thing he insisted on was sparing no expense for the girls. He had his own mama-san in Manila who would procure very young girls whom, *he always said,* had just reached the age of consent. Price was not an issue. The only requirement was that each and every girl had to be a virgin. Larry was terrified of getting AIDS.

Being an eccentric with an interest in vintage aircraft, sadly for him, this is the interest that did Larry in. It made me wonder; I mean, here was a guy with all the money in the world, and he died in a vintage seaplane crash. The accident happened May 21, 1995. His body was never found.

His untimely demise unfolded a most fascinating drama revolving around who would inherit his substantial estate.

In the end, DNA tests confirmed that four of the eight claimants to his estate were Hillblom's children. It was ultimately determined that a Vietnamese child, Lory Nguyen, two Filipino children, and a child from Palau, Larry Hillblom, Jr., were fathered by Hillblom.

In the final settlement, each of the four children received ninety million dollars, while the remaining two hundred forty million went to the Hillblom Foundation, which followed Larry's wishes and donated funds to the University of California for medical research.

Raoul in NYC, at the same time

I had a lot of time for one of the people at Deak-Perera—the head FX dealer, Raoul Del Cristo. Hailing from Cuba, Raoul ran a tight operation. Similar to Tony Pong in Hong Kong, he relished any time out of the office, entertaining clients and staff in luxury. Several nights a week were party time, and yet, miraculously, everyone was back in the office the next morning by 8:00 am sharp. You had to be sharp in this business.

Raoul understood the free market business well. If you asked him to undertake any task, the response was the same as Dirk Brink in Hong Kong, and later, my friend Rakesh Saxena in Hong Kong: "No problem!"

It became "no problem" for Saxena a couple of years later when he almost single-handedly caused the collapse of the Asian financial system by destroying Bangkok Bank of Commerce.

I often travelled to Bangkok during that time, and usually stopped by to see Rakesh and his lovely wife, Suvanna, at their house near the Ambassador Hotel. Rakesh would hold court nightly in the dining room with all kinds of high-flying financial wizards coming and going, consuming bottles of Johnny Walker Black Label and Throng Tip cigarettes.

In 1984, opportunities began to present themselves for me to transfer U.S. dollars from New York to Hong Kong, and, of course, the money was in cash. The first person I thought of to help was Raoul. I flew to New York that summer for the first of many "pickups" from my client who was staying at the New York Hilton. I remember it well, because the total amount of two hundred thousand US dollars was in one-hundred bundles of twenty-dollar bills. I had to leave the meeting to go buy a larger bag, so I could carry it all.

For Raoul, it was "no problem" to transfer the money to Hong Kong. The only problem was that it did not take a couple of days, or even a couple of weeks, as he promised. Two months later, after many calls and promises to send the balance, I had to fly back to America about another transaction in San Francisco, and decided to make a surprise visit to Raoul in NYC to see what the hell the problem was. I stayed in his office all day, until the balance was miraculously "discovered" in his account, and finally sent to mine. *No problem.*

Maybe it was a simple case of out of sight, out of mind?

Brother Jim

My brother, Jimmy, ten years my senior, had settled down in the family profession and had become a house painter. When he was growing up, he did some work for one of the local mafia guys, Mike Weido, who lived in our hometown. At age seventeen, he was driving stolen commodities around the area in his brand-new

Cadillac. It was a waste of time to finish high school, and there was no time for school, anyway.

When my money laundry business began to flourish, I brought Jim into my confidence because I needed a hand in America, amongst other things, to deal with Raoul on my behalf. He was in seventh heaven—painting houses, then taking a couple of days off to handle money. His wife, Louise, had a fit when she found out.

From time to time, I would stop by and leave a big suitcase full of cash in their apartment in Hasbrouck Heights, New Jersey, our hometown near the George Washington Bridge.

One day, Louise told Jim and I she did not believe us, and asked to see the money. Always careful with her budget as a good wife, she almost had a heart attack when we opened the big suitcase, and right in front of her was a couple hundred grand in cash.

It was a very big mistake.

She began having nightmares!

CHAPTER 11
Cowboys and Kiwis

Me mates!

I wish to take a slight diversion at this point in my story, because, as I was going there so often I came to love all my mates "down under"; so they deserve special mention. You had to pick up the vibes of both the country and the era. It was easy to love them. They naturally liked Americans, although, for some reason, they called a Yank a "septic tank" because it rhymed. Everyone had a nickname, which served as a convenient alias. And every character had a unique story.

Early "cowboys" in Australia were surfers and 1960's hippies who discovered the pleasures of smoking weed from surfing safaris and along the hippie trail which stretched from Kathmandu, Nepal, and Kabul, Afghanistan.

No gangsters or guns—only surfboards and Persian carpets.

Important trivia…

Hanging out with Aussies and Kiwis who lived in Thailand and the Philippines was a blast because they had interesting lives. Tony Douglas, Trevor (buried at sea), and the two "Gregs," one aka "Blondie" Timewell, and Patrick "Top Hat" Bowler, both kiwis, were all birds of a feather and flocked together in the same famous nightlife bar district called Patpong in Bangkok.

The Mississippi Queen, Roxy Bar, Pink Panther, and the Sugar Shack, were all bars owned by Aussies with Thai partners. Everyone was living on a puff of smoke, "Cloud 9," right under the nose of the DEA.   In a way, it reminded me of a similar, yet opposite situation that existed in Hong Kong. Just across the street from the U.S. Consulate on Garden Road was a building called the St. John's Building where the government agencies were all located in one place. There was a coffee shop conveniently located outside the lobby, and to observe the "who's who" of the U.S. government, all I had to do was sit there for a couple of days. This was local common knowledge.

Young Greg

I met a young Aussie bloke in Sydney, whose disarming smile and confident swagger immediately won me over.

"Young Greg" I shall call him, helped me out quite a few times, by holding cash until I could come get it and occasionally picking up cash from some of my clients while I was off in another country. Greg was clean cut, usually wearing blue jeans and a polo shirt that revealed a finely chiseled physique that was the result of many hours practicing martial arts.

When he moved to Hong Kong in the early '80s, we spent many afternoons at the gym and sipping good wine at Greg's flat. One day, one of his "mates" "turned" on one of his deals, and the police came knocking. Greg had been indicted in Australia, and they arrested him in Hong Kong where he would await his pending extradition. It was a sad time. I did not enjoy visits at Lai Chi Kok Correctional Institute in Kowloon.

Later, I found out that the police did not find his little stash of weed, affectionately known as "Bob Hope" or "dope" (Bugs Bunny was "money" and Oxford scholars were "dollars"), because the Chief Inspector plopped himself down on the sofa while the police searched the flat. Fortunately, they never looked under the cushion upon which the Chief Inspector had chosen to ensconce himself. Hallelujah!

Greg had been indicted because of the one weak link in the laundering and smuggling business: the snitch. It was simply amazing how many people would betray and roll over on their good friends.

Bob McGregor

Bob McGregor was a bespectacled chap about five feet eight inches tall and somewhat portly, with a contagious and friendly smile that spread from ear to ear, a very classy guy. With a brilliant mind and jovial personality, he had opened a commodity trading firm, Econotec Pty Ltd., distributing a daily worldwide message called *"Bob McGregor's Gold Alert!"* He was a commodity chartist genius, and after a couple of years of uncanny predictions calling the curves on gold, he had developed a huge following of paid subscribers who were making a fortune based on his advice.

On one occasion, Jenny and I flew to Sydney for a much-needed vacation, and spent two glorious weeks having fun. When I checked in with Bob after my holiday, he proudly showed me his trades. My account was up fifty grand. Life was so good I had to pinch myself.

I was indeed blessed to have known Mr. McGregor, one of the finest blokes I could have ever come across. Bob is one of those people who oozes integrity as well as humility—a stand-up guy in every respect, and he took no nonsense from anyone. Because of this, he attracted and was happy in the presence of all kinds of characters, from professional people to rascals.

Spider and the Duck

Others were the "Spider" or Surfin John", and the "Duck", Peter King. He had to be one of the finest people to ever grace the earth, and I was blessed to have him as a friend. We were all introduced by our mutual mate, Warren Magi, and had great times in Sydney and Hong Kong.

Warren orchestrated his own gold trading company called Mace Metals, and through sheer guts and brain power rose to joint venture with London's finest, Johnson Matheson, and AM/PM London gold fixing.

Peter was best known as the "Peking Duck." The nickname came from his name, and because he quacked like a duck. Peter spoke so fast, yet so quietly, that no one could understand a single word he said. The TGIF nights in Paddington with the Duck holding court were simply amazing.

I liked the Sydney social circles, for they were really classy with often lots of talk of horse trading and information floating around. Sometimes, who you know and what you hear, can make you a small fortune. Surrounded by a bevy of beautiful ladies spicing up the atmosphere, the tall and handsome Duck, a seasoned stockbroker, had his hands on more than just the pulse of money.

Whiskers

That's me! Aptly named by one of Greg's best mates, honest businessman Neil Hoffman, aka "Neil from Newcastle;" with my full beard, "Whiskers" fit me well. One day circa 2000, I decided to shave, and to my horror discovered I had another chin hiding beneath all those whiskers. That was the last time I did something that foolish.

Aussie style

Parties were the go.

On one trip in which Jenny joined me, we went to a great party on Shark Island in the middle of Sydney Harbor. It was a birthday party for a band—either John Paul Young or Rockwell T. James or Piggy Morgan—I can't remember which.

The party featured a barge with a piano played by Piggy, plus an organized cream-pie fight on the beach with all the girls in bikinis, the tops of which seemed to fall off effortlessly and at random.

I always had a blast going to Palm Beach on the Peninsula where another group of smugglers lived. I enjoyed the space, the beautiful drive over the Spit Bridge and driving up the coast to Avalon, Whale Beach.

The beat goes on!

The lifestyle of a professional money launderer does, of course, have huge risks and a serious side too. Paranoia must be avoided at all costs and you have to develop a sixth sense so you can "feel" whether any unduly nosey or inquisitive eyes are watching you, or listening to what you think are private conversations. You have to be alert to the presence of eyes and ears and noses that may have picked up your scent.

At times, I had to completely abandon a deal, because there was absolutely no way of depositing the cash into the ANZ Bank. Sometimes, it reeked with the musty mold smell of money that had just been removed from the ground in which it had been buried for a long time.

More characters than you can shake a stick at!

In this "noble" profession, characters seem to come out of the woodwork, and they range from the quiet to the bizarre.

"Mr. Paul Black," for example, was a good bloke, friendly, with a bit of class. Introduced by Cito, Paul was in deep shit circa the late '70s and early '80s. He had a small account with me.

One day we got word that he had been arrested in Malaysia concerning a big drug case, and we were horrified because the penalty there was death.

Several months went by when suddenly, one day, I received his call on my direct line. To my amazement, he had escaped from jail in Penang, and made his way to Bangkok where he was in a flea-bag hotel and flat-ass broke. I was practically on the next plane with his account balance in hand.

First Financial Services to the rescue!

Never a dull moment

The connection to Hong Kong and Thailand was always part of the scene; comfortable for smugglers and misfits trying to work the system.

Greg's good mate and mentor, Lionel Grant, was born in Tasmania and moved to mainland Australia after assaulting a local police sergeant with a fencing pole. He was a surfer and board maker who spent a year in Hawaii where he grew fond of the local weed.

Returning to Australia, Lionel began cultivating marijuana and became a major player in the distribution of the drug during the early '70s. He relocated to Thailand around 1975 with another Australian, Barry March. Lionel's bar, The Roxy, was famous as a meeting place for smugglers, local misfits and the *DEA*.

Manila Aussies, too

Kim Barnaby was an Aussie friend in Manila, and a rascal you could never forget. Having spent many hours at the bottom of the sea in a diving bell, when he did come up for air he was somewhere between man and animal. He was solid as a rock, and I loved Kim as a brother, but once on the "grog," anything could happen.

Like the time we were a party of eight in a Chinese restaurant eating a sumptuous meal, when Kim had had enough—cognac that is. He suddenly turned green and, without any warning, barfed spectacularly over all the food. Surrounding tables fled in horror.

On another occasion, in the Hong Kong America Club's main dining room, Kim became a bit too loud. Two elegantly dressed older Chinese ladies sat at the table next to us, and glared at Kim who was using foul language of every kind.

He turned toward them, and squinting through bleary, bloodshot eyes, tried desperately to focus, but he could not see. He rubbed his eyes and tried to focus again. After he blinked many times, his vision cleared, and then he asked slowly, with several seconds pause between each word, in a calm slur, "What...are...you...two...old, wrinkled, Chinese.......farts... looking...at!" They turned purple. I turned green.

We were asked to leave.

CHAPTER 12
Give that Man a Cigar! and More Untold Tales

Jim, my brother, and I relished every opportunity to smuggle a load of U.S. dollars back to Hong Kong in our respective Old Faithfuls. After one successful "double" trip, we were sipping shots of twenty-year-old Scotch whiskey at the Captain's Bar in the lobby of the Mandarin Hotel.

While observing Jim in some kind of ecstasy smoking his favorite *cohiba* Cuban cigar, I said, "Hey, Jim, the embargo of Cuba is really a load of bullshit, isn't it?" Jim nodded approval. "Let's smuggle in some harmless cigars!" Jim was ecstatic!

From that day on and over many years to come, the Old Faithfuls never returned to America empty. We filled them with dozens of the finest Cuban cigars, pre-sold to waiting friends in New York City. This enabled us to cover the expense of the trips and make a handsome profit.

It marked a major improvement in the former method of smuggling Cuban cigars by switching Philippine-made cigars for Cuban cigars packed in Philippine cigar boxes. We did not do it for the money; we did it for the fun.

The Captain's Bar was the location of a brief encounter that I shall never forget. Staggering out of the bar one night in a stupor, I literally bumped into two of the most famous people in the world.

There we were, just the three of us—the two of them and me, standing alone in the front of the Mandarin. My jaw dropped, and I blinked several times. I could only think to say, "Uh, hello, good evening." She gave me a broad smile. He gave me a glance of understanding annoyance. A limo pulled up, they got in, and I waved good-bye to John Lennon and Yoko Ono.

Orlando security, oh no!

My elder sister, Honey, always had a nose for smelling money, and was curious about what was in the stuffed Compass Travel bag I sometimes left in a corner of the condo I had bought for my mom. On one trip, she almost found out. I had about a hundred thousand dollars in the bag, in twenty-dollar notes, money collected in California and taken with me to Orlando, then New York.

I had decided to hand-carry the bag instead of checking it. It was a gigantic mistake that practically ruined me!

Honey drove me to the airport, and lovely little Mom, with her beautiful white hair, came along for the ride. Mom was chatting with the lady at the conveyor belt as the bag went through the X-ray. The lady looked at it and froze. "This is very dense," she said, "I cannot tell what it is. Please open it for me." Just then, my mom gave her a big smile, as I said,

"Sure, it is only brochures for a conference, and they are all wrapped."

"Brochures?" asked Honey.

"Yes, that's right," I said, "Travel brochures from Compass Travel." I stared hard at her, pretty sure I had, *Don't ask me to show you,* flashing across my eyes.

To my relief, the lady looked at my mom, smiled and said, "Oh, that is okay then, have a good day." At that moment, I said a silent prayer. I had taken a big risk, foolishly pressing my luck again.

Another memorable trip involved our mom's eightieth birthday celebration, July 14, 1983. Our mom's lifelong dream was to see Hawaii, so my sisters in Orlando put Mom on a flight to Los Angeles, where she was met by Jim (who happened to have three hundred thousand dollars in large notes checked in for the flight to Honolulu). I had arrived in Honolulu the day before with my family, and we were booked for several days at the Honolulu Hilton off Diamond Head. July 14th, 1983, was one beautiful birthday for our mom.

I really wanted to stay longer, but the money in the golf bag was burning a hole in it, and I had to get it to Hong Kong as soon as possible. Jim took our mom to a show in Waikiki, and we said our farewells as I rushed to catch the daily nonstop flight on Singapore Airlines, with Old Faithful securely checked in as baggage.

The $6,000,000 ride

In the laundry, there was hardly ever a dull moment.

On one occasion, a large deal presented itself from Jimmy, in Hawaii. Through his syndicate, a stash had arrived in California and had been turned into cash, to the tune of US six million dollars that had to be moved. At that time, we had discontinued making deposits (and sending cigars) to the Chartered Bank of London account.

The dollars had to somehow be moved from San Diego to Toronto, and plans were set in motion. In Toronto, we had a nice system through a friend's company into which cash could be deposited since there was no reporting in Canada. *Canada was civilized.*

Because it was Mother's Day, I was in Florida visiting my mom, and taking in the annual Bermuda investment conference sponsored by *The Bank Credit Analyst* of Montreal. Norm Ornstein was another attendee I knew from a previous conference. He later headed a Washington think-tank called the American Enterprise Institute.

I waited a couple of days for a phone call indicating the money had been moved to the expected starting point in Winnipeg. The call came, we were good to go. I had an open ticket, and the next day found myself happily flying from hot and sunny Orlando to pleasantly cold and beautiful Winnipeg.

The money had been faithfully transported by one of our good mates, Daryl, who had made some excellent connections and good friends in North America. He transported it without a hitch through the Indian reservation on the USA-Canada border. God bless the real American Indians.

'Hawaii' Jimmy and I hired a van and made the long drive, cautiously creeping closer to Toronto. I was enjoying the scenery while always keeping my eyes out for police or radar speed traps. For several days we were conservative as hell with our driving, stopping every few hours for coffee and a stretch. We checked into motels on the freeway for two or maybe three nights.

Jimmy was driving the last leg. Having been to Toronto many times, I was looking at the map, trying to get our bearings. Suddenly, coming over a big hill, we saw the skyline of Toronto. *Hallelujah!* Thank God we made it

Upon arrival, we both breathed a big sigh of relief. Within a matter of a couple of days, the money would be *cleaned* and transferred to Hong Kong.

Nonstop from Honolulu

In 1986, I had another close call.

I was looking forward to getting back to Hong Kong with four hundred thousand dollars in cash safely secured in my smuggling device of choice. Waiting to board the SQ flight from San Francisco, I called Jimmy in Honolulu. Since he was a night owl, and since my flight arrived in Honolulu just before midnight, *and* I had a two-hour layover, we agreed to meet.

Since it was a domestic flight, all I had to do was walk out of the airport and re-board in time for the departure to Hong Kong. With my briefcase, boarding pass and passport in hand, it was pleasant to stroll out into the beautiful Hawaiian night, smell the flowers, and be met by Jimmy in his convertible Mercedes. Off we went.

First thing Jimmy offered me was a spliff that we gladly shared, with one eye on the highway and one eye on the clock. "Maui Wowie" is very strong shit! We smoked another one. When I think of it now, that was such a stupid thing to do. Of course, Jimmy did not know I had checked a golf bag full of money. Anything could have happened, and it almost did.

We headed back to Honolulu airport. Without paying much attention to exactly where we were, we parked the car and walked up to the boarding gate together.

Then, a big sign caught our attention:

"WARNING! ARE YOU CARRYING OVER US $5,000 IN CASH?"

Blah, blah, blah. . . "It is an offense unless you report it under U.S. Treasury Regulations. Failure to do so will result in confiscation, fine and imprisonment, or both."

We both found this rather amusing, and started to grin too broadly while staring at the sign...*for a little too long.*

There was a man standing a few meters to the left who was equally interested, but staring at *us.*

As I approached the counter with my boarding pass and passport, he rushed forward. He was a typical government nerd who looked at me with venom in his eyes. Flashing a U.S. Treasury ID and Customs ID, he demanded to know if I was carrying over five thousand dollars, and that I open my briefcase. His eyes were as cold as steel.

I became instantly sober and turned to Jimmy with a wave saying, "Thanks for the beer, see you next year when I return to America, or better still if you come to Hong Kong."

The agent fumed when he found nothing special in my briefcase. I calmly stared at him, but my heart was racing. The agent reluctantly returned my briefcase to me, and I breathed a huge sigh of relief when we began to board. It was foolish. He took my name and passport details. He apparently was not willing to hold up the plane or take me and my luggage off the plane—thank God.

I would have to be more careful in the future, much more careful. But not quite yet.....

San Francisco Airport sometime in 1985, or was it '86?

It had been a great trip to America and I was feeling pretty good. I had stopped in San Francisco to visit a friend, and a real character at that. He was an American lawyer named Creighton Churchill, and he said he was a distant relative of "Winston" himself. Creighton always had some kind of a project going on that required funding, and we were looking at doing some business.

We always enjoyed going out to restaurants for dinner, and this time we went to an Italian beauty downtown.

I don't know what the distraction was, but for some reason, the next day I was bored, and decided to go to the airport to check in the "loaded" golf bag a few hours early, and spend a couple of hours at the bar. As always, I watched out of the corner of my eye as the golf bag disappeared into the belly of the cargo system.

After a beer or two, I switched to scotch, and with an hour to go before boarding, I was beginning to feel just fine. Before I knew it, an attractive young lady took a seat at the bar near me. We started a friendly conversation.

For the most part, she was an American Indian and very spiritual in her outlook. She looked me in the eyes and said my eyes were bright and clear, that I must be a good person, and to call her the next time I came to America. It was just conversation, until she mentioned she had a couple of joints with her and we should go outside and have a smoke. By that time, I could hardly say no. Off we went.

Returning to the bar, she offered me a pill she said would help me sleep on the trip back home. I told her I wasn't a pill dropper, so she explained it was a "Quaalude."

"Oh yes," I said. "I have heard of them, but never tried any."

With my judgment thoroughly impaired, I took one. What happened next was amazing.

I bid her thanks and good-bye, grateful as I was that she had chosen, so graciously, to spend her time with me. I suddenly found myself looking for the plane, as an announcement blared that boarding was commencing. I began to feel extremely drowsy. I could hardly move! Actually, I could barely keep my eyes open.

I found the plane, thank God. *Where is my seat?* I fought to keep my eyes open and function normally, until I could find my seat, fasten my seat belt and close my eyes. I made it. I was in Singapore Airlines business class on an aisle seat. I wished the nice lady sitting next to me in the window seat a pleasant flight.

Suddenly to my amazement, I woke up with a bit of a start as the plane experienced a hard landing in Honolulu. The lady next to me looked at me in shock and I could see she looked quite worried.

"Young man," she said, "I have never seen anyone sleep so soundly as you!" The stewardess agreed. I apologized for snoring, had I done so.

To my amazement, the plane had already taken off from San Francisco when the pilot had detected a small electrical fault and decided to return to San Francisco Airport for a part replacement. It had taken an hour. Then we had taken off for Honolulu again, and flown all the way without further problems. I, meanwhile, slept soundly throughout the whole experience, completely oblivious to what was going on around me.

I was to find out later that my guardian angel must have been with me, because mixing that little pill with alcohol (in my ignorance) was a potentially lethal combination, one from which many people have never awakened. I may have been very close to never making it home; and for sure, I realized that there must have been some serious underlying psychological reasons that had caused me to take such risks in the first place.

This *illegal* money moving business was taking a serious toll on my brain and on my spirit. Waiting at the luggage carosel at Kai Tak Airport in Hong Kong ten hours later, I shuttered to think that I almost did not make it, and envisioned my 'fully loaded with cash", Old Faithful, going around and around without me. Deep in prayer, I waited to collect it.

Never trust anyone from India

Dirk Brink's wisdom about getting behind an Indian when clearing customs worked so well that in places like Seoul, we would bring along one of our good Indian friends, a "token Indian" from Hong Kong, to create the diversion.

Truth is, we did a lot of business with very trusted and excellent Indian friends and partners in Korea and in Kenya and in Nigeria, via the Shahs and the Melwanis. But in Hong Kong, Brink said to never trust an Indian if he does not know how to wag his head when bargaining with you. Head-wagging was Brink's litmus test.

One day there was big trouble with a transaction done through an agent in Kowloon, a Mr. Patel. He was referred to me as someone who could reliably make payments in rupees in Bombay. Always looking for a new source, I told him I would keep his services in mind.

One day, an English gentleman arrived in my office and said he was referred by Howard Marks, aka *Mr. Nice*, and needed some funds in Bombay in rupees as soon as possible. Contacting Patel, I asked if he could handle a payment of approximately US one hundred thousand equivalent.

The client gave me the cash plus my fee, and flew off to Bombay. I gave Patel the instructions concerning who to pay and which hotel to use, and was assured it would be done the next day. Although I was a very trusting soul, and Patel was highly referred, I did, of course, check him out, making the effort before we did any business to visit his office in Kowloon and test all his contact numbers.

The next day came and went. I happened to be busy with my brother Jim arriving in Hong Kong with a loaded golf bag, and I had almost forgotten about the Bombay payment. Jim and I were leaving the next day to go to Macau, and I was really looking forward to the break; my nerves were becoming shattered. I felt at times, with two or more deals happening simultaneously, that I was heading for a big disaster.

Then it happened.

Jim arrived late that night and we dropped the golf bag at my office where it would be safe to process the next morning. The message light on my phone indicated over ten messages, and I wondered who the hell it could be. It was Bombay calling. The client had been sitting next to the phone the whole day waiting for a phone call that did not come. I was livid! Although late, I called Patel and left a message on his office phone, and called him at home as well. He did not pick up; I did not sleep well that night.

The following morning, I followed up again after apologizing to the client and assuring him all would be well. Patel finally arrived at his office just before noon. He apologized, but I sensed that he was stalling. Jim and I were booked on the 6:00 pm hydrofoil to Macau. I called Patel back every hour and felt I was getting the royal run-around.

Decision time.

"Jim," I said, "let's go to Patel's office right now and sit there until the payment is made. You pretend to be the client's partner, a Mafioso from New York, the tough guy."

Jim said with relish, "I can do that!"

In thirty minutes we were sitting in front of Patel. We totally surprised him. I don't think he noticed the resemblance. My brother just sat there and stared at him. Jim only said four words, "I'm from New York." It was enough. Patel got his agent in Bombay and my client in the hotel on the phone.

Within twenty minutes the agent arrived at the hotel, the payment was made, and Jim and I made it to the hydrofoil, and to Macau with time to spare.

Time for a sail

I was in desperate need of a break. Most Aussie golf-bag couriers like Graham Shields and Kim Barnaby were "yachties." To chill out, I joined Graham on a yacht delivery from Hong Kong to Sydney, meeting him on the boat in the Philippines at Surigao Del Sur, Mindenao, for the six-hundred-mile sail across the Philippine Sea to Palau, Western Carolina Islands.

Relishing the new experience and the beauty of the wide-open ocean, we did not check the weather carefully, and on the third day out, ran smack into a major typhoon. With thirty-foot waves, our pleasant journey quickly turned into a giant roller-coaster ride.

I found out later that Graham was very worried we were not going to make it. Navigating only by sextant, in heavy clouds and nothing to get a fix on, with no SAT NAV, we miraculously found the directional signal emitted by the Palau Airport beacon located on Koror.

The harbor master and customs (U.S. Trust Territory) could not believe their eyes when we sailed in through the storm on our thirty-footer, and in record time at that. They were naturally suspicious. In our ignorance, we had not applied for a permit. There was another yacht in the harbor, confiscated for arms smuggling.

Fortunately, by a stroke of good luck, I happened to personally know one of Palau's legislators, a fine man named Kaleb Udui, a Palauan attorney whom I met in Saipan years before when I worked on Guam. After speaking with him on the phone, the authorities rolled out the red carpet.

It was great to be back on land, and Palau was one of the most beautiful places on the planet. Most folks worked for the government.

Palau was renowned for growing some of the best "weed." Thus, we spent a pleasant few days lounging around with the locals, until it was time to bid farewell. Graham had to continue the sail to Australia. Our new local Palauan friends gave him a big bag of weed to tide him over on the long sail to Sydney. For me, it meant taking the Continental Air Micronesia "Island Hopper" back to Manila, and getting back to Hong Kong.

Although my profession was sometimes enormously stressful, and certainly destroyed millions of my limited supply of brain cells, my blind faith, coupled with a happy-go-lucky life style, insured that these were primarily very happy days.

CHAPTER 13
M.I.T. Financial Services

A partnership that starts in good faith but ends up in a vicious rivalry can be compared to a marriage and a divorce. I often wondered, lamented, how something like First Financial Services Ltd., which started with so much joy and enthusiasm, could succumb to the same sad fate.

Tom O'Donnell and I had been the best of friends, but when Bill Thomasson joined the partnership, circa 1983 the chemistry changed. While still partners, I happened to come upon the knowledge that Tom had opened another company for himself, M.I.T. Financial Services, and did it with my trusted auditor of many years—Armando Chung.

One day Tom and I had a heart-to-heart talk and Tom, frankly and in a matter-of-fact way, told me he was moving on. We were just about to open a commodity futures trading division. Tom later did this on his own and did very well. We both kept close tabs on trades and trading techniques, charting with our friend, Rakesh Saxena, although I myself had my hands full just looking after the money moving business.

Bill Thomasson also moved on. It seemed I could not satisfy his demands for bigger and bigger slices of the profit-sharing. I was on my own.

The hardest lesson I learned from my experiences was that in business, you really do not have many friends.

After Tom's departure, I noticed a sudden sharp decline in my money-moving business as a whole. From the Philippines to Australia, it began to evaporate before my eyes. An added shocker was finding out that several of my long-time trusted agents and clients had actually traveled to Hong Kong specifically to meet with Tom, and returned home without even calling me.

When I found that out, I asked Arthur in Manila and Ben Garcia in Sydney what the hell was going on.

"Bruce," they said, "business is business, and you taught Tom well and he learned well. He is offering your same services at a big discount." I should not have been so shocked, but being trusting and naïve, I was, in fact, stunned. No loyalty after so many years?

Outwardly, I shrugged it off. Tongue in cheek, I wished everyone good luck. I licked my wounds.

Little did I realize at the time, however, that Tom's moving on would turn out to be a blessing in disguise. Tom soon got involved with some nasty characters; specifically, one really quite despicable individual named Jack Corman. As a consequence of handling Jack's investments and laundering his money, M.I.T.'s office, unbeknownst to me, was raided by *INTERPOL* in 1985. Jack, it seemed, was not only a client but also a DEA *super-snitch*!

Over the next couple of years, I moved on with a handful of trusted friends like Brian, Tim Milner, and Robert Kimball (aka "Todd" aka "Nicholas Hardcastle") all of whom were real friends who would not think of jumping ship.

Tom O'Donnell prospered, having also taken with him his good friend, Mike Brennan, whom we had flown from California at Tom's request and given a job.

What happened two years later, however, was so shocking and heart-breaking that I cried. It can be summed up in the note written by a DEA agent just after the October 1987 stock market meltdown:

"Former First Financial partner, Tom O'Donnell, who started his own firm, MIT Financial Management, lost millions in the 1987 Stock Market crash, and who was also under a sealed indictment in Washington DC for money laundering, committed suicide in his Manila hotel room. He was set up by informant, Jack Corman, who

later was working together with another informant, Phil Christenson [sic]."

I was in London at the time I heard of Tom's apparent suicide. I had flown in from Canada after attending an investment conference in Quebec City, and was looking forward to dinner at the home of Sal Petrancosta and family. Sal was a dear friend, a financial analyst formerly based in Hong Kong.

On that traumatic day, a rare hurricane hit London and the taxi I was traveling in slammed into a tree on the way to Sal's apartment in Lexington. My guardian angels must have been trying to warn me.

My only thought was that if Tom had come to me with his problems, financial or otherwise, I would have welcomed the opportunity to bury the hatchet and start over again. The person who bears a grudge is the one who suffers.

I had fortunately avoided the stock market; I had plenty of liquidity and Tom was a very good commodities trader. We could have managed the clients' losses and rebuilt the company.

What I did not know at that time was that Tom had been indicted.

Thank you, Mike Brennan - Fast forward to early May of 1988

Fate's chance meetings seem to call the unexpected shots in life.

My wife Jenny and I rarely went out late at night; however, one night we joined some young folks visiting Hong Kong, friends of friends from Florida. We had a few nightcaps at a disco in the nightlife haven called Lan Kwai Fong. It was nearly 2:00 am, and I was very tired.

Just as I was motioning to Jenny that we should be going, I looked across the club. It was very dark, but in the flashing of the strobe lights on the mirrors, I spotted the reflection of Mike

Brennan. Mike, who could have been Dustin Hoffman's twin, was normally happy go lucky, but his face was ashen.

"Mike," I said pleasantly enough, "how the hell are you?"

Before he had time to answer, I added, "I am just leaving, but let me buy you one for the road."

In a state of surprise at having bumped into each other, we shared a drink and spoke of Tom and how badly he was missed. Then Mike, drunk, dropped the bombshell.

"Bruce," he said, "Do you know a fellow living in Bangkok by the name of Jack Corman?"

"Sure I do," I said, "and to tell you the truth I don't like him one bit. Why?"

"Why? Because he is *DEA,* and he set Tom up! Tom had been indicted in a big money laundering case in Washington, D.C. Corman had an account with MIT and lost a lot of money in the crash. But never mind that. He was setting Tom up the whole time. That can be the only reason Tom committed suicide; he was aware that he was going to be indicted, and because of the sentencing guidelines, he knew he would be sent to prison for a long time. He could not face it." Then he paused and added, "It wasn't suicide." Then he told me that Corman's actions had caused Tom to have a heart attack.

I said, "Thank you very much, Mike." But I wondered something else: *Was it murder?*

I must have been as pale as a ghost as I thought of the several times I had met Corman, the times he had come to my office, first introduced by Andy Rogers, a Bangkok based art dealer and client of mine, and the fact that I knew my good friend Brian was right now, at this very moment in early May, 1988, very deeply involved in some kind of a big deal with him.

I hoped and prayed that rumors about Corman were not true because, with a flash of horror, and a biting chill that ran down my spine, I recalled Corman forcing my staff to take a half million cash deposit at my office just before Easter weekend that past March, for transfer to Brian. More about this later.

All I could think of was that I needed to tell Brian immediately.

The case against Tom . . .

I would later read about the case against Tom from part of a sworn government affidavit against other defendants in his case.

It read in part:

*"In this case the evidence against the defendant is very strong and includes the testimony of **two confidential informants** (Christensen and Corman) who were initially planted at the Thailand end of the operation.*

Throughout late 1983 and 1984, the defendant made several trips to Thailand and Hong Kong to arrange the importation of twenty to forty tons of marijuana. The informants told the defendant they would need two million dollars front money. The defendant told them the money should be laundered in Hong Kong through a money launderer, Tom O'Donnell, and over one million dollars was fronted.

In March 1987, the informants, who were now working for DEA, tape-recorded conversations in which the defendant discussed the shipment seized by the Coast Guard.

On May 12, 1987, Special Agent Ogilvie (DEA) was introduced to the defendant at a hotel room in San Francisco. A co-defendant counted out three hundred fifty thousand dollars cash that Special Agent Ogilvie was to take to Thailand.

Tom had learned to launder well and was doing a good job for informants Christensen and Corman as they set up various drug smugglers. And all this was happening while at the same time there were other active scandals simultaneously swirling around

END OF PART THREE

The Cleaner

Part Four

More Characters Than You Can Shake A Stick At"

The Cleaner

CHAPTER 14
Nicholas Hardcastle

"Nicholas Hardcastle" was a good friend and former student at Stanford University. He was a brilliant thinker who, like another close friend and client, Howard Marks, had chosen smuggling as the most rewarding and direct way to riches and happiness. However, after Nicholas' arrest and conviction in Bangkok on a smuggling charge, he was sentenced to forty-five years in prison.

Only a miracle would save him.

Sometime around the mid to late '70s, when I was still an employee of Deak & Company, I met Nicholas.

"Nick" was introduced by our mutual friend, Bruce Miller, who was a client of Deak & Company in Hong Kong.

Bruce was living in Nepal and Bangkok, and traveled around the surrounding countries dealing in art or whatever he could find to turn a quid. He was the kind of person you were always pleased to see in town, and who always had something going on. He had a sharp mind and a sharp wit. What we all had in common was that we left America for greener pastures and never looked back.

I always enjoyed visiting Bruce's house when I was in Bangkok, especially with Jenny and our sons. The house was like an art gallery wrapped around a fish pond next to the living room.

One day my son Doug, then about four years old, reached in to try to catch a fish, and lost his balance. We heard the big splash, and all had a laugh, especially Doug who, dripping wet, goldfish slipping out of hands, found it quite hilarious.

When I became a free agent, I had more time on my hands and was able to get to know what business everyone was really in. This consisted basically of two groups: the dope dealers who smuggled pot, and the art dealers who smuggled art, normally valuable antique "tankas" from Tibet, by sewing it into their winter jackets.

Both groups smoked a lot of pot, and I assumed that is how they overlapped. Both needed to move money back and forth, and both needed ways to do so without going through the bank.

The best dealers in the black market in Thailand for baht were Deak's agent, ATB Finance in Hong Kong, the subsidiary of Asia Trust Bank in Bangkok, headed by its flexible and very likeable Chairman, Mr. Waloob Tarnvernichol; as well as a delightful lady named Kun Nathaya who had a money exchange and an antique shop near the Ambassador Hotel called Vasu Carving.

The black market in currencies, the desire to change Thai baht into US$, was something that was pretty well accepted, and as long as you could maintain an account in baht and the other account offshore, preferably in Hong Kong, then why not?

It's the same as in India, Pakistan, the Philippines, Singapore, and the Middle East, where it is known as "hundi." Hundi was no more than a swap, nothing more, nothing less, and often done within the same family. Money was transferred based on trust, and without any records.

Visiting Bruce in Nepal or Thailand, or Nick in Bangkok, was always a pleasure. Before figuring out what to do for the day, it was best to start off with a couple of strong "cups of mud" and half a dozen reefers. Hashish mixed with tobacco worked well in the mornings, and evolved into Thai Buddha by late afternoon. Or, was it vice versa? *Ah, the good life!*

Party on!

I had been visiting Bangkok quite often at that time, and on one occasion I remember in particular, there was a big party going on at Nick's house near Soi Pahoenyitin. Thai houses with their big gardens were such a pleasant change from urban Hong Kong. I loved them! (In Thai houses, you always remove your shoes before entering the house, which is such a civilized custom.)

On this occasion I had brought along two bottles of Glenfiddich Scotch and I was feeling no pain—that is until the next morning when I had to wake up and tried to catch the plane back to Hong Kong. I had one hell of a ferocious hangover and swore off scotch from that day forward. I decided to move on to "XO" cognac.

Chugging down cold water the next morning, I bid farewell to everyone with the parting words that we would soon meet again in Hong Kong and would carry on from there.

I was halfway to Hong Kong when I looked down and noticed that I was wearing someone else's shoes. Out of the dozen or so sets of shoes on Nick's front porch, I had picked up the wrong pair; mine had been brand new and these were very old. Stupid.

But hey, all's well that ends well. When Bruce arrived in Hong Kong a couple of days later, we looked down and discovered we were wearing each other's shoes. What goes around does come around.

Baht chains

I was experiencing a slow-down in my business at the same time Bruce Miller was looking for a way to cover his expenses. He was a clever man, and observed that you could buy gold bullion five percent cheaper in Bangkok in bullion baht chains, as compared to buying in Hong Kong. If you could absorb the exchange difference from dollars to baht, then back to dollars, you could make a tidy profit.

How to do the deal? I could not resist the temptation. The art of the scam itself was becoming irrestible.

Fly from Hong Kong to Bangkok, buy the gold bullion chains, and then fly back to Hong Kong and sell them, all the while hoping and praying the gold price would go up that day.

After a little checking around and a trip to the Bank of Thailand for a chat, one immediate problem was solved; it was not legal to take gold bullion out of Thailand, but it was perfectly legal to take bullion baht chains, because this was considered to be jewelry, not bullion.

One simply bought the chains and then brought the receipt to the bank and filled out a form—I believe it was called an "EC 63" at the time. After waiting a couple of hours, presto, you would be handed the Export Permit. Both forms were necessary, and both had to be presented to Thai customs upon departure. We had found an excellent little money earner and it was completely legal.

Armed with the paperwork, and holding a travel bag loaded with gold chains, we confidently approached customs at the airport. We arrived a bit early in case it took extra time. Customs was shocked! "What is this? You cannot export gold bullion without paying a big tax!"

"But this is not bullion. It is jewelry and perfectly legal. Here is the paperwork."

Well, the paperwork won out, to the amazement of us all, including the customs agent. Apparently, this had never been done before. Since we were able to make a tidy three percent and were quite broke, we decided that we should repeat the process every week. After a dozen trips in the span of a few months, however, they changed the rules; they imposed a limit on the number of chains we could take at one time, temporarily destroying our little business.

We looked for solutions to get around the little legal obstacle, and Bruce came up with the answer.

Bruce approached a goldsmith and placed an order. Could the goldsmith make chains for us? "Sure, no problem," was the reply. Bruce said he would never forget the expression of amazement on the customs agent's face when he showed up for what was to be the last and final transport.

"What the hell is that?" the agent asked as he stared at what was probably the biggest Thai baht gold chain ever made! The thing must have weighed a kilo! Wearing it around your neck for any significant period of time would have possibly resulted in a permanent and painful spinal injury or worse.

In a bit of a state of shock, and with no sense of humor, customs did not think it was funny. They flatly told us we better not ever try that trick again!

Game over.

Nicholas is? Robert is?

A book could be written about Nick, aka Robert Kimball , aka Robert Bland, and I sincerely hope he will write one. Nick and Robert, so it is not confusing, are one in the same. As for me, I can say that he is one of the most decent, intelligent and humble people I have ever had the pleasure to know. Both bright and kind-hearted, he did, however, live life on the edge and seemed to thrive under stress and great pressure. At first, I did not know what was causing the stress, but I soon found out.

Rumors from mutual friends connected Robert to Thai marijuana smuggling. Specifically, transporting to America and England, and transported by the quickest of means—air freight. Personally, I had no interest in knowing the truth, except I often felt that while visiting Bangkok, I should stay at a hotel rather than at his nice Thai house.

Then it happened.

Thank God I was not in Bangkok on October 20, 1980, when the Thai National Police seized approximately three thousand two hundred kilos of marijuana and twenty kilos of hashish, and arrested eight people at Nick's residence.

The smuggling operation had come under scrutiny due to its size and sophistication, with the goods being flown from Northern Thailand by military aircraft to a base near Bangkok; and then flown by commercial aircraft to countries like America and Australia.

Amazingly, the Thai military and Thai customs were in on the deals. Organizing such a team was a master stroke of brilliance. The airway bills, for example, would show the origin of the goods as Bahrain or Hong Kong so as not to arouse suspicion at Bangkok customs.

About a year later, on October 20, 1981, Robert and his colleagues were convicted and sentenced. Robert got the longest sentence: forty-five years imprisonment.

Don't be late

There is a very big difference in the way things are done in some Asian prisons compared to the way they are done in America or Hong Kong. Light years apart, in fact. In Asia you can make "arrangements" for some luxury to enter your life. In America, all they want to do is punish you.

To give you an example, Robert, for a certain sum of baht, could "take the day off." With arms full of a ball and chain, he would sneak out of the notorious prison from time to time in one of the guard's cars, accompanied by three or four of the guards.

Visiting the house of a mutual friend, such as Bruce, he could enjoy the finer things in life: steak, champagne, a good smoke, and make a few long-distance calls to his father in New York.

But time flies and Bangkok's traffic is notorious. Roll call occurred at the prison every evening at 6:00 pm.

One day when he was "out," the clouds opened up and it started raining like hell. The streets became quickly flooded. Traffic came to a standstill. Panic set in. Driving on all sides of the road and sidewalks and in between, pushing anything and everything out of the way, I was told "Robert" arrived back at the prison for the evening line-up just in the "nick" of time, with less than five minutes to spare.

You can't keep a good man down

Upon learning of Robert's arrest, I was very worried and saddened. His phone had been tapped, and many Americans and people of all nationalities had probably stayed at his house without realizing the danger. To have been there on the wrong day and time would surely have been a nightmare come true.

Over the next year or two, I was able to visit him at Bang Kwang Maximum Security Prison in Bangkok. He was resilient to the core.

Pierre Hotel, Central Park

A year prior to his arrest, I had come to know that "Robert" was working through a group in New York that would collect money and hold it for him. However, he was not particularly keen to go to America to collect it; he asked if I could help. Never saying no, I agreed to make a lightning trip to New York City, meet his contact at the Pierre Hotel in Central Park, collect US two hundred and fifty thousand dollars and bring it back to Hong Kong.

"Could you do it over the weekend? It's an emergency," he asked.

"No sweat. For expenses and three percent, you have a deal my friend!" He never was the type to quibble over fees. "I'll depart Friday night and have the bread in your hands Monday night."

"Deal!"

I left Hong Kong the next Friday on board a JAL flight, stopping in Tokyo to connect with the nonstop to JFK Airport in NYC. I arrived the same day and checked into my hotel.

All of a sudden, stricken by the food I had eaten during the flight, I was so ill I wanted to die. I called the contact and made an appointment to go to the Pierre Hotel in the morning at eleven. But I was up all night, spent most of it sitting on the toilet with my head in the sink, puking up some kind of green bile. What a nightmare.

The next morning, I could feel every heartbeat in my head. I could barely move. Eleven o'clock was approaching. Looking pale as a ghost, I showered, put on a suit and took a taxi to the Pierre Hotel.

When the lift opened on the tenth floor, I was shocked. The doorman was standing there as if directing traffic. The lift operator gave me a good hard look and mumbled something like, "Here comes another one."

"Pete" opened the door to the suite, and I found myself in a room full of people dividing up boxes of money.

"Here you go, Bruce!" he said, as he tossed over a couple of bundles of banknotes. "This is for Robert. Give him my regards. By the way, there may be fifty thousand more coming. Where are you staying?"

I hesitated, and had a very bad feeling when I told him my hotel and room number. *Stupid mistake. I must be very sick*!

In ten minutes I was out of the place and heading back to my hotel with two hundred fifty thousand in large bills. Just as the lift door opened, one of Pete's associates, a rough looking character, jumped in unexpectedly and asked me if I needed any help.

"No thanks," I forcefully declined. Then, I lied. "I have all the help I need waiting outside."

He split.

Back at the room, feeling sick and paranoid as hell and imagining the worst, I checked the time on the digital clock in the room: 1:30 pm.. First things first. I immediately took the cash out of my Compass Travel bag and threw the bag away. Reaching for Old Faithful, I took it apart with the rivet wrench, packed in the money and sealed it tight. I was sweating profusely. *Done.* I felt relief—no worries now.

I confirmed my reservation to Hong Kong for the next morning, Sunday; the 9:00 am flight. Then I collapsed on the bed, holding my throbbing head and tried to sleep. The phone startled me awake. It was pitch dark in the room, and the clock read 11:30 pm.

"Hello," I answered.

"Hello. This is Pete's friend. Remember we met today at the hotel? I am here in your hotel, and I have something important to ask you. Can I come up?"

"Hell no!" I said. "Give me ten minutes, and I'll come down to the lobby," I replied quickly. I was still getting dressed when there was a loud knock on the door. I looked through the peephole and there he was, along with a young lady. He said it was better not to meet in the lobby as there were so many prying eyes there.

"Okay," I said. "Listen, I'm tired. So what is it you want?"

"I want to *buy* the money, the two hundred fifty thousand dollars you were handed today. Do you still have it?"

By this time, I was very pissed off and keeping a close eye on both of them. "Sorry," I said. "It is long gone, and besides I would never bring it here. I am leaving in the morning. What the hell do you mean, you want to *buy* it?"

With a sorrowful voice, he proceeded to explain what a great deal he had for me. He was prepared to give me $2,000,000 in counterfeits for the two hundred fifty thousand. *Why me, Lord, why am I so lucky?* I asked myself. Good-byes were said quickly as he glanced around the room, probably looking for the Compass Travel bag. The golf bag was not in sight.

The next morning I felt much better, having recovered from the food poisoning, and settled in for the long trip to Hong Kong. About twenty hours later, I found myself once again standing in that most familiar place, staring down at the luggage conveyor belt at Kai Tak Airport, waiting for the appearance of my friend, Old Faithful.

Get stuffed!

What was to happen over the next couple of years during Robert's detention was nothing short of a miracle. Imagine yourself facing forty-five years in prison. Even though the Thai sentencing system gives you hope, just the thought of a forty-five year sentence is daunting—tantamount to a life sentence. But, as I mentioned, you just cannot keep a good man down.

Robert was out in less than five years. Here's how:

After some adjustment to prison routine, he got to work. Convincing the prison system, which needed money, that he could make money for them, he gave his sharp mind to a project that is hopefully still active today. The idea was to make stuffed animals; that's right, stuffed animals made in prison using prison labor, then sold in Bangkok department stores.

Before long, different varieties of the most beautiful furry and cuddly stuffed animals were coming off the prison production line, creating joy not only for those who bought them but also for those who made them.

With good behavior, each year at the time of the King's birthday, a deserving prisoner would get a reduction in his sentence. *All countries should do this.*

Soon, Robert had about two hundred happy inmates working for him, pumping out so many beautiful stuffed animals that the prison fund was in surplus, and he had caught the attention of the King. The King issued him a special Royal Pardon and he was suddenly a free man.

The miracle had happened.

As the story goes, however, it all came quite suddenly, and he was not ready to go. Who would take up the baton to ensure that the "business" would continue?

"I can't leave now!" were his parting words as he bid an emotional farewell to all his inmate mates. The fairytale ending to what seemed like a ghastly nightmare had come true, at least for a little while.

Birds of a feather

Initially, with Robert, and another aka "Todd," now out and about, it was not too long before the question presented itself: what next? I knew Robert and I knew Brian. They knew a lot about each other, even though they had never met. Both men were very experienced in their respective areas of expertise, and the bottom line was they were both really good people.

It was a fateful decision to make the inevitable introduction. I suppose there was a business motive in it for me. I thought, *it is karma they should meet*. If successful, there would be a couple of substantial investment accounts to look after. I would not need any more clients, and sensing the heat, I wanted FFS to be completely legit.

The road ahead would lead to Reno, Nevada.

CHAPTER 15
"Mr. Nice" Comes to Hong Kong

Raoul and Patrick in NYC and the wine country

In the money laundering business, relationships mean everything and all is well that ends well. From time to time, I would get a call from one of my sources needing to move two hundred fifty thousand dollars or more from New York.

I mentioned that my brother Jimmy lived right across the Hudson River in New Jersey. Of course, being my older brother, Jim had my complete trust. We made a great team. Jim loved the business, and relished picking up and delivering the cash. Jim earned a nice fee to do it, but he would have done it for nothing, just for the thrill.

On this particular occasion in 1985, I was visiting Raoul Del Cristo, Vice President of Deak-Perera NYC, and met a friend of his named Patrick Alexander-Lane. We all got on well, and since we would all be in California in a few days, we decided to take the opportunity to drive up to wine country. Seemed like a great idea. As it happened, I would also be paying a visit to Brian in L.A. the same day Raoul had an important meeting in Beverly Hills.

Raoul was very excited. As he told it, the Governor of Mexico's Central Bank was secretly driving up with some valuable information, namely, the date when the Mexican peso would be devalued. Armed with such inside information, Raoul could make a bundle.

Patrick and I had a chance to get acquainted during the drive up the coast. Everyone was in high spirits. Patrick told me that his brother-in-law often came to Hong Kong on business, and that he would ask him to pay me a visit. I told him I would be pleased to meet him and suggested we could also do some business.

"Excellent!" Patrick said. "Look for him on his next trip. His name is Howard Marks." *How small can the world be?*

Mr. Nice

A month or two later the phone rang at the office: "Hi Bruce! This is Howard."

We arranged to meet across the street from my office in a little wine bar in the Landmark. I liked Howard instantly. He dressed casually, spoke in a soft Welsh accent, and told me, with a wink, about the various projects he was working on. I believe one such project was an English school in Pakistan, of all places.

Howard needed to set up a Hong Kong limited company, so I pointed him in the right direction. He also expected to receive and to pay out sums of cash in U.S. dollars from time to time.

Perfect. This was my business at FFS, operating something like a private bank, not for the public, but just for the convenience of a few selected friends. I had the respected law firm of Baker & McKenzie review the way I operated to ensure I was not running afoul of any Hong Kong regulations—the Deposit Taking Ordinance, or Trustee Ordinance, for instance. Basically, everything was held in trust and in suspense, and I was registered as an Investment Advisor.

I loved Hong Kong's way of doing business then. If you needed to be an investment advisor, at that period of time, you filled out a one-page form at the government office and presto, you could soon expect to receive your beautiful official *Registered* Investment Advisor Certificate. No qualification was required. All one needed to do was register. Reputation was everything.

It was that simple

Howard and I never specifically discussed the nature of the funds that were in and out of his account. You make judgment calls based on the character and personality of the client, and Howard was obviously a very bright, very likeable and articulate fellow, a graduate of Oxford, no less. Little did I know that we had some mutual friends in the "business" of smuggling weed and hashish in large quantities. Need I say more?

The amount of funds moving in and out of Howard's account, except for the first deposit, was intentionally never too large, and transactions were infrequent. Howard was comfortable "parking" funds with me for safekeeping. On his occasional trips to Hong Kong, when we did meet, the nature of our meetings tended to be more social than business, typically making a quick trip to the bank, then sharing a couple of glasses of wine and a few good yarns.

Little did I expect that one day we would both be defendants fighting for survival in different prisons, connected by a web of intrigue and fellow defendants, even though the cases were separate.

Equally shocking would be the Royal Hong Kong police investigation that took place at a time when I was really beginning to feel the heat from scandals being exposed all around me.

In an interview dated September 30, 1988, with my disgruntled former secretary, Bernadette Layfield, regarding the account of Howard Marks, it was written: "Layfield remembers Marks because he was polite, and because his first transaction with the company was for one million US dollars cash."

This certainly did a lot to strengthen the government's belief that I was a major launderer of narcotics funds. At the time, however, I was completely unaware of the fact that I had been placed under a giant microscope.

I vividly recall Howard's first deposit. He appeared unexpectedly at my office after banking hours one Friday afternoon, and after exchanging pleasantries, the conversation turned to business.

"Bruce, I'd like to open an account with you here at First Financial. I may leave suddenly over the weekend, so would you mind holding on to this large briefcase for safekeeping, until you can deposit it?"

"With pleasure, Howard."

He pushed away the simple document I used for opening an account. Instead of signing it, he shook my hand, and we headed to the nearest bar.

Having just returned from a grueling four days in Sydney, I managed to hang out with Howard until almost 3:00 am. With heavy eyes, I vaguely remember saying good-night, and bidding farewell in a place called "Bar City" in Kowloon.

The Sydney trip had been tense. With no choice but to "just move it," golf bags loaded with two hundred fifty thousand dollars each had to be given to couriers Graham Smith, Kim Barnaby, and Ben Rego (or was it Greg Pozar?), who were all arriving and departing on consecutive days.

I had to change hotels four days in a row. After all, people notice the "unordinary," like folks with tattoos, or wearing hats. How about the guy who goes in and out all day with a golf bag wrapped around his shoulder?

Fully recovered and back in the office the following Monday morning, after my third cup of coffee I remembered Howard's briefcase behind the door in the pantry. It was heavy. I entered the encrypted combination written on a bar napkin by Howard. I entered "333," and presto. There, in front of me, was a pleasant sight—a cool US one million dollars, in nice circulated one-hundred-dollar bills. Howard left a note to credit $150,000 to his account and telegraphic transfer the balance, through my facility for hundi payments through BCCI, less my commission, to Malik in Karachi. Pakistan.

That's how things worked with Howard.

* * * * *

In time, I heard that Howard had been incarcerated in Terre Haute Prison in Indiana. Almost everyone I knew had either been indicted or incarcerated, and was trying to sort out his life while fighting to win back his freedom.

I did not actually see Howard again until many years later, after the success of his best-selling book, *Mr. Nice.* I read his incredible account and considered it an honor that Howard chose to even mention me and my company, First Financial Services Ltd., in his fascinating memoir, while keeping a secret his large first deposit.

CHAPTER 16
Nugan Hand - The CIA's Very Own, Very Private Bankers

At the same time….

My life had changed dramatically.

Deak & Company was experiencing liquidy problems, only to be cannibalized by a high-profile group of lunatics who ran a Hong Kong-based bank for the CIA.

Enter Nugan Hand.

In the late 1970s, a sense of gloom and doom pervaded the offices of Deak & Company (Far East) Ltd. in Hong Kong. Their world had literally fallen apart. The company had staked its future on gold and was overextended. Later, in 1984, Mr. Deak was murdered in his New York office, by a sole crazed, 'brainwashed' female gunman, at the same time parts of the Deak empire had become insolvent and were facing bankruptcy.

Even though I was thriving at FFS, the murder of Mr. Deak, a great man and good friend, cast a shadow over my life that would affect me for years.

In the late '70's, Deak employees were already starting to abandon ship and, sensing blood, Mike Hand of Nugan Hand scooped up many of the best and most experienced foreigners, like Ron Pulgar-Frame and Jill Lovatt. They knew how to manage customers Deak-style; and with Nugan Hand Bank paying ridiculously high rates of interest on deposits, they were attracting a lot of attention.

One day, Ron called me and set up a meeting with Mike Hand and Frank Nugan. "Bruce," he said, "you should come and join us;

this operation is better than Deak, paying double the commissions for attracting deposits."

In fact, in the preceding couple of years, huge sums coming out of Australia were laundered through Deak's secret "banking" facilities at ANZ Bank and via currency swaps.

As I said, at the time I was just launching FFS and doing fine, so I declined joining Nugan Hand. There was also something about the organization that spooked me. When they opened an office in Chiang Mai, the heart of the infamous, drug infested, Golden Triangle", they simultaneously telegraphed to the world that whatever they were up to, it was probably no good.

The spider web

There is fascinating background information concerning Mike Hand and Frank Nugan, much of which can now be found in the public domain.

Mike Hand joined the U.S. Army in May 1963, and won the Distinguished Service Cross (DSC) in Vietnam. According to the DSC citation, he almost single-handedly held off a fourteen-hour Vietcong attack on the Special Forces compound at Dong Xaoi.

In 1966, he left the army to work "directly for the U.S. government," supposedly employed on undercover missions for the Central Intelligence Agency in Vietnam and Laos. It was reported that he worked closely with the Air America crews and worked for the CIA's William Colby during the Vietnam War.

Mike Hand moved to Australia in September, 1967, and made contact with Bernie Houghton. According to Alexander Butterfield (of Watergate fame), Houghton worked with him as an intelligence officer in Vietnam, and was also connected to General John K. Singlaub, who ran covert air operations throughout the Vietnam-Laos-Thailand war.

Houghton established the Bourbon and Beefsteak Bar and Restaurant in Sydney, and in one interview admitted, "I had heard of Mike Hand's great combat exploits and courage, which were well-known in Vietnam."

The Bank

In 1973 Frank Nugan and Michael Hand established the Nugan Hand Bank (NH). Nugan was a lawyer whose company had a lucrative contract to supply goods to the United States Navy Base at Subic Bay in the Philippines. Another key figure in this venture was Houghton, who was closely connected to CIA officials Ted Shackley and Thomas G. Clines.

Nugan ran operations in Sydney, whereas Hand established a branch in Hong Kong. This enabled Australian depositors to access a money laundering facility for illegal transfers of Australian money to Hong Kong, often using the services of Deak. The Hand-Houghton partnership led the bank's international division into new fields: drug finance, arms trading, and support work for CIA covert operations. Hand told friends that it had been his ambition "that Nugan Hand become banker for the CIA."

Some years later, an investigation by the Australia/New South Wales Joint Task Force on Drug Trafficking discovered that the clients of the Nugan Hand Bank included several people who had criminal convictions relating to drug offenses, including Murray Stewart Riley.

It is a small world.

I had the genuine pleasure of meeting Murray Riley, a most charming and intelligent fellow, even before I met Nugan Hand. I happened to know his girlfriend, a lovely Aussie girl named Maggie Davies.

Maggie ran a very popular and delightful pub in the Roppongi section of Tokyo, called Maggie's Revenge. As an alternative to the Spanish restaurants where we met, this pub became the secret number-one drop box location for Father Jose and me to leave messages for each other during the drama and life of the Lockheed scandal. Small world indeed. It was also the favorite watering hole of Bangkok DEA Agent, James Conklin, when he was in town. More about him later.

You must be joking...

When Deak employee, Ron Pulgar-Frame, and Nugan Hand manager, Les Collings, and Mike Hand himself, told me about NH twenty-two percent deposit rates, I was shocked, to say the least. No wonder they were knocking down the walls to get former Deak employees to launder the funds. Plus, Deak had charged Nugan Hand five percent out of Australia, while they charged their customers twenty-two percent!

Former CIA agent, Kevin Mulcahy, later told the *National Times* newspaper about "...the Agency's use of Nugan Hand for shifting money for various covert operations around the globe."

It soon became clear that the bank was exclusively laundering CIA funds and drug profits. Even the IRS eventually announced that it was dropping its investigation of Nugan Hand because of "legal problems." According to the *Wall Street Journal*, the reason for this was "pressure from the Central Intelligence Agency."

During the years I worked as a free agent for Deak & Company, I had many conversations about Nugan Hand with Dirk Brink at Deak's Shell House office.

Mike Hand invited me to the NH offices in the Connaught Center for several successive Friday night cocktail receptions for "visiting dignitaries." It reminded me of my experiences with the military in the years I worked for AMEX Bank, particularly at

MACV Headquarters in Saigon. You could feel the "good ole boy" network, which was mighty tempting to join; but, on the other hand, by far the stronger pull was from my inner voice screaming at me that if I ever became too deeply involved with these folks, there would be no way out.

Meanwhile, Brink was furious about the long-serving, highly experienced staff that jumped the Deak ship just for higher commissions, and moved over to NH.

Consequently, after years of excellent service, Brink closed down the "laundry bank account" at ANZ bank in Sydney, and discontinued moving money and deals originating from the U.S. Consulate in Hong Kong, and the likes of NH. At the time, Mr. Deak had experienced a difficult time under the Reagan administration regarding Deak's business in South America. The bad vibes were spreading around the globe.

Then comes the shock! As reported . . .

In 1980, the Nugan Hand "bank" collapsed in sensational circumstances amidst rumors of involvement by the CIA and organized crime—rumors that could no longer be ignored.

On 27th January, 1980, Frank Nugan was found shot dead in his Mercedes Benz. With his body was a Bible that included a piece of paper; on it were written the names "Bob Wilson" and "Bill Colby." Robert Wilson was a senior member of the U.S. House of Representatives Armed Services Committee, and William Colby was a former director of the CIA.

After the death of Nugan, Wilson resigned from Congress.

The official inquest into Nugan's death in June, 1980, made front-page news amid testimony from Mike Hand that NH was insolvent, owing at least fifty million, and as much as hundreds of millions.

Mike Hand promptly fled Australia under a false identity on a flight to Vancouver in June, 1980, after destroying NH's remaining records. He disappeared until he was discovered living in Idaho in 2015. It is probable that as a CIA operative, he had re-entered the U.S. and was given a new identity.

In a mind-boggling twist, it was reported...in the Perth Sunday Times

"In April, 1983 a Perth businessman, Murray Quartermaine, testified to the Stewart Royal Commission on drugs, that Hand was living in Pretoria, South Africa under the name of 'Hahn.' Quartermaine's former business partner, Christo Moll, had been linked to the bank, and Quartermaine had won a four-hundred-thousand-dollar judgment against Moll. Quartermaine also told *The Age* that he had evidence suggesting that Frank Nugan's death had not been a suicide."

The remarkably similar circumstances that led to the tragic deaths of Quartermaine and Mr. Nicholas Deak, both victims of violent deaths at the hands of deranged women who seemed to have been "mentally preprogrammed" to do the dastardly deed, were never explained.

I still wonder.....

Who or what agency could possibly be capable of such abominable crimes?

Deak & Company was rumored for decades to be the unofficial paymaster of the CIA, and key to greasing the palms of those the government asked it to grease, no questions asked. Mr. Deak was known as the "James Bond of Money." But something had gone terribly wrong. In 1984, after a federal investigation into its ties to the laundering of cash from the drug trade around the world, and particularly from a non-drug related laundering operation out of Manila (the cash in manila envelopes non-reporting scandal), the company lost its support from the powers that be. Even Deak's close friendship with CIA director William Casey seemed suddenly useless.

Bizarre indeed was the story that a woman named Lois Lang would suddenly appear out of the woodwork, fly from Seattle to Miami where she met several Argentineans, pick up a pistol in Orlando, travel on to New York City, walk into Mr. Deak's office at 29 Broadway and shoot Mr. Deak and his secretary because a "voice" in her head told her to do it! I mean, were we born yesterday?

There is, however, a wealth of circumstantial evidence that points to a CIA-directed brain washing program. After the murder she took pictures of the dying Mr. Deak. Proof for someone perhaps? And upon being arrested as she left the office, she immediately cowered in the fetal position and said something to the effect that "He told me to do it!"

Who is the "he" that told her to do it? Mr. Deak was a truly amazing man. A multi-linguist with a PhD in Economics, he was recruited into the Office of Strategic Services, the forerunner of the CIA, after enlisting in the Army during WW2. One of his friends at OSS was Casey, future director of the CIA, and William Colby who later happened to be closely connected to the CIA bankers, the infamous Nugan Hand.

CHAPTER 17
BCCI of Pakistan and More…

With Nugan Hand now history, looming larger than life on a horizon full of scandals was Bank of Credit and Commerce International (BCCI) of Pakistan.

BCCI had purchased the Hong Kong Metropolitan Bank (HKMB); FFS operated a gold counter at the HKMB Hilton Branch. The bankers from Pakistan were smart, calm, very capable, and highly underrated. But there was definitely something strange going on. You could sense it, but could not put your finger on it.

Until one fine day…

The problem

It was a beautiful fall morning in San Francisco, circa 1985, in Northern California. I had a problem, and I just could not find a way around it.

The conundrum I faced was one of logistics, namely, what to do with volumes of banknotes that simply took up too much space? I didn't know what to do with huge piles of ten- and twenty-dollar notes. The Philippines had been my saving grace, of sorts.

Armed with a list of names photocopied from pages of the Manila telephone directory, I spent many hours going from bank to bank in S.F. and other cities, purchasing small money orders using the names of people I got from the phone book. I would send the money orders back to Hong Kong by DHL, and we would endorse and deposit them to our account at Hang Seng Bank, for immediate credit. But oh, what in-your-face exposure and tedious work it was.

All in the family

The first place to look to for help was naturally my Chinese family. By good luck, or by fate, my father-in-law, Mr. Cheung Ting On, was a merchant seaman. He was the chief steward on a ship owned by Swire—one of the old "Hongs" that made their initial fortunes, so it is told, smuggling opium.

The first time I met Ting was in 1971 when I was working in Saigon and dating Jenny during my visits to Hong Kong. They lived in a small fourth floor flat located at 933 King's Road, North Point, on Hong Kong Island.

Once, after a dinner date with Jenny, I was outside her home saying goodnight when the door suddenly sprang open. Ting screamed something in Cantonese that sounded quite vulgar to my ears, snatched his daughter away, and slammed the door in my face.

After Jenny and I were married, Ting and I laughed about it, and he and I became the best of friends.

He travelled the seas between Hong Kong, New Zealand and French Polynesia, with occasional stops in San Francisco. Upon returning to Hong Kong, we would often stop for a few beers at a girlie bar, the Two Dragons, owned by one of his friends in the red light district of Wanchai. In these ways, my father-in-law and I became good mates.

Ting was a likeable character who supplemented his income with some harmless smuggling whenever possible. One day, over a bowl of wonton soup, I confided in him that it would be great if I could find a "Chinese laundry" in San Francisco, one that could "wash" some money for me from time to time.

Contact Mr. Wong….

I vividly recall the day I stumbled into the "Hong Kong House," a tiny dim sum cafe just down a side street in San Francisco's Chinatown. I must have thought I was back in Hong Kong, because

I automatically ordered in very basic Cantonese, saying something like, *"Yut booi won ton meen, m-goy"* or "One bowl of wonton soup, please."

The cook and owner, Mr. Wong, laughed and said. "You must be Bruce!" He had been expecting me. We became instant friends.

Little did I imagine that Chinese restaurants all over San Francisco not only needed a Chinese laundry to launder their tablecloths, but a "laundry" to launder their money. Consequently, for several years after that first bowl of soup, either my brother, Jim, or I would stop by for a bowl of noodles while picking up a couple of hundred grand in small bills.

The final destination of this money - Toronto, Canada

My friend, Peter Cavanaugh, ran a sharp investment company, Cavanaugh Capital Management, in Toronto, that dealt mainly in managed gold trading accounts. We had much in common, both having been employed by Deak & Company prior to striking out on our own.

Peter was Swiss, and an excellent skier. In fact, as I recall, he was a member of the Swiss National Ski Team and one of the skiers in the opening sequence of the James Bond film, *Dr. No.*

Peter's company managed quite a few of my clients' investment accounts and did very well for them. He also assisted me with cash deposits from the San Francisco restaurant business, which perfectly legal in Canada. I was blessed to know Peter, a person of the highest integrity, ethics and ability.

Not exactly a stroll around the block

It took some teamwork and a trusted crew. First, I had to get the funds to Vancouver, and that was done by simply driving across the Canadian border. (Our modus operandi in those days was so simple.)

Northern California was full of laid-back folks—old Chinese friends of Mr. Wong, looking to supplement their retirement or help send their grandchildren to college. What better way than to create a neat little compartment under the back seat of their cars, enough to hold a couple of hundred grand, and occasionally drive to Vancouver for the weekend?

Either my brother Jim or I would meet them and fly the cash to Toronto using a routine domestic flight. Then it would be deposited with my friend's investment company.

The system worked like clockwork, laundering all that "restaurant" money back home to Hong Kong, tax free. However, the fact remained that small bills simply took up too much space. It would take the luck of the Irish to solve this problem.

I kept thinking, *There must be a better way.*

The streets of San Francisco, sometime in late '86

I could not believe my luck! Or was it fate?

It was a Friday afternoon in downtown San Francisco. Strolling around as the lunchtime crowds were beginning to swarm the streets, I felt the wonder of San Francisco. What a great town! If I ever returned to America, SF would surely be a great choice. Suddenly, while waiting in the crowd at the corner of Union Street, directly in front of me I saw a banking friend from Hong Kong!

"Louis!" I yelled.

"Bruce, how nice to see you! Let's have a coffee."

Louis was once a well-known banker in Hong Kong, formerly the Hong Kong representative of Bank of America. We first met in the late '70s when I was the Hong Kong representative for Bankhaus Deak of Vienna. Representative offices cannot do business as such, and actually do not do much more than meet once a month for lunch and develop personal relationships.

Louis was now working for BCCI in San Francisco. BCCI had purchased Hong Kong Metropolitan Bank. I explained my problem.

"Call this number and ask for 'Mr. Butt,' our head cashier. He may be able to help you."

Well, to make a long story short, I did call and he did help. He could *not* accept my large cash deposits and credit my account in Hong Kong without reporting them to the government, because BCCI had already been placed under a microscope by the U.S. Treasury. However, Mr. Amid Butt stated, "While I cannot launder your money, what I can do is to change it from 'small' to 'large.'"

Excellent!

On quite a few occasions, we handed Mr. Butt a large suitcase of small notes, and a couple of days later, for his small fee, received a small suitcase of circulated one-hundred-dollar notes in return. Later, when BCCI folded, all transactions came under scrutiny. We held our breath. We were never contacted, approached or questioned in relation to our dealings with BCCI after its collapse. No one ever knew. There was no paperwork!

Headlines and stories about BCCI came out of the woodwork regarding the bank, the U.S. government and the CIA, until the bank was forced to close in 1991. Details of the debacle made sensational reading.

Scandals!

1976: CIA and Other Intelligence Agencies Use BCCI to Control and Manipulate Criminals and Terrorists Worldwide

"With the official blessing of George H. W. Bush as the head of the CIA, a small Pakistani merchant bank, the Bank of Credit and Commerce International (BCCI), was transformed into a world-wide money-laundering machine, buying banks around the world to create the biggest clandestine money network in history."

The bank would solicit the business of every major terrorist, rebel, and underground organization in the world.

- 1984-1986: CIA Reveals BCCI's Drug and Terrorist Links to other U.S. Agencies, but No Action Taken.
- 1984 and after: BCCI Dominates Supply Chain of CIA Supplies and Weapons Meant for Mujahidin.
- December 12, 1985: Plane Crash in Canada Kills 256; Evidence Suggests Links to Iran-Contra and BCCI Covert Operations.
- Early 1986: NSC Uses BCCI to Illegally Divert U.S. Government Funds to Contras.
- February 1988-December 1992: Justice Department Blocks Investigations into BCCI.
- Autumn 1988: CIA Has Secret Slush Fund for Covert Operations at BCCI; Fails to Tell U.S. Customs about It.
- March 1991-December 1992: CIA Hides Its Relationship with the Criminal BCCI.

In March, 1991, Senator John Kerry's Senate investigation of alleged "criminal" BCCI heard about a secret CIA report on BCCI that was given to the customs service. Kerry's office asked the CIA for a copy, but was told the report did not exist. After months of wrangling, more and more information about the CIA's ties to BCCI came out, and the CIA eventually gave Kerry the report, and many other reports relating to BCCI. But the CIA did not share documents on CIA operations using the bank; this was a crucial piece of information.

Kerry's public report concluded, "Key questions about the relationship between U.S. intelligence and BCCI cannot be answered at this time, and may never be."

Never a dull moment...

I had been lucky operating as a "one-man band" and not becoming embroiled in tempting deals in Pakistan. I always enjoyed traveling there, most of all to visit my good friend, Illyas Butt in Lahore. He was my initial connection to BCCI, for many "hundi" payments, like the one I made to Malik on behalf of Howard Marks. Illyas was also the undisputed "King of Carpets" in Hong Kong.

Arriving in Karachi, we were always met on the tarmac by Illyas' friend, the Karachi Chief of Police. Our passports were conveniently stamped, and we were bustled into a limo, armed with as many bottles of Black Label as we could carry from the duty-free store. We were soon on the way to a huge party at the residence of the Minister of Finance.

By the mid to late '80s, while my company was rolling along like a well-oiled machine, I realized that this party could not go on forever. My gut feeling suggested, *You gotta know when to hold 'em, and you gotta know when to fold 'em," and that is before the shit hits the fan.*

I held 'em too long.

END OF PART FOUR

Bruce Aitken

The Cleaner

Part Five

Kidnappings, Casinos, and Stings

The Cleaner

250

CHAPTER 18
Kidnapped in Phuket

The press

August, 1986. Phuket Island, Thailand.

The drama that unfolded was reported widely in Asia, especially in Hong Kong's *South China Morning Post*, the *Bangkok Post*, and the following year in the *Sydney Morning Herald*. Given all the scandals that were unraveling at the same time, there was more publicity than we really wanted.

The kidnapping

August is the last hot and humid month in Hong Kong before the beautiful fall and mild winter. The day the drama unfolded, to be exact, was Thursday, August 21, 1986, and it was a day that would turn out to be far from ordinary.

Sitting at my desk on August 18th, the telex suddenly came to life. We still used telex in those days, and I liked it because it was a secure and easy way to communicate. It was just after 9:00 am, and I was on my second cup of mud. Patti, Jenny's cousin who served as our receptionist, brought the telex to me right away because it was from a coded account. I naturally assumed it was a payment instruction.

I glanced at it, and immediately recognized it had come from my friend, Tim Milner. Jenny read it at the same time. We both deemed it very strange because Tim was sending instructions to close his account and transfer the entire balance, as soon as possible, to an account with BCCI in Hong Kong called "Goldcore Ventures Limited."

My first thought, soon dismissed, was that as it was his money, he could spend it as he pleased. Moreover, it was quite possible that he had found a good investment opportunity.

My *gut* feeling was quite different. Obviously, something was not right. Our friendship and our business relationship went back many years and had been tried and tested. There was the "Cessna-Milner Affair" just for starters.

Tim was comfortable with his account with us and would not be taking out the entire balance in one whack without at least having a conversation and confirming. Y.C., our accountant, agreed, but was perplexed because the code word and test key were correct.

The message had to have come from Tim, and only Tim. The account balance was about US one million dollars in the form of two hundred twenty thousand US, about two hundred seventy-two thousand deutsche marks, and about sixty-nine million yen.

Suddenly, I was very worried. I replied and asked for verbal instructions direct from the horse's mouth, so to speak.

Then on August 21st, we received a second follow-up telex from KS&S in Thailand.

"Patti," I said, "please send a reply in code as follows: 'Tim, confirm receipt of your cable instructions just now. Please follow up with direct telephone call to my private line for reconfirmation. Thanks and best regards, FFS Ltd.'"

I also told Patti to send the telex to the address on the Thai number, and answerback "K.K.S." mostly likely located at a Thai travel agency or other business. Then we waited for his call.

The phone rang at 3:30 pm. For some reason, I made a point to jot down the exact time. I thought it was Tim, and indeed it was. He said he was calling from a direct dial IDD phone.

TM: "Hello, Bruce? Tim here."

BA: "Hey, Tim! How are you, mate?"

TM: "Bruce, I am in Pattaya and I sent you the telex. Please send the balance of my account."

His slurred speech was a bit of a concern.

BA: "Right, Tim. Are you okay? I thought I better ask you to call because…"

TM: "Bruce, I gotta go now. See you later."

BA: "Okay, Tim, first thing tomorrow morning."

TM: "Thanks."

He quickly hung up.

Jenny asked, "Was that Tim?"

"Yes."

"But you spoke for less than a minute!"

She was very uncomfortable about the conversation. "Something is really wrong, Bruce!"

YC said, "Let me have the instructions, because if we are going to credit the account at BCCI in the morning, I'll have to notify Hang Seng Bank right away to remit the money overnight from our call account in New York."

I immediately thought of Tim's best mate, Brian.

"Get Brian on the phone right away!"

We made several attempts to reach Brian at his office in Bangkok. Then, around 4:00 pm, we called again and he picked up:

"Hi Bruce, what's happening?"

"Brian, have you heard from Tim?" I filled him in, and his instant reaction was that Tim was in some kind of very serious trouble.

He said, "Do not send the money!"

"What should we do?"

Brian, thinking quickly, sprang into action. "What was the exact time Tim called?" We later found out from Brian that there was no direct dial from Pattaya, and this only further heightened our suspicions.

What happened next was a most amazing sequence of events. In Brian's own words, to the police in Thailand (as written by them):

... I (Brian) answered the phone call from Mr. Bruce many times. The first time was at 10:00 am, then at noon, Mr. Bruce told me that he checks Gold Core Ltd and found that Mr. Wolfgang and Mr. Michael were concerned in this company. These two people have German nationality. He told me their passport numbers.

Late that afternoon between 3:00-4:00 p.m., I received phone call from Mr. Karo Brown. He wanted to meet me about 5:00 p.m.

Mr. Karo Brown told me that phone number of the phone which Mr. Tim called to Hong Kong. He had checked this with the previous information I had given him. The address where the phone number is registered is: 66/2 Soi 39, Sukhumvit Road, Klong Toey, Bangkok.

Later about 6:00 p.m. August 22, 1986, I went to Thonglor Police Station to make a report that I believed something very dangerous was happening to Mr. Tim at the above address. The police questioned me until 10:00 p.m.

The police said they would send men to the address as a precaution that night and would go into the house to investigate the next day. Police General Montri and I went to the address the same night.

The next day at 6:30 am, I went to Thonglor Police Station as per my appointment, and met Major General Montri. Later, many policemen and I went to the address. It took about fifteen minutes to reach the address from the police station.

When the police knocked on the door, it was answered by one of the Germans who said, "Why do you come in here, who are you?" He shut the door and went inside.

I shouted at the house to let Mr. Tim out! We could not open the front door. Later on Mr. Tim was thrown out of the house. Strapped to a chair, he was tossed out of the second floor window, into a tree that broke his fall! Mr. Tim's physical condition was such that he could not speak coherently.

I took some clothes from my car to give to Mr. Tim.

Mr. Tim asked me to call Mr. Bruce to stop the telex transfer of the money! Later I went to Thonglor Police Station and I saw the suspects handcuffed there.

Fast forward almost one year later...

The two Germans were arrested.

The publicity regarding Tim's kidnapping for ransom was not welcome. The story was picked up in Australia. Much to our amazement, the Cessna-Milner Affair of 1979 was still alive and well, and it connected the three of us, along with a lot of other dots.

After the kidnapping, two members of the police force investigators from the Stewart Royal Commission flew to Bangkok to interview Tim. It is understood that he was tentatively offered immunity from further prosecution (they were fishing, he already served his time) if he would return to Australia and give evidence. He declined, although the police did not rule out the possibility that he might reconsider his decision.

Several months later, following the involvement of the State Drug Crime Commission in the Cessna-Milner inquiries, the Chairman of the Royal Commission, Mr. Bill Job, QC, also flew to Bangkok to interview Tim.

Our entire history was reported in the *Sydney Morning Herald*. The salient excerpts:

Sydney, Australia, July 25, 1987 –
Milner's claims of torture and drugged meals.

by Andrew Keenan

As a result of his (Milner's) investments with Deak & Co, Milner came to know one of the company's employees, Bruce Aitken, from about 1977. Judging from the statements and records of the interview, Milner became involved in smuggling marijuana to Australia during the late 1970s, although he made no reference to this in court. These activities culminated in his arrest with Ray Cessna in 1979. He served a short term and was deported in January 1980.

Later that year, Aitken established his own firm, First Financial Services, and Milner became a valued customer. Brian also became a client. Milner confirmed that he had referred Brian, whom he described as being involved in the gemstone business in Thailand, to Aitken's company. Milner also told the court that he did not realize that Aitken had been arrested in Australia in 1980 with $60,000 in his possession. The charge was eventually dismissed.

When I read this I had a terrible sinking feeling in my stomach. My company and I were now totally exposed. I felt that life was about to change dramatically.

Little did I know.

Who dunnit?

The entire experience was harrowing, and one we would talk about later over a few beers.

The Germans were tried and sentenced to long prison terms. They had come from Manila. Sadly, they had wives and young children they would not be seeing for some time. One was a medical doctor. Who had put them up to this kidnapping? We had our suspicions. We speculated. Could it have possibly been Australian intelligence?

No. That was too far-fetched.

Thank God Brian had been able to locate Tim. What if we had sent the money? Perhaps we would never again have seen Tim alive!

Revenge!

One year after the sentencing of the two Germans, an anonymous letter to the DEA regarding my business most probably came from the brains behind Tim's kidnapping. It was from someone who knew us all well, and who was probably very pissed off that we had foiled the kidnapping and had not paid the ransom.

The anonymous letter from Perth, Australia, in December 1987 to the DEA in Tokyo, provided intimate details of my operation.

Report of Investigation of Bruce Aitken

1/23/88
At: Tokyo, Japan

Details

1. On December 21, 1987, the Tokyo Country Office received an anonymous letter addressed to the Drug Enforcement Administration c/o American Embassy, Tokyo. The letter was post-marked from Perth, Australia, but the date was illegible.

2. The typewritten letter clearly indicates that English is not the writer's first language or a clever disguise to make it appear so. The author identifies an "aitkens" of "foirst financial hong kong" and others in his/her letter.

3. It appears that Bruce Emil Aitken, NADDIS 1066623 is the subject of the letter. Since Aitken is of interest to many offices, the letter is being distributed to offices mentioned in the file reference section of Aitken's NADDIS printout.

5. Tokyo Country Office will not attempt to decipher the letter or run exhaustive indices checks on the names and information contained therein. The letter has been distributed to interested offices for their own investigative analysis.

6. Tokyo Country Office will forward any subsequent letters received to the same offices.

Suddenly, the nature of the business had turned nasty, and the handwriting on the wall was not just screaming at me, but hitting me over the head.

The reader may be asking: What's the big deal with this report from the DEA about the letter? The answer: a NADDIS number.

*"The **N**arcotics **A**nd **D**angerous **D**rugs **I**nformation **S**ystem, **NADDIS**, is a data index and collection system operated by the United States Drug Enforcement Administration(DEA), comprising millions of DEA reports and records on individuals. NADDIS is thought to have become the most widely used, if least known, tool in drug law enforcement, by which, records about millions of individuals, many with no criminal history, can be reviewed quickly to locate complete reports on a subject of interest, their address or phone number." (Wikipedia).*

If you are in their system, they assign you a NADDIS number— the big deal was: I found out I had one.

Chapter 19
"The Summer of '87"

Who needs this!

The kidnapping of Tim Milner and the resulting publicity received by our friend, Brian, and me, was devastating. Pandora's Box had been opened. Sure, we had some concerns about this as it was happening, but we always assumed we would deal with the fallout later.

"Cito" (Ray Cessna) had flown in from Sydney. In a private conversation over a couple of bottles of Aussie Red, Cito, still shocked by the resurrection of the Cessna-Milner Affair, confided in me for the first time that the money I delivered to him in Sydney just before the trial, was given to Morgan Ryan so that "people could be looked after." So we celebrated first, then decided what to do next.

Funny how the story gets told, but the best part of it all was that we never lost our sense of humor. According to Brian, who was at the scene when Tim was unceremoniously thrown out of the second floor window, after clearing his blurred eyes, the first words he spoke were, "Did Bruce send the money?"

Justification?

No one felt we were in any kind of business that would cause us to lose sleep at night, that is, so long as the government did not get a whiff of our maneuvers. We actually thanked the government for making "weed" illegal, because it provided us with golden opportunities for good-natured people to supply it to those who wanted to smoke it—just like the "Roaring 20s" when nobody cared.

In our minds, it was identical to Prohibition when they turned most of the population into criminals. It was coupled with the "follow the money" paranoia that threw out personal privacy in the form of "cash reporting requirements."

Of course, the money to be made inevitably attracted real criminal elements that brought violence with them.

And then, of course, there were the snitches, that part of humanity that lurks in the "underbelly" of every deal. (Maybe they should be locked up forever, keys thrown away.)

Decision time

Brian, Robert (aka, Nick), Howard Marks and company were very busy spreading joy in the form of Thai sticks going to America and Canada via a web of people and networks.

I was happy to be involved along the periphery with a few good friends who needed to have the bread laundered. I never wanted to meet anyone other than those friends who had already become clients of my company. I knew I could make a decent living just by servicing them from time to time.

It was time to "retire" from carrying around money in golf bags or using other methods of deception to "clean" money; it was time to get out before I got caught. There had already been too many close calls, and the nerds in the government were definitely not stupid. Certainly, there were a lot of people out there who were talking too much. Why else would I get the third-degree search every time I cleared U.S. Customs and Immigration?

"That's it, Jenny," I told my wife. "The shit *has* hit the fan!" We struggled with the decision to close down and wind up First Financial Services Ltd. FFS had been a good friend—a mini Deak & Company. There was a tinge of sadness because we had worked very hard for years to develop a legitimate parallel financial services business with boring clients. However, the real breadwinner, the foundation of the business, had continued to be "the laundry."

But I had made up my mind.

I informed my clients and customers that First Financial was closing down with immediate effect; well, with *almost* immediate effect. I gave clients a month or two to give me instructions concerning where to send the balance of their accounts. I raised my fees so they would not delay. Trouble was, almost all of my best clients were in the smuggling profession, so I had to wait until they came to Hong Kong to pick up their cash in person.

What's wrong with parallel parking?

I suppose the temptation was just too great for me. Sometimes you just have to compromise, and that's what I did. *Why not have the best of both worlds?*

I decided to close down the ticking time bomb, First Financial, with great fanfare. Then, secretly and confidentially, I would keep one very big toe in the water by creating a parallel banking and laundry system just to handle the business of a handful of my biggest and best smuggling clients who were still in need. I did just that; I opened an account with a major Swiss bank in the name of my elderly Chinese mother-in-law, peace be upon her.

Meanwhile, out at sea

While my business was paralleling, several multi-ton shipments of Thai weed were either already on the high seas or in an advanced stage of planning.

One shipment had already arrived on the West Coast of the United States and the proceeds had been turned into cash, while another had already reached Vancouver and had likewise been turned into cash. I found out about these either from requests to launder the proceeds or from news reports that the shipments had been intercepted.

Similarly unknown to me, the mother of all loads was on the *Encounter Bay*, on its way to Seattle.

Actions and consequences…

From time to time, one makes a decision that has a major impact not only on one's own life, but on the lives of many others. I made one such decision that would require other people to make monumental decisions. Call it the "knock-on" effect, a "chain reaction," or such.

I don't know a better term. I do, however, know that the cumulative effect of a string of several incorrect decisions made by me and by others would bring down and unravel years of "hard work" in the centuries-old professions of smuggling and laundering.

Robert and Brian had put their heads together and made plans to do a number of smuggles to America. They were a good team. I knew all of their colleagues, as well, and was looking forward to assisting them with their future investments.

But the kidnapping of Tim and resulting exposure changed everything. It no longer made sense to take such risks. God forbid if things were to go wrong in America—I shuddered at the thought.

Could I help? Weed sails east, cash sails west

In conversations with Robert, I was sometimes made aware of a large amount of cash they were accumulating in America. I did not know where or how they wished to dispose of it, and I had no interest in becoming directly involved. The best solution I could offer, and the only deal in which I was willing to help, was a so-called "reverse smuggle." They indicated an initial amount of up to US thirty million dollars—it was tempting indeed!

The plan was to put the cash on a sea-worthy yacht which would be purchased in California. All the money would be sailed to Hong Kong, and once the cash arrived, I would "clean it" over a long period of time, perhaps a year; I assumed that most of it would be small bills. This transaction would be my only deal for '87.

It made good sense, actually: weed sailing east and cash sailing west.

Ed, the alternative?

Considering the fact that the risk was so high and the time frame involved was too long, the plan was rejected.

An alternative solution to the problem was to approach the only contact I still had in America, my old buddy, Ed Seltzer. Ed was a trusted and wise friend who was very savvy about our business. My relationship with Ed began in 1980, and we had a history of good experiences. Ed could be trusted one hundred percent. Robert would be introduced to Ed, with the important caveat that I have no knowledge. Should they come to an agreement, I did not want to know about it.

Ed was keen. There was a good fee to be earned. This decision was a fateful one that would have disastrous implications. It was a decision I would forever regret. But I confess knowing that if their deal worked out, one day Ed would show me his appreciation.

More disasters in progress

They say that things happen in threes. There must be some truth in this. The fall of '87 produced one disaster after another.

As part of the clean-up and cleansing of FFS, I had to wrap up a lot of loose ends. There was the matter of some funds I had committed to "pick up" in Vancouver. I planned to make this job the last of my money laundering days. The client had been introduced to me several years earlier from a good client and friend in Sydney, who went by the code name "Surfin," as in "Surfin John." Mention this code word and all is cool!

Anyway, "Surfin John" introduced me to Graham Burns, not his real name. Graham was an American living in Southern California. I first visited Graham at his home in Encinitas, on the coast, just south of Newport Beach. I felt entirely comfortable with this group.

The remaining money given to me was two hundred fifty thousand US dollars. I flew into Los Angeles and connected to San Diego, rented a car, and drove to Graham's house. The person who owned the money, as it turned out, was not presently able to communicate.

I had a bit of a sick feeling in my stomach when I learned Graham's "friend" was at that moment an indicted fugitive. We all met in his hotel, and I steeled myself for a surprise knock at the door.

Instead, we went to a beachside restaurant for a great California breakfast. I wished him luck and never asked his name. As planned, two of his lady friends were already driving his car up to Vancouver. They gave me their names and the name of their hotel. The instructions were simple. I would call and come to their room. They would give me the keys to the car and tell me where it was parked.

I checked into their hotel the following day and got the car keys. Sweating profusely, I had a hell of a time removing the carpet on the back left-hand side, unscrewing the floorboard and removing the cash.

They had parked shockingly close to the cashier booth! First, I had to drive up to the next floor in the car park, which must have looked a bit strange. I was then to leave the key at the front desk, and meet them yet again to explain where I had moved the car.

On to Toronto

The furthest thing from my mind at that point was the introduction of Robert to Ed Seltzer. I had in fact almost totally forgotten about it.

My only concern at the moment was to put this cash into my trusted Old Faithful, fly to Toronto, deposit the money and wait to receive the U.S. dollars telegraphic transfer to my account. After that, I would forget about it—and forget about it, I did.

I actually had some flashbacks. One was with Tommy Tuttle, a colleague of Robert.

One night in Toronto, while we were having dinner, I believe around '85 or '86, I had a premonition that one day we would be seeing each other in a prison somewhere. Around the same time, I had another premonition when visiting a friend at Lake Tahoe. We drove past a sign that said "Reno" and I got a sick feeling in my gut. Something told me that whatever happened, I should never, never, *absolutely never*, go to Reno. It must have been my guardian angels screaming at me.

If only I had listened.

Vancouver, BC

The summer of '87 felt like a roller-coaster ride in which I could not find my way off.

Although they had nothing to do with me, there were several boats, presently on the high seas, loaded with weed, that would result in piles of cash. According to the Royal Canadian Mounted Police investigation that occurred soon thereafter, I learned:

That between the first day of January, 1987, and the fourteenth day of September, at or near Vancouver, British Columbia, various persons, including ones known to me -- John Denbigh, Robert

Kimball, Phillip Sparrowhawk and Howard Marks -- were discovered to be trafficking in marijuana.

I personally knew everyone but Sparrowhawk.

It further stated that Sparrowhawk and Marks, along with other persons, were known to be in possession of proceeds from the sale of narcotics; the sum being around one million four hundred thirty thousand Canadian. An additional amount near one million three hundred sixty-five thousand Canadian, represented the sale of the marijuana.

Calm before the storm

Back in Hong Kong, I had no idea that the peace I was experiencing was the calm before the big storm. I prayed, and fantasized that all my problems would blow over.

I decided to take a well-earned break, and take a holiday with my family. Jenny and I took our sons to Orlando, and spent some time with my mom, their doting grandma and my two sisters and their families.

We flew business class on a North West Orient 747 to Honolulu, and spent a few glorious days at the Honolulu Hilton on Diamond Head. We had the whole North West Orient 747's upper deck to ourselves.

Later, sitting around the hotel pool, I reflected on the fact that life was incredibly good. Matt and Doug were seven and five years old; Jenny and I could not have been happier.

However, arriving in Honolulu had been an unusually disturbing hassle. In front of my family, I was pulled aside and placed in a room for questioning. I was tired from the flight. It was strange.

Sitting alone in the room, I suspected there was a hidden camera, because an agent came in and placed an open file on the desk directly across the room from me. I was very curious to have a look at it, but resisted the urge. After twenty minutes, I was told I could go, and I did. I went straight downtown to lodge a complaint at the U.S. Customs head office.

After a wonderful stay at home in Orlando, I went on to New York to see my brother and some friends. Time being short, I wanted to visit my friend, Matthew Wallace, who was a close friend of Bruce Miller. I returned to New Jersey the same day for dinner with another friend, Steve Deutsch. To accomplish our multi-faceted visit, we hired a plane at Teterboro Airport and made it a day trip—flew to the Hamptons and back.

Ah, the good life.

Robert Kimball on the line

To end the holiday happily, we went to Montreal and bided our time in the hotel before heading to a professional ice hockey match. The phone rang. It was business. It was Robert calling from a hotel in Vancouver, requesting my services. Thank God, however, I was being delayed by another unexpected, and very tempting transaction of US one million in Toronto.

I anguished over whether or not to do the Toronto transaction while on holiday with my family. It was a matter of meeting "Bill" from New York in Toronto, and delivering the cash to my agent. Bill always had perfectly organized one-hundred-dollar notes. I never saw his ID. His surname could have been Le Morte, another major smuggler, also done in by the same two super-snitches.

I rationalized that the three-percent fee of thirty thousand dollars would more than pay for our whole holiday.

By the time we arrived in Vancouver several days later, Robert had already checked out of the hotel and returned to America; -- twenty-four hours before the whole team in Vancouver was busted. They had been under surveillance based on information from the two DEA snitches, Corman and Christensen.

For some reason, I felt I was being watched for the two days we stayed at the Grandville Vancouver Hotel.

I rented a car and we went up the coast to go salmon fishing. The boat skipper noted we were novices, so he didn't have to take us very far; after all, the day before, he took out two Cathay Pacific pilots and they caught nothing.

He took us to the other side of the bay, towards the north. It turned out a school of whales had most likely come by the night before, because all the salmon turned north. In less than an hour we had caught the legal limit, and were back at the shore, giving salmon to a group of old ladies on a picnic. We packed or froze the rest, and checked it along with the thirty thousand dollars for the trip home to Hong Kong.

CHAPTER 20
Reno the Casino

November 5, 1987, a day I would love to forget

It was a beautiful fall day in Hong Kong and I was feeling good about my life. Although the future was uncertain, I felt "retired" from the profession of money laundering. It was a future most pleasing to contemplate.

On a personal level, there had been many trials caused by my travels and my propensity to live life as a "dreamer." In spite of starting with nothing and having accumulated a decent level of savings, and in spite of having a lovely wife and two beautiful young sons, I was always dreaming about doing something else or being somewhere else.

The root cause of my dreaming was probably a deep sense that I should have been a professional baseball player. I never found anything quite like baseball, so I found excitement in alternative ways, like making a profession of traveling and smuggling cash.

November 5, 1987, I dropped Matt off at school and headed to the office with Doug in my new BMW. For all intents and purposes, I had closed down the "laundry," while establishing the temporary parallel "laundry" to service my small group of friends.

All seemed well.

"Good morning, Y.C.," I said to my accountant, as I entered my office.

"Bruce," he said, "good morning, but there is something very urgent!"

"Oh?" My interest peeked.

"Bob Seltzer, Ed Seltzer's brother, has been calling every ten minutes for the past hour. He asked that you call him as soon as you come in." My heart sank straight to the floor. This did not sound good.

I dialed his number in California and he picked up on the first ring. "Hello, Bob?"

"Bruce, Ed asked me to call you right away! He said you would need to know immediately. Ed was arrested last night in Reno in an FBI 'sting,' attempting to launder over eight million dollars. It was a set-up. Ed told me you don't know anything about it, but you know the people involved."

Pangs of fear raced through my gut as I thanked Bob for the call, and asked him to tell Ed I was deeply concerned. I did not know what would happen next. I had hardly given any thought to the introductions I had made of the key players. What could have happened? Bob told me it had to do with a fake casino sting in *Reno*. The news was devastating.

Reno.

A dense black cloud descended over what had been a beautiful day; all I felt was fear. When Bob read the list of names of those arrested, my fear changed into deep depression and a feeling of sickness in my heart: Robert, David Bose, Tommy Tuttle, "Steve" (a young and innocent trusted employee of Brian's), and Ed himself; along with his supposedly excellent contact, William Harris, whom I had never met. *And* all the money—Brian's, Robert's, and who knows who else's!

All I could say was, "Oh, no, oh, no, OH, NO!" This time the shit had really hit the fan. I had an instantaneous throbbing headache; *I* had made the introductions.

Hey Ed . . .

Ed Seltzer had told me about his good friend, William Harris, aka "Sir William." It seemed they both had membership in the Knights of Malta, an ancient humanitarian and sovereign order (involved in charity works) from which you could even get a "passport."

It was, however, through this organization that Harris had carelessly broadcast that he was looking for help to launder up to fifty million dollars. Unfortunately, a character with a nefarious past took a bite: Joseph Stedino.

The web

Ed Seltzer's decision to bring Harris into the picture to clean the money for Robert turned out to be a decision we would all regret. Harris and his "casino modus operandi" would lead to Reno, where Joe Stedino resided.

The intertwining low-life world of informants, also known as "snitches," is a small world, indeed. According to private eye Jack Palladino, a background investigation done March 28th, 1988, revealed Stedino's work as an informant. To the grand jury, Stedino's opinion of himself was that he had his fingers on the pulse of Las Vegas:

> *"I'm a pretty well-known fellow. Somehow, I've managed to pick up a jacket as being a wherewithal person, meaning that I'm able to accomplish many things, find work for people, and do a lot. And sometimes people ask me to get involved in illegal activities and this happened to be one of them. I know the 'lingo' too! That's the way I talk, I grew up in the streets so I can speak any of their vernacular. I can speak with street people or with those who have been to college."*

271

It's all in the head

The report on Stedino from psychiatrist William O'Gorman, listed his complaint: "It is his belief that he is being harassed primarily so that he will turn informant for the FBI. Stedino's drug history encompasses a long list of pills, however, he denies using any narcotic. He drinks no alcohol, smokes three packs of cigarettes a day, and 'occasionally gambles on football games.' His joy is being a member of the 'Knights of Malta.'"

Rap sheet

There was a wealth of information about Stedino in Palladino's reports, which were done on behalf of Robert; it included possible Mafia connections.

Stedino's rap sheet revealed a conviction in 1969 for white slavery (Mann Act) that involved the transportation of women interstate for immoral purposes, for which he received a $1,000 fine and three years' incarceration at a Federal Reformatory at Chillicothe, Ohio. (Stedino referred to it as the "real estate" business as he was dealing in the "patch.")

"The sting" according to the FBI

According to the FBI reports, here are the main points of what happened:

"On October 13, 1987, Harris was called by Stedino concerning a legitimate business opportunity. Harris and Stedino had never met before but had mutual acquaintances through the 'Knights.' Approximately half an hour after Stedino's initial conversation, Harris called Stedino again and inquired if Stedino had any contacts with Nevada casinos in which to launder up to fifty million dollars in United States currency. Stedino told Harris that he was familiar with a casino executive who could handle such a transaction.

"During this and subsequent conversations, Harris told Stedino that an individual by the name of Ed, later identified as Edward Seltzer, an attorney from Los Angeles, had clients who wished to launder the cash funds. Harris also indicated another person was involved by the name of Bruce, who was from Hong Kong.

"On October 22, Harris and Seltzer traveled to Reno, Nevada, from Los Angeles via PSA Airlines Flight 1627. Stedino introduced them to an FBI agent named Daniel Camillo, who was acting in an undercover capacity and represented himself as a casino executive.

"...Camillo agreed to accept the cash, hiding it among the cash flow of his casino and then using his business accounts to wire it to Europe and Hong Kong.

"As a result of this meeting, it was agreed that the initial transaction would involve the sum of ten million dollars.

"When Harris and Seltzer arrived in Reno and met with Robert and David "B", they delivered what must have weighed in as a ton of cash. The money was taken to Room 352 at the Airport Plaza Hotel where Stedino and Camillo were waiting.

"Upon arrival in the hotel room... and more than 8 hours of solid counting, they decided they had a total of $7,618,570 in U.S. currency. It was 4:00 am, time to stop for a well-earned break. Camillo began to order drinks, but before he was half way to the door, it burst open. Twenty men, some in suits and some in body armor rushed in, guns drawn.

"FBI.
EVERYBODY'S UNDER ARREST.
GET ON THE FLOOR!"

CHAPTER 21
Reno Changed Everything

I need an "Alka" Seltzer

The news of the casino fiasco was devastating. I knew the ramifications would be terrible. Robert Kimball and David "B", aka "Benji," were in jail in Reno. Brian had lost a bundle of money and was in great danger. Ed Seltzer was in jail.

I was in shock. I could not eat or sleep. I felt sick, and I felt deeply responsible for introducing Seltzer to Kimball; however, I did not know Ed's friend from England, William Harris, and thankfully we had never spoken.

Bad news travels fast – the Kingpin

Brian first heard the news from our mutual friend and my client, Tom Sherrett, who was one of the most talented of the top distributors. Low profile, no law enforcement agency had ever heard of him. Within a few days, the newspapers were reporting that Dan Camillo, the phony casino owner, was actually an FBI agent.

In his very first interview with the FBI, William Harris had *"cracked like a dried twig"* and given up everything he thought he knew.

"Well, Seltzer," he stated, "the lawyer guy, he knows this guy by the name of Bruce, in Hong Kong. He used to launder money, but he doesn't do it anymore because he has a bunch of problems in the Far East. He's retired. You know, I think this guy Bruce, he must be the Kingpin."

The DEA report stated:

"Ever since the Cessna-Milner scandal and Tim's subsequent kidnapping, Brian's name had always been associated with that of Aitken, and the fact that his friend's name was now tied to the money seized in Reno was a massive cause for concern."

See no evil, hear no evil

Unknown to me at the time were the actual telephone conversations of the special agent and the informant tapes, and the list of co-conspirator hearsay statements (below) that I would later read:

Harris: And Ed, your Chinese guy (in Hong Kong), he's the guy who has done all this stuff before, tell him it's gonna cost him if he is getting anything out of it at all, I don't know.

Stedino: He's not.

Harris: Yeah, that was original talk from the Chinese, from Bruce in China. Obviously he does not have control of this thing either and is not interested. He's retired from the business.

Stedino: Must be Wednesday, and the delay so far, it's not your fault, Bill, it's Ed's fault. You have done everything you can.

Harris: Well, it wasn't, in a nice way, there wasn't a deal. You know, there was a deal, but it wasn't a deal. The big situation was that somebody from China said, "I used to do this business, and now our guy is over there who would still like to do it. But I'm not gonna touch it."

And also on tape, "The STING" in the hotel room

Seltzer: There is a reason because most of these guys have *one* person handling all their stuff. And that guy is not doing it now. It's a whole new ball game. He's out of business. See for years and years there was one guy that handled all this kind of business. Real funky and he catered to them. And he'd do it a lot cheaper. Uh, not real sophisticated...He could never handle this amount. But he would do one million dollars. For years and years, I would give him money and he wouldn't give me an accounting. Real private banker! And it was worth it. It was great for me. I used him for years, and now he is out of business. I never got an accounting from him. Some guys would keep millions and millions of dollars with him!

Camillo: I don't understand. Where did you meet Bruce?

Seltzer: You won't believe it. I met Bruce when I was running around Hong Kong, Singapore, trying to figure out how to float a bunch of bread out of Australia, at a time when they had restrictions. I had an appointment with these guys. So, I had appointments with three different people. Some were in Hong Kong some in Singapore, to float this bread out. I went in there one day, had an appointment, and Bruce was not even there. He had an office in the Wanchai District -- that was built during the war as a whorehouse district, so it's real funky! So I talked to one of his employees, an American guy named Tom. It's like a feeling. I had a quarter of a million in a bag. I said okay, he walks me over to his accountant to set up a company. Everything was just spot on!

Seltzer: It's really hard starting out and I gave them $10 million bucks! ...about 10 years ago. That's $50 million today. That was Australia money. I gave him all of that money and it really gave him the kind of credit he needed to become substantial. He did very well. And now, he is going out of business and I don't want to see this go by the wayside, this particular deal. So, I said please don't! You know I can find a way!

Stedino: So he is the one who controls Robert--and Robert is all right?

Seltzer: Well, he did, but he's out of the business now.

Stedino: I think I can tell you, I have no greed. Let me ask you a question…if Bruce retired someday?

Seltzer: No, no.

Stedino: He'll always be in it?

Seltzer: Yeah, but he, well…he's got to get his. I have to make sure he gets his. That's my friend. It's like buying his business.

Seltzer: I'm getting wacky counting this damn money! Oh boy, I'm getting tired.

Stedino: I counted $2 million in 45 minutes; I'm faster than a fart!

Seltzer: I'm getting slap happy. Need some coffee…run the count!

I'm in big trouble – time to take inventory!

People, places and things; these three elements are of great importance to a select few personalities who find excitement in the challenging world of smuggling and laundering of the proceeds; these elements are all part of the dance.

But when you dance to the same tune for too long, one fine day you are most surely going to bump into "the government" who will use every means possible to make you sit down, and sit down for a long time. Call it professional jealousy, of sorts.

Something deep down tells me most prosecutors, working long hours for government pay, envy the life of the smugglers they are after. And smugglers are a *boon* to the defense attorneys!

The "tool of the trade" of the establishment type is the indictment, which must be avoided at all costs. However, the reality is that the government could indict a ham sandwich if it really wanted to. So it's important to choose your people, places and things very carefully.

The grand jury is indeed a powerful tool of the prosecutor, more correctly referred to as the "persecutor." They convene, listen to "evidence" from one side, and decide whether you should be charged. And if there is no charge on the books, then one is created. It's all done in secret. Anyone can be called as a witness, with no lawyer present, and charged with contempt if they don't appear, and with perjury if they lie.

Although you may remain silent and take the Fifth Amendment, the grand jury can grant you immunity. Now you are in deep shit. Hold back to protect your mates, friends and family, and you may find yourself charged with contempt. At the same time, other witnesses, trying to save their own asses, line up to testify against you.

It's nice in the dark

Remember rule number one in the "bible" of the free market money exchange business "according to Deak? The one I inherited for my company? *Know your client!* But that's with the corollary that in some cases it is best not to know too much.

This was precisely the situation that existed at the time of the Reno disaster, and the one I found myself in during the swinging '80s.

There were over two hundred accounts held in FFS, all based on trust and with signed Confidentiality Agreements. I was looking after other people's money to the tune of US thirty or forty million dollars on deposit at any one time. That was a lot of money in the early '80s. The six or seven largest accounts were in the "know your clients but best not to know too much" category.

Cash reporting requirements changed the game completely. Once the U.S. enacted laws requiring banks and financial institutions to report cash transactions over five thousand dollars, "money laundering" became the focal point of criminal investigations everywhere. I never thought such a law would pass in America, and was I wrong.

In one swift stroke, a very important freedom of the individual, that of financial privacy, was completely trashed in the name of the "war on drugs." Of course, this law did not apply to other countries, so in a place like Hong Kong, the effect was just the opposite—it magnified its status as the ideal place to deposit cash and park your money.

I knew my clientele; I liked them all, I knew the business they were all in, and I felt no hesitation in looking after their business affairs.

Birds of a feather are superstars

Bangkok, Thailand, more specifically, Patpong, was the center of risqué bars and massage parlors; to be exact, the Club Superstar was the place to find both the hunters and the hunted. The hunted were composed of life-loving characters from all corners of the world, looking to make their fortunes smuggling weed.

Such people would become well known, like American Robert Lietzman, the Shaffer brothers, Englishman Michael Forwell, and my best friends and clients; the cream of the crop.

There was also a jovial local supplier by the name of Tony the Thai who was taken off a plane in Los Angeles one day with a big bag of undeclared cash. He died in a Los Angeles hospital in 1982.

A chap named Phil Christensen, a partner of Brian's, along with another "friend" named Jack Corman, would succumb one day, and flip to the other side. They became super-snitches instead of superstars.

The stumbles left a trail…and had long memories

Meanwhile, Brian had completely assimilated into the Thai culture and was as Thai as a Thai. He hung around with few foreigners, known as "farang," while revolutionizing the industry in terms of growing, harvesting and packing weed.

An accomplished sailor in his own right, he was always a perfect gentleman and a person of the highest intelligence, integrity and values. Brian was on his way to becoming the most powerful figure in weed smuggling in the world.

But trouble was always waiting like a cat ready to pounce.

In 1983, according to *Reefer Men*, "Brian was calling the shots, when Christensen contacted Chris Shaffer with the view to forming a consortium to smuggle twenty tons of top-quality weed into California. They were joined by a chap named La Morte and two additional investors -- Taylor and Ellis."

Taylor and Ellis were converted Sikhs who took the faith seriously; good people who believed in being healthy, happy and holy; they were into yoga and peace. Tom O'Donnell laundered all their money.

Fortunately, Brian was not a subject of interest at this point, unless there was a secret DEA strategy for setting him up. As for myself, I had no more appetite for excitement. An unbidden foreboding and sense of urgency told me the time for chilling out had passed.

All was not well in Dodge

While I was desperately trying to chill out, two separate shipments at sea were being compromised at the very same time by an incessant leak of information streaming to the DEA. In an amazing "O. Henry" twist, the smuggling ring had found the source of the leak, which allowed them to provide false information to the DEA, purportedly from the snitch. It resulted in an amazingly successful "reverse sting."

Having transferred the load off the coast from the *Stormbird* to a local fishing vessel, they landed one shipment right under the nose of the Vancouver authorities. The ring had lived up to all expectations, and the way ahead was up, up, up!

However, turned up even higher was the heat building up to a boil, and swirling around First Financial, that seemed impossible for anyone to control.

Looming on the horizon, in full progress, was the "big one" the mega ship, the 72 ton, multi-million dollar load on the "Encounter Bay"!

A lot of cash would need to be laundered by someone.

That someone was not me.

CHAPTER 22
1988 Everywhere on Tape

The view from the government...

Brian was one hundred percent true to his values, having provided the best legal assistance to his people who had been busted in Reno, while at the same time pressuring Tom Sherrett for a cash injection. He was confident that Robert Kimball would also do the best he could to raise cash, in spite of the fact that he was incarcerated. Robert was as honest as they come and would ensure Brian would receive any money he had been promised.

Have cash! The Encounter Bay

At the same time, the Colflesh brothers, Sam and Robert, and their partner, a very successful Michael Forwell, teamed up with Brian to do "the big one" on the *Encounter Bay*. The Colflesh brothers were also enticed to travel to the States to collect about US ten million dollars that were due to Brian from Thomas Sherrett.

At this point in time, Michael Forwell was sitting on heaps of cash, and therefore bought *Encounter Bay,* a large and powerful oil rig server, for three and a half million dollars. Just prior to this, in December '87, the snitches reported that Brian was visiting the Superstar Bar looking to meet Sam Colflesh for the first time.

This turned out to be a key moment in the history of Thai weed smuggling, with successful and experienced smugglers teaming up for the first time to handle the "mother of all loads." This was the load that was supposed to clear all slates and allow everyone to retire.

Tom Sherrett was invited to participate, but declined, saying it was "crazy." Brian was to purchase the goods from Laos, then pack and transport them across Vietnam for loading near Danang, where small boats would meet *Encounter Bay*. Thus, the biggest import in history, valued at about US$100 million, was about to get under way.

Snitches unchained

At the same time, Corman and Christensen were also very busy. Brian had been friends with them for many years, and he had no reason not to trust and confide in them. But the nature of betrayal involves stopping at nothing to save one's own skin. Maybe this kind of betrayal stems from a fear of spending time in prison. To me, it exposes a supreme form of weakness that describes the person in one word: coward.

The government's plan was taking hold. Brian needed help recovering the funds that were due him from America. Christensen had just the right fellows waiting in the wings, two "pit bull" collectors of money, Jim Robertson and Bill Bartelucci—*two government agents* from the Miami, Florida, DEA office.

Investigation Reporting from James Conklin, Bangkok DEA sums it up....

On January 26, 1988, Corman met with Brian at the Beer House German Restaurant, Soi 23, Sukhumvit Road, Bangkok, to discuss Thai marijuana traffic. During the meeting, he discussed the seizure of $7.5 million dollars in Reno, Nevada.

Brian related that six boatloads of marijuana were shipped to the U.S. in 1987; four of which were successful. He stated he was still collecting money for those loads.

He stated that over $7 million dollars belonging to the Shaffer brothers was seized in Reno, Nevada, and that two of his men were arrested. He stated that his profit for the portion of the marijuana was $22 million dollars. However, he would have to pay some money to help his men. He was presently trying to retrieve this money, and expressed interest in developing a new laundering system.

Brian said that for the past two or three years, he had shipped all his marijuana out of Danang, Vietnam, that he presently had 100 tons of marijuana under his control, and that he would be interested in a joint deal with Corman. They also discussed the kidnapping of Milner and who could have caused it.

During February '88

"Corman and Christensen met with Brian on numerous occasions. During the course of these meetings, Brian related that he presently had $15-22 million dollars in cash in the U.S. that he wanted to collect and move to Hong Kong to be under the control of Bruce Aitken.

"He stated that transportation of the marijuana will be provided by Bob and Sam Colflesh, two brothers who own the Superstar Bar, Soi Patpong, Bangkok.

"He also stated that he provided 42 tons of marijuana sent to the U.S. which he split with Christopher and William Shaffer. Robert Kimball was to collect the money and arrange to send the money to Bruce Aitken in Hong Kong. He stated that he presently has at least $15 million U.S. dollars in the U.S. he is unable to move to Hong Kong. He requested Corman to bring his financial experts to Bangkok for a meeting to explain the methods of money transfer to Hong Kong.

"On February 11th, both informants met with Brian and Tom Sherrett. Sherrett related that two of the defendants in the Reno case had begun to cooperate with the government, and that "it was only a matter of time before Brian and Aitken were implicated."

Audacious is the word

Incredible as it may seem, the two agents proposed that they meet Robert Kimball, who was incarcerated in Nevada State Prison, with a request from Brian to assist them in collecting nineteen million that was being held by third parties. This meeting took place on February 15, 1988, without the permission or presence of Robert's attorney, Jack Hill. This was a clear violation of Robert's constitutional rights.

Jack Hill was furious, and rightly assumed that they must be government agents. However, the DEA had already successfully collected six million from Sherrett in Portland, Oregon, and "laundered" a million, which had been made available to Brian. Fortunately, I was not present, nor privy in any way to what was discussed and planned, even though some of the meetings took place in Hong Kong.

In full confidence

The super-snitches, via their capable money laundering special agents, introduced two new agents to meet the Colflesh brothers in Bangkok. These two agents were hired to do the offload.

DEA Agents Larry Brant and Helmut Witt met with Colflesh and Forwell on 5 May, 1988, at the Peninsula Hotel in Hong Kong. Brian was present. I remember those days very well, because they were probably the only days Brian was ever in Hong Kong that we did not meet. I was not involved in this conspiracy, although I was later indicted in the case.

I am indicted!

The ongoing efforts to find the money were of utmost importance. When it comes to money, the government has no problem bending the rules themselves, as can be attested to by the outrageous fiasco of the two government agents taking the bold step of visiting Robert Kimball in prison.

As a result of other information gleaned from the DEA's covert investigation, a superseding indictment was returned against Kimball and his confederates on September 13, 1988. In addition to the counts charged in the original indictment, the new indictment accused Kimball of conspiracy to aid and abet the distribution of a controlled substance. But these charges created the need for separate trials—a set-back and impediment to the prosecution.

I soon found out that "the superseding indictment also adds Brian and another individual, Bruce Aitken, to the list of Kimball's alleged co-conspirators."

That mother of all loads

The *Encounter Bay* was eight hundred miles off the U.S. coast. Larry Brant of the DEA had been monitoring its progress. Captained by Sam Colflesh, it was halted dramatically; its engines fired on by the Coast Guard cutter *Boutwell*.

At that moment, a steady stream of communications was taking place between the agents and the informants. As the "minder" of the two informants, Jim Conklin, Bangkok DEA, was in the loop. The informants were also spreading conflicting information, stating that Sherrett was attempting to locate someone named Dan Hertog, aka "Dangerous Dan," who was allegedly holding the balance of the Reno money.

At the same time, the agents were attempting to entrap the "Two Jacks" (investigator Jack Palladino, and Kimball's attorney, Jack Hill) into a money laundering indictment.

Conklin reported that Brian expected to come to America to spearhead the collection of thirty million.

Dennis Cameron, FBI, Reno, reported that the "noose was tightening, the warrant was ready and just needed to be signed... once signed they will seal it."

The DEA plan: Fly Brian in. As soon as he gives us his date of arrival in Zurich, fire up the confiscated Lear Jet out of Miami.

Life must go on

I regretted having stuck my neck out way too far. There was so much activity swirling around me, and I had zero control. I just wanted to wake up and find this had all been a bad dream, especially for all of my good buddies.

It confirmed my worst fears, and as events and conversations flashed through my memory, I realized that my best friend, Brian, was in the most serious of circumstances imaginable, facing a huge disaster. I knew that he was scheduled to depart for Switzerland for medical treatment on a chronic old leg injury, then proceed to America.

A Welcome" Waiting...

Jack Corman had arranged it. Jack was to fly to Canada, then Jack would have a small plane waiting for he and Brian for the short flight across the border into the good old USA.

Throwing caution to the wind, I made a quick call and a quick trip to Bangkok to see Brian personally, and tell him about my conversation with Mike Brennan. But things had gone too far. Rumors alleging that Corman was a snitch had circulated in the past and had also been discounted. It could not be possible. Brian would have to trust his old friend and see it through to the end.

Brian departed for Zurich on July 4, 1988. The day before, the two agents, Bartelucci and Robertson, arrived in Zurich to see Brian and discuss his trip to the U.S.. Another agent was there: Jim Robertson, known as James Harper, DEA special agent.

Special Agents Thomas Harper and James Devaney were introduced to Brian by Corman as money launderers. At that meeting, Corman ended by saying he and Christensen were hoping to one day meet Bruce Aitken to discuss future money laundering.

Tom Sherrett in Hong Kong

When Tom Sherrett passed through Hong Kong, on a lightning visit to see Brian in Bangkok, he told me that he had met the "collectors" that Brian had sent in Portland. He watched them carefully as they pulled away in their government-issue type of van, and he felt that he had just handed over six million dollars to the government. He assumed that since he had not been arrested, that he still had a window of opportunity in which to flee.

Tom said he was worried that Brian did not seem to realize how much trouble he was in because of the "smuggle" he did separately with Robert which had subsequently led to the big-money bust in Reno. He said the authorities had a bank account number for Brian in Vienna, Austria. In addition, the English guy and the "other guy" arrested with him, had "*rolled,*" and were providing the authorities with further information.

Another lawyer involved in the case told Tom the DEA was sending a team to Hong Kong and Bangkok in February to continue a full-scale investigation.

On tape, Tom said that he had seen Bruce Aitken in Hong Kong to discuss the situation, since Aitken "handles" money for Brian and Kimball. He said Aitken was "sick" about these problems.

CHAPTER 23
The "Sting" at First Financial
Seattle and the "Phantom $500,000"

Easter weekend

My life was totally occupied with mind-boggling, serious concerns, and I was in dire need of a break. It was March 31, 1988, the last day of business before the long Easter weekend. Little did I expect the day would include a transaction taking place at my office that would have a major impact on my life.

This was exactly one month prior to the chance late night "Disco" meeting I had with Mike Brennan, Tom O'Donnell's former partner, at the disco in early May; informing me that Jack Corman was a snitch for the DEA..

I left for the office early. As I would later read from the tape transcripts, the telephone was already ringing at my home in Stanley Village, on the lovely south side of Hong Kong Island. It was "the snitch" calling. My son, Matt, answered the phone:

Matt: Hello, hello, hello?
Corman: Can I speak to Bruce?
Corman: Is he home?
Matt: No, who is calling?
Corman: My name is Jack. I am his friend.
Matt: You are my daddy's friend?
Corman: Yes, is he home?
Matt: No...you don't sound like my daddy's friend. You sound like a girl! (*Matt's laughter*)

Matt: No, my daddy went to the office. Good-bye! (*Matt laughs and hangs up.*)

Brian had asked me to please help him. One part of me wanted to help him as a brother; the other part of me wanted to avoid the whole damn thing because I had a strong negative feeling about Jack Corman. He was one of the few people I ever disliked from the moment I set eyes on him.

With these thoughts on my mind, I sensed trouble, so I intentionally lingered at the nearby coffee shop so I would arrive at my office late.

It must have been after 11:00 am when I arrived. My receptionist, Patty Wong, immediately handed me a bunch of messages. There were more than half a dozen calls from Jack Corman.

I called a meeting of my staff and explained to them that I greatly distrusted Corman. Whatever his request or purpose, we would put him off in a such a way he would not become suspicious.

Settling in at my desk, Patty came in and announced that Corman, in spite of being told I was not in, was sitting in reception. I let him come into my office. He asked me if I had any word from Brian to receive, then send him, five hundred thousand dollars. I truthfully said I knew nothing about it. I was just about to show him the door when fate intervened.

Patty knocked and entered my office. "Bruce, Brian is calling on your direct line and says it is very urgent!"

Shit. Here is Corman, his so-called partner, sitting right in front of me. *Was it fate? In another two minutes I would have had him out the door.*

Brian asked me to please do him this last favor, receive the funds from Corman and transfer them to Bangkok via the underground banking method today, before the five-day weekend.

I was caught between a rock and a hard place. My gut feeling made me decide against it. I decided to call Brian back later and find another way to help him.

Corman left. I had indicated to him I would have to receive the funds before 2:00 pm, which I knew was next to impossible. Then I immediately instructed my staff, my accountant Y.C., and Patty, that under *no* circumstances were they to take any money that came from Corman. I told them to tell him it could only be handled by me personally. As for me, I would not be back until 6:00 pm when it was impossible to do anything.

Here's how it happened...

Special Agent Henry Morgan (DEA Hong Kong) and Jack Corman, delivered $500,000 U.S. currency to the offices of First Financial Services Ltd. Around 2pm.

"At approximately 6:30 pm, Corman called Aitken at FFS. The call was recorded. Aitken said that he was expecting to hear from Corman earlier so that in case Aitken couldn't process the money he could give it back. Corman suggested that the problem was with Brian. Aitken said that he was 'not involved' in any way, shape or form. 'This was just dropped on me, it took my accountants a couple of hours to clarify it...I am not in the picture in any way, shape, or form whatsoever, I have no facilities.' *Aitken went on to say that through his staff the money got taken care of.*

With the closing of my business and my suspicion of Corman, I had decided to have nothing to do with this transaction. Consequently, I had purposely left the office and purposely returned after closing hours. To my horror, my accountant, knowing Brian as my good friend for so long, and in the habit of always doing his best to provide good service, and knowing that we had made this transfer many times in the past, received the entrapment five hundred thousand dollars cash and made the transfer to Bangkok.

This solo transaction was to later become the sole basis for a superseding indictment against me in Seattle, Washington, which would eventually pit my wits against a fascist prosecutor there.

And it did not help that...

On June 11, 1988, Corman and Brian met in Room 931 of the Mandarin Hotel in Hong Kong. Brian told Corman that he was concerned about a news clipping from the *International Herald Tribune* I had given him regarding a money laundering "sting" operation in Florida (Operation Pisces); I had read the article by coincidence.

According to the DEA Report, Brian asked Corman if he was sure of the reliability of undercover agents William Harper and James Devaney. They were from Miami. He said he was surprised that Operation Pisces had actually successfully moved money into the defendants' accounts for four months previous to their arrests. *(Sound familiar?)* Corman assured him of their reliability, and Brian agreed that he wasn't worried about them but insisted that constant caution be maintained.

He again reviewed with Harper and Devaney information he had recently received from Bruce Aitken and from Mike Brennan regarding the alleged cooperation of Jack Corman. Brian inquired whether the S/A's or U/C (undercover) Morgan in Hong Kong had any dealings with Brennan. S/A Harper informed him that he would advise Morgan to be wary of Brennan. He indicated that he did not personally know Brennan, but that Aitken had flown to Bangkok to pass the above information along to him just prior to his departure for Switzerland. Brian expressed concern over the continued rumors in Bangkok and Hong Kong of the alleged "Corman" cooperation.

At the same time

The Feds were now in fast-action mode, and most of the action stemmed from the Reagan administration's attempt to end the drug menace by establishing a two-hundred-million-dollar Federal narcotics task force. They had the resources to go after non-violent hippie pot smugglers by infiltrating their plans with low-life snitches and fake money launderers.

This is when Brian decided to make the trip to Zurich, Switzerland, then continue to America to meet up with Corman.

Tom Sherrett, naturally, vanished from the face of the earth. In fact, the agents wanted very much to arrest him earlier when he handed over the money in Portland, but it would have blown the *Encounter Bay* sting. They searched his house. Apparently, Tom packed out in such a rush, he left a receipt for repair of the *Lloyd B. Gore*, two hundred seventy-seven thousand in cash, two pounds of pot, and sales records.

The sharp-eyed prosecutor in Seattle, Peter Mueller, followed this lead immediately and learned that the boat had just come ashore on July 27 in Vancouver, B.C. Seizing the opportunity, the Canadian Royal Mounted Police were contacted, and the "smuggle" was busted just as the crew was in the act of off-loading the weed.

All of this happened while we were traveling home from our holiday, via Vancouver.

On the way, the worst news of all...

I was still sorely in need of a vacation, and getting away with Jenny and the boys to Phuket, Thailand, was just what the doctor ordered. My rest, however, would be short lived.

The nightmare saga of *"The United States of America vs. Bruce Aitken"* was soon to begin.

I just didn't know it yet.

CHAPTER 24
Kata Beach, Phuket, Thailand – Late July, 1988

We loved staying in this little resort at Kata Beach—the Kata Thani on Phuket, better known as "James Bond Island" from one of the famous movies filmed there.

It was 6:00 am and the tropical morning breeze was softly tossing the palms trees outside the entrance of the cottage. A shadow from the fading moonlight danced across the ceiling as night turned into day. It was so good to be on a holiday with my family. I was worried about so many things, and my life had slipped into chaos. While events were beyond my control, I should have been wise enough to see trouble approaching.

Next morning, while outside practicing Tai Chi to clear my head, I heard the phone ring. It was strange that anyone would call so early. No one in Hong Kong knew where we were. I listened to Jenny speaking in her usual friendly voice.

Then she stopped talking.

I waited for her to hang up, and when she opened the door, I could see a look of shock on her face.

"Tim Milner just called. He is on the way over. He said to get today's *Bangkok Post* and read the front page headline. He wanted you to know that yesterday, Brian was arrested in Zurich, Switzerland."

Sweat started to pour down my face; everything about me sunk, a chill ran up my spine; I was intensely sick to my stomach. I knew that life would never be the same. Through a mental fog, I heard Jenny. "Bruce. . ."

Tim arrived within an hour with the *Bangkok Post* in hand. My heart sank even further. Brian was accused of being the kingpin mastermind in a seventy-two-ton shipment of Thai marijuana to Seattle. I remembered the handwriting I'd seen written on the wall the last time I saw Brian—just days before his departure.

"Bruce. . ." I heard Tim call my name as I finished reading the article in the *Bangkok Post*, "This is big trouble." Yes, big trouble ahead. No way around it.

I turned to Jenny. "Let's pack up and get back to Hong Kong; we'll deal with whatever happens from there." I had wound up the business of First Financial and broken no laws, so, although scared within, I thought I had no worries. *Right?*

It was early afternoon, and while we were getting ready to check out of the Kata Thani, the phone rang again. This time it was Maria, Jenny's sister in Hong Kong. The Hong Kong police had raided my office and my flat, and had taken all of my records. *All my records? Oh shit!* I had over two hundred clients' records in FFS, all under confidentiality agreements.

In a panic to protect my clients, I made a decision: destroy all records in storage; I asked Maria to make the necessary phone calls. (This decision would later result in serious repercussions.)

By the time we had flown from Phuket to Bangkok, we decided it was best for Jenny and the boys to fly back to Hong Kong on their own because I had no idea what was going to happen next. Surely, if I returned to Hong Kong, I would be arrested. I needed to figure out where I stood.

A funeral of sorts…

Filled with a whirlwind of paranoia, I had another concern— Old Faithful. When I imagined it being taken or opened, I felt incredibly sad, and a eulogy flashed through my mind: *"Old Faithful, R.I.P."* I needed to dispose of it as fast as possible, toss it in a dumpster somewhere.

After the family departed, I walked from the international departure terminal to the domestic terminal, took a flight to Songkla in the South of Thailand, and checked into the Florida Hotel. By chance, I befriended a couple of Malaysian fellows who were driving to Penang; some good luck—they invited me to join them; it was much easier to cross the border in a private car than on the bus.

As we drove along, I assessed my situation.

I had been winding up First Financial Services for the past year. The "best" accounts I had inherited from Deak were in the export business—exporting Thai weed, that is. Our relationships started out innocently enough, and being naturally friendly people, we got along well—we became friends. I organized my business so no laws were broken; in Hong Kong, that is. With signed "Confidentiality Agreements," I felt no compunction to give out client information to anyone under any circumstances without the client's specific authorization. I thought I was covered.

On the run to nowhere

As the serious nature of my situation sank in, I found I could not sleep soundly. When I woke up early the next morning, my first thoughts were of Jenny and the boys, but I dared not call home for fear the phone was tapped. At that moment, I felt very lonely, and I wondered if I had made the right decision in not returning to Hong Kong with my family. Foremost in my mind, of course, had been my sons; I could have been arrested at the airport and I did not want my sons to witness such a humiliating experience happening to their dad.

At 8:00 am I was already in the hotel coffee shop waiting for the new friends who had given me a ride. I had left them in the bar the night before, as I was in no mood for music and conversation. Reading the newspaper, unable to focus, I was well into my third cup of coffee when they appeared, slightly hung-over, but no worse for wear.

Being Muslim, they confided to me, their occasional business trips to Thailand were the only chance they had to have a few beers and let their hair down.

The border checkpoint leaving Thailand and entering Malaysia was only a few kilometers away, but on the way, I sensed my new friends were suddenly concerned about my presence. I sensed they felt something was very strange about my leaving Thailand this way, and I could feel their eyes on me as I handed my passport to the immigration officer. The official took longer than usual to check the computer, then glanced at my picture, stamped my passport and returned it to me saying, "Have a nice day."

Driving over the big bridge to Penang, I felt a temporary sense of relief. I soon found myself at the train station waving good-bye to my new friends as I boarded the train to Kuala Lumpur. As planned, when I arrived in "KL," I checked into a cheap hotel just before midnight and called a friend's mobile phone that Jenny had arranged to borrow.

To my great relief, Jenny answered the phone. She had arrived safely with the boys; however, the police had called first thing in the morning and asked both her and Maria to come to the Wanchai Police Station at 10:00 am. They were asked about my whereabouts, arrested for the suspected destroying of records before the statutory time limitation, and had to post a bond of HK five thousand dollars each.

Jenny said the police could hardly be bothered, except that the request had come from the USA and I was the only person they were after. "Where is your husband and why did he not return to Hong Kong with you? Did you know that your premises had been searched?" Jenny said she had no idea about any of it, and that I had continued on a business trip. They said to give them a call when she knew I would be flying back to Hong Kong.

Over the next several weeks, I found myself becoming more and more consumed by my problems. The next day, I took a flight from KL to Kota Kinabalu in Eastern Malaysia, and a few days later took another flight on to Manila where I had many friends. From Manila, I could contact the lawyers involved in the case and call Jack Hill for Robert Kimball and find out what was happening with Brian. I certainly needed to get some good advice myself.

With a total breakdown of routine, living in small hotels and out of a suitcase, the days in Manila passed slowly. It became difficult to think clearly. I had no appetite. I could not sleep.

After two weeks, I extended my visa because Jack Hill was in Hong Kong and wanted to come to see me, along with my newly appointed Hong Kong barrister, Gary Alderdice. They both encouraged me to return to Hong Kong as soon as possible; however, I wanted to know more from America first.

The stifling heat in Manila was getting to me. I flew on to Taipei, Taiwan, and checked into a small hotel about one block from the Taipei Hilton where I had stayed in better times.

By then, I had heard the news that I had been indicted in the money laundering fiasco in Reno. A deep depression set in over the following few days as I tried to think. I could stay in Taiwan out of the reach of America because there is no extradition treaty. My purpose was not to avoid the problem, but to deal with it from a position of strength.

I had the law on my side, because while the horrendous U.S. justice system indictments charged me with many counts, there was only one count on which they could charge and extradite me. All the others would have to be dropped because no such "money laundering" charges existed in civilized Hong Kong. *All I had to do was stay away from America, and let time pass so the case would be dealt with in my absence.*

But then, add a little fuel to the fire!

But more bad news came, and from a very unlikely place.

The last thing I needed was more publicity and for the ancient Cessna-Milner Affair to be resurrected and regurgitated, but there it was again. This time the whole history was repeated in excruciatingly minute detail.

"Cessna-Milner's Money Mover Raided"
Sydney Morning Herald
Monday August 29, 1988 - By ANDREW KEENAN

The Hong Kong offices of Bruce Aitken - the American "mystery-money-mover" in the controversial Cessna-Milner drug affair - have been raided at the request of the U.S. Drug Enforcement Administration (DEA). It is understood that they were part of continuing investigations into one of two major drug syndicates uncovered by the DEA in recent weeks. Although the recent DEA activity is not related directly to the Cessna-Milner case, it might inadvertently prove to be the catalyst for yet another investigation of the nine-year-old affair...

The extensive report read like a rogue's gallery of characters. It rehashed and made current lots of information about the past and about many relationships with account holders of previously esteemed FFS.

The report exposed my relationship with Howard Marks, Cessna-Milner, solicitor Morgan Ryan, the Milner kidnapping, the fact that Deak and Company was identified in a 1984 report of the U.S. President's Commission on Organized Crime as providing a money laundering facility, and the fact that the Costigan Royal Commission had found that Deak laundered money for Nugan Hand; last but not least, the sixty-thousand-dollar fiasco.

Message from the super-snitch

Jack Corman.

Of course, Jack Corman was the mongrel of a dog who had come to my office on many occasions and tried to entrap me. The *first* time he came to my office, he was introduced to me by Andy Rogers, an art dealer out of Nepal and Bangkok. Nice work, Andy!

I decided to give ole' Andy a call.

All I said was his name: "Andy," and I could hear the surprise in his voice.

"Bruce!" he shouted, "Where are you and how are you?; everyone is concerned about you!"

"Well, Andy, (*you arsehole*), you should know why I am calling."

To make a long story short, Andy agreed to fly to Taipei and meet with me to discuss something very important that he could not discuss on the phone, *provided I paid his expenses. Seriously?*

Two nights after the call, I was waiting for him in the lobby of the Taipei Hilton. To make sure he was alone, I stayed at a distance and watched him check in; then I startled him when I came up behind him. "Hey you, what is your room number?"

"Bruce," he said, "Shit, you look so thin!"

No kidding? (I was down to a hundred and forty pounds.)

Over the next few hours, Andy was to repeatedly express how great a person Jack Corman was and how he did not know he was working for the DEA.

So, let me see now just what a great fellow this was: a cowardly low-life super-snitch who set up Brian, my partner Tom, and so many more. Oh yes, Jack was a wonder, all right.

"Get to the point, Andy."

"Well, Jack has a message for you."

So, the message went something like this:

Listen, Bruce, the government knows that you were not a major figure in all of this, and that you had nothing whatsoever to do with drugs. In fact, they are not really very interested in you at all. What they are interested in is your money laundering expertise, and since you handled so much money that was drug related, just cooperate and tell them where it all is.

Really? All I had to do was give Jack the nod and he would do the rest? In a matter of days, I could return to Hong Kong, meet with the DEA and work out a deal, just like he did, to *roll over on all my friends* and help the DEA set up more stings. Gee, what a deal; roll over on all these good people and then live the rest of my life feeling like a rat!

I laughed out loud.

"Andy, tell Jack, that no-good, low life chicken-shit bastard, to drop dead!"

I could, of course, clearly hear, taste, see and smell the approaching tsunami.

CHAPTER 25
The Fear Factor

The old adage "Don't do the crime, if you can't do the time"

Fear is the thing that motivates people to turn on their friends and partners—sometimes relatives. Fear of loss of freedom and financial meltdown seem to be among the biggest motivators; but for some, personal character, integrity and self-esteem outweigh such considerations. These people have become an *endangered species*. My experiences in dealing with large sums of cash had brought me into contact with both types.

Of course in many situations, fear of the power of the criminal justice system—the government—takes over. Once the government has succeeded in getting an indictment against you, you are in deep trouble. You can easily be charged with a litany of multiple "counts," a list of violations that seem to be non-existent in statutes and have been pulled out of thin air—each carrying a long prison sentence.

Another weapon in the government arsenal is the "plea bargain." You need money to negotiate the best result, either in the form of restitution to the government or in the form of hefty fees to hire the best defense lawyers.

Of course, you can always go to trial.

It's a long shot, but you may even be able to win.

The "good guys" – bite the bullet

Three cheers for the "good guys!"

The phrase is most memorable to the generation brought up during the 1950s and 1960s. That generation grew up in an age when a "snitch" was considered to be the lowest form of filth on the planet. No one, and I mean no one, would have snitched on a friend, or risked being ostracized.

I think of how America has changed. It now seems to be a nation of snitches who are simultaneously glorified and despised by the government; glorified if snitching "for" the government; despised if whistle-blowing "against."

Super-snitches

The super-snitch group contained the likes of Jack Corman and Philip Christensen, who went out of their way to ruin as many lives as possible—went way over and above what was necessary to save their own necks. Surely they tried to rationalize their consciences, if they had any, by deluding themselves into thinking they had miraculously awakened one morning, seen the light, and morphed into secret DEA agents.

And the "not-so-super"

I never had the "pleasure" of meeting Joe Stedino or William Harris who starred in the Reno casino disaster. Harris was never even mentioned in the Reno case as a co-defendant, except to say that he was sentenced to the *lightest* sentence of three years. He was certainly not evil, but he had made a terrible mistake in judgment. His words did great damage to me personally when he stated that "Bruce, the guy in Hong Kong, must be the *'Kingpin.'*" Thanks a lot, Bill.

To his credit, however, after some excellent investigative work done by Jack Palladino, he later recanted this statement and said that

I had no involvement at all in the Reno affair, at least to his explicit personal knowledge. We never met or spoke.

Much to my chagrin, I would later find out that other snitches had come out of the woodwork and turned against me in order to secure a better deal for themselves.

My observations

Formerly in the air force, Jack Corman was comfortably and safely stationed out of danger in Thailand during the Vietnam War.

A heavy drinker and drug user with a special love of cocaine, he was the type of character the government loves to have as a snitch.

To be a good snitch, a person has to be willing to "do the crime but not the time." Jack had gotten caught in a minor case of smuggling cocaine into Florida; he instantly repented and decided to devote the rest of his life to setting up and entrapping colleagues and friends, for and on behalf of the government. That's when he officially came out of the closet as a pseudo-DEA agent. The DEA realized they had a pit bull on their team: wired, frothing at the mouth, always ready to prove his worth.

Poor Jack.

Phil Christensen

Birds of a feather.

When interviewed, Phil Christensen mentioned his military experience of a dozen years, involving heroic raids behind the lines in Vietnam, Laos and Cambodia, and leading Montagnards—all adventures that he included as part of his job as a Forward Air Controller. Christensen's actual duties were clerical rather than heroic.

He stated that he began snitching to the government not because of any pending charges, but because, "I realized it was time to get out of the business." More likely, since he was Corman's partner, he had no choice since Corman would have soon been snitching on him.

But don't take my word for it

All the shocking details about Corman's past, his questionable military history, his drug dealing, his Florida indictment for cocaine, his "deal" with the DEA, his snitching on so many people, were given under oath at the Vancouver hearings; plus there were defense impeachment themes and fascinating interviews with those who knew him best. Here's a sample of the recorded testimony to reiterate the point:

"Under questioning, Corman stated that he had initially had a meeting with the DEA in November 1986 in the Bahamas, in which he had decided to turn in his friends and colleagues immediately after learning the charges against him from the DEA. Again, 'Your deal' was to set up people so the DEA could charge others and you could save your own skin!"

Under further questioning as to Corman's future obligations to the DEA, he stated that he was due to give evidence in Reno: "the Kimball case: I guess it also involves Brian, the Khalsa case in San Francisco, and the Rabreau case in San Diego…and others in the future."

They kept him very busy.

The irony is that the outrageous and unethical methods chosen by the government can sometimes backfire on them and actually assist the defendants, as in the situation I described when two agents visited Robert in prison without his lawyer present. Here is how it was reported:

Synopsis by the Reno Gazette Journal, September 9, 1989...

"Federal agents illegally tried to get evidence in a multi-million-dollar money-laundering and drug-smuggling case in Reno, a federal Appeals Court has ruled.

"By sending two undercover agents into the Nevada State Prison to talk to defendants in the case without their lawyer's knowledge, the government interfered with the defendants' constitutional rights, the U.S. 9th Circuit Appeals Court said. The ruling on Thursday involves a case in which eight men are charged with attempting to launder $7.6 million in 1987 through a non-existent casino that actually was an FBI front.

"While it does not affect the money laundering charges, the ruling effectively keeps the government from pursuing an allegation that the men also conspired to import tons of high grade marijuana from Thailand. Reno Federal Judge Howard Mc Kibben, who was backed up by the decision, has ruled that the eight men should be tried on the money laundering and drug charges separately."

Let's get Jack Hill!

"Reports of Investigations" throughout this saga were replete with references to Brian's communications and meetings with Jack Hill, the attorney representing Robert Kimball; also, the efforts to collect monies. Jack Palladino was also enlisted to look into the matter of locating and collecting the millions of dollars in cash still being held by trusted friends of Robert Kimball.

As a consequence, based on Corman's snitchimony, I mean testimony, the government actually tried to have Hill removed from representing Kimball, and was equally keen to try to indict him for aiding and abetting money laundering.

Being no fool, however, Hill was shocked by the fact that Kimball was visited in Nevada State Prison in Carson City by two "money collection agents" sent by Brian. He was convinced they were government agents. He also insisted that Palladino not be involved in any collection activities.

The bottom line was that, he, Hill avoided the agents' attempts to entrap him. He avoided them like the plague; however, that did not stop the government from trying to get him.

Corman was called to give evidence in Vancouver in November and December 1988, and at this hearing his true character appropriately was exposed.

CHAPTER 26
Rakesh Saxena: One of a Kind and Kind of a Friend

It was around the same time, a friend of mine was in the initial planning stages of a mega project that would cause the *Wall Street Journal* to describe him as the "Mrs. O'Leary's cow of the global financial crisis." With a mind as sharp as a tack, he was in Bangkok birthing the mother of all scandals.

Rakesh Saxena is probably best described as a rogue trader; willing to take on any risk, provided, of course, it was with other people's money. Over time, Rakesh tired of his job and the dull level of activity at his employer's, WOCOM (Hong Kong) Ltd.He had even applied to work for me as an FX trader. Then, one day he suddenly packed up and moved to Thailand.

We stayed in touch, and I would often see him on my trips to Bangkok. I was always welcome at Rakesh's home. He was heavily involved with Bangkok Bank of Commerce big-wigs, all sitting around a table drinking Johnny Walker Black Label and smoking Cuban cigars.

Unbeknownst to me, in the next room, one of the biggest frauds in banking was being perpetrated right under my nose. When the shit did hit the fan, it hit hard.

But as usual, there was an amazing twist.

Jack is everywhere!

One Sunday night, over a couple of drinks, Rakesh told me an astonishing story. His wife, Suvanna, had a brother who was becoming involved in some nefarious activities, having met an American in a bar in the red-light district called Patpong.

The Yankee said, "If you are looking to make a bundle, and make it quick, I have a deal I would like to invite you into."

The American claimed to be very successful in shipping multi-ton loads of high-quality Thai marijuana sticks to the West Coast of America. They needed an investor for the next load, and asked if Suvanna's brother would be interested. Interested he was! For an investment of US one hundred thousand, he was promised a return of ten times that amount. The meeting to commit to the deal and hand off the money was scheduled for the very next night.

"What's the name of the American?" I asked Rakesh. "I'll check it out for you."

"Great!" he said, without hesitation. "His name is Jack Corman."

"Who did you say! *Jack Corman*? Holy shit, Rakesh! You have to tell him to pull out of the deal immediately! Corman is the number one DEA super-snitch!"

"Oh no!" Rakesh's jaw dropped.

I could not believe Jack "Wear-a-Wire" Corman was still out and about setting traps for good people. That guy really got around! In a state of shock, Rakesh called Suvanna into the room and she immediately called her brother. He did not believe me.

"No, impossible; it could not be!" He had been to the bank that day and completed the withdrawal of his life savings, sold his stocks and converted it all into cash on the black market. The money was sitting in his briefcase.

Needless to say, the deal was called off. I returned to Hong Kong and faxed Rakesh a copy of the indictment against Corman.

On my next trip, the brother-in-law thanked me profusely, and even tried to offer me a reward. My reward and his was to keep him from being set up in a sting and spending the next twenty years in prison.

As to what happened, at first he told Corman that he was having trouble raising the hundred thousand dollars. A week passed and Corman followed up again, pressing him mightily. This time the brother-in-law told him very frankly that regrettably he had changed his mind. He decided he did not want to start in the dope business after all. He did not want the risk of spending his life in jail.

Rakesh and the BIG deal

It turned out that the visitors who plied the scotch at Rakesh's house were also mostly up to no good, and in due time his world was to come crashing down around him.

"Don't do the crime" rang true, although the truth did not come home to roost until many years later, as reported:

Reuters – June 2012:

"A Thai court jailed an Indian financier for 10 years on Friday for massive embezzlement that helped bankrupt a Thai bank in the mid-1990s and spark a crisis in the financial sector that spread through Asia in 1997.

"Rakesh Saxena, 59, was found guilty on five counts of securities fraud between 1992 and 1995, having siphoned off tens of millions of dollars from the now defunct Bangkok Bank of Commerce, where he was employed as an adviser.

"The scandal that engulfed Bangkok Bank of Commerce caused a run on bank deposits and led to the bank's collapse, contributing to the devaluation of the baht and the regional crisis. Saxena was arrested in 1996 but was extradited from Canada only in 2009.

"The Bangkok South Criminal Court heard how Saxena had set up 60 businesses in Thailand and used them to secure loans from the bank to cover debts and running costs, but instead channeled the money into personal accounts, mostly in Switzerland.

"'The defendant clearly demonstrated his intention to take funds from the damaged party to invest for his own personal use, depositing the funds into several overseas accounts,' the judge said in reading the verdict.

"Estimates of the money he stole from the bank vary from $60 million to $82 million. The court did not give a total.

"Saxena, wearing orange prison fatigues and in a wheelchair, appeared frail and confused as the sentence was passed. He was also ordered to pay 1.13 billion baht in damages and a 1 million baht fine."

I was not surprised to read that Rakesh, after all those years on bail and allowed to live, but not to leave, at great expense, in a luxury condo under 24-hour guard and monitoring, had been extradited to Thailand. I only marvel that he had not been sent back sooner. I thought of a visit I made to see him at his Vancouver condo several years later, in 1998; I was looking for a way to get back on my feet, and make some money; however, Rakesh seemed more bizarre and risk-inclined than ever, running all kinds of deals in unstable countries in Africa.

His beautiful condo was itself a prison of sorts. You could look out the window or stroll out on the porch overlooking the water and the marina, but you could not set foot out the door. During the almost eleven years he lived that way, Rakesh kept his busy mind active by doing deals wherever he could. He never skipped a beat, dealing electronically by email and phone—the consummate deal-maker. The weekend I visited him, I believe to impress me, he told me of his frequently calls with the likes of Saudi billionaire and "partner"Adnan Koshoggi and the wife, for some unknown reason, of convicted Brexel Burnham Lambert "Junk Bond King", and wealthy philanthropist, and partner, Michael Milken.

With failing health, an apparent stroke a year or two later, he was definitely better off in Bangkok where his family and children could visit him. There, he would have plenty of baht, and still might hopefully find something of real value in his life; something that couldn't be squandered by an addiction to the thrill of the game.

CHAPTER 27
Listen to Whom? The Nightmare Unfolds

After the "bust" in Reno in the fall of 1987, it was apparent to me that I was in a great deal of trouble. I needed a good lawyer. What was unknown to me at the time was what exactly in God's name had happened in Reno; I had no idea at the time what was said by whom, much less about my introduction of Robert Kimball and Ed Seltzer. I had to assume the worst-case scenario.

It was no coincidence that soon after I returned to Hong Kong, Kimball's attorney, Jack Hill, conveniently introduced me to one of his colleagues who "just happened" to be in Hong Kong and staying at the same five-star hotel, the Regent in Kowloon.

Attorney "Marcus" (not his real name), out of San Francisco, was a very sharp fellow. I took an instant liking to him because I was in a very vulnerable position. I felt like the Sword of Damocles was hanging over my head. Marcus had spunk, and I felt he was a fighter who would make a good defense lawyer should I need one. In early 1988, I needed one.

I placed Marcus on a fifty-thousand-dollar retainer and asked him to monitor the Reno situation and keep me apprised. This he did very well, and as events unfolded, he assured me that he had a close communications relationship with both the prosecuting U.S. Attorney in the Reno case, and U.S. Attorney Jeff Russell in San Francisco. This gave me quite a bit of comfort.

Jack Hill and Gary Alderdice, my barrister in Hong Kong, had traveled to Manila to brief me on the government's cases against me. Gary Alderdice came to see me again in Taipei, and a second time with Marcus. I was lucky indeed to have Gary. He was introduced to me by a long-time mutual friend, a lady named Teddie Thunder, based in Hong Kong.

Occupy my mind - occupy my life

My occupation was changing into a full-time self-survival job. Not being a believer in keeping a lot of paperwork around, and preferring to do business on a handshake with people who had complete faith in me, meant that record-keeping was basic. The numbers had to be correct for audits, but the sleeping devils were in the details, or rather in the lack of details.

Boring stuff--but very important are "the facts" because...
"Facts are stubborn things" – John Adams

First Financial Services Ltd. was analyzed and taken apart, laid bare for the whole world to see, and its methods had to be justified under the law. Fortunately, I had done my homework and had hired a top international law firm in Hong Kong to organize my business so it could stand up to all legal scrutiny in Hong Kong.

My first task was to detail the whole FFS operation, and step my solicitor through the processes I used for all types of transactions. Glass Radcliffe & Co Ltd., my auditor, was run by a pleasant chap named Robin Radcliffe; Robin needed to prepare all kinds of special opinions and certify copies of everything—client accounts, confirmations, certificates, everything except the rolls of toilet paper.

For Marcus' eyes only, all the cash transactions were listed in detail.

Rakesh Saxena, of all people, had not yet caused the Asian financial crisis, and was high on my list as an expert witness as to how cash money was routinely moved in and out of Hong Kong.

The list of tasks seemed endless. The fight was on!

She remembered...

As I had requested, Maria had called our storage company, Crown Pacific, to have all previous years' FFS records destroyed. Under the company's ordinance, the documents should have been kept longer, and destroying them early turned out to be a big mistake on my part.

The Hong Kong police could keep me on a holding charge and monitor my movements until America decided to extradite me, and worse, it placed a cloud of suspicion over me as a presumption of guilt.

My motive at the time was simply to protect the confidentiality of my legitimate clientele, just in case the day came when things fell apart.

That day arrived early.

Timing IS everything

An important factor in this whole unfortunate saga was a stroke of luck regarding timing. America was undergoing a completely vicious period of "punishment vindictiveness," as a sort of pendulum swing resulting from the tolerant and lenient days of the '60s.

Under the new "Sentencing Guidelines," crime punishments were paid in spades. Bottom-line sentencing included throw-away-the-key thinking, and judges had almost no leeway. But thank God, our "crimes and indictments" had to be judged using the *old* guidelines.

Fasten your seatbelts

Marcus spoke frankly and did not pull any punches—I liked that in a person, especially a defense lawyer. I recall phoning him one day and discovering he had gone for a walk by the ocean that morning so he could think about how to fight our case. That was very comforting, but the thought of going to trial made me feel quite ill. Criminal indictments do not just go away. They are nightmares.

Meeting in Taipei, Marcus informed me that we had some major evidentiary problems:

1. The five-hundred-thousand-dollar transaction that had occurred in my office.

2. The hearsay tapes in Reno between Harris, Seltzer, and the informants.

3. The newspaper article I had read describing how the DEA out of Miami was setting people up using entrapment money for laundering services (Operation Pisces) *exactly* like the service Jack Corman had arranged for Brian. As soon as I read it, I had faxed it to Brian, and he brought it to the attention of Corman, who immediately brought it to the attention of his "minders" in the Bangkok DEA.

4. The "Brennan" incident; my trip to Bangkok to inform Brian that Corman was a DEA informant.

5. Hearsay from other informants; the list of defendants and others willing to testify against me grew bigger by the day.

6. Early destruction of the documents in Hong Kong.

On the run, sick and homesick

I was not feeling well at all, as I was alone in Taipei and unable to sleep, unable to eat, missing my family, missing my life and feeling like a fugitive. I was desperate to return to Hong Kong, since the first order of business would be to face the music there. That is exactly what I did. My barrister was to write:

316

"Bruce Aitken returned to Hong Kong on the evening of October 3, 1988 and predictably was arrested for the offense of 'perverting the course of justice' in relation to the destruction of documents of First Financial Services. "

Counsel met him at the airport and went with him to the offices of the Commercial Crimes Bureau where he was initially interviewed 'off the record' about the American offenses. Even 'off the record' no statement was given and no admissions made."

The interesting feature of this informal interview was that the Hong Kong police passed on an offer apparently made by the DEA that they were willing to deal as far as my involvement was concerned. Their indication was, although the Hong Kong police could not give any guarantees, that if I decided to give full assistance to the DEA and act as a State witness, in return I might not be required to plead to any charges. In addition, there were suggestions of a possible suspended sentence.

Obviously, the U.S. prosecutors wanted to make some kind of offer; however, Marcus told me we could not decide until he saw me to discuss in person. Although momentarily comforted by a possible way out, it was an offer I could not possibly accept, for reasons already stated.

The strength of my legal position was that I could not be tried on thirteen of the fourteen counts in the Reno indictment because they were non-extraditable. There are *no* such equivalent "money laundering" laws in beautiful Hong Kong. *This was my ace in the hole.*

I had to completely avoid the United States until the Reno case of my co-defendants had been tried or otherwise dealt with. Then, the first count against me in the drug conspiracy would automatically fail because it was total bullshit and the prosecutors knew it.

If I was extradited on the one drug count, it was an absolute no-brainer that the indictment was faulty and the government had no case. This was the sole reason they were sitting on the extradition warrant, and the Hong Kong police were well aware of this, and consequently treating me with civility.

My attorney wrote to my barrister, Alderdice:

"We have received and read the preliminary police reports in this case. It appears our client's alleged role is strictly limited to currency transactions and in no way involved the possession or sale of illicit drugs. Moreover the only direct contact Mr. Aitken had with the DEA was in a currency transaction of a nature which appears to be legal.

All other evidence is in the form of hearsay statements of various persons beliefs regarding Mr. Aitken.

I note that the drug charge (21 U.S.C. 846) in the indictment as concerns Mr. Aitken relates in substantial part to the disposal of monies generated from the sale of marijuana. My assessment is that the government's evidence is quite thin."

We spoke often by phone...

The gist of these conversations (I kept meticulous notes) was that the government's case remained weak, and any "provisional warrant" was four to five weeks away, after the "persecutors'" planned visit to Hong Kong.

Marcus said that under no circumstances, absolutely none at all, should I entertain any conversation about the "local" problem or he would break my arm. Our strategy would be to move for the dismissal of the "846" drug indictment.

Bottom line, things were well under control and not all bad. Marcus had spoken to the prosecutor and they had agreed not to do anything immediate about the warrant. They wanted to talk to him after they heard from the Hong Kong police.

There was no evidence regarding the Hong Kong documents disposal problem and it was only a technical charge.

When the phone rings at 2:00 am, I jump! The update...

"The prosecutor Russell agrees that Bruce Aitken is the only one in this case 'who has any life.'" Marcus stated that his office was right across from Russell's, and that I was "a nice guy." *This was amazing good luck!*

Jack Hill had been waiting for either Kimball or Brian to "roll over," and Hill's dismissal hearing as Kimball's attorney had been set for November 2, 1988. Hill was under suspicion for aiding and abetting money laundering. Marcus arranged for Hill to be represented by Peter Robinson. Corman and Christensen and the two agents out of Miami who were setting Brian up had to be there. This was a chance to observe firsthand what sleazes Corman and Christensen really were. Peter Robinson, on behalf of Jack Hill, would have a chance to memorialize some statements from those two snitches.

In addition, Marcus would go to Zurich to seek information in my favor from Brian; this was most urgent and *very* important. Jack Hill had apparently served as attorney for both Kimball and Brian, and Brian now had his own attorney, Bill Beard.

"Bruce, you have three alternatives at this crucial time." (Marcus)

1. Go to Borneo forever. (Not an option.)
2. Marcus would inform the U.S. Attorney that I would cooperate for any benefit I might receive (however, they did not need my evidence against Robert and Brian). (Not an option.)

319

3. Battle. For the government to prove conspiracy, they had to have specific criminal intent evidence. (What did they have?)

My daily consciousness was now totally smothered by monstrous nimbus clouds hanging over my head. I knew there was to be an extradition hearing soon, but I would not give any evidence at that hearing. I would simply state, *"On the advice of my counsel, I don't wish to say anything at this time; if I am later charged with an offense, I will explain in court."*

The "good news" tape

My attorney was keen to say he was in close touch, almost on a daily basis, with Jeff Russell, the head U.S. Attorney handling my case, hoping to gain more time while making the case that I was not a bail risk.

However, of great interest to me were the tapes that Corman had clandestinely made in my presence. At one meeting in Bangkok and Cha Am, Thailand, the tapes were unintelligible and of such poor quality they could be considered worthless.

My instructions from Marcus were exactly this: The prosecutor will try to surprise us, so under no circumstances should I agree to be interviewed by anyone. Under no circumstances should my wife, Jenny, be interviewed by anyone. Absolutely no exceptions! No provisional warrant had been sent, and none was expected for the next thirty days.

With no offer from the government, we had to wait and see if either Robert or Brian would talk. "Talk about what, Marcus?" I said. "You don't understand. We are all brothers." I was completely at peace.

My position was clear: the tapes were worthless, the situation was stable and positive. I told Marcus that, in fact, I believed the tapes could help me because there was never any talk about drugs or money.

At the same time, unfortunately...

Important investigative work being done by Jack Palladino, retained by Robert Kimball in support of the cause, indicated that I was, in fact, in very serious trouble.

From what Palladino told Gary Alderdice, the count they were using to proceed against me was "Continuing Criminal Enterprise," so-called RICO, which is the most serious of all possible charges the government can possibly make. Sickening news.

And then some good news!

Palladino expected the Reno indictment to be settled soon, following grand jury hearings in Seattle. He had interviewed both Harris and Seltzer and had copies of their statements which completely exonerated me and explained why they used my name as revealed by the prosecution evidence. The contradictory statements obtained by Palladino would negate that evidence.

Palladino further stated that, from the point of view of my Reno co-defendants, including Kimball, they were all anxious to have a trial proceed without me because a lot of potentially damaging evidence against them could be introduced which would show their financial transactions using First Financial Services.

This must have been my sub-conscious reasoning when I decided to have the records destroyed.

Gary Alderdice on developments: "I'll inform Marcus" and ask...

"Can you confirm that the prosecution's strategy is that the government is trying to consolidate all into one indictment which would affect Bruce in a RICO [Racketeer Influenced and Corrupt Organization Act] charge and probably a lesser charge of conspiracy to import and distribute the 72-ton marijuana shipment into Seattle?" *Can you imagine that is considered a lesser charge?*

> *Alderdice wrote, "I do not see from the materials I have considered so far that there is any evidence whatsoever against Bruce in relation to the 72-ton shipment. It seems to me that the entire prosecution case is based on the records of First Financial Services which were seized here and the evidence of the 1988 payment of US $500,000 in Bruce's office!"*

The beat goes on

Sensing that the prosecution would file the extradition warrant early in 1989, Marcus delayed coming to see me until around that same time. Then our primary strategy would be to file a major motion in the court in Reno to block my extradition; he said not to get my hopes up. He still felt that eventually we would have to fight everything, based on the facts, at a trial.

Marcus was pleased at our seeming ability to control the timing, allowing us to prepare. We needed more specific information and expert opinions from my local legal team regarding the perfect legality of the five-hundred-thousand-dollar currency transaction. The trial, if and when it proceeded in Reno, would be over in ten days. I made a note to call Marcus in San Francisco every Friday at noon—4:00 am Hong Kong time.

Hong Kong time, 4:15 am

Word was that Jack Palladino was in Vancouver, BC, investigating Corman and Christensen at the hearing of Jack Hill. We hoped this would provide important impeachable information. Our strategy was to wait for the trial and delay, delay, delay.

Sometime early in the New Year, 1989

Thankfully, Gary Alderdice confirmed some good news regarding the Commercial Crimes Bureau criminal charge:

"It appears that the police are now considering a substitute charge other than attempting to pervert the course of justice. It is suggested that he may be charged with an offense contrary to Section 121(1) of Cap. 12, namely, failure to keep proper books of account which would make him liable to imprisonment for six months or a fine of HK$10,000 (US$1,300)

"You will note that the Section refers to a person being a 'director' of a company. It seems to me that a person who is not a director of a company has no responsibilities to comply with these provisions and if it transpires that Bruce Aitken was not a director at the material time [I was not] *then he ought not to be charged as he has not committed any offense."*

While I was sitting on the edge of my chair...

Marcus suddenly called. He talked and I listened intently. He had met with the prosecutors and the prosecution indicated a desire to cut a deal. What were they offering? Marcus told me the range: "They want to send you to prison, and we want the entire matter dropped. They are bluffing! They won't act on the extradition one way or the other until after coming to speak with me here in San Francisco."

Before that happened, he intended to visit Brian; the Swiss had approved the visit for February 3.

Brian was as stand-up as they come. No doubt about it, he would help me. In fact, I learned later that through his lawyer he made a statement to the court stating that I had no knowledge or involvement in his business.

Marcus was to come see me in Hong Kong towards the end of February. All was in order, not to worry.

February Aquarius…my confidence in Marcus was complete

Then he called again. He had a family emergency so had to change his schedule; he would not be going to see Brian. Instead, he would meet my lawyers, have dinner with Jenny and me, and return to San Francisco the next day. Lightning visit! Marcus was concerned about what the Hong Kong police were doing holding me on a short string, but didn't want to talk about it on the phone.

He suggested I meet him in Canada or Mexico from then on; but on second thought, no, maybe I better not.

Meanwhile, life had to go on somehow.

The Hong Kong police saw me as I was: a businessman. I needed to get back to my business. Upon Gary Alderdice's request, Inspector Chan, after discussion with Chief Inspector Howard, agreed to return my passport. I could keep it and travel any time by giving them forty-eight hours' notice.

Ten days passed before Marcus called

Marcus started the conversation by asking me if I had been able to ensure that Gary Alderdice would be in Hong Kong during his visit; he said things were accelerating rapidly and we needed to get together as soon as possible. Just then, a crack of sorts appeared in our "solid as a rock" relationship.

Marcus said something very forcefully to the effect that I had to get my finances together *immediately.* Somewhat taken aback, I said that I needed to be brought into the picture first. How can he talk about more fees until I knew what had been done and where I stood? I wanted to know how he had used my fifty-thousand-dollar retainer. I needed to make an intelligent decision about how far to take things.

Our understanding regarding fees was that the maximum would be a whopping three hundred thousand dollars plus expenses for "the whole thing," including the worst-case scenario, a trial.

We had put a cap on fees for the sake of my family.

Then came surprising and unexpected news...

Brian had been extradited to America and would be in the USA the following week. It was a relief that it would no longer be necessary for Marcus to go to Zurich, and Marcus also postponed coming to see me in Hong Kong.

At the same time, Teddi Thunder, a friend of Andy Rogers (the naive fool who brought Corman to my office), had a message for me. Teddi knew the Asia crowd and was a lady beloved by all; a real friend, always making her flat available in Hong Kong for friends without hotel bookings or money.

To my surprise, the message from Andy was from Jack Corman. Andy said, "Jack still has an open offer to assist you in some way." I think Jack must have been feeling the heat because by then all of Bangkok knew he was an informant.

Assist me?

"Yes, thanks for the message, Andy. You can tell him to drop dead!"

The visit! At last, the visit we had been waiting for...

Another month passed. My hopes were up.

Then Marcus arrived with various documents: The 'Hill' discovery regarding the informants' degenerate pasts, plus a lot of useless fluff from the investigator, plus the three garbled tape transcripts from Bangkok, including the one where Corman visited my office. On the latter tape, I am heard clearly replying to Corman's entrapment attempt: *"Sorry, I can't help you in America. Because of reporting requirements, that's one country in which I never touch the money."*

Marcus also met with Jenny, Gary Alderdice and Tony Polsky, a reputable Hong Kong business consultant I had hired, who might serve as an expert witness.

Tony was physically handicapped, short, overweight, and walked with a cane, and yet possessed a brilliant mind. By complete coincidence, he was from Portland and a good friend of Tom Sherrett; and more amazingly was once a sports editor for the *Bergen Record* in New Jersey—he was also aware of my baseball history.

I guess my expectations were too high because I would soon be very disappointed by Marcus' visit. I felt that almost all we discussed and accomplished could just as easily have been taken care of by telephone and fax. No offer had yet been made by the prosecution; so my offer to them, therefore, was exactly the same as it had been all along: ZERO.

Marcus advised Gary Alderdice that I would be extradited soon but not necessarily to join the trial of the others; the judge would not wait for me. As for me, it was recommended that when I got to the USA I should go to trial as soon as possible. I could expect to be flown to America in July, 1989, and all would be finished in September or October.

I never questioned Marcus' integrity or ability. Everything was his call and he represented me well. My anxiety and expectations were those of a novice and extremely worried defendant.

The next thing I knew... May 10, 1989

I received a FedEx letter from Marcus informing me that he had spoken with Jeff Russell regarding my case. I cautiously opened the letter and read that the prosecutors were not willing to dismiss the charges, and would commence with formal extradition proceedings.

That sick feeling returned to my stomach.

Another shock! Discovery of more documents!

Gary informed me that the DEA and one of the prosecutors were in town at the same time having discussions with the Commercial Crimes Bureau. The agents were Brant, Mueller, and Brady.

To my shock…

Gary wrote, *The Commercial Crimes Bureau has in fact recovered documents which were not destroyed and these represent the 1986 records of First Financial Services Limited. The DEA are here for one week inspecting thousands of pages of documents!*

What to do now?

I had two months at most until the expected July extradition request. I was very aware of the potential danger, but until extradition, I would keep busy and try to carry on with the business trips I had planned. Little did I realize what was waiting for me when I made my decision to travel on business to Vietnam the first week of June, 1989.

Guy Coombs, my trusted friend and agent from DHL in Manila, had expressed a desire to visit Saigon with me to look into some business opportunities. The idea was that Tim Milner and I would go first, then report back to him.

Didn't quite happen that way.

END OF PART FIVE

The Cleaner

Bruce Aitken

The Cleaner

Part Six

Free Trip Home

The Cleaner

CHAPTER 28
Disaster Strikes. My Nekba, As They Say in Palestine

Bangkok, Thailand, June 8, 1989

I arrived in Bangkok late at night, after meeting Guy Coombs in Manila, and cleared customs and immigration uneventfully. I was oblivious to the fact that the United States of America had just revoked my passport, based on two lies: one, that I was a fugitive, and two, that I was a felon.

Morning of June 8

Tim Milner and I were caught in the usual Bangkok traffic snarl, and it was our fate to arrive at the Vietnam Embassy at 11:45 am, only to find that it had closed at 11:30. We decided to return to the Suri Guest House off Soi 38. Tim wanted to buy a briefcase on the way. It was a beautiful sunny morning and I was feeling at peace. In fact, I felt great.

"Hey, Bruce...!"

"Yow, Tim...what's happening?"

"Something very strange," he said. "The car next to us and the one behind us have U.S. Embassy plates. I haven't seen so many Yanks in one place since the Fourth of July!"

We laughed, but suddenly I did not feel so good. But why? I had spoken to Marcus just before I left Hong Kong and he said there was nothing to worry about. I had notified the Hong Kong authorities of my travel plans as required.

As we neared the guest house, Tim noticed one of the embassy cars pulling into the parking lot of the Ambassador Hotel; a few minutes later we noticed the other embassy car following close behind.

Stopping at our guest house, I went straight to my room, #22. In less than a minute the phone rang; it was Sompong, the front desk manager. "Bruce," he said, "please come down; there are people here to see you."

Returning downstairs a few minutes later, I was met by two Thai Special Branch Police. They approached me.

"Is your name Bruce Aitken? Please come with us."

"What's this all about?"

"You entered Thailand last night on a revoked U.S. passport and you are under arrest!"

Surely they were joking.

"You must come with us to see the U.S. Embassy officials, and after a talk you will probably be back." This didn't make much sense because they asked me to bring all of my belongings.

Tim was in a state of shock. I had entered Thailand the night before with no problem clearing immigration. Not knowing where I was staying, but *somehow* knowing my plans and itinerary, they had staked out the Vietnam Embassy, waiting until I turned up to collect my visa. How did they even recognize me? I can only assume that Jack Corman was in one of the embassy cars, staying out of sight in typical cowardly form.

I sensed I was in big trouble, and shuddered at the thought that the State Department had cancelled my passport. Because a passport is a very personal thing, I felt a massive sense of outrage and betrayal.

In a daze, with thoughts whirling through my mind, I did not notice where we were going—a Thai immigration compound where I was taken into a room to await the Americans. Little did I realize this was the beginning of the most difficult ordeal I would ever face, a nightmare becoming a skin-crawling reality.

I was seated at a desk in a large room bantering with the Thai police for a couple of hours, all the while looking for a way to escape.

They brought me drinks and offered me cigarettes.

Enter the DEA…

Finally, two Americans appeared: Jim Conklin, head of the DEA in Thailand and Mike Seamen, DEA from Hong Kong. Conklin handed me some papers to read and said, "You won't like this very much but you are going to the USA on the first flight tomorrow morning."

Over my protests, Conklin said, "It is people like you who manage money that keep the drug dealers in business. Don't you know that the laws changed in 1986? You should have known!"

They departed with a gesture indicating I had no rights and said, "Have a nice evening!" And with that, the Thai police took me to another office.

I was not allowed to have a Thai lawyer. I was not allowed to make a phone call. I was not allowed to appeal the decision, an act which would have automatically kept me in Thailand for sixty days.

Eventually, the policeman watching me permitted me to make a local call to an American friend living in Bangkok, Mark Schatten.

I asked him to call my wife Jenny in Hong Kong and let her know what had happened. I was experiencing both nausea and an unnamable trauma regarding what was happening; I couldn't believe the USA would stoop so low for so little. My sense of outrage nurtured a seed of resistance and endurance I would ultimately need to counteract the humiliation I would soon be experiencing.

A policeman escorted me downstairs, past a courtyard filled with women and children playing. My heart sank to the floor. I recalled the vision of my own boys as I said good-bye to them the morning before, and remembered my hesitation in leaving my family on that beautiful day. (*Sick feeling again.*)

As we drove to the airport, tears flooded my eyes. It had been a particularly beautiful morning in Hong Kong and I had wanted to cancel the trip, but instead, I justified leaving: what was there to worry about, it's just a business trip, my appointments are already set up, I'll be back in a few days.

As I was being driven in the "doom car," all I could see in my mind's eye was Douglas waving good-bye from the second story window of our home while Matt ran down the driveway waving until I was out of sight.

I had also driven myself to the *Star Ferry* where I said good-bye to Jenny, and parked the car before jumping into a taxi to the airport. As I turned around and waved to Jenny, I thought how pretty she looked and how fortunate I was to have such a fine woman. My heart was sad that I had drifted away from her and put her through hell during the last few years; we had just started to heal the wounds I had inflicted.

My attention drifted to my flight—PR 306 to Manila—the meetings I had yesterday, and the late-night same-day departure to Bangkok, where I proceeded to the Suri guest house, guzzled a beer with the proprietor and was asleep by midnight. I had had no idea what awaited me the next morning.

Walking across the courtyard, I realized I very much needed to pee, but decided not to say anything. I was surprised I was being treated like a criminal: handcuffed, photographed and fingerprinted. My small hand-carry luggage and belongings were taken away, and I was walked into the Immigration Holding Cell.

Bangkok Immigration Detention...

The "cell" was a microcosm of human survival and suffering under difficult circumstances, and an exercise in human cruelty. I had been naive. It was shocking to see how the gentle Buddhist Thais treat people who are immigration violators. Shame on them!

The physical plant consisted of one very large room with a few toilets and two shower stalls, all to accommodate seventy-three hapless souls of various nationalities. I learned that it sometimes housed up to two hundred for periods as long as eighteen months.

The "room" had no provision for sleeping; standing room only. You sat on the concrete floor cross-legged unless you could find a space to stretch out.

It was hot and humid and the ventilation was poor; everyone had stripped down to their underwear, and rolled their clothes into pillows.

As for food and water, forget it. If you had no money, you were at the mercy of those who did; they were the acknowledged leaders.

Entering the almost pitched dark room, I surveyed the seventy-three pairs of eyes that were surveying me. A quick tally indicated that most of the population was of Pakistani origin; a handful of Arabs, two or three Europeans, a group of Chinese, and the rest was a mixed bag.

A tall and thin Pakistani, who had a small mattress and a few belongings, immediately motioned to me to come over and sit next to him because he was the chief. He told me the police had told him to look after me. Not knowing exactly what that meant, I thanked him and I told him straight out that I was capable of looking after myself.

He shrugged and said, "Okay, just come over and sign in the book."

As I approached I saw that he had a large, soiled book, like a telephone book, listing the names of everyone who had passed through this hell-hole. I signed in: "Bruce Aitken, Hong Kong, British Crown Colony," placing my name on auspicious page number 108, amongst a long list of fellow human sufferers.

He told me to find a place to sit, and if I had some baht I could buy coffee and cigarettes. With cigarettes, I could buy tea with a bit of sugar. Looking around, I squinted in the dim light, and purposely avoided the group in the far corner, an obvious pocket of homosexuality.

Since I could speak some Mandarin, I gravitated to the sound of Chinese. My new Chinese friends, economic migrants waiting to be deported, shared their food and encouragement with unreserved generosity.

At 11:30 pm the chief told everyone to stop talking, to only whisper, so everyone could sleep. My anger began to swell as I looked around at the group of pitiful, harmless characters I was to sleep with that night.

Did I say sleep?

What were my options?

I told Conklin before he departed to go to hell. But, if I resisted boarding the plane, I would rot in this room indefinitely, and when I got to America, I would have no chance for bail. I told myself I would eventually be acquitted against these faulty indictments.

Four o'clock in the morning and, bidding everyone farewell, my mind began to focus on the next chapter of this very bad dream.

Enter Mike Ogilvie, DEA, along with the Hong Kong agent, Mike Seamens (the "Two Mikes"), who escorted me to America.

Ogilvie played the tough guy, refusing me any rights, threatening me with bodily harm, to bind and gag me and do whatever it took to return me to the USA. He wore a brown safari suit, the kind that was in style in the '70s.

"Cowboy" Mike had on his cowboy boots, jeans, and an old shirt with a torn pocket.

Handcuffed and bundled into a car, I watched the sun come up as we drove to Don Muang Airport, while it dawned on me that I was being kidnapped and arrested on foreign soil by fellow Americans.

Having resolved not to resist, I had no option but to fight the battle in the courts; I would have to suffer through the humiliation of being transported to America against my will. All I could think about were the boys and Jenny.

Confused, tired and frantic, I wondered if, by taking some action now, I would make things worse or better. I decided to put my faith in God to show me the way to face this dehumanizing battle. I decided to face the United States because there was no way I would ever run away from my problems; and with a family, there was no way I was going to consider looking over my shoulder for the rest of my life.

After checking through immigration, I waited handcuffed in the departure lounge with my two minders, silently wondering what lay ahead. My children were asleep in their warm beds in Hong Kong. Soon they would be getting ready for school. There were only three weeks of school left and we were planning a summer of swimming, building models and playing baseball.

Still wearing the clothes I was arrested in, I remember a very pretty stewardess looking at my face and asking me, as I boarded, whether I was feeling well. Unbeknownst to me, many friends and a Thai lawyer friend were frantically trying to find me.

No, I did not feel very well.

The Northwest Orient flight was packed with a group of elderly American tourists, nice white-haired sweet grannies who reminded me of my mom. They smiled at me until they glanced down at the handcuffs.

The flight landed in Tokyo five hours later. On the way, I was praying for engine trouble, or that the typhoon that was passing by the Philippines would divert the plane to Hong Kong. *There I would be safe.*

In Tokyo I was escorted by the goons and two Japanese plainclothed policemen to a waiting room. They offered me an orange juice, and I chatted with them, speaking a few words of Japanese; they politely asked me about Hong Kong and my family.

I sensed that I needed to make some kind of move to find a way out, but if I refused to board the plane, I would definitely be denied bail in America as a flight risk.

When it came time to board the flight to San Francisco, the Captain, a tall, handsome Scandinavian-looking fellow had to take a look at me before I could board. I walked up to him; he gave me a somewhat sympathetic glance and told the goons I could take my seat.

I must be dreaming

In the days to come, I would remember a dream that had occurred several weeks prior to the disaster.

In the dream I was at Tokyo Airport without a passport, but did have my permanent Hong Kong ID; I was boarding a flight to Hong Kong. I don't know why I did not recall the dream when it proved itself true in Tokyo. Was it exhaustion? I can only assume that God did not want me to go in that direction. I would spend a lot of time agonizing over this, and it haunts me still today.

Could I have explained to the Captain that I was being kidnapped against my will and did not want to board the flight? I was not technically under arrest, I had no passport, and was in transit. Could I have purchased a ticket on my American Express card on Cathay Pacific and returned to Hong Kong?

I kept wanting to fly home to Hong Kong. Arriving at immigration would have been a bit of a hassle, but in a few hours I could have been walking up the lane to surprise my wife and children.

I agonized whether I made a big mistake in not trying, but then I remembered another dream, one in which I was vindicated and was walking away from an American courthouse a free man; armed with a new passport, looking back through the airplane window at the coast of the USA, probably for the last time.

Which dream was true?

Having decided to bite the bullet and return to America, the clincher was actually the publicity. All of Hong Kong would have been reading about my case in the *South China Morning Post.* I would have been ruined, and my children would have suffered as a result. Without a passport, I would not have been able to travel out of Hong Kong, and I would have been extradited anyway.

My life was now in the hands of my faith in God. *Faith had always seen me through.* Had I been wiser, I would not have gotten so close to the dealings of some of my friends; but the facts would come out.

All the times I had lived on the edge also flashed before me; all the risks and chances I had taken in Asia. I had been a very lucky man. But times had changed and maybe I had not kept up with the changes.

The complexities of my life, my personal faults, being a "dreamer," and being unable to find a personal peace of mind, all were factors that played a part in putting me in that airplane seat headed for America.

I had no one to blame but myself.

If only I had been wiser. If only I could have another chance. Things would be different.

Or would they?

CHAPTER 29
Welcome to the United States of America

San Francisco International Airport, June 9, 1989

As we crossed the International Date Line, I realized I had to live through two disastrous "June 9s" (two time zones, both with a June 9). The second June 9 was as horrific as the first, but by then I was numb.

During the long flight from Tokyo, I had little conversation with the agents. They pretended to be trustworthy and tried to lure me into talking about my business and contacts. Ogilvie was civil enough, telling me how he had been a New Orleans policeman for over twenty years before joining the DEA. He said he was completely and utterly amazed I had come to Bangkok.

Why didn't my attorney tell me this could happen to me?

Ogilvie asked why didn't I renounce my citizenship? Why did I cooperate? He had even said that it was important that I separate from the others.

Yes, I had the best lawyers looking after my interest in Hong Kong and the USA. Conklin, at the Immigration Detention Center, and the Cowboy both said "bullshit" when I told them that. Conklin told me he had not known I would be traveling to Bangkok, but that he had been notified by the Hong Kong police. This time *my* response was "bullshit." Cowboy eventually stumbled, and said he knew the lawyers were dealing with it, and said the prosecutor was non-committal; however, he let the cat out of the bag and said they would probably drop all the charges and indictments against me in return for my cooperation.

I said, "That's news to me."

Sensing my chance

While the agents slept, I slowly opened my briefcase and took out my phone book and various secret papers. Soon my pockets were stuffed full. I went to the toilet, tore all the notes into shreds and flushed them all into the antiseptic innards of the plane.

We had all reached the same conclusion, perhaps unfairly. Perhaps my attorney wanted me to go to trial because it was in his financial interest. The agents had told me he knew that the government had a faulty indictment against me.

I recalled Marcus saying, "You are in great trouble and therefore need a first-class lawyer to represent you, to solve your problems, and this requires a first-class fee." That was the three-hundred-thousand-dollar fee. I looked at it as taking food out of my family's mouth. In the end I dismissed such hearsay thoughts about motive because I thought so highly of Marcus.

Upon arrival at San Francisco airport, I was met by another group of agents. Things then got much worse; this was the American gulag.

At this point I was really beginning to feel like shit. I had on the same white pull-over cotton shirt with thin blue stripes and black pants that I had used as a pillow in the Bangkok immigration jail. After a seventeen-hour flight, I was at U.S. customs and immigration smelling very foul, indeed.

Just after the other passengers departed the plane, the Cowboy arrested me and read me my rights. He also asked me if I wanted to talk to the prosecutors before talking to my defense attorney. If I was willing to cooperate, maybe we could have the whole matter dealt with then and there.

After what they had just put me through, I thought they had a hell of a nerve. The torment had strengthened my resolve. I already told them I would not testify against anyone, and contrary to their implied belief, I did not know the whereabouts of huge amounts of money, or have huge amounts of money myself.

More good news

I recalled Cowboy's words as soon as we cleared U.S. Customs. "For the last time, you can talk to the prosecutor and *maybe* spend the night in a hotel; or you can spend the night in jail. Which will it be?"

My reply was short. "I don't know what the hell you are talking about."

It was a cool morning in San Francisco. Cowboy commented that there is no fairer system of justice in the world then in the USA. He was totally oblivious that he had just been an accomplice to my kidnapping.

America, since the demise of the Soviet Union, had become the world's only remaining "super" hypocrite. *Just ask any Palestinian!* Ironically, Russia is now more like America used to be, and America is more like Russia used to be, and much more so since 9-11 and the unconstitutional and unpatriotic "Patriot Act"!

But I digress.

Cowboy and company had a car waiting for me. It was parked somewhere; somehow they forgot where. This in itself was not all that surprising.

Meanwhile, I was being paraded around for all to see, like the North Vietnamese used to parade POWs around the streets of Hanoi. Down the escalator, up the escalator. Out the door. Back inside. Up the stairs. Out the front door. Back inside. Down the same stairs, out the other doors. Round and round we went.

After twenty minutes, their legs were beginning to tire and, presto, they found the car.

They opened the trunk and dropped in my little hand-carry luggage. This was the exact moment that Cowboy was savoring to repeat, *yet again,* in front of all to hear.

"Oh, by the way," he said casually while all the others laughed, "Did I tell you? I may have forgotten. I have some more good news for you. You just got indicted in Seattle!"

It was true; a "Sealed Indictment." I replied that years earlier I had read a book called *Bonfire of the Vanities*, where it pointed out that a grand jury in the USA could indict a ham sandwich. I said, "Now I know what a ham sandwich feels like." It went over their heads. A rogue prosecution, a rogue system of justice, a rogue government!

It was close to noon when we arrived downtown at what I was told was the Federal Building; I had a sinking feeling as we drove into the underground car park. (My mood contrasted totally with that of the almost festive mood of the agents. They were so proud of themselves.)

I said to myself, *"Don't let the bastards grind you down."*

Proceeding into a lift, the door suddenly opened and a lady agent in her mid-thirties with blond hair that looked like it hadn't been washed or brushed in weeks, entered, took a long hard look at me and said, "Got one, huh?" They proceeded to talk about me like I was some object—a piece of dead meat or some dog shit they had stepped in.

Placed into a small cell with only a wooden bench, I waited to be fingerprinted and photographed yet again. As promised, I asked, and was allowed, to make a call to my wife in Hong Kong. A quick calculation through my weariness told me it was about 7:00 am Hong Kong time. It had been more than forty-eight hours since I was arrested in Bangkok, and I'd had no sleep; I knew those hours had been miserable for Jenny.

When I started to dial the phone, Cowboy told me to be sure to "make the call collect." I told him I knew the government was bankrupt, but I thought they could afford a phone call. I ignored his request. It was so good to hear Jenny's voice. Of course, she asked where I was. I could hear the tiredness in her voice.

"San Francisco, in the Federal Building, awaiting something called *arraignment*."

My conversation with Jenny was held under the stares and bent-over ears of three agents cowering behind me.

I told her that I had been indicted in Seattle, too. With a strength found only in my good Chinese wife, she offered me great encouragement and support. I told Jenny not to worry and to look after the boys. That's all that mattered: "Just tell the boys I am away looking after Nana for a few months."

Hanging up the phone, I looked at the listening agents whose faces had turned dour and mean; my spirit remained unencumbered because I had no fear of their lies and hostility. But I *was* exhausted and contemplating the next trauma, and the most important matter in my life—the legal battle ahead and who would represent me.

Being represented by Attorney Marcus had been a pleasant experience to-date. He had given me confidence but the relationship of trust had changed dramatically. Even with my assets, I began to realize I could not afford him. "Good lawyering is expensive," kept ringing in my ears.

I thought of his second trip to see me in March of 1989, which accomplished nothing. I had been waiting in anticipation to learn what "the deal" was, what interest the government actually had in me, only to be told they were non-committal. This information contradicted what the agents told me. At the same time, changing horses in mid-stream would be risky; something akin to walking through a mine field.

To my utter surprise, I had two attorneys at my arraignment. One was Dan, an associate of Marcus' firm. He arrived first, giving me a good deal of comfort and confidence, while informing me his boss would come visit me Saturday morning. It was now Thursday. Since Marcus and I had been drifting apart and not agreeing on the fees, I was really not expecting anyone.

At the same time, I had received an urgent message from a good friend who knew of my plight and made arrangements for a San Diego attorney to represent me.

Phew! I had no idea what to do except pray. I did: *Oh please, dear God, take this burden off my shoulders. But Thy will, not my will be done.* I prayed to God as I had many times when I was in trouble in my life; I put my life in God's hands.

At the arraignment, the courtroom in the Federal Building was packed. The DEA agents, plus some other obviously interested folks with unfamiliar faces, the clerk, the prosecutor, the judge were all evaluating me; and I them.

The indictments were read. I was asked if I was Bruce Emil Aitken. We moved to have a bail hearing postponed, while we were to decide on jurisdiction; decide whether to go to Reno or Seattle.

Then, I was turned over to the U.S. Marshals office in the same building, but on a different floor.

Emptying my pockets into something like a large plastic baggie, I was allowed to keep nothing. There was a short list of questions that Cowboy asked the marshal to read off to me. Was I ever convicted of a crime? No. Was I gay? No. Did I have any contagious diseases? No. The answers were all "No"…except one. Was I an escape risk? Cowboy checked yes! My attorney and I looked on in disbelief. *The bastard.*

My attorney asked me, "Why did he do that?" I replied loud and clear, "Because he is an arsehole."

The old black dude marshal, who was checking me in, then gave me a real evil look and said, "We'll be tough on this one."

I noticed a twinkle in the old black dude's eye. Finally, after a pause, the old black dude marshal said the agent wanted to make it damn tough on me by saying I was an escape risk. "You are from Hong Kong? Well, you don't look Chinese and you don't look like an escape risk to me."

He took my good leather belt as a souvenir and placed it in his drawer. He stole it. I didn't care.

Just like in the movies, I found myself locked in a jail cell waiting for transportation to the Oakland County Jail. But first they put a chain around my waist and threaded it into itself like a needle. Next, handcuffs were placed in the middle and closed around each wrist. Next, "foot cuffs" similar to handcuffs with a short chain, were locked around my ankles. That's it.

You cannot move your hands more than six inches in any direction and you have to walk in short steps or else the cuffs cut into your ankles. You can't scratch your nose, or anything else. Takes some getting used to.

It was around 5:30 pm when I took off in a caged van with three other souls. It was a clear, sunny evening and soon we were smack into rush-hour traffic, heading toward the bridge that connects San Francisco with Oakland. As I peered into the surrounding traffic, I wondered when I would be free, when would I see Hong Kong again. As I watched the Americans driving home to their families, I suddenly felt devastated.

Oakland County Jail

Oakland County Jail was no picnic. After being placed in a cell for two hours, someone realized that I was a federal prisoner. My clothes were taken away and I was issued prison clothes: blue pants and shirt, socks and rubber sandals.

Then, clutching my only belongings (three photos of my children), I was escorted into a large dorm with fourteen bunk beds and a TV. Fortunately, all the beds were occupied, so several of us were moved to a smaller room with only four beds. This was to be my home for the next five days until I could return to court in San Francisco with my attorney and move to have my bail hearing heard in Reno.

I chose the closest lower bunk and introduced myself to a mixture of characters. I quickly learned how people who have been detained for some time survive having their dignity and humanity slowly stripped away: you make friends without asking too many questions and you learn the routine—you support and encourage each other not to give up or lose hope against the system. Everyone was suffering silently, but would not give up.

Since I hadn't had a meal that day, I was offered a few crackers and a candy bar, a cigarette; but I had no appetite for anything.

Somehow, sometime during the night I fell asleep from sheer exhaustion. It had been three days since I was able to lie down or shower and I didn't care about anything at that moment. My attorney's assistant had visited me and I told him frankly I wanted to fight the case and that my life was in his hands.

The next morning, Friday, was the day before Marcus was scheduled to meet me. San Diego attorney Michael Pancer came to see me first. Then it was time to make the most important decision of my life; I had twenty-four hours to make up my mind.

Michael was someone I liked instantly; sharp as a tack and humble in his demeanor. I felt his sincerity. It turned out he could represent me for less money, since there was an indication coming from some of my co-defendants that they would assist with his fees.

On Saturday morning Marcus arrived and I was not in a very good mood. I asked him what the hell happened. He had told me when we were in Hong Kong that he had a close relationship with the prosecutors and because of that I was being dealt with favorably. What was so favorable that they cancelled my passport so as to have me deported from Thailand?

The meeting quickly came to a head because Marcus became quite angry and surprised when I informed him I was speaking to

347

another attorney. He said something to the effect that I must decide *right now,* and so I did: *Michael Pancer.* Mightily pissed off, Marcus left abruptly, huffing and puffing venom while sarcastically wishing me good luck. As I was escorted back to the room, I prayed to God I had made the right choice.

My four temporary soul and cell mates were a mixed bag. One was in for drug trafficking (smuggling pot), one was a bank robber, one a counterfeiter, and the other a jewel thief.

The daily routine sucked and so did the food. You had a total of fifteen minutes from the time you left the cell to get a tray of food, eat and get back to the cell. I learned to eat quickly.

What left the greatest impression on me, however, was the nature and mentality of the prison staff.

As a general rule, they were all sadists in varying degrees (the job did entail the threat of violence against them). My conclusion was that you had to be a bit weird and unbalanced to gravitate to the prison "profession;" however, a job is a job, and not easy to find sometimes. The key to some peace of mind was simple: avoid staff in every possible way and they will avoid you; don't ask for anything because the answer will probably be no; stop existing.

The torture of the Oakland County Jail is that you never see daylight. There are no windows. If you want to know if the sun is out, watch the weather report on TV.

After a few days I was becoming disoriented, and tai chi saved me; I practiced it in the small space next to my bunk daily. Tai chi would prove invaluable to my physical and mental health in the days and months to come.

On the sixth day, with ten minutes' notice, at 6:00 am I suddenly found myself being taken to the caged van. The driver was a young marshal in his early twenties, assisted by a girl about the same age, who blasted the radio so loud that it would make a dog howl.

The first stop was at a correctional facility near the airport to collect three others, all of us destined for locations unknown.

Soon I realized why I was whisked out of Oakland so instantaneously. To avoid any escape when transporting prisoners, they kept you in the dark; even the telephones were switched off. They didn't want anyone to have time to plan any escapades. Something told me that this lesson had been learned the hard way.

McClellan Air Force Base

An hour passed as we drove down the highway in the direction of Sacramento. I was focusing my eyes as far as possible on the horizon. Soon we approached the entrance to a U.S. military installation (I think it was called McClellan Air Force Base) where I observed first-hand the power of the government.

As we wove our way down immaculate streets, I recalled other air force bases I had seen in Vietnam, how organized they were. Stop signs and speed bumps at every intersection. It occurred to me that America itself was a pseudo-prison of life control; everyone had their lives controlled by the government; federal, state and local, everyone living in straitjackets of varying degrees.

The greatest and most valuable freedom in America was the freedom to leave and see the rest of the world. I considered myself to be, deep down, a patriot who loved his country the way it was before all the control was installed into the system. At that moment, I would have given anything to have the freedom to go to the airport and board a flight to Hong Kong.

Before I knew it, we had entered the airfield itself and were driving on the tarmac past hangars with fighter jets. I watched several F-16s take off and land. Just then, a car pulled up beside us, and a marshal inside motioned that he was the transportation from Reno.

Just as suddenly, a white Boeing 727 landed and taxied right over to us. Simultaneously, several gray air force pick-up trucks approached and circled the plane. The occupants of the pick-ups got out and surrounded the plane, assuming a type of battle stance around the perimeter. Had it been a lot warmer, and had the plane been painted camouflage, I would have thought I was back in Vietnam on Tuy Hoa Air Force Base near Nha Trang.

Overhearing the marshal's conversation, I learned that this aircraft had been confiscated by the government from a South American smuggling operation and was now known as "Fed Air," ferrying federal prisoners around the country like a domestic CIA Air America. Eerie.

I soon found myself in the back seat of the caged U.S. marshal's car headed for Reno, Nevada. There was little conversation until halfway through the three-hour trip, which included a stop during which the marshals bought each of us a coke. These guys were decent and civil, heads above the ones I had met in California. One guy mentioned that he almost had the chance to come to Hong Kong to collect me. The other fellow had spent time in the military and had been to Hong Kong several times.

It was good to be out of the Oakland County Jail and I was thankful for small things—like kindness and a coke.

With some trepidation however, I recalled the inner voice that had whispered to me long ago—perhaps it had been my guardian angel—warning me about something dark and daunting in Reno, Nevada.

CHAPTER 30

Welcome to Reno-grad

We arrived at the outskirts of Reno around 1:00 pm. The Washoe County Detention Center was a brand-new "only-opened-last-year" thirty-four-million-dollar concrete and steel monster with strange small windows and a lot of surrounding fencing.

They were expecting me. I felt I was considered to be some sort of an alien, a strange creature all the way from the other side of the planet who suddenly dropped out of the sky and landed in Reno.

I entered, stepped in front of a camera, and was told to walk to the carpeted side of a large entrance hall. I could use any of the telephones for a collect call or watch TV. Was I hungry? They had water and soft drinks, sandwiches and potato chips.

The place was high tech, which unsettled me; a space-age computerized people processor. But it was very clean, and the people were civil enough. I could not help but wonder what lay ahead for me in the labyrinth that extended behind all the automatic glass and steel doors that stood in front of me.

I wondered: am I lucky to be in this sort of place in which society has spent a fortune to look after its growing number of misfits? I was to learn, however, that it did not take much effort to be housed here. All you had to do was jaywalk, and you could find yourself spending a few days as a guest of the State. *Jaywalk?* Hilarious.

I roared inside with laughter, envisioning the whole population of Hong Kong stuffed into paddy wagons, no one left unscathed. I shared the joke, but no one laughed.

Another way to land here was to be caught in public with an open can of beer in your hand. God forbid! Presto, you are in the slammer.

No doubt about it, America had become a "no-common-sense" hypocritical police state. I was beginning to feel a knot in my stomach. *What kind of justice could I receive in such a place?* Just a few miles down the road in California, possession of a joint was a fine; here, it was a felony. I felt nauseated; claustrophobia was setting in and my breathing quickened.

Entertainment consisted solely of TV, the mind-numbing electronic teat, which made you ill, serving up huge portions of police-state garbage (violence and police, followed by more violence and more police). "Miami Vice" is child's play compared to watching live roadblocks looking for drunk drivers; live drug busts in Miami on "America's Most Wanted" and "The Reporters."

But no problem; here in Reno you can smoke all the cigarettes you want, get a heart attack and cancer, drink until your liver dies, gamble your money away, and fornicate until your testicles fall off because prostitution is legal. But don't walk across the street with a Goddamn open can of beer! You'll ruin our children! For Christ's sake, man, have some decency and use your common sense; put it in a paper bag!

But who am I to judge?

Enter

When my name was finally called about two hours later, I was asked a few questions and fingerprinted yet again. Down the corridor, I turned into a small lobby with a row of plastic seats against the wall, across from a supply room with a wall-to-wall shelf counter, and a row of shower stalls. I was asked my size, handed clothes, told to take a shower and place my present clothes into a hanging plastic bag.

352

The clothes I had on my back were still the same unwashed clothes that I had been wearing when I was arrested in Bangkok. *That* must have been why everyone was staring at me when I came in.

The first real shower in two weeks felt so good, but the bright orange clothes felt lousy. Suddenly the marshal shocked me and shouted out the command, "Grab your family jewels and cough!" Since he could not see in, I decided to only cough. *Screw you!*

After passing through more doors and checkpoints, I arrived at Housing Unit #2. My first impression was that it was not crowded.

It was a very large, diamond-shaped room with a twenty-foot high ceiling, a perimeter of two floors of cells connected by metal stairways on both sides, fifty-six rooms in all, identified by large orange numbers.

The center area was an elevated platform divided in half, with plastic chairs and tables; each side had one color TV.

Before entering and being assigned to Cell #23, I was directed to a small conference room to view a ten-minute video describing the life at the facility, and given a booklet entitled "Inmate Information Handbook." Looking again at my new attire, I started to dislike the color orange.

Having some space and privacy was a bit of a respite. The last time I lived alone and spent time with myself was in Vietnam many years before. What would I learn about myself? What would I dislike? This was a chance to do some soul-searching that would test my mettle, but the truth was I did not know if I could handle it.

I felt enormous pressure; the fabric of my mind and philosophy of life should have been well-developed by now, giving me an anchor of sanity. Peace of mind was something I had not had since last September when I phoned Jenny from Manila and learned of the Reno indictment. I knew it was bullshit, but how do you get out of this kind of bullshit? The government does not play with a full deck and the odds are stacked against you. A grand jury really *can* indict a ham sandwich.

Many thoughts would cross my mind in the privacy of the square footage of my cell. If I had been wiser I would not have gotten into this mess in the first place. I was not guilty in my opinion, yet I felt so guilty. I did not have Jenny to rely on. I did not have my sons' companionship. Over the weeks that would pass, the times I felt overwhelming grief were the times I thought of my children. Of course, they needed their dad, but oh, how much more I needed them. The closeness, the physical contact, tickling each other, watching them sleep.

Our family had made some wonderful summer plans. And although not religious, I had just gotten into reading a beautiful children's Bible to the boys at night before they slept. We had planned to swim, cycle, and hike; just the week before, I had purchased two nice folding tents, good enough for us to camp in the county park. We had models to build. Oh, my boys—my love and my life!

I Resolved somehow not to let the bastards grind me down, I thought, *I am going to kick their ass in court. This experience will not destroy me.*

Even though I had not been able to walk away from the world of business and the "funny money" with its many festering problems, I was determined not to let this ruin me. Even though I had been a fool, I had to believe. I believed it was not too late.

Bail

The foremost objective in my mind was bail and to get out of jail. It was June 1989. Since my return from Taipei to Hong Kong to face the indictment, every legal step and advice from lawyers in the U.S. and Hong Kong had been taken to create a favorable situation for bail. I never thought I would spend a single day in prison. I thought I'd done everything properly.

I had been charged in the Reno indictment with only one count that was extraditable. Having been basically kidnapped and returned to American soil, I was facing all fourteen counts, plus the newly unsealed indictment in Seattle. The nightmare I dreaded had become a reality. *Lord, this time you gave me a mountain--a mountain too high to climb.* What the government had done to me was outrageous—applying ultimate pressure to force me into some type of cooperation.

Much had to be done and the first order of business was to prepare for an interview with a person who would check on my background and make a recommendation about bail. Her name was Mary Callahan and she had a reputation of extreme bias in favor of the government. Her report was crucial.

Somehow, I sensed that the tide was very much against me. I was not the first person the USA had kidnapped. I had learned that no one previously kidnapped had been granted bail, as all were considered flight risks, a danger to society, or both. (No United States warrant or request had ever been issued and sent to the Hong Kong authorities. I was, in fact, kidnapped.)

The purpose of going before the magistrate was to request that my bail hearing be delayed until I could obtain the assistance of my Hong Kong barrister, Gary Alderdice, to appear on my behalf. It was important to show that I was aware of the indictment, had dealt with it under the best legal advice and to the letter of the law, that I was not a flight risk, and I was waiting for the extradition procedure to come to America and face the charges.

I slept badly the night before speaking to Callahan. My voice was raspy. In fifteen minutes we covered my whole life, and I would discover that my intuition had correctly told me the obvious: Callahan had already formed a prejudicial and biased opinion about me before we even met.

The day of the hearing came and the magistrate, a lady named Atkins, listened to both the prosecutor (who read the charges) and my defense attorney, Michael Pancer. I agreed to the delay and to being incarcerated another two weeks to allow time for Mr. Alderdice to arrive. I also needed the time to prepare myself. What if bail is denied? Reno was beginning to feel like a pit of quicksand.

Being confined, particularly being confined in a maximum security prison, lends itself not only to restrictions to physical movement, but to verbal communication among the incarcerated. There are a few important rules to follow. Survival can depend on following them.

The Primary Survival Rule

The most important of all rules, and you can forget the rest, is never, absolutely never, under any circumstances, discuss your case with other inmates. For that matter, don't discuss it with the marshals either.

The reason for total secrecy is that prisons reek of informants; snitches are lurking everywhere. There are desperate people who will lie and swear under oath to anything if it helps them get closer to their day of freedom. Apparently, the prosecutors and judges just love to set such scum free.

In the jail, the snitches have their own section segregated from the general population, with better facilities and treatment, but they get no respect. When they transfer to other prisons or end up returning to prison, they are marked just like cattle are branded.

Housing unit number 3...

This situation lasted five days, then I was suddenly transferred to Housing Unit #3. Thankfully, HU#3 required my clothes to change from orange to British racing green—so much easier on the eyes. Most of the folks in my new quarters were either those who had been found "guilty as charged" and were awaiting sentencing, or were awaiting bail, like me.

I was one of about a dozen Federal prisoners being housed in a State facility. Since the Federal government pays the State something like seventy-seven dollars a day for Federal prisoner maintenance, the State does not like to let us go. The profit motive is alive and well in the correctional institutions system.

I was still wearing bright orange when they took me to HU#3, so I had to stand there looking like a neon traffic cone in a field of green grass. As I stood at the entrance surveying the crowd, I saw at least seventy-five tough-looking characters.

The place was full, so I was told I had to share a cell and to proceed to Cell #9; I put my mattress and the few personal belongings I had on the floor. I couldn't wait to change into my new green suit so I would blend in with everyone else. All eyes were watching me.

I stopped in front of Cell #9, and raised my hand...the door buzzed open with the loud sickening sound only a prison door can make. I heard a murmur of voices coming from the direction of the TV; inmates watching me. I thought, *Oh shit! They must be putting me in the same room with some maniac or a raging faggot.*

It turned out the fellow there was another Federal prisoner who had been in and out of court for over a year. I soon saw the humor. I was sharing a room with the *real* "Mr. Clean"—the cell was spotless! I didn't even want to pee in the toilet for fear of messing the place up.

My roommate for the night (the very next day someone transferred out and I moved to Cell #39) offered to share his food and his books, and turned out to be a very decent fellow; no complaint that someone was sleeping on the floor and taking up ninety percent of the remaining space.

A few days later, another prisoner arrived who turned out to be a co-defendant in my case, a chap and friend, Tommy Tuttle.

Strangely enough, quite a few of the inmates were familiar with our case. I was told to forget about getting bail from Magistrate Atkins, and that my barrister may as well stay in Hong Kong. I was also told to go through the motions and set up a good case to get bail on appeal from a real judge in the 3rd District Court of Appeals in San Francisco —just spend a few more weeks in jail and then get bail. Atkins was a prosecutor's mouthpiece ad nauseum who, as it was told, bolted for her chambers for a shot of Johnny Walker Black every time there was a recess.

That explained her bulbous red nose.

CHAPTER 31
Politics and the Battle for Bail

Ah, prison! It is an experience that most sensible people dread, even fear—all those worst-case scenarios portrayed in the press and Hollywood.

At the same time, other than the loss of freedom or fear of violence, as I said, few environments give you such an opportunity to test your mettle. On the list of "things to do in life," at least I can scratch this one off.

I soon learned that most of the people I met in prison stood in stark contrast to the stereotypes portrayed in movies and other media. Most inmates were non-violent ordinary people who had done a lot of things in life, including committing a crime, but were unlucky enough to get caught.

Day in court

The day finally arrived for my bail hearing, and I entered the courtroom with a heavy heart. I studied Magistrate Madame Atkins' face intently. She wore black judge's robes, which contrasted sharply with the gray bouffant hair that surrounded her round face and pale skin that had never seen the sunshine. She had that red-faced, alcoholic look.

While I suspected the next four hours would be an exercise in futility, I was shocked at how biased and unfair she actually was. She was a prosecution mouthpiece and *only* a prosecution mouthpiece; an anathema to the system of justice that America stood for—or the one I remembered, anyway.

Gary Alderdice had flown in from Hong Kong and met with Michael Pancer and me the night before the hearing. It was great to see him; we had become good friends over the nine-month ordeal. A New Zealander, Gary was familiar with the evidence and discovery and knew that I was no criminal. He flew all the way to Reno for a modest fee and returned to Hong Kong immediately after the hearing.

Gary had brought me two letters from Jenny that I had to speed-read, and some beautiful color drawings from my sons. This greatly raised my spirits. I wanted to retreat into the privacy of my cell to read them over and over. The top of the drawing read, "To my beloved Dada." I had to cry. The marshal took the drawings and letters away, and I was never to see them again; the pervert wanted to apply more pressure on me, but the opposite happened; it made me stronger. *Truth be told, it really, really, really pissed me off.*

The hearing

Present for me were Mr. Alderdice and Mr. Pancer. My dearest friends, Mickey and Chato Howard from San Diego, had braved all to come as character witnesses and to offer their home as surety. Surely no better friends existed on the planet Earth. Against the advice of his lawyer, Mickey had come to visit me the week before.

The government had two prosecutors, Jeff Russell and Brian Sullivan, supported by an assortment of spooks in the gallery, and the tomato-faced magistrate, Atkins.

The prosecutor from San Francisco, Russell, had the floor. I tried to catch his eye to see what kind of person he was but he totally avoided looking at me; a dangerous robot. The Reno prosecutor, Brian Sullivan, at least exchanged a nod with me. A human. I felt no animosity; they were doing their jobs.

I quickly realized I was in a war and the courtroom was the battlefield. Russell took the offensive and *was* extremely offensive.

He proceeded to vomit out an arsenal of lies, a picture of deceit, portraying me as a monster, a flight risk and a danger to the community, who was facing up to a life sentence in prison. He was an artist with a poison brush. It is amazing that in a courtroom, *everyone* does not have to be under oath!

Indictments had been returned against me by two grand juries, he roared, as if this in itself had some credence to it. I had that "ham sandwich" feeling, again.

Russell "pre-offered" most of their discovery and I felt the hearing dramatically shift gears from being a bail hearing to a trial.

My sins:

1. I was a "foreigner," he said, who left the United States over twenty years earlier; who had lived in Hong Kong for the past sixteen years! (Oh, no!)

2. I was a person who traveled a lot. Here, he showed a copy of my passport with additional pages, recording my travels since 1985. Just *look* at the multiple stamps--over thirty-four countries! Oh, no! Since when is "traveling a lot" a crime?

3. Informants said that I identified them as being informants to one of my co-defendants.

4. An informant had executed a financial transaction in Hong Kong at my office in the amount of five hundred thousand dollars— "half a million." This, he said, was money laundering. In fact, *you are looking at the Meyer Lansky of money laundering*! All attending the court gasped out loud, and with malice aforethought, stared at me as if I had just landed from outer space.

5. When I became aware of the indictments, I did not rush back to the USA to face them immediately.

On and on he went, presenting a bent and twisted version of the truth and facts. What a pervert!

Next, Gary Alderdice took the stand. He certainly was an excellent witness on my behalf. He had been a prosecutor in Hong Kong for fourteen years. *He was particularly familiar with extradition and had just handled two U.S. extradition cases.*

Mr. Alderdice went on to explain how we had met in Manila; how I had first called him from Manila; how he did not know me before that date. He explained that when I learned of the indictment, I had acted immediately to obtain legal advice.

When we met in Manila, we discussed alternatives and I was well aware that I could have chosen to stay in countries that had no extradition with the USA. I could have stayed in the Philippines; I could have stayed in Taiwan, a country that has no extradition with anyone; I could have gone off to live in Vietnam.

Instead, I returned to Hong Kong, to my home and to my family. To do so would have meant facing the extradition process, perhaps a six-week process, before I would have been returned to the USA under Count #1 of the Reno indictment. I could not have been extradited or prosecuted for the other thirteen counts; they would have been dropped.

I was following my legal rights under the Extradition Act and had always cooperated with the Hong Kong police. He reiterated the fact that they had returned my passport to me so I could travel on business at any time.

Mr. Alderdice had no doubt that I would have immediately gotten bail. *How could they refuse me?* I had already been allowed to travel on many occasions; therefore, I could not possibly be considered a flight risk.

Of importance was the fact that Alderdice's testimony mentioned that I had not been charged with "perverting the course of justice" in Hong Kong; however, the police wanted me to plead guilty to "not maintaining proper records." When the prosecutor took his turn again, he stressed the fact that my records had been destroyed, contradicting his earlier statement that he had examined my 1986, and 1987, records in May in Hong Kong and deemed them to be intact.

I was the last person to be called to the stand, and by that time I was not feeling at all well; very emotional at that point. I told Michael Pancer that I did not think I would be able to control myself. He said I would be a good witness for myself and we proceeded.

Michael began by asking me some questions about my background, my family, where I grew up, and my life suddenly began opening up before me. With every eye in the packed court room staring at me, *suddenly I could not speak.* I had to turn away from the court because I almost choked on my emotions. My body had simply had enough... the lies, the humiliation, and the anger. I felt like I was about to experience convulsions. A five-minute recess was called so I could drink a glass of water and regain my composure.

Then the prosecutor asked me questions under cross-examination, and when it got to First Financial Services, he asked if I took deposits—and all hell broke loose! My mind went totally blank, and I couldn't understand the ramifications of the question. My attorney instructed me not to answer; this was beyond the scope of the bail hearing!

Prior to this, there had been another heated exchange regarding who had told me about my indictment. My attorney objected, saying even he did not know the answer to the question, and the matter should be saved for trial. The objection was *overruled,* and I had to answer. I couldn't think! I answered that my wife had called me in Manila and told me, and the questions stopped there, because as to who told her would have been hearsay. *God must have put the right words in my mouth.*

Soon, four hours had passed and it was 6:00 pm. The prosecutor reiterated that I was a flight risk and a danger to society.

My attorney reviewed our efforts to address the problems legally and pointed to the fact that I was a decent person.

Magistrate Atkins obviously needed time to write an opinion and consider the evidence, so she decided to make a decision the following day. (I sensed she was in dire straits for another stiff drink.)

On July 3 I received a message at 1:30 pm: be ready for the hearing at 2:00 pm.

After being chained and shackled and going through another humiliating check-out, I was put in the prison van and taken to the courthouse holding cell—the kind with bars like you see in old western movies.

My attorney had gone back to San Diego and sent an assistant, and the prosecutor did not bother to attend. I was inwardly pleased that my attorney chose not to attend. It showed that we knew what to expect from a kangaroo court.

I listened passively as I was pronounced as *both* a flight risk *and* a danger to society. Now I would really have something funny to tell my friends in Hong Kong.

I thought how humorous it was that Atkins pulled into the courthouse parking lot at the same time we drove up. She could not look me in the eye as I shuffled along in shackles. I could sense she felt extremely uncomfortable; it must have been her conscience. She bristled when the marshal's car radio suddenly came to life, crackling loudly, asking where the hell we were.

One said, "I don't think he will be released today," to which the one in the car replied, "Well if he is, I'll only have to re-arrest him and send him to Seattle!" Laughter!

Back at the jail, I was greeted by a tall black marshal who asked, "Is this guy coming from the laundry?"

Somewhat bewildered, the other marshal replied, "No, from court."

"No, I mean, can this guy take care of the laundry, as in 'money?'"

Really funny.

The reality?

Something sinister had unfolded, no doubt about it. Clearly, the government wanted something; but whatever it was, I could not accommodate them. Although they knew I had absolutely nothing to do with drugs, they falsely assumed I could lead them to tons and tons of cash belonging to my clients.

The drug counts in the indictment were one hundred percent faulty; and not to belabor the point, the remaining money laundering counts would have had to be dropped without any such counterpart in Hong Kong. *Cancel my passport and kidnap me and then I would have to face them all. I would have to fight for my life.*

How did they do it? They did it with that phony letter from the U.S. Consulate in Bangkok to the Thai Immigration general requesting that I be deported, based on two lies: first, that I was a *fugitive* and second, that I was a *felon.* In the court hearings and on appeal, I would be denied bail three times because I traveled a lot and had access to other people's money.

Leon Richardson: A most reluctant "expert" witness

I needed expert witnesses for my defense, and there was only one person who knew how Deak & Company handled cash in Hong Kong: Leon Richardson, a friend and prominent businessman. We knew it would not be easy to explain these matters to someone from Reno, and hoped Leon could help.

The bottom line, however, was that Leon felt my barrister, Gary Alderdice, was much more qualified to act as an expert in the law and the Banking Ordinance than himself. He also felt the prosecution would tear him apart since his credentials and qualifications were only his experience and based on hearsay. Leon also offered some very interesting insights into the seriousness of my predicament.

He wrote:

"Mr. Alderdice, I realize the severe problem that Bruce Aitken is facing in the U.S. I would like to help him in every way I can, however, the fact that I am well qualified by hearsay and the fact that I am a non-professional financial advisor, again with no academic qualifications, would not be accepted by the prosecutor who is naturally trying to rule out any evidence or witness that could be for the defense."

And he emphasized:

"At this time, money laundering is an exceedingly HIGH POLITICAL ISSUE in the U.S.

...the administration is doing everything possible to go after others such as what they are trying to pin on Bruce Aitken

"I think they would not listen to any facts even if you or I told them that what Bruce Aitken did in Hong Kong was not illegal and was not money laundering, due to the fact that Bruce is a U.S. citizen."

In the magistrate's findings

The courtroom was crowded and hot, and the room smelled of stale air and government injustice. My breathing quickened, and although I already knew the forgone conclusion, I steeled myself.

After a reading of the facts, she stated:

"I have considered the cases and exhibits provided by both sides and feel that I have no other choice but to detain you Mr. Aitken where there is a presumption to believe the person has committed the crime where the maximum term of imprisonment of ten years or more is prescribed..."

And for good measure she added:

"Even assuming that the Government had 'kidnapped' defendant Aitken in Bangkok, Thailand, and brought him before this court, such action would not justify the dismissal of the Indictment against him. Under the Ker-Frisbie Doctrine, the personal presence of the defendant before the Court gives the Court complete jurisdiction over him even though the defendant may have been abducted, illegally arrested or improperly extradited."

Something definitely is not "kosher" here...

The truth is, the option to return voluntarily was never seriously discussed, and not one offer was ever placed on the table from the government and *communicated to me.*

The words of Magistrate Atkins were quite revealing...

"There were a number of contacts over the next weeks and months between the government and attorneys for Mr. Aitken in an effort to have him return voluntarily to stand charges, but this was to no avail."

"In about March 1989, Mr. Marcus traveled to Hong Kong to meet with defendant Aitken and after his return to the United States he advised the government that his client was not interested in working anything out."

"Contrary to present counsel's contention, there was absolutely no agreement of any kind between the government and defendant's former counsel Mr. Marcus."

Bail denied and denied! A sign of the times

Being denied bail, a basic right of a citizen of the United States of America as guaranteed under the Constitution, was a humiliating, degrading and depressing development that deserves analysis.

It had a profound effect on my respect for the U.S. justice system and revealed how its henchmen operated.

The two indictments against me were faulty and they knew it. Reno was based primarily on hearsay from the indicted William Harris, who suggested I was the commission-earning "Kingpin." In Seattle, charges were based on one transaction that was not money laundering.

Early on, I had first-class legal representation and our strategy was always to talk to the government so that, should the government move for an extradition hearing in Hong Kong, I would immediately be admitted to bail in the United States.

My decision to follow this sound advice was a no-brainer, since after all, "I have an excellent relationship with the prosecutor Russell," bragged my former attorney Marcus. "I can assure you, there will be no surprises."

Glad I wasn't holding my breath.

CHAPTER 32
Back to the Future in Jail

The fat one

Returning me to prison after the failed bail hearing, the fat Italian marshal named Lou said to me, "Why don't you just tell them about your friends and where all their Goddamn dope money is, and then you can go home to your children?" I remember telling him that I was innocent and would fight to the end, and that I would never let the bastards grind me down.

We discussed Vietnam and for some reason he got very angry. He was under the impression that I had been working with the enemy in *North Vietnam*! He was a vet who had been wounded, and had been rewarded with a purple heart for a scratch on his forearm. (Kinda like a certain Secretary of State.)

Jail is a form of torture

All people in prison are under great pressure. Some cope, others suffer a lot; you observe and pity them, but you have your own suffering to bear. You turn to your faith. If you have not developed faith in God before you arrive, then you are in big trouble. It is the only thing that will save you, your spirit, your humanity, your sanity. By that time in my life, I should have been much better prepared.

A lot of it had to do with being surrounded by so many stressed-out men all day, men with serious problems who were under great pressure. Rainy days made everything worse.

I needed a miracle.

On the surface, the charges I faced spelled doom. My loved ones were on the other side of the planet. Loneliness set in. On the other hand, my karma was good and many people were rooting for me. I knew I needed to pray for my tormentors, for those who were persecuting me. I had to force my mind to think pleasant thoughts, think about things that were true, noble, right, pure, lovely, and honorable; I knew it was the only way peace would be with me.

Free as a bird...

A little bird came to visit me every morning, perching on my small slanted and barred cell "window." I had the habit of resting my eyes from the interior constant glare, and looking out in the distance because I could see a highway far away and cars going to and fro. This little bird, tiny and free, seemed to have pity on me in my human cage, and it brought back one of the most pleasant memories I had:

When I went to Chiang Mai in Northern Thailand with my son, Matt, we visited a Buddhist temple. At the base of the temple was a very large bird cage, filled with several dozen little birds. Their lovely little chirping sounds were irresistible. For a few baht donation the door of the cage was opened and all the birds flew away, and you were left with a feeling of real goodness in your heart. It didn't matter that the birds would fly back to the cage in time for their next meal and to wait for the next kind-hearted person to again set them free—a beautiful experience!

I wished it would happen the same way for everyone in the prison.

I thought about the Seattle trial. If it took place without me, I would benefit from the "discovery"; exactly what was the government's case against me.. Also encouraging was the thought that a jury is composed of twelve persons and their decision to convict has to be unanimous. Jury selection was crucial.

"J.D." was one of the marshals and he was a really good-hearted person, sometimes asking after my family. He said he knew it was tough. The government had endless resources at their disposal; tough to beat. He gave me some sound advice. He said that although the place was not bugged, if anyone were to ask what we talk about, the answer is "Hong Kong and tai chi." He told me he had heard about my case; that the government was clutching at straws. If I did not do it, great; and if I did, don't tell anybody. (The marshals, it seems, do learn a lot about the inmate cases.)

The same day I was called down to collect a big box of discovery, I was asked to immediately call my lawyer, Michael Pancer. He was coming to see me Sunday because he had reviewed everything; he sounded very confident and upbeat.

In the meantime, I needed to sit tight and try not to watch the endless violence on television. (I thought about the song, "God Bless America," but gave the tune new words: *"God help America..."*) No matter what I did, my mind raced, and I sometimes felt I was close to the edge. I was forty-four years old, facing twenty-plus years in prison. *Could this be possible?* In Reno, it is possible.

Of course, I was terrified of having a bad influence on my sons. I spoke to Matt and Doug one day.

"Mommy is coming to America to see you," Doug said. "Can Matt and me come too?"

He asked if I was staying at the same hotel as Mommy.

I needed to get bail!

Some days are better...

Jenny came from Hong Kong on two occasions. What a woman. What a wife. She looked great, but I was not allowed to give her a hug.

I had been busy reading through three big boxes of "discovery," all bullshit about me and my fellow defendants. I didn't feel sorry for myself, but I did feel sick. It was so obvious that they were trying to apply maximum pressure to break me. Thank Heaven for Jenny; she was so positive.

When Jenny left, crying, for Hong Kong, the blues hit me hard, although all I had to do was think of her and I would bounce back. Jenny's words gave me strength and restored my faith: *"We are proud of you."*

Every time I read Jenny's cards and letters, I had to steel myself:

> *"On days when you are low, just try to think of the fun things and good times you will be sharing with Matt & Doug. These two wonderful and precious boys are the source of your joy and happiness. You must fight to the end! Don't for a moment give up hope. Remember you are now at the bottom. You have no choice but to go up. Yes, it will be very painful to fight against a mountain of fabricated lies, alone, without the family around. We are not physically with you but you are always on our minds and in our hearts. Be strong, keep your chin up, let your spirit flow free and you will win. Try meditation and to relax and be calm; take it easy, Bruce...we all love you. Love, Jenny"*

Not getting bail applied the worst pressure. The reason they wanted me to testify against others was because they thought an informant in the case, Phil Christensen, might change his mind; and the other snitch, Jack Corman, was such a dirt bag they were afraid they would lose their case in the 9th Circuit.

A positive lesson in all of this misery, was a lesson in perseverance—to wait without a feeling of impotence or anger—to wait with a sense of purpose. To do this, I had to practice correct thinking, and I really had to *work* at it to overcome the things that were trying to drag me down. I discovered that my free spirit was not built for being in prison for very long, and despite my efforts, I began to feel like a caged animal.

One day, I received legal mail that included a very interesting letter to some folks in Washington, D.C., concerning having the Seattle indictment dropped. Michael had correctly pointed out to the Justice Department that both cases against me were in essence, based on the same set of facts, and therefore, one must be dismissed. The news gave me hope for a breakthrough.

CHAPTER 33

Help, I need somebody!

I finally realized that if I didn't win, I was a dead man. That's all there was to it. The horror of the thought of not seeing my children grow up, and the realization that my life was at stake, made it clear I needed to get reference letters for the next bail hearing. I didn't feel I could ask Jenny to help because she was under enough pressure already.

With a feeling of desperation, I made a conscious decision that I needed help and decided to call my friends in America, tell them of my predicament, and ask for their help in the form of a reference letter.

I made the list: Mickey Howard, Steve Deutsch, Chuck Nordquist, Roger Slater, Norm Wolfinger, Ron Langa, John Schofield, Jim Wooten, Father Jose. I gave all the information to Mike Pancer on a call to his office in San Diego, and called him back two hours later, as requested. Michael works fast. The first returns were coming in and all of them were positive.

So the cat was out of the bag: *Bruce is in prison.*

Help from home sweet home…

I asked my mom to call Ron Langa and John Schofield, who would inform former Senator Lou Frey. Ron, my oldest friend in Orlando, almost fell off his chair with concern. He called Michael Pancer in San Diego, and immediately faxed his recommendation. My mom also called my dear friend, Norm Wolfinger, who, as a Florida prosecutor himself, wrote me a wonderful recommendation.

I called Ron and spoke with him. It felt real good to have his and Norm's sincere good will and friendship; true friends indeed.

Father Jose wrote a wonderful letter on my behalf.

Steve Deutsch sprang into action, and both he and Mickey Howard courageously attended my hearing. True friends!

What affected me most was Ron's willingness to do more, asking me to let him know whatever he could do to assist me. I told him I appreciated his letter.

"I know that," he said, "but what more can I do?" He said he would pray for me; he could do that.

I could not have asked for more at the moment; people were out there praying for me.

Florida revisited

My friends in Florida got hold of the indictments against me and were rightfully horrified.

Lou Frey contacted Washington, D.C., and held a meeting with the local FBI and DEA, whom he knew well.

John Schofield was told I had been offered the witness protection program. This was news to me. John said what they wanted was my cooperation. Since it was not forthcoming, I was right in thinking that was the reason for all of the pressure.

Jim Wooten, in a show of support, attended my hearing. He could not believe the flimsy case the government held against me. He told me he would inform everyone in Florida.

Bottom-of-the-barrel night

One night, I was feeling so low that I have labeled it "bottom-of-the-barrel night." I could not seem to shake the doldrums and was having an absolutely terrible time with myself. I would walk outside in the cage, but I couldn't stand it for long. I'd walk for maybe ten minutes, then go inside, drink coffee. I felt the walls closing in on me. Around and around I went until I thought my head would explode, along with my heart, which felt like it would burst with frustration; I was terribly lonely.

In a state of despair, I placed a collect call to my mom, although it was almost midnight in Orlando. At age eighty-six, Mom was a fighter and firmly believed in her son. She had been praying for hours that I would call because she had some news to tell me and she was very excited. John and Lou had actually pulled some major strings in Washington.

Almost immediately, however, unbeknownst to her, John received a phone call from the DEA, or was it the FBI, in Washington. Someone by the name of "Agent Coombs" told him to back off because "Bruce Aitken was photographed on the smuggle ship, *Encounter Bay*!" Lies, lies and more damn government lies!

God damn it! What was I to do!

Tale of two letters

I realized I needed to get hold of myself so I could fight; I could not show weakness.

I had made it a habit to write home every day—two letters. In the first, I would write about my frustrations and how miserable I was feeling. Then I would tear the letter up and write another one that was positive in every way—no use putting Jenny under more pressure. Crucial was my decision to either go to Seattle and fight the indictment, or remain and fight the indictment in "Reno-grad." One of the cases had to be dropped; my life depended on choosing the right one.

I gave my full attention to the pile of shit they called "cases" against me, and forced myself to believe both cases would start to crumble soon.

Turn–the-corner day

Regardless of what would happen, getting bail or going to Seattle, I knew I had to accept the challenge and prepare myself and participate fully in winning my case. Seattle or Reno or both, bail or no bail, I knew I had a personal hell to pass through. I locked my mind and resolved, *pass through it I will!*

The word coming from Washington, D.C., confirmed by Lou Frey, was that "since I did not take the immunity, then they were going to throw me in prison until I broke down."

Nightmare unfolds…

There were times I felt brain-dead; actually, I must have been brain-dead since 1987 to have exposed myself and my family to the dangers that were staring me in the face. I wondered if the good fortune in my life had finally run out. I thought I was basically a good man, or at least not a bad man, so why was I facing spending more than twenty years, times two, in prison?

Horrors! They found more boxes!

The destruction of my company's documents turned out to be a double-edged sword. To my massive surprise, the Crown Pacific had overlooked the destruction of ten more boxes of my records from 1987, which was when I was winding down the business. My first reaction was shock. Then I felt it was *karma;* I knew things would either get much worse or much better.

The "flight risk" learns how to fly

Then the most amazing development outside of my case occurred; it would sustain me until the end.

A fellow inmate started to appear at the same table where I sat for breakfast. It took time for us to have a conversation because he was a very quiet and reserved fellow; but after some time, I learned a lot about "Mike" and his amazing background. Of all the topics I could have used to start a conversation, I chose Vietnam. Soon, we were friends.

Mike was an amazing person and a very experienced pilot. While flying a Falcon jet from Canada, he had suddenly been ordered to land at Reno airport where he was detained and the plane impounded. Heresay was that apperently there was some kind of a lien on the aircraft. Instead of calling a lawyer, he made one call to his partner in Los Angeles. The partner flew to Reno with a spare set of keys, and while the paperwork was still being done, filed a flight plan and took off with the evidence—the Falcon jet. Simply amazing. I loved it!

Mike also told me about his experiences in Vietnam. He was a Phantom jet pilot in the U.S. Navy, flying off aircraft carriers in the Gulf of Tonkin and flying missions over North and South Vietnam. He had been shot down—not once, but twice.

I told him about my interest in flying. I was working on my private pilot license in Australia until I had that $60,000 legal problem that discouraged me from returning there. He told me they could use a good pilot to fly a chartered Falcon out of Singapore, and encouraged me to give it a try. At first, it sounded like a fantasy.

What happened from that point on was truly a work of inspiration through the single-handed efforts of Mike "Roger That." Mike created an entire pilot's course, including making planes, instruments, navigational equipment, and a pilot's test; we made all sorts of stuff from the paper and cardboard we could scrounge up.

Where would you like to fly tonight?

Mike was a great teacher with an amazing memory. He would give me assignments, then we would sit down at night and I would "fly." The deputies were so impressed with this activity, they gave us the use of the lawyers' conference room. The lawyers' room was a glass room next to the deputy station and they could see in. They would often come by early and remind us that it was time to shut down for the night, "time to land the plane."

I believe this diversion was a grace given by God to help me through all those days when, shocked and disappointed in myself for my weakness, time seemed to stop and my suffering seemed unbearable.

In a couple of months, I completed Mike's course, took the test, and passed with flying colors.

Be careful, stay sane…

A crucial fact involved Judge Harold McKibben denying my bail "without prejudice to return again." He informed the prosecutor that the evidence regarding me receiving a commission on the Reno casino sting was hearsay, and that it may very well be inadmissible.

In fact, the U.S. Assistant Attorney in Reno, Brian Sullivan, was in a panic. He sensed I might be given bail, and suddenly told the judge that another person, named "Bender," in San Diego, had delivered money to my office with Tom Sherrett on one occasion and was prepared to testify against me. All of this—out of the blue.

The judge decided not to grant me bail. However…

With an annoyed tone, Judge McKibben expressed serious reservations and said he was going to call for an evidentiary hearing; said for me to come back and try again after one month. Jenny gave me a reassuring smile at the end of the hearing.

As I returned to my cell, I had a feeling that a crack had opened up in the government's case; the tide had started to turn.

CHAPTER 34

The deal... So much to live for...

From my Diary: "I am writing tonight because we are in *lockdown*; after dinner a spoon was missing and 'life' will not return to normal until it is found..."

Fortunately, I had had fantastic conversations with Jenny and the boys earlier in the day. And Jenny's letter reassured me: "I'm sure that *something* will be happening soon." She emphasized strength, courage and persistence; there is a light at the end of the tunnel. She only asked that I not give up hope.

> *"Every time you are down, you must get up and start all over again. It is tedious but in the end you will reach your goal and be vindicated. The boys, you and I have a strong bond and it will pull us through.. Call whenever you need to talk to us, write also.*
>
> *Love, Jenny*

> *"PS: Bruce, I know that lately you have been feeling low and depressed, which is natural. But I want you to shape up, for our future with the boys. You have your whole life and your future at stake. You simply can't give up. If you do, I will not forgive you. Please get out of any depression you may be getting into. Take things one day at a time, do it for the boys. We love you!"*

I made my own poem: *"For God has sent me a trauma of a grave and heartless kind, to test my strength of being and the fabric of my mind. I search my soul to find the answer, how I will survive. It's my faith and love of family--that's my goal to stay alive."*

Caught between a rock and a hard place

Months passed, with hopes being raised and dashed. Late fall of 1989 had arrived and along with it a great impatience. It was time to become proactive and tell the tale. At the same time, the appeal to the 9th Circuit Court for bail would soon be heard.

Robert Kimball had won his case when the outrageous government agents visited him in prison without benefit of counsel, a clear violation of his constitutional rights; school children could have figured that one out. This meant that all the cases could now move forward; the coming months would be very important.

My meeting with my investigator

My investigator, Steve Swanson, visited to discuss my case. About five foot eleven, athletic in build, with piercing blue eyes; attired in blue jeans, and a gray flannel shirt, his appearance and demeanor and pleasant personality reflected a very cool and savvy guy. He told me that one of my co-defendants' lawyers, Ed Chesnoff, had met with Sullivan and they were discussing a negotiated settlement. Chesnoff and all our lawyers wanted these indictments to come under the old sentencing guidelines because it would yield a more favorable classification for sentencing. This was good news for all defendants.

Steve contacted a lawyer friend at television's *60 Minutes*. He thought they might be interested in taking a hard look at my case, publicizing it.

Michael Pancer said not to get my hopes up for the 9th Circuit Court because there was little chance to win and he did not want me to be disappointed again. I wanted to go on record as saying that justice was no longer alive in this country. Indeed, I saw firsthand how morally corrupt the justice system and the government had become.

Justice Brandeis sums it up

"If the government becomes a lawbreaker, it breeds contempt for the law; it invites every man to be a law unto himself. It invites anarchy. To declare that in the administration of the criminal law, the end justified the means – to declare that the government may commit crimes in order to secure the conviction of a private criminal would bring terrible retribution.

The misconception behind the existence of the CIA is a simple one. The misconception is that it is possible and proper to turn over to a group of men the kind of authority and power the U.S. Constitution was specifically designed to prevent. In fact, the very existence of the CIA is a monument to the failure of recent and present generation of foreign policy makers in government to take the basic philosophy of the nation seriously.

The main work or principle that emerged from the work of the Philadelphia Constitutional Convention was that the biggest danger to human freedom was represented not just by bad men at the heads of bad governments but by good men who were put in positions where they were able to operate outside the law. The founding Fathers didn't have to be told that extraordinary situations would arise in which extraordinary authority might be required.

What concerned them, however, was that the existence of such situations might stampede and mislead men into creating a mechanism that in itself would be subversive of Constitutional government."

How right he was. Today the mechanism includes not only the CIA, but the Executive Branch, the U.S. Congress, and the court system itself. Does the "Patriot Act"after 9/11 ring a bell?

One day in the middle of November

I got a call at twelve noon informing me to be in court at 12:30 pm. I had no idea as to why.

It transpired that we were going to hear a motion to transfer my case to Seattle. I called Michael Pancer's office in San Diego. Michael had told Annabelle Hall, my local Reno attorney, to tell me but she did not.

After the court hearing, I was brought back to detention by the same marshal, Lou. He asked why I was in court again, to which I sarcastically replied, *"for the monthly airing of the innocent."* He said if I were innocent, all would be okay, and if I weren't, then the time I had already spent inside would count against my sentence. He asked my opinion of the prosecutors. I told him that the prosecutors have a *sleazy* job and they did it quite well.

Back at the jailhouse, just before dinner, it happened again. For the second time in one day, a fork had gone missing and we were back in lockdown. All I could think was, *I have to get out of this place!*

Soon thereafter, there were talks of a deal being offered if I pled to some technicality. "Depends on what the technicality is," I told Michael. I could save a bunch of money from a costly trial, and return to my family with just some damage to my reputation. If I gave the pit bulls a few crumbs to satisfy their blood lust, I could get out of the zoo!

Michael came to see me because the defendants were tabling their offer before Reno prosecutor, Sullivan. We spent an hour and a half going over everything, and I was able to stay upbeat for a change. Michael and Attorney Chesnoff (representing "Benji") were to meet with Sullivan. I was to call Michael back at home in San Diego around 8:00 pm that evening.

The rest of my day was spent in a mood of high anxiety until 8:00 pm rolled around. I held my breath as I heard the phone ring at Michael's residence. He initially said that things did not go as well as planned, but there were some positive points.

In essence, the government was reasonably satisfied with the financial side of things—the settlement with my co-defendants. It was a sizable sum, between ten and thirteen million dollars, in addition to the seven million six hundred thousand they already had.

The *problem* was the time in custody. It was a mountain of time for my co-defendants.

As for me, myself, and I...

I simply could not believe it! For me, they asked for eight years. I was not able to "fly" anywhere that evening. They said they wanted me to do some years to learn my lesson. I would most certainly lose focus and at some point "auger in", the polite term for crashing the plane. Eight years, eight years…the number struck me in the gut. In eight years it would be 1997, Hong Kong would have reverted back to China and I would still be in prison! I was feeling mightily pissed off and my temperature rose vertically.

The positive news was that the Seattle prosecutor, Mark Bartlett, did not want me to transfer there, and he agreed to go along with whatever they agreed to do regarding a settlement in Reno.

I was crestfallen, but in a moment I told myself: *the war has begun.* Michael indicated to me that their offer was made tongue-in-cheek, and he wished that I had been there. It was more like they had just gone through the motions so their superiors would be satisfied.

Next time, we would get closer to reality, and that reality was already sinking in. Steve Swanson had gained some insight and came to discuss matters in depth. Michael, or I believe it was Steve, who suggested a counter-offer: *I would accept eighteen months, of which I would have to do twelve, less what I had already done; and after a period of bail, I would be allowed to do the remainder on a farm.*

I told them that I would not make such a decision because the government were hypocrites and I wanted to fight. *Let's go to trial and defeat them! Force them to move to Seattle.* Finally, Michael cleverly said he would write to them and tell them I wanted bail before I would consider any type of settlement.

Michael followed up with, "Okay, let's go to trial! You are a good man."

Michael knew I was standing up for principles, and he confirmed that the case was a winner. There was no deal to negotiate. For me to have pled guilty at that point would have justified all the unjust actions of the government. No, thank you. *Use ordinary force to engage them, and extraordinary force to defeat them.*

Of course, I felt circumstances had definitely changed in my favor. I knew I had to focus on all of the positive aspects of the case.

God please give me courage and see me through this most difficult time in my life.

Did I have anything from the past?

I desperately needed a carrot to dangle before the government, and Steve Swanson raised the topic with Michael. It involved an approach that made sense to all, because it concerned the many clandestine payments of which I not only had knowledge, but had also made for and on behalf of the U.S. government while working for Deak & Company in Asia.

I gave Steve the particulars about the payments to John Clutter of Lockheed, the CIA connection, and the commissions paid to Korean generals; all supposedly sanctioned by the U.S. government.

My position is clearly stated...

At the same time, the following letter was tabled from Defense Attorney David Chesnoff to Reno U.S. Attorney B. Sullivan – November 30, 1989:

> *"As to Mr. Aitken, his attorney could only recommend a plea bargain that allows for his release from custody. He may have served the equivalent of an eighteen month sentence depending on credits for time served. Mr. Aitken has not agreed to any deal at this time, but his counsel would recommend a plea bargain in which Mr. Aitken was released from custody pursuant to a no contest plea to a currency violation. (Mr. Aitken has indicated to counsel that it is his firm belief that all the charges against him should be dismissed.) Mr. Aitken is the only defendant that has not had his motions heard. If he prevails as to the motion to prohibit admission of co-conspirator hearsay pursuant to the Silverman decision, there would be no trial evidence left from which he could be prosecuted."*

December

There was a long meeting at the prosecutor's office and the only hang-up seemed to be in Seattle. Michael told me some *very good news* about the so-called informant "Bender" in San Diego.

Michael spoke to Bender's attorney. Bender confirmed that I never made those statements regarding the money that he and Sherrett brought to my office in 1986; something to the effect that I would hold the money until the "mother ship" was loaded. He said it never happened, and honestly it *never did* happen. This accusation had been the basis for denying bail. He did say that he brought funds to my office; however, this was far less damaging testimony.

Michael spoke to Reno prosecutor, Brian Sullivan, and he said they seemed to be reaching agreements with everyone except me. There was a big problem, however, with the Seattle prosecutor, Peter Mueller. In confidence, Michael passed on the information about Bender to Sullivan, who promised to pass it on to Mueller to see if he would then come around.

The first of December was a day to remember. I spoke to Steve Swanson at home. He said he knew the Bender information had been totally discredited; it was a very important development.

The tension is rising!

Something was happening, something called a "status conference." The Seattle prosecution (Peter Mueller) had been holding things up and taking a hard line. It was up to Sullivan to contact Seattle.

The day was traumatic. I was brought to court; it was very difficult to witness all of these people in the courtroom, especially my friends, co-defendants, listening to the attorneys and prosecutors.

As a result of the conference, the government's offer to me was suddenly, to wit:

"Five years! To plead guilty to one felony count, a currency violation, with 4-1/2 years suspended and a fine of $250,000."

Bullshit prevailed during the negotiations; the whole system of justice was based on bullshit, fraud and, primarily, *greed;* government and prosecutor greed and ambition. They had never wanted to go to trial.

Back in prison that night, I had a visit from Dwayne, Steve's partner. Dwayne said the offer was actually very good and I should not be too concerned as there would be help coming with regards to my fine from the other defendants.

Focus on the fact that the deal will get you released immediately, he stressed. Get out, go home and never come back; it's a great deal!

I spoke to Jenny about it. Like me, she was not happy. It was giving the government several more pounds of flesh than I could bear. I had dreamed of being home for Christmas, but would instead be happy to look at the Christmas drawings I received from Matt and Doug.

The same day, a new deputy locked us in our cells for twenty-four hours; he was a sadist.

I was not going to eat.

Mentally, things were going badly.

I had been waiting to hear from Michael Pancer about accepting the deal according to the other defendants. At that point, I would have to decide.

Christmas passed.

I was experiencing painfully volatile mood swings. I needed to pick myself up and reunite with my fighting spirit: *It is only from the grave that no one returns!*

January 3, 1990

Steve came to visit me again. We went over some accounts and had a very frank talk. Then I spoke to Michael, and he said things were happening fast. He must have ruffled some feathers, because all the defendant attorneys were in Reno talking to Sullivan before going to see Robert. Michael and Chesnoff came the following day.

Steve, after pleading with me no end to accept the offer, let the cat out of the bag. *"Look," he said," they just can't drop it, not after they have made you serve almost ten months and practically destroyed you!"*

I looked him squarely in the eyes for a full minute before I replied. My mind was racing. "Okay, okay, I will consider it," I said, as the possibility of going home actually seemed to be a reality.

The main point was that all my co-defendants and the government had agreed. Their deals would fall apart if I did not agree. This was something like government blackmail. It was all or nothing. That's how the system was rigged.

"Bruce," he said, "Frankly, you may not think so, but the biggest danger you face is going to trial."

A trial would be dangerous for two important reasons.

First, the sentencing guidelines; if I were found guilty under the new guidelines, there would be little flexibility and I could very well be sentenced to twenty years.

Second, facing a jury of "peers" from Reno would be to my great disadvantage, given the amounts of money involved and the nature of the drug charges. I would not stand a chance against all those cowboys trying to understand what I was doing in Hong Kong. They would tend to side with the government. To go to trial in Reno would be an absolute and total disaster.

Finally, Steve said emphatically, in fact screaming at me, "Look man, I am from Reno. There is no way in hell you are going to win here. There is no fucking way in hell. Do you *get* it? There is absolutely no question in my mind that the jury here will not hesitate to find you guilty. The judge will have no choice. You'll be doing ten to twenty years for sure. *Wake up!* The marshall on duty tapped on the glass of the Attorney conference room indicating to Steve that the whole floor could hear him shouting! In a softer voice, he continued, "If you accept this deal, although it is not perfect and you feel humiliated, you can get out of jail next week!! If you miss this chance, with no bail, you'll rot in here for most of the next year, even before you get to a trial! Others will help pay the fine! Here are the facts, man, the bottom line..."

"Look again at what you are facing!"

Steve continued with our list of problems:

- In Reno, the double hearsay about "commissions," plus the "Layfield" statement regarding Howard Mark's initial $1,000,000 deposit.
- Although the commission evidence was recanted by Seltzer and Harris as building in bigger fees for themselves, if it was allowed in, I was screwed right there and then. Game over!
- Bender's false statement. This was later recanted; however, if it were to be allowed, it would be another major strike against me.
- The $500,000.00 entrapment by the government for which I had been indicted in Seattle and was facing twenty years. One of my co-defendants in Seattle, Brian Merrill, was prepared to testify against me and say that I knew what the money was for.
- *Most important of all,* the Seattle prosecutor had indicated off the record that many more of my clients would become defendants. They were literally coming out of the woodwork, ready and willing to testify against me. This was by far the greatest danger I was facing.

Who were they?

For starters, they were comprised of my "friend" and client B. Merrill, and also Howard Marks' partner, "Sparrowhawk." Howard Marks had already been sentenced. Sparrowhawk had nothing to lose. Merrill would testify that I knew about the Seattle shipment and tie it to the five hundred thousand dollars dropped on my office.

And who else? Who else? Who else?

We talked; Steve pleaded with me. "Man, please don't blow it. Trust me! This is your one and only 'get-out-of-jail' opportunity!!!"

Loose ends galore

In fact, there was also a diabolical and confidential caveat, impossible to stomach, that was tabled in the negotiation with my attorney and the prosecutors. It was the "proffer" that I would be debriefed about my knowledge of money laundering methods as part of my plea bargain.

Via my lawyer, I swore that as far as I directly knew, none of my clients (the names of whom the government had obtained from my files via the Hong Kong police) were involved in the drug business; none, absolutely none. I would, therefore, not be telling them about anyone, nor would I testify against anyone. I would not.

So what was the big problem?

Several of my clients had decided to sing like birds against me.

Michael pointed out to Sullivan that I had served time which was already beyond what he was asking for. Steve's words kept ringing in my ears as I weighed the options. Of course, I struggled with my emotions; the thought of not seeing my sons grow up always sent a tremendous shiver down my spine, and when I came to my senses, it was a no-brainer. They were right. I should take the get-out-of-jail card; however, something in my consciousness screamed "Beware!"

I heavily considered the advice from Gary Alderdice, my barrister in Hong Kong, who thought Michael had performed a miracle to get me out of the jaws of the monster. In time, I would come to realize that he was absolutely right.

In Gary's opinion, the risk I was facing:

"Bruce would have a felony conviction in relation to one of the money laundering charges. As to the fine, anything would be better than spending time in custody; and the sort of sentence he can expect to receive if he is found guilty on these charges could range from eight to twenty years.

"The main danger is in relation to the conspiracy to import cannabis count, although Bruce is completely innocent of this. This proposed plea deal would settle both indictments in Seattle and in Reno. That will mean that all the proceedings are completely finalized against Bruce and there are no further outstanding matters.

"There is a very real risk that if the statements of Seltzer are admitted into evidence against Bruce, then this in itself is sufficient evidence for a jury to convict him on the major charges in relation to the trafficking conspiracy and the subsequent money laundering exercise."

The letter concluded:

"I am not trying to influence Bruce who maintains his innocence to plead guilty to something he strongly asserts that he has not done. I am trying to point out the factual realities of the situation. I believe Michael Pancer has achieved all he can in negotiating this proposal and I can see no reason why Bruce should not accept it."

Finally! Plea agreement

A salient point was the fact that if any defendant chose to withdraw his individual plea of guilty, as set forth, the entire plea agreement as to each and every other defendant who is a party to the Joint Plea Memorandum shall be null and void at the discretion of the U.S. Attorney.

To my amazement, the government stated:

"Through a plea agreement, the government has offered Mr. Aitken the opportunity to be placed on probation after a term of incarceration. This short term of incarceration has already been satisfied by the approximately two hundred and fifty days of custody Mr. Aitken served in Reno, Nevada. Mr. Aitken anticipates returning to his family in Hong Kong. Mr. Aitken is considered to be one of the less culpable individuals in this money laundering case and that participation reflects his favorable deal with the government."

On January 16, 1990, Gary Alderdice informed Chief Inspector Howard that all indictments had been dealt with by way of prosecution accepting a plea of guilty for aiding and abetting others in the laundering of money.

"His sentence was imposed to enable him to be released immediately from custody. He has been in custody and his entire personal and business life has been completely disrupted as a result. I would hope that having regard for all the circumstances of the case, the Commercial Crimes Bureau can safely and correctly take a decision to his benefit, in other words, that the Hong Kong 'holding charge' should not proceed."

On reflection, had I not traveled to Vietnam last June, since no such money laundering statutes existed in Hong Kong, I believe I could have well avoided the whole nightmare. Always an optimist, I had high hopes that somehow some good would one day come out of the horrific and challenging experience.

The one and only good day in court

I did not sleep well the night of January 12, 1990, as court proceedings were to begin at 11:00 am on January 13.

The U.S. Marshals who drove me to court applied the usual customary harassment.

"Hey, Aitken, how do you like it here in Reno? How's the family doing in...where is it? Hong Kong?"

They always pronounced "Hong Kong" incorrectly with their honky-tonk accents on the first syllable "Hong," instead of evenly on both "Hong" and "Kong."

"How come you don't live here in America? You got no patriotism, man? Man, why don't you just tell the prosecutor where all the Goddamn money is and you can go home!"

They continued to play the "good guy, bad guy" routine all the way to the courthouse."I don't know what you are talking about," I said.

"Bullshit! You are going to rot away here in cowboy land!"

That did it; I couldn't resist and finally fired back.

"That's fine; right along with you bunch of rednecks!"

Once there, I tried to focus on each and every word being said—I seemed to be in some kind of trance. Before I knew it, it was 5:00 pm.

The judge accepted the *Plea Agreements*--I was sentenced to time served and the fine, most of which would be paid by my co-defendants. In effect, everyone got their deal.

In a tragic footnote.....

The advice of Steve Swanson not only turned out to be correct, it turned out to be prophetic to his very own future, albeit ten years later.

It was written in *Drugging America,* by Rodney Stich:

"After Swanson's retirement in 1984, he combined investing in California and Nevada real estate with working as a confidential informant for DEA.

"Under whistleblower legislation, Swanson filed a claim for a percentage of the money that a defendant forfeited to the government after his arrest. That claim would greatly reduce the windfall that the government receives. Possibly for this reason, government personnel turned against Swanson. (Swanson had been awarded US $8 million in 1996 by the Washoe County District Court in a civil suit.)

"In 1998, Department of Justice prosecutors charged Swanson with drug money laundering and racketeering, along with two others.

"The alleged drug offenses were part of a sting operation that Swanson was carrying out with DEA agents. DOJ prosecutors ignored the fact that he was cooperating in the sting operation with DEA agents and actually working with the federal government.

"The stress during the trial and the prosecutors' alleged false statements, the perjured testimony, were compounded by much greater stress arising from his wife's terminal cancer condition. She had a metastatic brain tumor and needed expensive medical treatment and the retirement income from Swanson's retirement as a DEA agent. Those benefits and the retirement income would be lost if he was judged guilty in that trial.

"In March 2000, during the trial, the federal prosecutors concluded their closing argument to the jurors, inflaming the jurors with the way they misstated the facts. Swanson, fearing that if convicted he would lose the medical benefits that his wife so badly needed, decided on an immediate course of action.

"He borrowed the keys to his lawyer's van. He left the courtroom, drove onto fast-moving Interstate 75, parked the van, and walked to his death in front of an incoming 18-wheeler. Swanson was killed instantly, thereby insuring that his wife's medical treatments would continue, along with his retirement benefit."

When Michael Pancer introduced me to Steve Swanson, I felt I had the best combination of investigator and lawyer on the planet. Street-smart, experienced, savvy and connected on the inside and outside. I respected him totally.

Had I not taken Steve's advice and instead used my stubborn fighting-Irish nature to fight the case, and had I ignored Michael's frank appraisal that the government saw me as a major launderer of narcotic funds, I may well have spent twenty years in prison.

Consequently, it was with some trepidation and a chill down my spine that I was shocked to read about Steve's fate. His advice to me about the dangers of going to trial in Reno and the viciousness of the prosecutors turned out to have tragic consequences for himself.

CHAPTER 35
A New Life

What a strange feeling!

So there I was, sitting in the courtroom with all the lawyers and defendants. Judge Harold McKibben had accepted the pleas from all the defendants. In my strange trance, all I wanted was to be out of the glare of the situation and alone in my cell; I had already become somewhat institutionalized.

While nine months of literal time had passed, it had seemed much longer because of the environment—something akin to being in a psycho ward. I always suspected there was something in the food to make your mind dull. But you had to eat.

More than shocked…

The hearing had taken six hours; then, there I was returning to the marshals' van to be taken back to jail for the last time. The marshals were speechless.

I had not yet been released and checked out, so I was still in custody, shuffling along in leg irons and handcuffs.

During the thirty-minute drive back to the detention center, we ran into heavy traffic. I sat there in silence. I had a totally surreal sensation of relief, mixed with unbelief; something like a feeling of detached awe. Feeling as if a weight had been lifted off of me, I no longer felt any animosity towards anyone.

Was I guilty?

Technically, perhaps, of many things; however, my conscience was clear. I looked out the van window at the freezing tarmac and smiled at the marshals.

Processed in and buzzed back into the "comfort" of my Housing Unit #3 Main Wing, dinner was just winding up. As I entered, escorted by one of the marshals with my release papers in his hands, the buzzer rang loudly.

There was a moment of utter silence as I faced the other ninety good souls living in that unit. I paused for what seemed to be a moment frozen in time, and gave them the thumbs up! Pandemonium broke out in the form of a massive roar! The duty marshal announced loudly that everybody better shut the hell up or they would be locked down for twenty-four hours. I was not given a chance to say good-bye to anyone. Instead, I was told to hurry.

"Get your personal belongings from your cell and get back here in five minutes, and don't talk to anyone!"

My cell door buzzed open; in ten minutes, I had all my belongings: a box of legal pads, a book or two, my notes, and photos of Jenny and the boys. That was about all.

The cell doors with reinforced glass windows are purposely constructed at an angle, designed that way by some moron jail-building architect so that you cannot see anything ahead unless you place your face against the glass and squeeze your eyeball until it hurts. As I walked down the metal stairs, I saw many eyeballs being squeezed and wishing me well. I turned to each cell that I passed by and again gave everyone the thumbs up. The roar continued until I cleared the unit!

That good-bye was an exhilarating experience; a magical sound that I shall never, ever forget.

About 8:00 pm

I had not seen my personal belongings in two hundred and fifty days. Upon checking out, I was handed plastic bags containing my wristwatch, about twenty-five hundred dollars in cash, and some Thai baht left over from when I was arrested in Bangkok.

There was my favorite blue polo shirt, rolled up and wrinkled. I recalled that I had worn it for about five sweaty days in a row, including on the airplanes to the U.S. It had never been washed. I stared at it for a moment and chose to put it on. I'll leave just as I arrived.

It was cold outside, but I did not give a damn! They offered to let me wait in the lobby entrance until my lawyer picked me up; I preferred to wait outside, alone in the snow. It was about twenty degrees Fahrenheit, and although I shivered like hell, I was at peace.

So many thoughts flooded my brain. I could not wait to call my mom in Florida, to call Jenny, to soak in a hot bathtub and have a good meal and an ice-cold beer. I would soon be booking a flight to San Francisco to arrange for a new passport and take the first available flight to Hong Kong.

But it wasn't over yet . . .

The feeling of euphoria I experienced was coupled with a great deal of concern, because I knew surviving probation for four and half years would be like navigating through mine fields. The Seattle prosecutor, Peter Mueller, who I emotionally referred to as the "Nazi," was a particular worry. The prosecution had heaps of evidence and documents about what I *supposedly* did and what I *supposedly* knew; and it was obvious he was absolutely furious I was getting out of jail.

Mysterious "others" had been arrested and were ready to testify against me at the drop of a hat to earn less prison time. Only people like my Reno co-defendants had the guts and integrity to remain silent, and for that, some paid the price of being incarcerated for many years.

Accepting the plea had been the most difficult decision of my life. I was certainly aware of my good fortune—the fact that a plea had been offered at all. Mueller had been away from Seattle, and it was done in his absence by U.S. Attorney Mike Bartlett, forever bless his soul.

A choice that was not...

The government knew it would be difficult for me to refuse my friends and force them into deals that might be worse. Per the Plea Agreement:

"If any defendant chooses to withdraw his individual plea of guilty, as set forth, the entire plea agreement as to each and every other defendant who is a party to the Joint Plea Memorandum shall be null and void, at the discretion of the U.S. attorney."

Kimball, Bose, Tuttle, and Seltzer, had all agreed and negotiated their pleas. I knew that part of their deals would be additional credit for time off, provided they would forfeit additional funds. Harris had disappeared.

The tipping point to my decision to take the plea was the fact that if I did not take the deal, *nobody* had a deal.

How could I know about the drama that waited just on the other side of the hill?

But first...

I must have been a wretched sight!

There I was, checking in at the crowded Reno Hilton lobby trying to look inconspicuous, wearing a smelly, wrinkled short-sleeve polo shirt in the dead of winter. To my surprise, the counter staff hardly noticed, gave me my key and said to have a nice evening.

I immediately called my mom, then eighty-seven years old; she was unbelievably happy and relieved. Through the entire ordeal, I had been worried about her more than anyone. Her son in prison? If anything had happened to her, I am sure I would have never been able to recover.

My room in the Reno Hilton overlooked a busy street strewn with glittering lights. I sat on the edge of the bed and dialed. She picked up on the fourth ring.

"Hello, Mom."

"Oh," with a sad voice, "Hello, Brucie." (I will always be her little boy.)

"Mom, are you okay?"

"Oh…"

"Cheer up, Mom! I'm out! I'm calling you from the Hilton Hotel in Reno."

Silence. My mom started sobbing uncontrollably; it was at least ten minutes before she could even speak.

I was crying, too.

"I'll be going to San Francisco, Mom, to get a new passport, then going home to Hong Kong. Then I'm coming back to see *you*!"

Next, I called Jenny.

Jenny answered the phone on the first ring. She was so surprised, and pleased it had happened so unexpectedly.

"I'll get to Hong Kong as soon as possible."

Next came a long-awaited soak in a hot bath tub; surreal; nice surroundings, able to do what I wanted to do, which at that moment was *nothing*. But, of course, my mind wandered through a list of facts and scenarios, remembering that some of my friends had gotten sentences of twenty years, thinking about how the system *tries* to break people. I kept thinking about all inmates back in the detention center, both the ones who were dreaming of their coming freedom, and the ones who had already been sentenced to decades or "life".

Then I snapped back to reality; I had to focus on a meeting I was required to attend the next morning at the Federal Building; hello probation.

Mr. Momerack & J.D.

I did not sleep well, and the first thought of the morning was for my friends still in prison. I went for a jog through a small park, where I was startled to come upon a couple of empty beer cans on the path next to a big pool of blood. *Shit!* What the hell could have happened here last night? I needed to get the hell out of Reno!

Not knowing what to expect, I arrived at the office of the head parole officer, Wayne Momerack, before my meeting scheduled for 9:00 am. If I were a minute late, I figured they would send out the marshals.

Mr. Momerack was expecting me.

"How long have you been in Washoe County jail?"

"Since I arrived on June 15, 1989."

"What!! Since the day you arrived!?"

"Yes, sir."

He seemed surprised and sympathetic to my having had to spend my entire stay in Reno doing "hard time" in the Washoe County Detention Center.

Because I would be living in Hong Kong, my probation would be "unsupervised," which meant I had to complete a monthly form advising him of what I was doing and listing my income. That was it. Should any inquiries come up regarding my probation, he would be the person who would communicate with me. To my recollection, we shook hands and said good-bye and good luck.

We did not meet again, although at times I was concerned that it would be reported to the court that I was not sending back the monthly income report timely or not showing sufficient income; but Wayne Momerack was a very decent fellow doing a tough job well. I liked him.

That evening I had the pleasure of having dinner with J.D. Wallace. "J.D." was the marshal that I had come to know, trust and respect. His kind words of support (*Hang in there, man!*) when I was at rock-bottom always gave me the strength to snap out of it.

The first day, I spent a lot of time feeling like I was disembodied; living in a surreal world. Twenty-four hours earlier I could not so much as have my own spoon; and yet, there I was with J. D., sharing a happy, peaceful evening—I even had a dinner knife! It was getting late when J. D. and I heartily shook hands and wished each other well. I had found a real friend, a kindred spirit; I knew God had sent him to help me. (God bless you, J.D.)

Passport office, San Francisco

The next morning I went straight to the passport office; first in the queue. Based on the documents I was given by the government in Reno, obtaining a new passport should have been routine, but what can I say—when dealing with the government, nothing is routine.

The first task was for the staff to enter my name in the computer. Well, as soon as that happened, all hell broke loose! I thought I was about to be re-arrested. *We have to check this out! Wait right here and do not leave.*

"No sweat," I said. I didn't intend to leave without my new passport.

Calls were made to the prosecutor in Reno and to the State Department in Washington; I sat silently saying to myself, *Go ahead; knock yourselves out!* After about an hour, they had done just that—knocked themselves out; then, in a calm and friendly manner, they issued my brand-new U.S. passport.

Sayonara America… for now!

Taking the deal and getting out of jail, in spite of the fact there might be battles ahead, did turn out to be the right decision. With about half a dozen "friends" waiting in the wings to testify against me, it would have been almost impossible for me to have survived a trial in Reno.

Agreeing to accept the felony conviction and fine was a lot more than the government deserved; they lamented letting me off easy, and could try every way they could to get me back in jail. However, I would be back in Hong Kong with no intention of returning to America for many years to come—even if I was served a subpoena. I would *disappear*, and Vietnam was as good a place as any to fade into. In time, everything would pass away.

I admit I did not anticipate the insane tenacity of the Seattle prosecutor. I was a money launderer, so what? Were my clients involved in smuggling drugs? He said so, but technically his guess was as good as mine. I never saw any drugs. I only saw cash. Talk of drugs was non-existent. Of course, in reality, I knew otherwise; I was not a fool.

I could tell my version of this truth, but I believed without a shadow of a doubt that the government was not at all interested in hearing the truth from *"the Meyer Lansky of money laundering."*

END OF PART SIX

The Cleaner

Part Seven

Out of the frying pan, into the fire!

FLIMFLAMMED AND SLAM-DUNKED

The Cleaner

Chapter 36
1990 – Out of the Frying Pan

The first shock...

January 13, 1990, should have been the happiest day in my life; it was not. I was about to be released from the prison gulag, however, the devil was in the details of the plea agreement.

In court and *seeing for the very first time the exact wording* of part of the plea, I had to agree *before* sentencing to face a debriefing in Reno prior to my departure, and another *if* required in Seattle. Since I had always professed my innocence, it was assumed that this would not be a problem. There was nothing to hide. It was a mere formality according to my attorney Michael Pancer, my investigator Steve Swanson, and my barrister in Hong Kong, Gary Alderdice.

The government wanted to know about all the money laundered for my clients, wanted me to *throw them a crumb*. I had to make a quick decision. This crumb-throwing was against all of my principles, and all I felt was sick. I mean, all the defendants had agreed; this was prosecutor coercion.

It was ironic that, in prison, I had peace of mind from not having to communicate with the government regarding its witch hunt. Because of the people chomping at the bit to testify against me, I could see I would have to face one battle after another.

I needed another miracle to win the new battle.

Michael Pancer reassured me that this was the best deal he could have possibly negotiated. He assured me we would get through both meetings with the prosecutors and I could put this experience behind me forever. It was supposed to be a piece of cake. All I had to do was tell the *truth*. Of course, in theory, he was absolutely right, and I respected that, but I knew I would have to use every bit of strength and wit to survive the sentencing period and probation.

First in Reno...

I had gotten through the Reno meeting with ease, offering and saying nothing. It was just like Michael and Gary said—just a face-saving exercise. Did I plan to be in Vietnam? It is closed to America. Keep us informed if you see anything. *Don't hold your breath.*

The Reno prosecutor, Brian Sullivan, was civil. I smiled when his wife suddenly appeared in his office, stopping by to see what I looked like. Apparently, I had been the number-one topic at the dinner table in the Sullivan household for quite some time.

During our meeting, Sullivan played a tape that Corman and Christensen had made while meeting with Brian and me at the coffee shop in the Hyatt in Cha Am, Thailand in 1988. Not one word had been mentioned about drugs or money laundering. The tape completely exonerated me.

To everyone's credit, the meeting was more of a formality than an interrogation—even somewhat cordial.

It is interesting to me that when Brian and I were in Thailand, we visited a temple where we individually asked a Thai monk about our futures. When we shared our experiences later that day, our faces turned ashen: the monk told each of us we would go to prison.

Seattle...

By late February, I had made a return trip to America to see my mom, then made a point of facing Mueller. *Let's get it over with.*

Michael Pancer made the arrangements.

First, to ease the tension, Michael took me to a Seattle Supersonics basketball game. (I couldn't watch much of the game.)

Peter Mueller was the Seattle "*persecutor*" who reminded me of Jack Corman with his whining voice and dour demeanor; another squeaking balloon that made your skin crawl.

I felt his tenaciousness and zeal to do his job.

The duel begins

Seattle was the complete opposite of Reno, and it did not take long before the kitchen got hot. That is also when I realized the challenges facing me in regard to the agreement..

The concern was how to dance around Mueller, because there was no doubt in my mind he would be thoroughly disappointed in the outcome. As a matter of fact, he was mightily pissed off and spewing venom as soon as the pissing contest began. He was disillusioned because he had totally unrealistic expectations; there was no meeting of the minds. *We were worlds apart, as far apart as night and day.*

Mueller's office was cluttered with files. His pale face was etched in a way that suggested a dour, driven personality. (probably because It rains a lot in Seattle.) At the onset, Michael Pancer protested vigorously that any violation would not be determined by Mueller (*God forbid*) but by the judge in Reno. Mueller reluctantly agreed and began the interview, or shall I say pissing contest *interrogation.*

This first decision was to become the major factor that saved me from what was to become Mueller's constant accusation that I was holding back information, and his zeal to revoke my deal. He wanted so badly to incarcerate me and charge me with additional offenses.

War.

Two months later, breach of plea already

There was no way I could satisfy Mueller's blood lust, and I didn't even try. His methodology was to go over all the client records I had at First Financial, one by one.

From the beginning, I had blocked out any memory of anything that could hurt someone, whether Mueller liked it or not. I was determined that absolutely no one would suffer as a result of my explanation of First Financial's accounts. He was wasting his time.

I kept my answers short and my knowledge non-existent. This truth was difficult for Mueller to comprehend, and he became more furious with each moment.

"Sorry, Mr. Mueller," I would say. "Truthfully, I have no idea about the business of this person and I certainly do not have any idea of the whereabouts of that person's money."

I was beginning to sound like a broken record because I was speaking just like a broken record. I could not wait to get out of there and return to Hong Kong.

When I did return to Hong Kong, Mueller was still communicating with Michael Pancer. The communications relayed to me from Michael usually started with the words, *"Bruce, Peter Mueller says the government has information that you knew about..."* whatever.

I had to say the same thing over and over; even my April 11, 1990 letter to Michael Pancer and Gary Alderdice had clarified my intentions:

> *"I want to mention that in spite of all the difficulties I was facing in prison, I would never have entertained any agreement if I thought my statements could hurt anyone, especially since the questionable people I know have already been dealt with. So far, this has been the case. I will never testify against anyone!"*

410

I'll get by with a little help from my friends

Mueller continued to ask me about each account, all of which I confirmed were clean as a whistle and not tainted with drug money *that I had direct knowledge of.*

One of my clients and friends, Brian Merrill, had been introduced to me by Tim Milner and was a known associate who had been indicted because of the *Encounter Bay* bust. Corman had confirmed, in conversations with "Brian," that he was on the boat off the coast of Vietnam, that handled the transfer to the *Encounter Bay.*

I knew nothing about this. I had been to dinner and visited Merrill and his girlfriend, Susan, on several occasions while they were living in New York. He was a master carpenter and was building his own pleasure yacht, *Glide,* to sail around the world. Absolutely *no* mention of drugs.

When Mueller asked me about him, I gave him my canned reply: *"Brian Merrill, a really fine fellow, excellent sailor and yachtsman, small account and not drug related that I have explicit personal knowledge of."*

I never was so rude as to ask my clients personal questions about the source of their funds. Deak & Company had taught me well. Never listen to hearsay. I was not paid to be a policeman. I was in Hong Kong.

He said what?

Michael Pancer called one day and told me that Peter Mueller was about to have a stroke because *Bruce lied* about Merrill. In an apparent effort to save himself in the Seattle indictment, Merrill had informed Mueller that he was prepared to testify against me, saying that I knew he was involved in smuggling drugs, and that the money in his account with First Financial Services was *all* from the sale of drugs.

Sad—all I felt was sad. This was totally out of character for Merrill. I could only assume he had been put under unbearable pressure.

Mueller immediately accused me of violating the plea agreement *that in spirit, I never agreed to.* And to make matters worse, another defendant and client and "friend" supposedly expressed his willingness to roll over on me. Now I was in very big trouble, facing a nightmare as big as the one I had experienced the previous year.

Mueller and Sullivan team up against me...

In a telephone conversation, Michael told me he talked with Sullivan in Reno and learned that Mueller now had very grave concerns about the workability of the proposed resolution of Bruce Aitken's "violations" of the plea agreement. Per Mueller: "The problem is that there is no guarantee that Aitken is potentially subject to any meaningful penalty for the violations."

Mueller said that I had lied about Merrill, and insisted I sign a written stipulation, which would be presented to the court in Reno, that these lies constituted a violation of the plea agreement, which the government had discretion to bring before the court at a later time in the form of a motion to revoke my probation and to incarcerate me without any preconditions.

I was about to ask Michael Pancer to politely tell him to go to hell (or worse) when things suddenly *got* much worse.

Michael was very concerned. He said he hoped we could get back on track and keep me out of jail.

"When I first met with Peter Mueller," Michael said, "he was adamant that you would have to be incarcerated even if you cooperated in the future. He called me the next day and basically said that he had been flimflammed in that you did not cooperate with the government, and yet there doesn't appear to be any detriment to you as a result of your failure to cooperate. It is really touch and go.

"Mueller also had questions concerning Howard Marks. He wants you to know that Marks got a twenty-five year sentence and may well be debriefed. He also wanted you to know that Marks' brother-in-law, whom you know, Patrick Alexander, is in jail and may be debriefed. In other words, we don't want another Merrill situation!" I assured Michael not to worry about Howard Marks, a brother of the highest ethics and integrity.

He continued, "These are not all of the government's many areas of concern, but they are the main ones."

I thought to myself, *this is unbelievable! How did this happen?* Michael was besieged with a pile of "dog shit" from Mueller and Sullivan that forced us to immediately switch into "saving me from incarceration mode; at any cost mode."

With more and more people coming out of the woodwork, Michael was wisely looking for a second chance to go back and correct the alleged "mistakes" and save me.

His concern for me was genuine—and spot on.

Shock and awe and another chance...

Michael replied that we needed to proceed with the sentencing in Reno. However, we would stipulate before the court as follows:

"That Bruce Aitken did not disclose all relevant facts concerning Merrill. We will stipulate that there had been a breach of the agreement by Bruce Aitken and as a result the government had the right to take advantage of that portion of the sentencing agreement which would allow Mr. Aitken to receive a full five years in custody.

"However, and this is a big 'however,' we will also inform the Court that the government does not intend to make that request at this time. The Court will be informed that the government has agreed with our request that it will wait until Mr. Aitken has been further debriefed. The Court will be informed that it will be entirely up to you, Mueller, as to whether or not you wish to have the sentence imposed and that it is your intention not to do so as long as Mr. Aitken is entirely cooperative and truthful from here on.

"There will be other changes of the original agreement. As a result of Mr. Aitken's failure to disclose all relevant information, Mr. Aitken may be called before the grand jury in Reno as well as in Seattle.

"The above-mentioned changes in the original agreement are substantial. In addition, it should be mentioned that the government has not waived its right in the agreement to try Bruce Aitken for making a false statement in Seattle. It is my understanding that will not be done as long as Mr. Aitken will be cooperative and truthful in the future.

"Mr. Aitken's stipulation will contain a paragraph that he has been advised by me that the Court can impose a sentence of imprisonment as a result of his failure to abide by the terms of the agreement. His stipulation will further state that it is at his request that the government is not at this time requesting a period of incarceration to be imposed, and he understands the Court has full authority to impose that incarceration at a later date.

"This should cover all the matters discussed and it would appear to give the government all the necessary protection in this matter. I believe it is to everyone's interest to get this matter back on track."

My blood was boiling!

I suddenly felt like I was walking on paper-thin ice. While I sincerely appreciated Michael's effort to go for _one more last_ *chance* based on a ton of incriminating garbage Mueller had puked up, I could never bring myself to say I lied and sign any stipulation to this effect—such was alien to my chemistry.

What to do?

I called on every fiber of my being and decided to fight the bastards! I pointed out that all Mueller's ancient-history-questions about Merrill took place before the Seattle conspiracy of which I had absolutely no knowledge of his involvement.

I responded to Michael:

"I will never stipulate that I did not disclose all relevant facts about Merrill and will not agree to a full five years in custody. I will never agree to let Mueller unilaterally decide and take this matter out of the hands of the judge. I do not agree to the changes in the plea agreement regarding testifying against individuals in Seattle and Reno. I will not sign any such statement agreeing to the changes.

"I hope you will fully support me in this big fight because I think it has only begun!"

The reasoning and the logic

I was relieved when Michael said he had no problem proceeding as outlined in my letter:

"You may be assured that you will be fully supported. It was my thought that if we could put this matter behind us without risk of incarceration, then we should do so. You make a lot of sense in your fax and I am happy to fight for you.

"Finally, my letter to Peter Mueller in no way binds you to anything. Nor is it an admission by you. It is merely an attempt to reach a settlement which has not succeeded.

"I am sorry that you and I had a misunderstanding as to how we were to proceed, but be assured that you are not committed to any course of action at this time. When I met with Peter Mueller, he

415

showed me enough of the transcript to convince me that we will have great problems prevailing at a hearing concerning whether or not we complied with the plea bargain.

"Merrill is going to testify and contradict a number of statements concerning him. The essential contradictions could be concerning whether or not you believed he was a drug dealer. In addition, his testimony concerning cash payments to you will also be considered a violation of the plea agreement.

"It is my thought if we have a hearing before Judge McKibben in which he believes that you not only violated the plea agreement by leaving out material facts concerning Merrill, but also further believes that your testimony in his court in that hearing is equivocal as to your contacts with him, then the judge will reflect that disbelief in his sentencing of you, should we lose the hearing.

"In addition, I am absolutely convinced that we are in many other Merrill situations just waiting to happen!

"I did inform Peter Mueller that you had been interviewed by that other agency, the CIA. If they wish to do anything on your behalf, now is the time. You may want to contact them."

Yes, this is a carrot I could dangle in front of them. The CIA agent I met in Hong Kong asked me to keep in touch should I come across any "information" about MIAs in Vietnam. Although I knew chances of this happening were completely "nil", I had a carrot to dangle.

Michael continued:

"Bruce, it seems to me that if we modified the agreement to state that you left out some information, then we will not be giving the government much in return for avoiding a hearing at which we are an underdog. Also, we do not know what else Peter Mueller is holding back."

Utter dismay

I knew I would never be able to perform what the government defined as "fully." My memory is poor, and the amount of material I had to cover was staggering and ancient. I had many accounts, and I did not go following my clients around prying into their affairs. My conscience was clear because whether I knew about their business or not was immaterial to me.

I don't believe I would have ever considered the plea agreement had it not applied to all defendants and had I been separated for trial and granted my constitutional right to bail. The government's use of coercion as a policy is shameful!

Critical decision

I did not tell Michael, or anyone for that matter, but I made a critical decision at that moment. If necessary, I would do a runner—go to Vietnam and stay there indefinitely. They would have to kidnap me a second time, and if they tried it, they would find it to be very difficult.

Willing to forgive in exchange for more blood

Mueller: "The government considers that Mr. Aitken, pertaining to his denial of knowledge of any involvement by Merrill in the illegal drug business, has breached his plea agreement and will request a date be set for a hearing on revocation of probation on account of the alleged breach."

Mueller wrote to Michael Pancer:
"I told you the government has no interest in Bruce Aitken's 'cooperation' if it is not given wholeheartedly without reservation. We have spent enough time cross-examining and

fencing with this individual, while he endeavors to tell us only those things he thought we could otherwise prove and held back the information he believed we didn't have, or couldn't get otherwise."

However…

"Finally, after our conversation, it occurred to me [*Mueller*] that provided he is truthful and cooperative in the future, there might be one circumstance in which the government could agree *in advance* not to seek imposition of a prison sentence on account of Mr. Aitken's plea violations relating to his knowledge of matters concerning Merrill. That circumstance would be if he can now proffer and provide current useful information of major importance to law enforcement, such as information leading to the apprehension of a major fugitive like Thomas Sherrett or the Shaffer brothers, or significant information relating to the current operation of an important drug smuggling enterprise."

Facing a rabid dog…

I informed Michael that what was most important was that *none* of the inconsistencies were in any way material to the Seattle conspiracy. What was material was that Merrill came to Hong Kong during the conspiracy. What was material was the fact he did not contact me and I never saw him during the conspiracy period.

What were the *petty* violations that Mueller was complaining about? From the transcript of the Seattle interview with Mueller:

Q: After visiting Merrill in New York in 1985 or '86, when did you next see either of them [Merrill or Crooke]?
A: I haven't seen either of them since.
Q: In person?

A: In person.

Q: After visiting them, have you communicated with them in any other way?

A: I have not.

Q: Have you spoken to them on the phone for example?

A: I have not.

Q: Do you know from any source as to Mr. Merrill's involvement and his whereabouts from the time of the seizure of Encounter Bay at the end of June 1988 until today?

A: I have no idea.

In my fax to Michael, I had pointed out, "What is my motive to lie about Brian Merrill, knowing very well during debriefing that he was one of the Seattle defendants I would not testify against? There was *nothing* material in Mueller's allegations!

"Let's cancel the 'plea' agreement and go to trial!"

What were my choices, Michael?

Michael stated:

"After numerous telephone calls and Faxes among myself, Sullivan and Peter Mueller, I can define your alternatives:

1. You can admit to the court that you held back information about Merrill and hence have violated the plea agreement. The government will tell the judge that they are going to give you an opportunity to continue to cooperate; but they can, if they wish, ask the Judge to revoke your probation. The government would agree, however, that they are not going to pursue the charges in Reno or Seattle *unless you again* violate the conditions of the plea agreement. You would then be entitled to a hearing before Judge McKibben.

2. Your other alternative is to not admit that you held back information about Merrill. In that event, the government would set a

419

hearing date at which they would try to convince the judge that you did hold back information. If they were successful at the hearing, they would then institute the charges in Reno and Seattle; and in addition, they would try to prevent you from withdrawing your plea. They would then ask the court to sentence you under the plea agreement to five years in custody. This will then be followed by prosecution in both Reno and Seattle.

"It is my recommendation that you choose alternative No. 1 since the last thing we want to do is to face the most serious charges in this case. I know these are not ideal alternatives, but they are our only choices."

In my opinion both alternatives sucked! I wrote...

"Alternative No. 1:

In my opinion the Merrill matter does *not* amount to a violation of the plea agreement. It is inconsequential and immaterial. Therefore, it is the government that is not acting in good faith in this instance. If the government can, if they wish, ask the judge to revoke my probation, they will surely find a technicality to do so later or use this "power" to intimidate me further.

"Alternative No. 2:

I did hold back information about Merrill but I cannot admit that I did. If I win at the hearing, I have no real benefit; but if I lose, the government can destroy me. I am prepared to fight Merrill over this!"

I reflected that the problem went back to the wording of the original plea agreement that I had only a few minutes to consider before accepting.

There was no meeting of the minds in the agreement. All this government talk about prosecution in Reno and Seattle, and now it's only me? It was simply further intimidation.

In addition, by chance, I met Don Taylor, a defendant in another case in Bangkok. He said that Mueller had pressured him mightily about me, but that he told the truth—I knew nothing about his money or his business; that, in fact, a stipulation of meeting me was a promise *never* to talk to me about his business.

Michael replied…

"There is one concession that I believe I can get from the government. That concession would be that you admit to a violation; then they can never prosecute you under the original charges. That is, they will have the discretion to go to the judge and ask that five years be imposed at some time in the future, but they can never reinstate the charges in Seattle or Reno.

"I believe it would be a terrible mistake to not accept the bargain if we could have that thrown in. That means your total exposure would be forty months in custody of which you have already done 9 months, and it is far from certain the judge would impose that sentence because you held back information about Merrill.

"It is quite possible that the government would prosecute you in either Reno or Seattle. *They do believe that you are a major launderer of narcotics funds. Do not assume they will not prosecute you.* In Reno they would only have to prove that you intentionally held back information. In any event, it is important that we try to resolve the matter so we can plan for either alternative.

"*Bruce, the government saw you as being much more involved than Ed Seltzer. That is why their best offer to you was eight years.*"

Can things get much worse?

Telephone conversations between myself and Michael Pancer reflected my disgust in dealing with the debacle in which I found myself. I knew Michael was right, but I couldn't accept it. What the hell to do?! Mueller told Michael they had at least nine or ten additional major problems with my statements, because everything I said was *no*.

Honestly

My real dilemma had to do with my upbringing in the good ol' USA. Ingrained into the sinew of my being was the fact that you never, *absolutely never*, snitched on anyone. I kept thinking, *How had we become a nation of snitches? Screw the prosecutors!*

There was much, of course, that I did not tell them that was purely circumstantial or hearsay, because thankfully they did not ask the right questions, and I truthfully did not remember.

Help would come from an unlikely source (a friend and client who was still a fugitive), and definitely delivered via an *act of God*.

Taking inventory, I decided that my very survival depended on staying out of reach of this vicious prosecutor (Mueller), even if it meant spending long periods of time away from my family. I was in a war of wills and wits and did not know where to turn for relief.

It was a depressing time.

CHAPTER 37

Back to the Future in Vietnam. Time to Disappear.

I needed a miracle and another "carrot" to dangle

I reflected deeply during this time and remembered a conversation I had with Steve Swanson. He provided an interesting insight and way to communicate with the government in clandestine areas. After all, he was highly experienced and highly regarded, having been "on the ground" for years in Marseilles, France. His undercover exploits were documented in *The French Connection*. He had advised me to look for a way out; said the government had a weak case against me.

However, in a trial with a jury composed of locals from Reno or Seattle, I would not stand a snowball's chance in hell!

Think! What did I have to proffer from the past? I immediately thought of John Clutter and the Lockheed scandal in Japan. I was assuming Clutter was the CIA Station Chief who ordered payments made on instructions to Deak & Company from the U.S. Consulate in Hong Kong.

While I understood Michael's contention that I would be in a better position if I limited my exposure to a few years in custody rather than the twenty-five year possibility, I felt I should follow my instincts; there could be room for further negotiation.

Michael wrote to the government and told them we were prepared to go ahead with a hearing, and not attempt to revoke the plea bargain.

Michael wrote to me: "In essence I am recommending a conservative approach to avoid exposure to the longer term in custody. You have every right to reject that approach because you are correct in that it does mean that there is a greater chance you will do the smaller amount of time in custody. This disagreement will not make me any less vigorous in my defense of you."

I felt great comfort in his words, however…

He continued: "At this time, the only violation I know for sure the government will allege, will be misstatements concerning Brian Merrill. However, Peter Mueller informed me by telephone that he believes he found many other examples of your failure to be truthful.

"If you are successful in the hearing, then you will be in the position you were prior to the hearing. If you are unsuccessful, the Judge will incarcerate you for some period up to five years at the conclusion of the hearing. The court has made it clear that there will be no further delays in your sentencing because of the numerous delays that have occurred so far. One way or another, this matter will now be resolved."

Yet, I lamented the situation I now found myself in. I kept reminding myself that I wanted to fight the "flimsy" cases that the government had against me; in Reno based on possibly inadmissible "hearsay" evidence and in Seattle, based on one forced intrapmant transaction that was not money laundering. I wanted to win all the marbles.

At the same time, I woke up in the middle of the night in a cold sweat every time I thought about going to trial and the high stakes gamble I would be taking. Should the jury foreman, at the critical moment the judge asks for the verdict, utter the word "guilty", I would be inside for the next ten years at the minimum.

Shaking myself back to reality, I pinched myself. I'm out. And I'll do whatever it takes to stay out!

I am badly in need of that carrot!

Enter my good friend and fugitive Tom Sherrett. Mueller had indicated many times to Michael Pancer that he was salivating to receive any current information on Tom Sherrett. Tom had simply vanished into thin air. Exhausted, Mueller had run out of patience. I had done nothing to help. However, I did have some very confidential and well-hidden tidbits of information to discuss with Michael Pancer on the phone, and now was the time to do it.

Tim and I had found a reason to make several return trips to Saigon to work on a wild idea we presented to the Saigon Sports Department: to organize, of all things, an international marathon. Saigon offered an escape and a repose from the incessant whinning and threats from the tenacious Mueller. I never told anyone that I had met Tom Sherrett in Saigon about a year earlier. At the time, Tom was aware that I had been traveling to Saigon. He found me by checking my name at Vietnam Airlines every day until I arrived. This was not difficult, as few Americans were visiting Vietnam at that time.

One morning the phone rang around 7:00 am; I picked it up and immediately recognized Tom's voice. He was calling from the hotel lobby.

Over coffee and breakfast, we shared each other's serious concerns. I was happy to see him even though it was not a happy time. Tom was tired. Being a fugitive takes its toll. He was looking for solutions but was facing a nightmare indictment and a very long prison term. He knew that the government had interviewed me, and that the government could not be trusted and was full of leaks.

I assured Tom truthfully that I knew nothing and said nothing about his Vietnamese wife and brother-in-law being involved in his business or in carrying money to Hong Kong. That said, while still on probation I was also in a highly sensitive position should it ever be known that we had met.

Now, after almost ten months of "dragging Mueller along" and not having seen Sherrett since that day, informing the government of the meeting was the only carrot I could dangle in front of them in order to buy time, and at the same time do no damage to Sherrett. I was sure that Tom was long gone from Vietnam. He is a good friend and would understand.

I spoke to Michael, gave him the information, and asked him to pass it on. He did.

The effect was electric!

Chapter 38

Did we hit a "Mueller" nerve? He wrote...

"On April 29, 1991, you called me and indicated that Bruce Aitken had recently acquired information which he believes might be useful in apprehending a DEA fugitive whose name you provided me.

"We are very interested in apprehending the fugitive in question and would like to receive Mr. Aitken's information as soon as possible. We would agree to the final dismissal of the above-mentioned Seattle and Reno charges if the information Mr. Aitken provides results in the apprehension of the named fugitive.

"However, if Mr. Aitken provides such information and assistance but the fugitive is nevertheless not apprehended we are not willing to agree to the dismissal of the above-mentioned charges. In short, we will agree to provide the consideration you seek in return for results and not merely for information."

Dear me

Mr. Mueller's letter did not even warrant a reply in my estimation. Requesting proactive assistance? After all we had been through he still didn't understand—I was totally exasperated.

Michael replied.

"You proposed that Bruce Aitken return to Reno and be sentenced pursuant to the plea agreement. He would then meet with the agents and give them whatever information he has concerning the major fugitive in which you are interested. If that fugitive is apprehended, then the only charges Bruce Aitken could possibly face would be a false statement charge in Seattle.

"I have stated that, in fairness, if you want to proceed in this fashion, Bruce should be in no worse legal position if the government moves to revoke the plea agreement after May 30th. I explained to you that that meant we would agree to withdraw the plea if you attempted to both violate the agreement and try Bruce in Seattle and Reno on the underlying indictments. I also stated that we would not attempt to withdraw the plea agreement if you indicated you did not intend to try Bruce on the underlying indictments. Bruce Aitken and I do not want to risk incarceration while trying to defend two major indictments."

Michael told me that if we lost at the hearing, Peter Mueller could seek to indict me for making a false statement and could reinstate the original indictments. But, he did not think he would do all of that.

Michael called his bluff...

Concerning the status of my plea agreement and the sentencing procedure, Mueller wrote:

"Mr. Aitken will promptly provide to the government information he currently possesses which he believes may be helpful in apprehending a specific DEA fugitive whom you have named. If assistance is feasible, Mr. Aitken will provide it at such time that the agents with whom he will be working decide would be most productive.

"Mr. Aitken's sentencing will proceed as scheduled on May 30, 1991. The government will agree to his being placed on probation at that time as called for in the plea agreement.

"Mr. Aitken realizes that the government believes he has violated the agreement and agrees that the government may ask the court for a hearing to establish such violations and to revoke probation at a later time."

Michael advised me...

"We have agreed to go forward as per the last letter from Peter Mueller. You are not giving up anything and they are not giving up anything. You are both reserving all of your rights, but they will not allow you to escape responsibility for past misstatements.

"Most importantly, on the other hand, you are not going to face a hearing next week that at its conclusion could find you incarcerated for five years and facing trials in two cases. In addition you are only going to speak to him about one subject. Nowhere does it say that you have to testify against anybody."

Michael kept talking to me.

"Bruce, we have made the best deal we could. God knows I tried for better, but Peter Mueller is intent on incarcerating you. Possibly, when we are all in Reno, I can negotiate further.

"All of your Reno co-defendants have been sentenced. All of your Seattle co-defendants are cooperating with the government. Bruce, when last we spoke on the telephone, you said we would proceed as planned. If you are changing your mind, call me."

The decision was easy

Michael's sharp mind miraculously saved me again. Still, I was mightily pissed off at Mueller; I had had enough of his vindictive bullshit over nothing material. I was beginning to hope that he would have a stroke.

I decided to take the next step into the abyss based on Michael's advice, which would thankfully commence the period of probation and dismiss the superseding indictment. This huge and important development was in my favor in a spectacular way.

As in a boxing match, I had to win the fight one round at a time. The skills I learned in tai chi kept coming to my rescue: let them expend their energy; give them little or nothing in return.

The sentencing in Reno... let's do it!

I did not relish returning to Reno for sentencing.

That day is etched in my mind. Present, were Judge Harold McKibben, Michael, the prosecutor Sullivan, and a menagerie of spectators and government types waiting to hear the proceedings.

I listened intently as Judge McKibben read and accepted the plea agreement and sentence. I responded in the affirmative. At the conclusion, he asked me if I had any statement to make.

This was it—my chance to make a statement; you could have heard a pin drop.

"No, Your Honor; I have nothing to say." It was true, as when in court before, my mind had gone blank.

I really could not think of anything to say.

I also realized I needed to keep my wits about me because they were expecting something "concrete." It was simple. Should I run into my friend Tom Sherrett again, I would simply tell him what I told him when we met in Saigon: "Don't get caught! If you do, they will throw the book at you."

Not long after, the shit hit the fan–again

Next, Mueller ordered me to meet with DEA Agent Conklin, Corman's handler in Bangkok. I refused. He just could not get it through his thick skull that I would not lift a little finger to help him. Back in rabid dog mode, he wrote to Michael:

"I am quite unhappy with Mr. Aitken's evident uncooperative attitude and am nearing the end of my patience in dealing with him!!"

The sneak and the threat

In fact, after checking my travel plans, Mueller made a special unannounced trip to Bangkok at a time he knew I would be there in route to a marathon organization committee meeting in Saigon. I met him briefly at the Ambassador Hotel coffee shop.

As I watched him puffing away on one of those strong Thai cigarettes, *Krung Tip*, I wondered if he knew the dangers of smoking tobacco, but I could not get a word in edgewise over his ranting.

He was furious that I had absolutely nothing to report about Sherrett in Vietnam other than I told him I supposed he was now long gone. In frustration, he told me not to get my hopes up... about my project in Vietnam [because] "Most likely by then you will be back in prison."

By this time...

I was seriously considering taking my family and moving to Saigon on a permanent basis. My undelivered reply to Michael for Mueller, "Tell him to go to hell!" was not working too well.

It was now August. The Seattle prosecutor's office sent two photographs of Sherrett and simply asked that I show them around Ho Chi Minh City. I showed them to Tim Milner.

"Tim, have you seen this fellow in town recently?"

Tim dutifully replied, "No, not me; never saw the guy before."

I reported to Michael in late August: "no developments," and fervently prayed to God for a miracle. How long could this go on?

After weeks of silence, I heard from Michael

The passing of time was my best weapon and I knew something would eventually have to turn in my favor; it did. Out of the blue, Michael sent me a fax:

> *"Our war of attrition seems to be turning somewhat in our favor. The government did not wish to keep our trial indefinitely on calendar in Seattle. Hence, they are willing to dismiss the case as long as you waive your rights to a speedy trial and to any statute of limitations arguments.*
>
> *"I strongly advise that you do so since they can just continue to keep the indictment on calendar. However once it is dismissed, it is my understanding that they would have to re-indict the case to prosecute you and that would be an impediment to their ever going forward with the case. Hence, please sign the enclosed waiver as it is greatly to our advantage to do so."*

I couldn't believe it; I signed that beautiful document as fast as I could, and for the first time since I was released from prison I felt at peace. I was in heaven. It was a miracle.

DISMISSAL OF INDICTMENT
United States District Court Western District of Seattle, USA,
Plaintiff v Bruce Aitken, Defendant
Pursuant to Rule 48(a) of the Federal Rules of Criminal
Procedure and by leave of court endorsed hereon the United States
Attorney for the Western District of Washington hereby dismisses
the:
SUPERCEDING INDICTMENT
Against: Bruce E. Aitken, Defendant
Dated this 9th day of September 1991
Mark Bartlett

1992. What would it bring?

I was looking forward to the New Year. Jenny and I spent New Year's Eve having a quiet dinner at home. Our sons were doing well in school. I was living on savings, but the cash was getting lower all the time.

There are not too many job offers in the classified ads for former money launderers, especially ones with a felony conviction, and I felt a slight sense of panic at the thought of being broke and unemployed at the same time.

I had the specter of probation hanging over my life until 1996, along with concerns about my cases continuing to raise their ugly heads.

Soon back in Saigon, in early January, I was having a beer at the roof-top bar at the Hueng Sen Hotel when Jenny called, her voice full of concern; she had gotten an urgent fax from Michael; the sickening knot returned to my stomach.

Chapter 39
Sparrow Who?

Expect the unexpected...

The urgent fax from Michael read:

"Peter Mueller telephoned me today. He has unfortunately *not* forgotten you. He told me that the little information we supplied to him about Tom Sherrett has proven to be totally worthless, and he is apparently preparing to take some further action in your case.

"He tells me that an individual by the name of Philip Sparrowhawk has told the government he gave you money on numerous occasions on behalf of Marks and Kimball, and other persons who were associated with an individual about whom you gave false information."

Part of the transcript Mueller sent...

"I Phillip Sparrowhawk of the Metropolitan Correctional Center, in the City of Miami, in the State of Florida, state that:

"From 1979 I usually traveled under the alias 'B. Meehan.' I obtained a false Irish Passport in that name in 1979.

"I have known Bruce Aitken since approximately 1984. I was sent to his office by Kimball to deliver $75,000 cash, which represented the purchase price of the 3 and ½ ton shipment of cannabis going to Australia. I have visited (with cash) Aitken's office at 1415 Connaught Centre, 1 Connaught Place, Central, Hong Kong on approximately 10 occasions, and have also met Aitken in Bangkok and Toronto. Aitken told me that he was an American citizen who operated several financial and investment businesses in

434

Hong Kong, including First Financial Services. Aitken is known to have the nickname 'Brubaker' from Kimball."

Michael continued:

"Mr. Sparrowhawk is scheduled to be returned to Canada and hence a deposition to preserve his testimony had taken place on January 21, 1992, at 10:00 am. The deposition took place by telephone conference call.

"Mr. Mueller said it would be the government's intention to use this deposition at a hearing in Reno to revoke your probation and at a trial in Seattle where you will be prosecuted for giving false statements to government agents.

"He did not mention reinstituting the indictment that was dismissed in Seattle. As you know that was the greatest fear in terms of a legal action that would expose you to a long period of time in custody.

"In any event, I need all the information you could supply concerning Phillip Sparrowhawk. The government is going to send me his prior statements, which I will fax to you."

The mother of all depositions and the fallout

From Micheal:

"The deposition of Phillip Sparrowhawk took four hours and forty-five minutes; Peter Mueller is without question the most thorough lawyer in the world. The deposition was also taped, and I will send you a copy when received.

"I told Peter Mueller he was required to tell me exactly what charges were being investigated by use of this deposition. He said the charges are false statements and the particular statements referred to are as follows:

- *Repeated statements by you that you terminated business in 1986.*

435

- *Statements indicating that the closing of accounts were not accurate.*
- *Statements concerning associates of Kimball and Howard Marks that did not mention Sparrowhawk or a guy who came to visit with funds for Richard Kimball.*
- *Statement that you did not know who delivered the false passport of Kimball.*
- *Failure to disclose knowledge of facts relevant to the Vancouver case.*
- *Failure to reveal Wylie as false identification of Kimball.*
- *Denial of facts or knowledge of Denbigh's and Mark's involvement in drugs.*
- *Failure to disclose a $1,000,000 cash transaction with Sparrowhawk in Canada.*
- *Failure to disclose knowledge of the Sparrowhawk bank account.*

Who the hell is Sparrowhawk?

Sparrowhawk was squawking about some large transactions that I allegedly handled for Kimball. I'd have to listen to almost five hours of tape and read hundreds of pages of transcripts in order to refresh my memory. *No problem.*

Of course, I was worried about Mueller's intentions. Just when I began to see the light at the end of the tunnel regarding my prospects for the future, presto, "another Merrill," but far worse, appeared out of the woodwork.

I responded. "Michael, only now do I know that this person named 'Brian Meehan' is Sparrowhawk! Sure, I remember him. I wouldn't lie to you! I always thought he was a nice guy. I would never snitch on him!"

The tapes arrived. I spent hours listening, locating holes in them wherever possible. This fellow Sparrowhawk had a memory like an elephant. I assumed Mueller couldn't stop salivating over all this information spewing out against me. I needed another miracle. *Surely God was tired of me asking!*

Just when I thought Mueller was down for the count, up he jumped right at the count of ten. I was secretly beginning to have a hidden respect for his tenacity. When we met in person, he seemed not a bad sort, just unhappy and dour with some kind of massive chip on his shoulder. I even felt a bit of pity for him.

As for Sparrowhawk, he was soft-spoken and likeable and I considered him a friend. Again, I imagined how pressured and desperate he must have been, otherwise, he would never have said anything against me. I could forgive this transgression, but the violations enumerated in the Sparrowhawk deposition were totally overwhelming—and they frightened me.

Dare I pray for yet another miracle?

Think! I told myself. *How the hell am I going to get out of this one? This time I am in very big trouble.* I kept a suitcase packed so I could make a quick exit.

Almost two months passed before I heard back from Michael. *I had spent almost that entire time hunkered down in deep prayer.*

He wrote, "I have not heard anything from Peter Mueller, and I like it that way. It would be most unfortunate if we did anything that brought your case to the attention of Peter Mueller or the court. If I hear anything, I'll let you know."

I breathed a silent sigh of relief.

We learned why Mueller had been so quiet...

Michael received a call from Assistant Attorney Mark Bartlett. It was his hope that the reason we had not heard from the government was that they had decided to put my case to rest—not true.

Mark informed Michael that the delay was because of an act of God: "Peter Mueller was involved in a very serious automobile accident two months ago." He had been out of the office for that period of time. I felt no personal joy in hearing this news. Mueller was due back in the office in one month. According to Michael, "He informed Mark Bartlett that he intends to prosecute you for false statements when he returns unless you have provided information of some importance to the government."

On the plus side, it did not appear as if they intended to reintroduce the Seattle indictment. That, of course, would have presented our most serious problem.

Two months passed before Mark Bartlett called Michael. Apparently he was being prodded by Peter Mueller to take some action in my case.

He offered three alternatives:

- *The first alternative was to go to Seattle and plead guilty to having given a false statement to a federal official. I could receive a sentence of up to five years in custody for that count.*
- *His second alternative was to do nothing and be indicted for numerous false statements.*
- *His third alternative was for me to return to Seattle and finish my debriefing, correcting any misstatements and telling the whole truth.*

Michael explained to Mark on my behalf that I recalled events of many years ago as best I could and any inconsistencies in my testimony were based on failure to recollect rather than intent to misrepresent.

He said to me, "Of all the alternatives, I like the third alternative the best."

The torture continued... August 1992

My policy of not asking questions of my clients continued to work against me. I saw no point in having another interview because my recollection had diminished over time. Of course, part of my "poor memory" had to do with feeling outraged over the government's initial and continuing methods and tactics.

"Please tell the government that my feelings are that any doubts are due to poor recollection on my part, and a totally distorted picture of me on their part. I feel that I have paid in full with the time I was denied bail and incarcerated in Reno."

The month of September

Michael replied that he conveyed my concerns to Mark Bartlett. "I have also told him we assume that if they start debriefing, that they will not be seeking to prosecute you. The reason I made a case for debriefing is that the government is considering two alternatives: (1) debrief, (2) prosecution."

Given that those two alternatives are on the mind of Peter Mueller, I decided to push for alternative (1).

Of course Michael was absolutely right.

Then everything goes quiet again…

Several more anxiety-filled months passed, slowly destroying my brain cells. Michael wrote, "I have not heard anything recently but it is hard for me to believe that Peter Mueller will let you slide." So ended 1992, a year in which success could only be positively measured by several miracles that allowed me to stay out of the United States and out of jail!

Early in 1993, Michael and I corresponded…

"I get nervous every time I receive a fax from you. I haven't heard anything from the Seattle U.S. attorney's office, but it is difficult for me to believe that they are going to forget you. Peter Mueller just doesn't seem like the type of person to forget anything."

"Funny," I replied, "I also get nervous every time I receive a fax from you! Although it has been silent, I completely agree with you about Peter Mueller and I am always prepared for the worst."

On April 2, 1993 – Mark Bartlett wrote:

> *Dear Mike:*
> *I wanted to write you a brief note concerning your favorite client and my favorite "cooperating" witness, Bruce Aitken. Although Mr. Aitken has consistently withheld substantial amounts of valuable information from the government in violation of his Plea agreement, he is like "a cat with nine lives" that always gets one more chance.*
> *In this instance the chance to avoid prosecution in the Western District of Washington comes not from our office but from the Western District of Oregon. As you may know, Assistant US Attorney Charles Stuckey is proceeding to trial*

this year on defendants being prosecuted in the Western District of Oregon for the Sherrett conspiracy. In the upcoming weeks, AUSA Stuckey and his investigators will be traveling to South East Asia to speak with various witnesses. They would like to meet with Bruce during their visit.

I view this as Bruce's last chance, a chance that in all honesty, he does not deserve. If Bruce, however, undergoes a change of heart and provides truthful, honest and complete assistance to the District of Oregon prosecution, our District will forgive his past sins.

Michael's response to me...

"Please find enclosed a letter I received from Mark Bartlett. While you may not think so, this letter is good news. I honestly thought that there were no conditions that would prevent Peter Mueller from going after you. He put quite a bit of work into building a false statements case and I didn't think he would abandon it.

"But apparently there is a good chance that we can put the whole matter behind us. I am trying now to find out who is being prosecuted in Oregon. It is quite possible that your 'truthful, honest and complete assistance' will be easy to give, hurt no one and as a result as Mark Bartlett says 'our District will forgive his past sins.'

"I will write to you as soon as I have heard from Mr. Stuckey."

April showers bring the flowers

He wrote: "The names of the individuals indicted with Tom Sherrett in Oregon were Mr. and Mrs. Vo Minh and Dr Vo Qui. I will let you know when I hear from the government again."

I immediately felt relieved and happy because I could finally tell the truth and return the "favor" to my good friend Tom Sherrett.

I informed Michael I was aware of the indictment filed before the statute of limitations against Tom Sherrett's girlfriend, Mrs. Vo Minh, and her brother Dr. Vo Qui)

I was asked about them before by Mueller in Seattle, and stated clearly and truthfully that I only saw them in Hong Kong on two or three occasions socially when they were there with Sherrett. I was not aware of any business they did, and I had no business relationship with them.

Happily, my comments will only help them in their defense!

August 18, 1993. Michael's sound advice...

"We are on the verge of truly concluding your case. Please go out of your way to satisfy Al Santos. While I know you have nothing to tell him, the appearance of being eager to help can be of great benefit to us.

"I consider it most fortuitous that the government has not tried to revoke your probation or charged you with making false statements. It really is *out of character* given the tenacious nature of the Seattle United States Attorney's office.

"So let's do everything to make sure they have no reason to go after you. What it takes to put this matter behind is that there is something that you need to do. Please attempt to be as friendly as possible.

"A lot of times prosecutors will help someone who has not helped them just because they like the individual. If you can convince Mr. Santos you really want to help but just don't have any information regarding those individuals, he will report back to Seattle that you appeared to be cooperative.

"If he senses your distrust, he may believe you are withholding information for that reason and it would make our job in Seattle more difficult. Basically the purpose of this letter is just to try to inspire you to put your best foot forward."

I told Michael…

Not to worry; I would definitely put my best foot forward. That was a promise. That the government was willing to forgive my past sins was another timely, desperately needed miracle; I thanked the Lord and the prosecutor, too.

In late September Al Santos visited Hong Kong. He was not like Mueller; he was decent; I told him straight up and politely that I had no knowledge of Tom Sherrett's Vietnamese friends other than having met them briefly and only socially. Naturally, I was so happy to be actually telling the truth.

To say I was glad to see the back of 1993 would be a great understatement—it had been yet another year living with a Mueller sword hanging over my head.

I was aging rapidly.

Chapter 40
Hallelujah!

Probation

I spent 1994 and 1995 quietly scratching out a living and filing the monthly probation report stating my income which, by the way, was steadily on the decline. The months passed uneventfully until the day I had been waiting for finally arrived...

United States District Court
District of Nevada, Probation Office
JANUARY 30, 1996

Re: <u>**TERMINATION OF PROBATION**</u>

Dear Mr. Aitken:

Thank you for your monthly supervision report for December, 1995. We would like to confirm that your expiration date from supervision was December 6, 1995. You have completed the supervision term as ordered by the court and we would like to express our congratulations. Best wishes in all future endeavors.
Sincerely
(s)
WAYNE L. MOMERAK
Senior U.S. Probation Officer

I was *THRILLED*.

There were steps the government could have taken to prevent my termination, but hallelujah! they chose not to! One can only imagine my shock when Michael told me the matter might not actually be closed:

"If you will recall," Michael wrote, "prosecutors in Seattle were threatening us with a 'false statements' case. Given the passage of time, I believe that case is probably dead. However, they may wish to have you testify in one of the other pending cases and may attempt to use those potential charges as leverage. Or they may just subpoena you to testify. Our greatest ally in all of this is the passage of time.

"When all of the prosecutions in Seattle are over, I believe I could then tell you that the matter is totally behind you."

Fast forward. It's about the money, stupid

I found that crime does not pay *if you get caught.*

The smugglers of weed and art and those who launder the proceeds were in it mostly for the money; non-violent, good folks for the most part, and friends. The karma was harmless.

The government, for the most part, created the criminality and the parallel cottage industry that underpinned it: the judicial system, the booming business in prison construction, and the agents. All were after the same thing: *money.*

Some of my friends did time, others lost their lives; life kept rolling on. With the passage of time and some reflection, I can honestly say I felt no bitterness towards anyone personally. My family had suffered, of course, and that hurt; however, only one person bore the responsibility for that state of affairs and that person was me. I had spent my life blatantly violating currency regulations.

I would try to make it up to them in the future.

Chapter 41
Reflection and Revelation

My future? It's an illusion

After probation ended, I seemed to drift like a ship without a rudder. Nothing seemed to matter. I felt utterly lost. My positive outlook was evaporating along with my savings.

What skills did I have? What talents did I possess? I took inventory and found myself sorely lacking. A mild panic set in and I turned to my last resort to show me the way: my faith. My spirit was hungry, and the material world was slowly escaping from my consciousness.

In searching for answers, I realized I was a consultant of sorts, so I tried to put together deals on a fee basis; but they were few and far between. I yearned for the good old days. In laundering money, I had stumbled upon *(or was it fate?)* one of the best "professions" in the world. It was impossible to continue in that vocation..

What do you do after you've lived like that?

To Russia with love and thanks

Picking up the pieces, there were lessons to be learned about the realities of life, human nature and survival. I had lived my life believing I could control my destiny, but I developed serious doubts. *Is there such a thing as fate?*

What were the options for my future? I searched my mind with the sole purpose of taking stock of myself with an initial sense of terrifying foreboding. Beads of sweat formed on my forehead at the thought.

I desperately needed work for my family's future.

It was now 1997 and the previous four and a half years spent on probation were totally consumed, in one battle after the other, avoiding incarceration. Shattered was my real hope for a complete change in direction.

"Mike" my pilot friend and instructor in prison, made me a fascinating proposal. Corporate aviation was expanding fast in Asia. His company would be expanding. In a few years, I could be based out of Singapore, flying a Falcon 500. I would have to begin training immediately in Aspen, Colorado. Instead of spending my probation years learning how to fly and accumulating hours, I was forced to stay away from America, off the radar, in Vietnam.

The "Vietnam Follies" as Tim and I affectionately came to refer to our sports promotion business, had also run its course for me personally. It was quite the adventure, from 1990-1996, we orgnanized some amazing events, like the International Marathons in alternate years in Saigon and Hanoi. Plus, a world class Surfing Championship at China Beach, Da Nang; a Brian Adams Concert, a Hong Kong to Nha Trang Yacht Race, and more! In fact, the bi-anual Hong Kong-Vietnam Yach Race has become the stellar race in all of Asia.

We laughed at some unique memories, like bumping into General Norman Schwartzkopf and Dan Rather in Saigon on top of the Rex Hotel roof garden. We wanted to announce our ground-breaking Saigon '92 Marathon. They freaked out! The embargo of Vietnam was still on. What were we thinking? Organized by two former convicts!

We'll always cherish the sight of over one million Saigon '92 Marathon specators lining the streets, or the poignant meeting at the VN Ministry of Veterans Affairs, when one of our American and one former Viet Cong wheelchair athletes, discovered they were both injured on the same day in the same battle. They embraced. Not an eye was dry. War, what is it good for, absolutely nothing!

I was spending more and more time in Vietnam, and away from my family. There were no international schools there. I decided to look for work in Hong Kong, while at the same time, search my soul for some real meaning and purpose in life.

Returning to Hong Kong, I was mysteriously and inexplicably drawn to look to the church, my last resort. I had heard that to "serve the Lord' is the highest calling.

In my search for peace and happiness, I began to attend Sunday Mass. Suddenly I was praising God. Through a friend I met at St. Joseph Church, I secured a much-needed employment opportunity, consulting for a local Russian-based company, making chips for watches and calculators from Integral, out of Minsk, Belarus.

Prayer answered.

This kept me busy for several years, traveling to Moscow and Minsk for friendly negotiations, ending with a lavish party at the dacha. Memorable experiences! I surreptitiously learned that by taking the overnight train, I could make several trips back and forth between Minsk and Moscow on a single-entry Russian visa. It seemed that the train ride, but not the airplane flight, was domestic, with no customs or immigration.

Despite the work in Minsk, I felt my life was going nowhere. I had totally lost interest in work or anything else, for that matter. The world had changed dramatically—I felt *off* all the time.

I needed something to anchor me and give me hope for the future.

Turning Point

The Lord finally called me to serve. After my baptism on December 15, 2000, I attended a rally in a packed Hong Kong

Stadium hosted by El Shaddai Prayer Partners, with the charismatic founder, "Bro Mike," Z. Velarde, that lit a spark in my spirit.

Joined by two long-time friends, Kamran Hashmi, a Muslim turned Baptist pastor, and Jacqueline Chan, the Chinese wife of our mutual friend, Illyas Butt, peace be upon him, we opened a kiosk in the open air spaces next to the Macao Ferry Terminal. And presto, "Happy's Kitchen," cleverly named by my son, Matt, was born. Illyas and I had been great friends ever since the first day we met, around 1975, when he came to Deak and Company to change his money. I always enjoyed visiting him when he was at his home in Lahore, Pakistan. In fact, he was my initial introduction to BCCI in both Karachi and in Hong Kong

With a stage right in front, we had choirs and bands performing on weekends, drawing huge crowds playing praise and worship music. Simple Pakistani and Filipino food was served. Our goal: help yourself, no price; just leave what you want in the big glass jar. Beggars joined the flock of domestic helpers, served by waiters who were their employers, who packed the place.

All was well until the SARS epidemic hit in 2003. The trembling public, all wearing face masks (except me, of course, I had faith, and the luck of the Irish) evaporated into the night, taking Happy's Kitchen along with it.

What to do? We prayed.

The idea come to me to play this beloved "praise" music on the radio. On Palm Sunday, April 6, 2004, the "Hour of Love" Radio program was born, and has become my vocation until the present.

The Cleaner

Epilogue

America had changed so gradually it seemed no one noticed or cared. But I cared.

It seemed to me that I had grown up in America's *golden age*. The Korean War ended in 1953—I was eight years old. In school, we pledged allegiance to the American flag and said the Lord's Prayer and read verses from the Bible. God had not yet been cast out of the schools and people's lives. Life was lovely. We were poor; so what? There was baseball, and cats and dogs; if we could recite a Bible verse, we could swim on hot summer days in Mrs. Earl's pool, one of the big rubber ones—but no verse, no swim!

It was a life of honesty and integrity, ethics, and justice. America was the greatest country in the world. I believed it wholeheartedly because it was true. There was absolutely no doubt in my mind that America would go to the rescue of anyone in need and suffering injustice. With particular gusto, America would first and foremost always be the champion of the underdog. Always!

From the outside looking in

Remember Vietnam and the peace rallies, "Make love, not war?" Well, the "pot-smoking hippies" were right about that; however, they lost the "war" to the nerds in the government.

Having lived outside the States looking in for over forty years, I really understood the words, "The Good Old Days."

I recall the days when there was no TV and no psychologically insane mass advertising; when businesses were closed on Sunday, which was a day of rest for all; when Palestine was on the map;

when the dollar was backed by gold and not hot air; when abortion was not a choice; when prayers and God were allowed in schools; when far fewer souls were in prison; when wars were to be avoided.

Give me the good old days.

And make these two goals politically correct: *Bring back our beloved Constitution. Return to righteousness.*

Fate & Karma

My life as a professional launderer of money provided many wonderful experiences. I traveled the world over, logging more air miles than most professional pilots. I was blessed to meet many amazing people, good people. Money was made and money was lost. It became a commodity that was oftentimes very heavy to carry around.

Other people's money given to me on a handshake, accentuated a feeling of personal satisfaction because of the high degree of shared trust. My own money was, therefore, hard-earned. The lessons I learned at Deak & Company served me well. The bottom line was that there was no evil in cleaning money, and cleaning it was technically a "tort" and not a crime.

Justifying cleaning money never haunted me because I felt I was doing it for the right reasons—to support my family and to help others in need.

It was often my fate to take the road of risk instead of the road of wisdom. Risk and greed showed me the other side of life, where people could do more harm than good and forsake their principles for money; and worst of all, for pride. They often forsook their honor for power, while inflicting pain and suffering on others.

My "baptism of desire," my epiphany, changed everything.

I grieved for my past mistakes, and I felt the wretchedness in my soul. I extended an invisible spiritual hand through the cosmos and touched those I hurt along the road of life and asked for forgiveness. A new peace was born in my heart. Suffering and failure happened for reasons that would turn out to be valuable for the development of my soul.

Prison showed me where justice was lacking. The helpless feeling of loneliness made me feel as if my luck had run out. That experience exacted a heavy cost because of the suffering I knew others experienced as a result of my decisions. The effect on my wife and children, my co-defendants and best friends, made me realize that I had lost my innocence. Those tough times showed me I'd lost the confident swagger that seemingly put me in the right place at the right time. They also taught me survival— to be brave, and reminded me that I was a fighter.

The horror I felt while on the run in Taipei provided me with solitude and filled me with all-consuming thoughts of my family and an unquenchable longing to see and touch them. The loss of my freedom and the feeling of shame caused me to panic at the thought of never seeing them again. My brief "fugitive life" was not romantic. It was unbearably lonely. I learned that suffering is the way we test, realize and value our love.

I learned the value of real friends and how rare they are, those who would put themselves out on a limb for you. That's something I learned in prison, too. You cannot hide, and you must be tough. Friends are there if you look out for them. It is not hell.

I also learned to forgive and not to hate those who hurt me, like the abominable snitches—they are the minority. They would have to live with themselves and with their own fates. As I have said a thousand times, where I came from, you did not, under any circumstances, inform on anyone. My brothers shared this bond and a history of integrity that can only be understood by survivors of our experience.

My life had been shaped by events, some of which had been within my control, some not.

I had lived an exciting life. The black market held an irresistible glamour that had drawn people to me like a magnet. I think it was my destiny to be in it. Because of my experiences, nothing would ever be the same again.

My dream became bigger: I wanted to change the world. Everything up to that point had just been a prelude and preparation to make a positive impact before the end of my life.

When all is said and done, all you need is love

How to change the world ?

It is now time for the silent majority in the whole world to peacefully rise and use the powers of the spirit. In our clarion call to action let us examine ourselves until we find the Holy Grail in our lives—our true power and charisma and collective destiny. We must relearn the spiritual language that has been forgotten, each person in conversation with God.

When we are true, God responds to desires and eliminates our fears; as we come to understand our lives in the Spirit, we are changed into forces of goodness and caring and forgiving that open rivers of flowing grace. Such grace cannot be measured in the material sense, because happiness, joy, goodness, trust, and truth cannot be measured—but they can become our life experience. We can make it hard, but it's easy: focus on love and forgiveness.

We have the power to make the world a better place if we surrender to the simple life, dedicating ourselves to our families and to society. These endeavors open endless possibilities and can create a positive fate, collectively changing the world by each and every kind thought, each and every act of love reaching out for the universal good.

I went through a lot to learn some powerful lessons. Faith and events showed me that to serve the Lord *is* the highest calling—the best thing in life is to get high, not on drugs, but instead get high on love.

"If all the religious traditions worked together to combat the brokenness in our world, there would be a tremendous outpouring of goodness and love, of compassion and mercy, of forgiveness and reconciliation, and of justice, respect and dignity for all. The result would be universal peace."
Scarboro Missioner.

My invitation

I invite the kindest, most generous, compassionate and good-hearted people on the planet, Americans, empowered by the miracle of social media, to join me in changing our great country for the better. To make a difference together!
God bless America.

The Cleaner

Final Thoughts

Thank you for reading my very personal tale of faith.

I hope you have gained some insight into the life and times I lived, and the problems faced by people who have had the unfortunate luck to be thrown into the court systems of today—people who are up against the government.

I broke the law, made a bunch of money, lived a lifestyle very few ever get to experience, and, like Icarus, flew too close to the flame and came spiraling down in a ball of flames.

Luckily, it worked out for me. I am free; I have my life, my lovely family and friends. It could have worked out very differently.

My life as a successful money launderer taught me many lessons, the most important one of which is the value of the spiritual over the material in the world; the value of people, as opposed to the value of things.

For that, I am eternally grateful.

One last bit of news...

One day, while sitting in an office shared with a friend, I was holding my head in my hands and *wishing I had some money to launder*, when the phone rang. It was the United States Consulate, Hong Kong. I could not believe my ears.

"Yes, Mr. Aitken, that's correct. We have received seventeen boxes of documents from the United States addressed to you." *Seventeen? That is too many.* "Where do you want them delivered?"

The boxes arrived, and what a treasure trove it was. Not only were all my documents there, the clerk who packed the shipment was kind enough to include all the FBI reports, DEA reports, DEA handwritten notes, CIA reports, "snitch" handwritten notes, and more.

That's when I thought, *One day, God willing, I must try to write a book!*

You can learn more about what I am doing by listening to the radio program I produce and host every Sunday night from Hong Kong:

The "Hour of Love" with "Bro Bruce"
Sunday, 9:00-11:00 Hong Kong time
"Soothe your soul, lighten your spirit and gladden your heart"
AM 1044 Metro Plus

Or contact me at:

WORSHIP MUSIC SOCIETY
GPO BOX 11685, HONG KONG

I also invite you to visit the website for information about the challenges, the struggles, and the most outrageously hilarious, sometimes deeply moving experiences encountered by Sports Asia Ltd in Vietnam.

More....

For additional documents mentioned in the book, please go the web site: www.TheCleanerBook.com

The Cleaner

Author in Dirk Brink's office - circa 1977

Saigon, Viet Nam 1994

Author at grand opening of American Express
office in Chu Lai, Viet Nam. Circa 1971

Author with Brian Adams, first International artist to perform
in Vietnam since 1972. Circa 1994

Baseball at Florida Southern 1967

Tony Pong, Bruce Aitken and Nick Deak in Hong Kong, 1976

Sydney after a pick up - 1980

Bag full of money

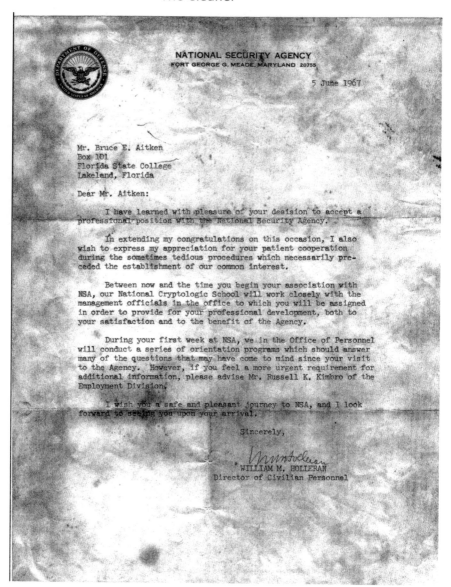

NSA Letter

Author in Moscow, Russia circa 1970s

Embassy of the United States of America

Bangkok, Thailand
June 8, 1989

Police Major General Kriengkrai Karnasutta
Commander, Immigration Division
Royal Thai Police
Soi Suan Plu
Bangkok 10120

Dear General Kriengkrai:

I am writing to inform you that the U.S. passport number Z4979990 and any other U.S. passports in the possession of Bruce Emil Aitken, an American citizen, who was born on February 7, 1945, in New Jersey, U.S.A., has been revoked by the Department of State. This action is based on the fact that Mr. Aitken is the subject of a United States Federal arrest warrant, issued on September 13, 1988, by the U.S. District Court for the District of Nevada, charging him with conspiracy to distribute marijuana, in violation of 21 United States Code 846. He is also charged with conspiracy to defraud the U.S. government and to launder money, as well as interstate travel in aid of racketeering.

Mr. Aitken is a fugitive felon who has entered Thailand without a valid travel document on June 7, 1989. Accordingly, the Embassy would appreciate your assistance in returning Mr. Aitken to the United States. If you consider Mr. Aitken deportable as an undesirable illegal alien, the United States Government will pay the costs of his transportation and provide agents to escort him to the U.S. It would be greatly appreciated if Mr. Aitken could be held in custody until such arrangements are finalized.

The Government of the United States would welcome the deportation of Mr. Aitken. However, because of the limitations imposed by U.S. law, we would not be able to guarantee reciprocity if the situation were reversed.

Mr. Aitken is described as a white male, 173 centimeters tall, weighing between 75 and 80 kilos, with brown hair, hazel eyes, and possibly wearing a beard or moustache.

I wish to express my deep appreciation for your assistance in this matter. You are most welcome to contact me or Consul Carmen Martinez if you require additional information on this case.

Sincerely,

Wesley H. Parsons
Wesley H. Parsons
Deputy Consul General

Revocation of Passport

Bruce Aitken

Visit the web site:

www.TheCleanerBook.com

Printed in Hong Kong
by The Green Pagoda Press Ltd.
13 February 2018

84212916R00288